the
COMPANY DIRECTOR'S
GUIDE

I⌀D

The Institute of Directors

The Institute of Directors (IoD) is a leading membership organisation representing over 50,000 company directors in the UK alone. Among its key objectives, the Institute aims to 'raise the professional standards of directors and help them attain high levels of expertise and effectiveness by improving their knowledge and skills'.

The Institute therefore publishes a number of authoritative business publications, written specifically for practising and aspiring directors, offering practical advice on the benefits and potential pitfalls of a range of business practices. The IoD also offers high level training and development programmes to raise the professional standards of business leaders and to help them reach both business excellence and personal success.

For more details on the Institute of Directors, its books, development programmes and the benefits of membership please contact:

Institute of Directors
116 Pall Mall
London SW14 5ED
Tel: 020-7766 8866

the
COMPANY DIRECTOR'S
GUIDE

YOUR DUTIES, RESPONSIBILITIES & LIABILITIES

Published by the Institute of Directors
The UK's leading organisation for company directors

IØD

Tony Renton and John Watkinson

KOGAN
PAGE

First published in 2001 by Kogan Page for the Institute of Directors

Kogan Page Limited
120 Pentonville Road
London N1 9JN

Institute of Directors
116 Pall Mall
London SW1Y 5ED

No responsibility for any loss arising as a consequence of any person relying upon the information or views contained in this publication is accepted by the Institute of Directors or the authors.

British Library Cataloguing in Publication Data

A CIP record for this book is available from the British Library.

ISBN 0 7494 3325 6

Typeset by JS Typesetting, Wellingborough, Northants
Printed and bound in Great Britain by Clays Ltd, St Ives plc

Contents

List of Tables

Table of Cases

Foreword

This *Company Director's Guide* builds on earlier work, supported by the government, to develop the widely used handbook *Standards for the Board*.

I warmly welcome the continuing efforts of the Institute of Directors to encourage and disseminate good practice in corporate governance in the private, public and voluntary sectors.

The Rt Hon Stephen Byers MP
Secretary of State for Trade and Industry

Preface

This book represents a collective view of law and good practice drawn from a broad cross-section of company directors, shaped considerably by surveys of IoD members, focus groups of experienced directors and input from academics. Strictly, it deals only with limited companies incorporated in the United Kingdom under the Companies Acts for business purposes and is primarily addressed to the directors of such companies. However, many of the duties and responsibilities they must accept, the tasks they must perform and the liabilities to which they are exposed are common to the governors of any type of organisation, however constituted and whether or not it has commercial objects.

This volume brings an earlier publication of the IoD, *Guidelines for Directors*, up to date. Some of the material in the latter has been re-ordered and the legal material, particularly that in Chapters 8, 9, 10 and 15, has been revised and updated. However, there are a number of significant changes from *Guidelines*, which was restricted to consideration of a director's legal duties and potential obligations only. This volume is greatly expanded and is concerned with a body of knowledge, not just legal matters, which a director ought to have about a company, its board and its directors.

Direction is not an easy task. The State, by means of law and regulatory agencies, sets standards of behaviour for those who direct businesses, with the intent of protecting customers, employees, those who supply goods and services to the company, and many other parties with a stake in a company's activities. At the same time directors are charged with the task of trying to ensure the survival and commercial success of the companies they direct. The result is that a director must not only exercise commercial judgement, but must also fulfil his or her obligations to others. This *Guide* tries to show how a director should go about balancing these many different factors.

The chapters are organised under four main headings. Part One, *The Company*, comprises two chapters on what companies are and the constitution of companies. Part Two, *The Board of Directors*, contains four chapters dealing with the purpose of a board, board members and their roles, how the board operates and board appraisal. The chapters in Part Three, *The Individual Director*, deal with the selection, appointment and removal of directors, a director's legal status, duties and responsibilities, extensions of directors' liabilities, directors and interested parties, disqualification of directors, directors' remuneration, directors and shares, taxation issues, and insolvency. Finally, Part Four, *Related Matters*, consists of two chapters dealing with family companies and with the broad issue of corporate governance in general.

The book will be useful, we hope, as a concise, readable and accurate guide to law and good practice for use by company directors. This was our main aim. However, it is only an introduction to the governance of companies; it does not claim to be a comprehensive survey. The book is concerned predominantly only with governance issues that result from the separation of ownership from control; other issues which may be important in a board's decision-making – for example, the whole field of business ethics – have been excluded. Every subject with which we deal is better known to some others than to us. We are conscious that many useful matters have been excluded and that the treatment of some issues may be over-simplified. It is difficult to draw a line between too little detail, whereby the text becomes overly simplistic, and too much, whereby the text becomes inordinately long and specialist. However, a line had to be drawn somewhere. This is a general guide, then, and no general guide can deal with every permutation of facts and argument. **In particular, this book is not a substitute for taking appropriate professional advice when necessary.**

The government is currently considering a major revision of the framework of corporate governance in the UK, and especially a simplification of the requirements for small private companies. A White Paper is planned for 2001 as a preliminary to new legislation. As an initial step the Secretary of State for Trade and Industry has established the Company Law Steering Group to review company law and consider, among other things, how company law might be modernised and what is the proper relationship between company law and non-statutory standards of corporate behaviour. We have not tried to anticipate these changes, though in places the tone of the discussion reflects some of the questions the Steering Group is considering and some of the evidence the IoD in particular has given to the Group. We have tried to state the law and good practice as at 1 December 2000.

The laws of the Westminster Parliament since the Union of the Parliaments of England and Scotland in 1707 apply *prima facie* to Scotland; if not, the Act usually contains an express provision that it does not extend to Scotland. The Companies Acts apply to both Scotland and Wales. Matters of company law in Scotland are reserved to the UK Parliament under the *Scotland Act 1998,* and company law matters were not transferred to the Welsh National Assembly under the *Government of Wales Act 1998.* Companies in Northern Ireland are regulated under Orders which fully reflect the *Companies Acts.* The contents of this book are therefore applicable throughout the United Kingdom, save for a very few matters (referred to in the text) which are particular to Scotland.

This *Guide* is the result of extensive consultation. We have drawn heavily from the work of course leaders teaching the Institute's Company Direction Programme and various IoD publications, particularly *Guidelines for Directors.* The work has benefited greatly from numerous suggestions made by many members of the IoD. We wish particularly to thank Chris Pierce and Alan Turner, who read and commented on most of the book. We acknowledge the comments and advice offered by Daniel Summerfield, Jonathan Trouncer and Richard Baron regarding various chapters. Vanessa Crichton cheerfully and efficiently helped with secretarial and administrative tasks.

Finally, throughout the book all references to the masculine gender include the feminine.

Tony Renton, Institute of Directors, London
John Watkinson, InterConnect Communications Ltd, Chepstow

Technical Preface

LEGAL DISCLAIMER

This *Guide* is, as the name suggests, for guidance only. It reflects the law of England and Wales as at 1 December 2000 relating to companies and directors of a company incorporated under the Companies Act 1985, other relevant statutes and case law. This law is applicable, with minor exceptions, to Scotland and Northern Ireland. The *Guide* also reflects accepted good practice in corporate governance.

Whilst every effort has been made to ensure the accuracy of the contents, neither the authors nor the publisher accept responsibility for any loss arising to anyone relying on the information contained herein. Company directors should seek appropriate advice from their legal advisers about the applicability of the content of this book to any particular matter or circumstance.

HOW TO USE THE *GUIDE*

- To refer to a particular subject, use the index. References in the index to the text refer to the page.

- Examples of statements, board papers, etc. are highlighted in the text by being printed in a tinted box.

- References in square brackets, thus [ ], in the text refer to the books or articles listed in the References at the end of the book.

- References, thus { }, in the text refer to Court cases listed in the Table of Cases on page xii.

- Further reading suggestions are listed at the end of the book.

Part 1

The Company

Chapter 1

What is a Company?

1.1 INTRODUCTION

Every association or organisation, from a humble social club to the largest international company, needs a governing body to direct its affairs and be responsible for its survival and prosperity. The governing body of a company is its board of directors. This chapter provides an introduction to companies and thus a review of the context within which the board of directors works.

1.2 WHAT IS A COMPANY?

The legal framework for companies is provided by the *Companies Acts* of 1985 and 1989, which enable companies not only to be formed, but to be formed easily, speedily and cheaply.

The word 'company' is often taken to imply a group of individuals with a common purpose; the *Companies Acts* refer to 'the company in general meeting' and refer to shareholders as 'members'. The concept of the company as a group of people is misleading, however. (As a matter of fact it is possible for a company to have no individuals as members – for example, some subsidiary companies are wholly owned by a parent company). It is more important to understand that a company is something over and above the group of people who associate together to found it. Once registered, a company has an independent legal personality, with a wholly separate identity from those persons who own it, work in it, direct it and deal with it. At registration a 'corporate veil' is drawn around the company; a company, like a person, can own property, be a debtor or creditor, employ people to work for it, enter contracts, and sue and be sued. This principle was established a century ago in the most famous case in company law:

> The company attains maturity on birth. There is no period of minority – no interval of incapacity. I cannot understand how a body corporate thus made 'capable' by statute can lose its individuality by issuing the bulk of its capital to one person. . . The company is at law a different person altogether from the subscribers to the Memorandum [the first shareholders of the company who give birth]; and, though it may be that after incorporation the business is precisely the same as it was before, and the same persons are managers, and the same hands receive the profits, the company is not in law the agent of the subscribers or trustee for them.
>
> (McNaughton LJ, *Salomon v Salomon and Co Ltd* {40})

The principle of legal personality applies to all limited companies, even though it may appear difficult to disentangle the company from a majority shareholder (especially if the shareholder has given personal guarantees of its obligations), and even though *de facto* control of a subsidiary may rest with a holding company.

EXAMPLE

The case of *Lee v Lee's Airfarming Ltd* {23} illustrates the separation of the company from other persons associated with it. Lee owned 3,999 shares out of 4,000 in Lee's Airfarming Ltd. He was a director and employee of that company, the business of which was crop spraying. Lee was killed in an air crash whilst engaged in spraying crops. It was held that Lee's wife could sue the company for compensation on the ground that the company was negligent, as the company was separate from Lee as a shareholder, director and employee.

It is this independent corporate existence that distinguishes a company from a partnership, which has no separate legal existence and is merely an association of persons carrying on business together.

1.3 LIMITED LIABILITY

1.3.1 WHAT IS LIMITED LIABILITY?

Limited liability refers to the limitation of the liability of the members of a company (i.e. shareholders) in the event of a claim against the company. The extent of the liability is to pay up the full value of the shares that have been taken up by the member. Beyond this, the debts of a company cannot be enforced against shareholders. Their liability has been limited.

When you take shares in a company you will normally acquire multiples of £1 shares. The £1, or whatever denomination is attached to the shares, is the nominal value stated on the share certificate. If the full nominal value of the share has been paid to the company the share is 'fully paid'; if not, it is 'partly paid', the remainder being 'on call'. The nominal or par value of the share is stated in the Memorandum of Association. The market value of the share will depend upon the market's valuation of the assets that the share represents. Shareholders receive dividends and capital growth from their shares in the good times. But if the company becomes insolvent, they are protected and do not have to contribute anything as shareholders of the company towards the creditors, whose claims are on the assets of the company. The shares may be worthless, but the shareholders' loss is confined to the value of their shares. By contrast, if a sole trader or a partnership fails to pay its debts, all the assets of the owner are at risk.

The 'Ltd' (Limited) or 'Plc' (Public limited company) part of the corporate name can thus be seen as a warning to potential creditors that, if the company cannot pay its debts, the shareholders may not be pursued for those debts.

> The unsecured creditors of A. Salomon and Company Limited may be entitled to sympathy, but they have only themselves to blame for their misfortunes. They trusted the company, I suppose, because they had long dealt with Mr Salomon, and he had always paid his way; but they had full notice that they were no longer dealing with an individual.
>
> (McNaughton LJ, *Salomon v Salomon and Co Ltd* {40})

Note that the liability of the directors is not limited. The privilege of limited liability granted by the law applies only to the shareholders of the company. Limited liability does not prevent the imposition of liability on those who direct and manage the company for any wrongs that they may perpetrate. Those who direct the company may or may not be the same people as the shareholders, but as directors their potential liability is unlimited.

A consequence of the rule of limited liability is that there must be no ambiguity as to the identity of the company. All company invoices, business letters and cheques must contain the full registered corporate name. Not to provide such information is a criminal offence and can give rise to substantial personal liability. For example, where a director of the company signs a company cheque with the incorrect corporate name and the cheque is not honoured, the director may be personally liable for the amount on the cheque. Further, the business name should not lead potential customers to think that the company is another company with a similar name.

1.3.2 APPLYING LIMITED LIABILITY IN A GROUP OF COMPANIES

A group of companies can often organise itself so as to avoid liability for parts of its activities. The 'group' itself does not have a separate legal identity; it is a collection of companies linked by shareholdings between various companies, whether a vertical group of wholly owned subsidiaries controlled by one holding company or a cross-shareholding arrangement with no overall holding company. In such a situation creditors of an insolvent subsidiary company are not necessarily entitled to payment from the other group companies for the debts that are owed to them by the insolvent subsidiary.

There would be a potential liability to contribute to the assets of the insolvent subsidiary only where the liquidator was able to prove both that the holding company was in fact a 'shadow director' of the subsidiary (see section 8.1.3) and knew that there was no reasonable prospect of avoiding insolvency, or that unlawful activity had been undertaken at the behest of the holding company. Further, if a subsidiary company does engage in unlawful activity on the instruction of a holding company, then, although in principle the law will allow the veil of incorporation of both companies to be set aside and for action to be taken against the holding company, in practice this is likely to be a difficult and lengthy process.

Thus, if your company is about to engage in a commercially risky venture, for example the introduction of a new drug, you should consider establishing a subsidiary company to operate that venture. The risks should then be confinable to that one company. However, any such 'ring-fencing' will be evident to other companies or persons who undertake a due diligence search before entering into a business relationship, and they may demand guarantees or other arrangements which negate any 'ring-fencing'.

1.4 COMPANY FORMATION

1.4.1 INCORPORATION

Companies are formed or incorporated by a process of registration at Companies House. The process is formal: particular documents must be signed and filed; the documents are reviewed by Companies House and, if they provide adequate and appropriate information, result in the registration of the company. A certificate of registration is issued and a number given to the company on the face of the certificate. The company is then in being and may trade.

1.4.2 WHAT ARE THE REQUIREMENTS FOR THE FORMATION OF A COMPANY?

Any two persons associated for lawful purposes may, by subscribing to a Memorandum of Association and complying with the requirements of registration, form an incorporated company. The *Companies Act 1985* states:

> *Any two or more persons associated for a lawful purpose may, by subscribing their names to a memorandum of association and otherwise complying with the requirements of this Act in respect of registration, form an incorporated company, with or without limited liability.* (s.1.1)

(It is possible also for there to be single person companies.)

The documents to be sent to Companies House must include:

a) a Memorandum of Association;

b) the Articles of Association;

c) a statement setting out:

  i)   the first director(s) of the company (names, addresses, nationality, business occupation, other directorships);

ii) the first secretary of the company;

iii) the intended situation of the registered office.

The documents must be signed by the subscribers to the share capital and by those persons who consent to being director and/or secretary.

A Statutory Declaration has to be delivered to the Registrar of Companies House by a solicitor or director that all necessary steps to registration have been complied with. If the Registrar is satisfied, the company is registered and a Certificate issued.

These technicalities are not difficult, but they are time-consuming, especially if undertaken alone by an individual. The process can be obviated by putting the task in the hands of specialist companies which concentrate on company formations. They undertake the work; you need only sign a few documents. These companies, in the course of their business, form scores of companies which they hold 'on the shelf'. These 'off the shelf' companies can then be sold to others (the price is usually about £200) and the transfer processes take only a short time. The transfer processes usually involve changing the name of the company, the resignation of the existing directors and secretary and appointment of new directors and a new secretary, and the transfer of ownership of the shares to the new owners. The documents bringing about these changes must be signed and then sent to the Registrar at Companies House. The Registrar will issue a new Certificate with the changed company name on it.

Thereafter, companies have to keep, by law, so-called 'statutory books'; these are:

a) *The Register of Interests in Shares*

Private companies must list all their shareholders and their holdings; public companies need to maintain a register of holders of more than 3% of the issued shares who have notified their holdings in accordance with the law.

b) *The Register of Directors and Secretaries.*

c) *The Register of Directors' Interests in Shares and Debentures.*

d) *The Register of Members (shareholders).*

e) *The Minute Book.*

Minutes must be kept of shareholders' and directors' meetings.

f) *The Register of Charges.*

All companies must keep a register giving details of all charges (for example, mortgages) on company assets.

g) *The Register of Debenture Holders.*

This register is not mandatory in law; but, if it is kept, it must be available for inspection.

1.4.3 WHAT NAME CAN A COMPANY HAVE?

A company can be registered with any name, subject to a few minimal restrictions. These are:

a) The company name must not be the same as, or too similar to, the name of an existing company.

b) The proposed company name must not be offensive or give rise to a criminal offence.

c) In addition, certain names require approval by the Secretary of State for Trade and Industry, particularly words which point to national or international prominence (for example, 'British'), words which imply business prominence (for example, 'Authority', 'Council'), words which imply specific meaning (for example, 'Charity'), and certain other words (for example, 'Royal', 'Police', 'Bank').

1.5 WHAT ARE THE DIFFERENT TYPES OF COMPANY?

1.5.1 THE DIFFERENT TYPES OF COMPANY

There are many different types of company within the UK, and there are many different ways in which companies can be classified.

No single classification is correct or relevant in all circumstances. It is sometimes informative to classify companies according to the degree of autonomy that the board of directors of the company has. Does the board make its own decisions or is its freedom of action heavily circumscribed by external bodies? Are shareholders members of the board or not? The answers to these questions determine the parameters within which the board operates and the mix of legal, structural and leadership characteristics that will affect the role of the board and therefore the role of a director. A director of a multinational holding company, a national subsidiary of that company and a family company which supplies the subsidiary all have different roles, though there are substantial similarities and common principles. A simple classification is to differentiate corporate bodies according to their legal status. In this sense, there are five types:

1. Limited by shares

Companies limited by shares are either

- Private Limited Companies, *or*
- Public Limited Companies.

The differences between these two are described in section 1.5.2 below.

2. Limited by guarantee

The members of the company guarantee a sum (for example, £1) in the event of insolvency should there be any creditors who cannot be paid from the assets of the company. The members' liability is limited to the amount the members agreed at the outset to contribute to the assets in the event that the company is wound up.

Companies limited by guarantee are used by such bodies as professional and trade associations, charities, Training and Enterprise Councils, clubs, and management companies for blocks of flats.

Members of companies limited by guarantee obtain limited liability. Those who trade with such companies should be made aware by the status of 'limited by guarantee' of the companies' limited funding and possible incapacity to meet their debts in the event of being wound up.

3. Unlimited companies

An unlimited company is a company in which the members have unlimited liability. It does not normally need to file annual accounts at Companies House and has greater freedom in repaying capital.

Such companies are rare; the lack of the basic protection of limited liability generally makes them an unattractive option.

4. Incorporated by charter

Some corporate bodies are incorporated by charter, such as Universities, rather than through incorporation by registration with the Registrar of Companies. The Institute of Directors is a chartered corporate body.

5. Incorporated by statute

Some charitable bodies, housing associations for example, register under the *Provident Societies Act 1965*. In Scotland a charity may be established as a company.

In this *Guide* attention is focused on companies limited by shares.

1.5.2 PRIVATE AND PUBLIC LIMITED COMPANIES

Public companies are companies limited by shares which must satisfy certain conditions. These are:

a) The Memorandum of the company must state it is a public company.

b) The company must have an issued share capital of at least £50,000, of which 25% is paid up on each share.

c) The company requires a trading certificate from the Registrar before it can undertake business.

d) The company must have at least two directors.

All companies that are not public companies are private companies. Private companies therefore include companies limited by guarantee and unlimited companies. Private companies usually have at the outset a small capital base with a limited number of directors. The shares are owned and controlled by private persons. Such shares are not traded on any Stock Exchange; a company cannot be a private company if any part of the capital is offered to the public.

The private limited company is by far the most common form of company. There are 1.3 million registered companies in England and Wales of which only about 11,600 are public limited companies; the rest are private limited companies, mostly either subsidiaries of larger companies or companies where the capital is held by a small number of individuals who for the most part have an active role in the management of the company.

The main distinguishing features in terms of regulation between public and private companies are that:

a) Private companies are designated as 'Limited' or 'Ltd'; a public company's name must end with 'Public Limited Company' or 'Plc'.

b) A Plc must have at least £50,000 of capital, of which at least £12,500 is paid up, at the time of incorporation. There is no restriction on the amount of a private company's capital.

c) A Plc requires a trading certificate; a private company does not.

d) A private company may have only one director; a Plc must have at least two.

e) The *Companies Act 1985* imposes more rigorous provisions on Plcs in a number of areas, including the maintenance of capital, distribution of profits, payment for share capital, accounting requirements, loans to directors, and financial assistance for the acquisition of shares. In general, the reporting requirements on Plcs are more onerous than those on private limited companies. In addition, small and medium-sized private companies are exempted from the requirement to produce some financial statements.

f) Private companies can waive some procedures with the unanimous consent of the shareholders, dispensing with:

   i)   the need to lay annual accounts and an annual report before the general meeting;

   ii) the holding of an annual general meeting;

   iii) the annual appointment of auditors.

   The shareholders can elect to waive these procedures either in a general meeting or by written resolution. The auditors must be informed of any written resolutions; failure to do so is a criminal offence by the directors and company secretary.

g) A Plc must call an Extraordinary General Meeting when its net assets are one-half of its called-up share capital; private companies need not do so.

h) Private companies may give financial assistance for the purchase of their own shares; Plcs may not.

i) Unlike private companies, Plcs may issue shares to the public, usually by being listed or quoted on a recognised stock exchange. Private companies cannot.

1.5.3 THE LISTED PUBLIC COMPANY

It is important to remember that a Plc is not automatically a listed company, that is, a company quoted on a Stock Exchange. Companies listed on the Stock Exchange are Plcs, but most Plcs are not listed as in practice the capital requirements for a listing far exceed £50,000. (In 1999 the minimum for a listing on the London Stock Exchange was an expected market value of the shares to be listed of £700,000.) At the end of 1999, of the 11,600 registered Plcs, only 2,450 Plcs were listed on the London Stock Exchange, 400 were quoted on the Alternative Investment Market and about 50 were quoted only on an overseas market.

It is therefore prudent, before dealing with a Plc, to check if it is in fact listed on a Stock Exchange. The term Plc has come to imply size and strength. This may not be the case.

Seeking a listing on a Stock Exchange is an option pursued by many successful private limited companies and public limited companies. It facilitates the raising of funds to enable the business to expand and it enables shareholders to realise the value of their investments. However, before pursuing this course, owners of unlisted companies should be fully aware that, once their companies are quoted, they have added responsibilities to the market and to their shareholders to deliver up profits in the form of dividends. There is, in effect, a public scrutiny and accountability exercised through the stock market which some entrepreneurs find unwelcome. For example, in 1998 Richard Branson bought back from Virgin shareholders the company he had floated only two years previously, saying: 'Being an entrepreneur and the chairman of a public company just doesn't mix.' Similarly, Sir Andrew Lloyd Webber floated The Really Useful Group Plc in 1977, but bought it back eight years later; the flotation was, he said, 'an absolutely enormous, crashing mistake' (interview in *The Times*, 1 April 1995).

Listed companies must comply with the provisions of the Listing Rules of the Stock Exchange (London Stock Exchange [1999]). These are very detailed and are not dealt with in this *Guide*. Listed companies are also required by the London Stock Exchange, as a continuing obligation of listing, to make a statement in their report and accounts regarding compliance with the Combined Code (London Stock Exchange [1998]), a summary of which is set out in Appendix B, and to give reasons for any areas of non-compliance. Companies which have not obtained a full listing and which are admitted to trading on the Alternative Investment Market are subject to the provisions of the 'AIM Rules', which apply the provisions of the Listing Rules subject to specific amendments. The administration of the Listing Rules was transferred from the London Stock Exchange to the Financial Services Authority on 1 May 2000.

A number of distinguishing features of the listed company which affect the role of the board and the skills required of the directors may be itemised. These are:

- the expectations and concerns of institutional investors as shareholders and the special role of the chairman and/or chief executive as the contact person with institutional shareholders;

- the impact of the stock exchange listing agreement and the panoply of rules that accompany a listing, including non-statutory codes such as the Combined Code (London Stock Exchange [1998]);

- the constant scrutiny which the company and its directors are under as a result of a share price which can fluctuate by the minute, with a particular premium being placed on security of board discussions and the integrity of the directors;

- a body of shareholders which probably intervenes only rarely in the direction of the company, so the board enjoys a high degree of autonomy;

- a board which normally includes a significant number of non-executive directors;

- boards tend to be larger; the average size of a company board in 1996 was 8 directors for all quoted companies and 12 directors for FTSE 100 companies.

1.5.4 THE SUBSIDIARY AND HOLDING COMPANY RELATIONSHIP

The Registrar of Companies estimates that two-thirds of the 1.3 million companies registered in England and Wales are subsidiary or sub-subsidiary companies. Many large companies – household names – have a myriad of subsidiary companies. Rexam, for example, contains 420 companies, of which 200 are overseas; Reckitt and Benckiser Group contains over 200 companies, of which three-quarters are overseas companies; BP Amoco Group contains

1,300 companies; and Unilever comprises 800 companies, of which 300 are overseas subsidiaries. Asea Brown Boveri (ABB) is an extreme example: it is a giant electrical engineering conglomerate with total group sales of $30 billion; it is made up of 1,300 separate companies and a very small head office function (171 people from 19 different countries out of a total group workforce in excess of 200,000).

The statutory definition of a subsidiary (s.736 and s.736A of the *Companies Act 1985*) is based on the concept of control, rather than ownership. A company is a subsidiary (S) of a parent (P) if:

a) P holds a majority of the voting rights in S; *or*

b) P holds shares in S and has the right to appoint or remove directors having a majority of voting power at S's board meetings; *or*

c) P holds shares in S and controls a majority of the voting rights in it under an agreement with other shareholders; *or*

d) S is a subsidiary of another company which is itself a subsidiary of P.

The role of the board of directors of a holding company and of any of its subsidiaries varies according to the relationship that exists between the companies. For example, a subsidiary company may exist as an independent subsidiary of the parent company or it may be merely in effect a divisional organisation with a board structure of its own. Many multinational companies exemplify this latter type of organisation. The key issue in deciding the true nature of the subsidiary is whether or not the subsidiary company's board has a real strategic role or is just an operating arm of the corporate group. Which role the board has depends to a large extent upon the reason for creating the subsidiary. This, in turn, determines the types of directors that are appropriate for those boards.

The reasons why subsidiary companies are created may include:

a) *Autonomy*: to provide greater autonomy for a part of the business, whether by horizontal or vertical separation, thus giving managers of those subsidiaries the ability to control more of their own revenues and costs and exposing them to directorial responsibility.

b) *Succession*: one way of resolving succession problems in a family company is to divide the business up into subsidiary companies, each one managed by a different family member. The holding company may have no other

15

role than to develop group strategy and to receive the profits from the subsidiaries and distribute them to family members in accordance with their shareholding in the holding company.

c) *Overseas operations*: subsidiary companies operating overseas often bring a number of advantages:

   i) Differences in tax regimes mean that there may be tax savings if business is conducted through a local company registered in the country of business, though careful attention to the exact form of corporate structure is necessary in order to avoid, for example, tax on dividends paid to the parent company.

   ii) Some countries require that business is conducted through national companies with a majority of shareholders from that country (for example, Iran, China), forcing the parent company to set up a local partly-owned subsidiary.

   iii) In practice it is often politically astute to operate joint ventures with a local company rather than to operate a wholly owned subsidiary, particularly if part of the business comes from government contracts or is reliant on the granting of licences. Local subsidiaries often serve as a mechanism for coping with host country legal and political pressures.

d) *Market sensitivity*: often, it is simply a matter of good business in that subsidiaries are closer to, better informed about, and more sensitive to local markets. Overseas subsidiaries may be a valuable source of local economic information. In addition, support from local interests is often more forthcoming if there is a local company.

e) *Mergers and acquisitions*: subsidiaries often proliferate simply because a group expands by the acquisition of established businesses. Whatever the initial intention, there is usually resistance post-acquisition to any immediate or radical changes in established structures. This is often in part due to a strong desire among executives to retain or gain the status of director, which can be met by leaving lower-level corporate subsidiaries in existence even if they are functionally redundant.

f) *Protection of a name*: a simple way of protecting a trade name or to register a patent in a new market is to establish a company with that name in that market.

g) *Insolvency risk*: often, an important reason for setting up a subsidiary company is to protect the *group* against insolvency. High-risk operations are often set up within a subsidiary structure in an attempt to insulate the holding company from the possibility of major loss.

h) *Buying and selling businesses*: it is much simpler and more clear-cut, particularly from a legal point of view, to buy or sell a company as a going concern than to acquire or sell assets.

i) *Joint ventures*: similarly, joint ventures are difficult to arrange unless a separate legal company is involved, and practically impossible in another country without one.

The relationship between the boards of subsidiary and holding companies varies considerably. How it is defined depends on the particular circumstances. At one extreme, the parent company operates simply as owner, reserving for itself only the highest-level decisions. Sometimes the parent board will retain exclusive decision-making power in relation to capital expenditure and disposals exceeding a certain value, and senior appointments. The parent board may determine dividend policy, the capital structure of the company and any financial matters having third-party relevance. The parent board may or may not allow the directors of subsidiaries to play a strategic role in the development of their part of the group's operations or to take an independent stance where social considerations come into account, particularly the special considerations which may need to be considered when operating in a different culture.

Whatever the relationship between holding companies and subsidiaries, a subsidiary is, nevertheless, a legal entity independent of its holding company. The company (and the parties associated with it) to which the directors of a subsidiary owe duties is the subsidiary, not the holding company. This can cause problems for persons who are directors of both the holding company and the subsidiary or for directors of subsidiaries who are accustomed to taking directions from the parent. In such a case there is a danger that directors may breach their duties to the subsidiary; they may find themselves with responsibilities (for example, for the welfare of creditors, employees or consumers) which they are in practice unable to discharge. On the other hand, the parent may become a 'shadow' director of the subsidiary and, as such, assume certain duties in relation to the subsidiary (see the discussion in section 8.1.3). This factor, along with the benefits that may stem from the properly delegated exercise of local initiative, should be borne in mind when responsibilities are assigned to subsidiary boards and their directors.

1.6 SUMMARY

1. A company is a separate legal entity. It is separate from all the persons who associate with it – for example, directors, shareholders, employees, suppliers and customers.

2. Companies are formed (businesses are incorporated) through registration with the Registrar of Companies at Companies House.

3. The shareholders of private limited companies and public limited companies, whether or not quoted on a stock exchange, have limited liability.

4. Limited liability applies to shareholders, not directors. The liability of directors is unlimited. The extent of shareholders' liability is to pay up the full value of their shares.

5. Companies may contract as separate persons with other persons and companies.

6. In a group of companies, all companies are separate entities and their shareholders are limited in their liability. Subsidiary companies of a holding company may become insolvent without damaging the separate holding company.

Chapter 2

The Company's Constitution

2.1 WHAT IS THE CONSTITUTION OF A COMPANY?

Private and public limited companies conceal a great variety of corporate structures and therefore, in order to accommodate this variety, the constitution of a company must exhibit significant flexibility. A director needs to be aware of the opportunities that this flexibility offers and be prepared to recommend to shareholders alterations in the constitution of the company to match changing needs.

The constitution of the company comprises two documents:

1. the Memorandum of Association;

2. the Articles of Association.

The Memorandum regulates the external affairs of the company; the Articles of Association regulate its internal affairs.

These two documents state where authority in a company lies. They also provide important practical details relating to the operation of the two key constitutional organs of the company: the board of directors and the general meeting of shareholders.

2.1.1 WHAT IS THE MEMORANDUM OF ASSOCIATION?

The Memorandum of Association is a document which primarily sets out the purpose of a company. It must state:

a) The name of the company

The name of a private company which is limited by shares must end with the word 'limited' and, if a public company, with the words 'public limited company' (or abbreviations 'Ltd', 'Plc', or similar). The index of company names can be inspected free of charge at Companies House.

b) Registered office

If the company is registered in England or Wales, then the registered office will be situated in England and Wales. Companies registered in Scotland will have their registered office in Scotland.

The registered office of a company is important because it indicates where the company is always to be found and it is the location at which, if documents are delivered, they are deemed to have been delivered to the company. This is why it is to the registered address that legal documents, for example writs, are delivered. Most companies have their registered address at their headquarters where the company secretary or the managing director is located. Registered offices are also frequently found at the offices of the lawyers or accountants of the company – so as to secure the fullest attention to any documents served on the company. It should be noted that Scots companies which carry on business in England and Wales may be served with writs or other processes of a Court at their principal place of business in England and Wales.

The registered office is also significant in that it tells the world in which jurisdiction or legal system the company resides. If a company is based in a foreign jurisdiction, for example the Isle of Man, the Channel Islands or France, then Court actions may well have to be started in a foreign jurisdiction under a foreign law. Actions in a foreign jurisdiction or country are both more difficult and generally more expensive than bringing them in your home country. It is therefore necessary to take care before entering into a contract with a foreign company. From a legal point of view, the Isle of Man, the Republic of Ireland and the Channel Islands are foreign jurisdictions with different legal systems. Also, you may find that your insurance company may demand an increased premium if you do business in certain countries. In the USA, particularly, any company is always at risk of litigation and accordingly you may have to pay extra for insurance cover.

c) Objects clause

Most of a company's Memorandum is taken up with a myriad of clauses which state that the company has the object of undertaking a whole host of activities. In general, a company has no power to do anything other than the objects for which it is incorporated. If the company acts outside its objects, it is acting beyond its powers, or *ultra vires*.

The original intention of the objects clause was twofold:

● to protect investors in companies by ensuring that the companies in which they had invested did not act beyond their powers, thereby enabling shareholders to be sure of the purposes to which their monies were to be applied; *and*

● to protect persons dealing with the company, who could infer from the objects clause the extent of the company's powers.

The Memorandum of Association should provide an assurance that if, for instance, you invested in a paper converter your investment would not be diverted into a travel company. If the paper converter did start to run package holidays, any shareholder could initiate proceedings to stop the company from engaging in that business.

It would therefore appear that the objects clause should be studied closely. In practice, however, this is not the case. The reason is that, in order not to fall foul of the *ultra vires* rule, those who set up companies now nearly always write the objects clause so generally that such clauses reveal little meaningful information. Typically, objects clauses today contain such vapid information as: the company may enter into contracts, the company may employ other persons, the company may enter into mortgages, and so on.

The importance of the objects clause has been further undermined by the ending of the *ultra vires* rule as it affects customers. It used to be the case that if a company entered into a contract which was *ultra vires*, then if the company breached the contract the other contracting person could not sue the company. Now, however, a person dealing with the company in good faith is protected by the fact that companies can no longer escape their contractual responsibilities in this way (see section 2.7).

In general, it is wise to draft the objects clause as widely as possible, giving the company substantial authority to do almost anything, so as to avoid the danger that the company may inadvertently act *ultra vires*. Paradoxically, it also assists those who are trading with companies as they do not have to check every transaction against the company's Memorandum to establish if the company has the power to engage in a particular activity.

Nonetheless, a director who causes the company to enter into a transaction which may be beyond the company's authority in the Memorandum can still be made liable for breach of duty to the company. Insofar as outsiders are concerned, transactions can be enforced by them so long as they acted in good faith and they are not connected with the company.

d) Share capital

The Memorandum sets out the amount of the share capital with which the company proposes to be registered and how that share capital is divided into shares of fixed amount.

e) Subscribers

The Memorandum must be signed by at least two persons (or by one person if sole shareholder). Such persons are the subscribers to the Memorandum.

2.1.2 WHAT ARE THE ARTICLES OF ASSOCIATION?

The Articles of Association are subsidiary to the Memorandum.

The Articles are detailed rules concerning the internal affairs of the company. A model set of Articles is Table A to the *Companies Act 1985* (see DTI [1985]) and the majority of companies have Articles that adopt most of Table A subject to some exclusions and alterations.

The Articles usually include provisions dealing with such matters as:

i)   Share capital and variation of rights.

ii) Transfer and transmission of shares.

iii) Alteration of capital.

iv) General meetings.

v) Votes of members.

vi) Borrowing powers.

vii) Appointment, power and duties of directors and managing director.

viii) Disqualification of directors.

ix) Proceedings of directors.

x) Secretary.

xi) Dividends and reserves.

xii) Accounts and audit.

xiii) Capitalisation of profits.

xiv) Special provisions relating to winding up.

The sort of questions answered by the Articles are, for example,

- *How are directors appointed?*
  Directors are normally appointed by the board and their appointment confirmed by the shareholders in general meeting.

- *Who has the casting vote at board meetings?*
  The casting vote at board meetings and at general meetings will normally be held by the chairman of the board of directors. But a company's Articles may stipulate a different requirement. For example, if there are only two directors and neither of them wants to cede dominance, the casting vote clause may be deleted completely.

- *Can directors vote and be counted in the quorum at board meetings if they have declared an interest in the matter to be voted upon?*
  Table A states that directors cannot be counted in any quorum if they have an interest in a contract which is being voted upon at a board meeting. It seems fair that any director who has a personal interest in a decision should not be allowed to vote. However, this can cause difficulties in small companies as there may be no quorum for board decisions. Therefore it is quite usual for small companies to allow directors with an interest to count in the quorum and even to vote.

2.2 WHO OWNS A COMPANY?

A company is owned by its shareholders. This is *not* to say that the shareholders own the business or the company's assets. Because a company is a separate legal entity, the company itself owns its assets. (Directors and boards, who govern a company, should never forget that they are in charge of property and assets that do not belong to them.) Even collectively, shareholders do not own the company or its assets outright. A share in a company is merely a bundle of rights, on which a monetary value can be placed, to participate in the company on the terms set out in law and in the Articles of Association, not an asset of the company. The bundle of rights will normally include the following main elements (though many of them may be excluded or modified in the case of a particular company or class of shareholder):

- a financial return, normally in the form of a proportion of the company's distributable profits (i.e. a dividend);

- a right to transfer their ownership to another person; *and*

- a right to vote in general meetings, enabling shareholders to participate in decisions on the size, shape and scope of the company and in particular in decisions to dismiss and appoint the directors, change the company's constitution, and liquidate the company and distribute the value of the assets among themselves.

Shareholders are not, in the eye of the law, part owners of the undertaking. The undertaking is something different from the totality of the shareholdings. (Evershed L J, *Short v Treasury Commissioners* {45})

2.3 THE TRANSFERABILITY OF SHARES

Shares in a company are transferable; they can be bought and sold or given away. This essential feature of companies confers a number of advantages:

1. The membership of the company can change without affecting the company's management or organisation. The members of listed comp-anies change on a daily basis, as shares are bought and sold. But the directors do not change every time someone buys or sells shares; the company and the board of directors have the capacity to continue unchanged. Obviously, major changes in the shareholding may give rise

to significant board changes, but the two events are independent. If a particular shareholder's voting rights exceed 50% of the total voting rights of the shareholding of the company, then he may change the composition of the board of directors if he wishes, but this does not have to happen. By contrast, where there is a change in the ownership of a partnership, there is generally a change in the management of the partnership as every partner is entitled to a say in the management of the firm. This can create difficulties, so that complex partnership arrangements which create the equivalent of a board of directors, comprising selected partners, conferring powers that all the partners have on this group, have been developed for large accountancy and law firms. However, from 2001 partnerships have been able to limit the liability of the partners through the formation of a new form of business association, a limited liability partnership.

2. Transferability encourages investment and trade ventures which investors would either be unable or unwilling to take on alone. For example, it would require an extremely wealthy individual to establish and run an aluminium smelter. But if thousands of people contribute equity capital by buying shares in the company, this enables the venture to take place without the need to find a wealthy investor. Additionally, if there is easy transferability, as provided by a stock exchange, then the investment can remain highly liquid. Approximately 60% of the value of UK and US share investment comes from institutional investors (for example, pension funds, insurance companies) who need to invest their available cash somewhere. They want a transferable share so that they can move their portfolio of holdings around depending on their view of a company's fortunes and prospects.

3. The transferability of shares is fundamental to the pooling of assets in a collective economic enterprise in order to carry on a business venture. The transaction costs of combining many individuals' capital outside of the corporate framework would probably exceed the costs of forming a company. Each institutional or individual investor would need to agree separate terms and conditions for investing in every business that they hold shares in. It would be as if every bus passenger had to negotiate the terms of his ticket with the driver before travelling.

4. For private companies transferability, though it may be limited, provides a necessary flexibility when changes in ownership and succession issues are looming. Succession planning is complex and is dealt with in Chapter 16, but without transferability of shares little planning is possible.

2.4 WHO GOVERNS A COMPANY?

In general terms the board of directors is responsible for a company's governance.

The responsibility for a company's governance has been put this way:

> *A company may in many ways be likened to a human body. It has a brain and nerve centre which controls what it does. It also has hands which hold the tools and act in accordance with directions from the centre. Some of the people in the company are mere servants and agents who are nothing more than hands to do the work and cannot be said to represent the mind or will. Others are directors and managers who represent the directing mind and will of the company and control what it does. The state of mind of these managers is the state of mind of the company and is treated by the law as such. So you will find in cases where the law requires personal fault as a condition of liability in tort, the fault of the manager will be the personal fault of the company. . . So also in the criminal law, in cases where the law requires a guilty mind as a condition of a criminal offence, the guilty mind of the directors or the managers will render the company itself guilty. . . . Whether their intention is the company's intention depends on the nature of the matter under consideration, the relative position of the officer or agent, and the other relevant facts and circumstances of the case.* (Denning L J, *H L Bolton (Engineering) Co Ltd v T J Graham & Sons Ltd* {5}).

The officers of a company, then, are those who are regarded by the law as being accountable for the company's actions. For example, the *Companies Act 1985* contains many criminal offences for which any officer of the company may be liable, although some apply only to directors (see Chapter 8). Furthermore, the financial statements of a company must disclose various transactions with a company's officers (see Chapter 9). The expression 'officer of a company' also points to the persons who are responsible for the welfare, survival and prosperity of the company.

2.5 WHO ARE A COMPANY'S OFFICERS?

The *Companies Act 1985* (s.744) defines the officers of a company as including the directors, managers and the company secretary. The company's auditor may also be regarded as an officer. A company's bankers and solicitors will not usually be officers except in the improbable event that a Court judges they have such other duties that they occupy a position in the company different from that of a normal banker or solicitor.

The roles of directors, managers and secretary are dealt with in Chapter 4. The provisions relating to auditors are, briefly, that:

- Auditors must be appointed at each general meeting before which accounts are laid, to act until the next such meeting when they can be either reappointed or replaced. If the auditors retire between AGMs, then the directors of the company may appoint new auditors to hold office until the next AGM.

- An individual can act as an auditor only if authorised to do so by a Recognised Supervisory Body.

- Auditors must not be an employee of the company.

- The job of the auditors is to form an independent opinion, based on their audit, and to make a report to members on the company's accounts stating whether they have been properly prepared and whether they give 'a true and fair view' of the state of the company's affairs. Auditors have the right to attend and speak at all meetings of the shareholders.

- Auditors have the right of access at all times to the company's books, accounts and vouchers, and the right to require the officers of the company and any subsidiary undertaking of the company to give them whatever information and explanations they consider necessary for the execution of their duties. It is an offence for a director knowingly or recklessly to give misleading, false or deceptive information or explanations to auditors. The auditors must report any failure to obtain all the information and explanations they think necessary. They also have a duty to consider whether the information given in the directors' report is consistent with the accounts.

2.6 WHAT IS THE BOARD'S RELATIONSHIP TO THE SHAREHOLDERS?

There are two distinct constitutional organs of the company – the board of directors and the general meeting of shareholders. They have different functions and powers, so it is important not to confuse the two in practice.

In larger private companies and public listed companies, the distinction between directors and shareholders will be clear-cut because there will be a large number of shareholders. In some companies, however, such as family companies, the composition of the board of directors and the general meeting may be the same and the shareholders/directors may get into the habit of ignoring the distinction between the two organs of the company. When these people get together, perhaps around the breakfast table or over Sunday lunch, it may be difficult to know whether they are merely taking a meal together, making decisions as a board of directors, or making decisions as a general meeting of shareholders. But this is a mistake. It is important to know when decisions are being made by the board and when decisions are being made by the general meeting, for the two have different functions and powers.

Smaller private companies often do not have a formal board system. However, it is extremely unlikely that a company can comply with its legal obligations in letter or in spirit, whether imposed by the general law, including the *Companies Acts*, or by its own Memorandum and Articles of Association, unless certain acts are performed collectively by its board of directors. Secondly, it is also unlikely that the directors of a company which became insolvent and did not have a formal board system would be able to avoid personal liability for 'wrongful trading' under s.214 of the *Insolvency Act 1986* or mount a successful defence against disqualification under s.6 of the *Company Directors Disqualification Act 1986* (see section 15.3).

Again, it might be, for example, that outsiders with an interest in the company – for example, a liquidator or a potential buyer of the company – may suspect a director of making a personal profit out of a company contract, say, and if the informality of the company and board meetings means there is no record of a declaration of interest, then the director may be liable to pay the profit to the company. Minutes of the separate meetings should therefore be maintained.

There are two main areas where it is important to know in what capacity individuals are making decisions. These are:

● voting rights;

● competencies.

2.6.1 VOTING RIGHTS

Shares in a company have a monetary value. The nominal or authorised share capital of the company is the number of shares which the directors are authorised to issue and their value at incorporation. The issued share capital is the shares actually issued by the company.

There are many types of shares, but the most common are:

- Ordinary shares, which are paid dividends and carry voting power;
- Preference shares, which, as their name denotes, are paid dividends in preference to or before Ordinary shares.
- Redeemable shares, which are shares which do not carry voting power but which have to be paid back at a certain time.

Shares denote ownership rights in the company and therefore, most importantly, they carry voting rights. There are two important distinctions between votes at board meetings and votes at shareholders' meetings:

a) First, the voting rights of the board are independent of any shareholding. Each director normally has one vote on the board and the chairman will normally have a casting vote, although it is possible for the Articles of a company to state a different practice. In the general meeting of shareholders, on the other hand, the normal practice is for matters to be decided by a poll; each shareholder therefore has as many votes as are attached to his shareholding. On occasion a vote at a general meeting takes place on a show of hands, when the number of shares a person holds is not taken into account.

Most listed companies have one vote attached to each share and this includes any proxy votes registered by those not attending the meeting (subject to the Articles). Whether or not, and in what circumstances, a vote on a poll can be demanded will be stated in the company's Articles. It is also set out in the *Companies Acts*.

The board of directors may want to know who controls the votes at a general meeting. One of the statutory books that must be held by the company is the register of members, listing who owns (and how many) shares of the company. Different types of shares may have different voting rights, but the Articles will reveal any differences. In larger Plcs, with many thousands of shareholdings and institutional nominee accounts, shareholder analysis is essential and is often professionally managed.

b) Secondly, most importantly, directors voting at board meetings are legally bound to act and make decisions in the best interests of the company and not for any ulterior motive, such as personal gain (this obligation is discussed in Chapter 8). By contrast, the shareholders can vote at the general meeting for their own interests if they wish.

When a director votes as a director for or against any particular resolution in a directors' meeting, he is voting as a person under a fiduciary duty to the company for the proposition that the company should take a creative course of action. When a shareholder is voting for or against a particular resolution he is voting as a person owing no fiduciary duty to the company who is exercising his own right of property to vote as he thinks fit.

(Walton J, *Northern Counties Securities Ltd v Jackson and Steeple Ltd* {26})

2.6.2 COMPETENCIES

When the company meets it is not the directors who are meeting, it is the shareholders. And when shareholders meet they do so in general meetings of the company. Each company, unless there has been a special vote, must hold an Annual General Meeting (AGM). Whenever the company is meeting at other times, it is an Extraordinary General Meeting (EGM) of the company.

The general meeting and the board of directors have distinct powers.

In broad terms, all powers of the company are vested in the board unless they are reserved to the general meeting by:

- the Memorandum and Articles;
- the *Companies Acts;*
- directions from the general meeting given by special resolution.

The general meeting delegates the management function of the company to the board of directors through the Articles of Association.

The main items that are reserved to the general meeting are:

- approving the company accounts;
- declaring a dividend or otherwise;
- altering the Articles or the Memorandum;
- changing the company name;
- changing the rights attached to capital;
- authorising the directors to issue, repurchase or cancel shares;

- increasing or reducing the capital of the company;
- authorising a purchase by the company of its own shares;
- appointing and removing auditors;
- dismissing the directors;
- voluntarily winding-up the company.

These are important topics; general meetings matter. When the company is prospering shareholders generally leave directors alone to make profits. But if the directors fail to deliver profits, then shareholders will demonstrate where ultimate power lies – namely in the general meetings of the company. The general meeting may change the company's policies and it may dismiss directors.

In company meetings a simple majority is usually sufficient. In limited circumstances, special majorities are required. To wind up the company or to change the Memorandum or Articles a 75% majority is required.

2.6.3 RATIFICATION

If directors exceed the company's powers but the shareholders are willing to accept the act as the company's own, the *Companies Act 1985* provides that such an *ultra vires* act may be ratified by a special resolution of the shareholders. However, a separate special resolution is required to relieve directors from any liability arising from such an act. The power of shareholders to ratify other breaches by directors of their duties to the company is derived from common law and is subject to certain limitations – for example, breaches involving dishonesty by the directors or illegal acts by the company cannot be ratified (see section 8.9).

2.7 WHO ENTERS INTO CONTRACTS?

2.7.1 THE COMPANY

It is the company that enters into contractual arrangements for the supply and sale of goods or services. If such contracts are broken, it is the company that is either pursued or decides to take action itself.

> Suppose, for example, that Fine Cakes Ltd supplies cakes to a supermarket under a contract between Fine Cakes and the supermarket. There is no contract between the supermarket and the directors or shareholders of Fine Cakes.

If the cakes are mouldy, then the supermarket has a grievance against Fine Cakes and any formal action by the supermarket would be against Fine Cakes, not the directors or shareholders of Fine Cakes. The supermarket will no doubt complain to whoever is responsible within the company for the contract with them, but these persons are not legally responsible for the mouldy cakes – Fine Cakes Ltd is. Similarly, if the cakes contain slivers of glass which injure the supermarket's customers, those customers can certainly pursue Fine Cakes for negligently allowing the glass to get into the cake. They will be able legally to pursue the directors of Fine Cakes only if they are able to show direct personal negligence by the directors.

This is why directors are often asked by banks to give personal guarantees. If Widgets Ltd borrows money from a bank, there will be a contract between Widgets Ltd and the bank as regards the conditions attached to the loan. If the company is unable to provide sufficient security for the loan, the directors and/or shareholders will probably be asked by the bank to provide a personal guarantee such that the bank may seize their personal assets if the company defaults on the loan. The reason for this is simple: banks or other providers of corporate finance are well aware that companies have limited liability for their debts but that directors do not. In effect, then, the bank supplements its contract with Widgets Ltd for the repayment of the loan with another contract with the directors or shareholders.

Owners and directors are often persuaded or forced to give up the protection of limited liability. For example, in a survey of small companies (Freedman [1994]), 66% of respondent shareholders stated that they had incorporated in order to attain the benefit of limited liability, but 54% of these owners had provided some form of personal guarantee for the debts of their company. The majority of individuals who established these companies were, therefore, not enjoying perhaps the main benefit for which they had incorporated.

2.7.2 THE DIRECTORS

The company is in a sense a legal fiction. Although it is a legal 'person', it is not corporeal. It can think or act only through individual human agents.

This applies to any situation, including criminal liability of the company, where actions of the company are in question; they can be assessed only by looking at the conduct of relevant individuals within the company. Therefore, in order to decide whether or not the company has committed itself to any contract, Courts or other interested parties may well have to determine the following: 'Who has the authority within the company to commit the company to contracts?' Similarly, if the contract is broken: 'Who has the authority to decide whether or not the company will take action?'

It is a part of the responsibility of the board of directors to ensure that there is internal guidance about the authority of individuals to bind the company into commercial arrangements with third parties. The board must ensure that rules of guidance are in place so as to minimise risks to the company. The risk is that officers or staff of the company may commit the company to obligations that it cannot meet. The board may delegate the development of these rules to an audit committee of the board (see section 5.7.2), but it is necessary to have such rules in all companies, however small. The rules should incorporate statements clarifying exactly what authority individuals (including directors) have within the organisation, particularly setting out in what circumstances and to what extent they have the capacity to bind the company without referring to the board of directors for approval. For example, it is normal for a company to place limits on the authority of directors to hire and fire staff, to enter into contracts valued over a certain amount, and to commit the company to loan arrangements.

The circumstances in which a director exceeds his powers, and the possible legal consequences thereof, are discussed in section 8.2.

2.8 CAN WRONGS BE INFLICTED AGAINST A COMPANY?

In broad terms, there are three types of wrong that can be inflicted upon a company. These are:

a) An *internal irregularity* involving failure to comply with the company's internal procedures as stated in the company's constitution. An example would be the failure of the chairman to call for a vote on a poll instead of a show of hands at a shareholders' meeting.

b) *Civil wrongs*, for example:

   i)   conversion or misuse of corporate property;

   ii) breaches of contract;

   iii) negligent action which causes the company loss;

   iv) negligent advice provided to the company which causes the company loss;

   v) breach of the company's copyright or patent;

   vi) trying to pass oneself off as the company by using a variant on the company's name or business name.

c) *Criminal wrongs*, for example:

   i)   theft of corporate property;

   ii) fraud on the company.

Where a wrong is perpetrated on the company it is the company that initiates any action. The board must decide, therefore, what action is to be taken by the company. The board is instrumental, but it is the company that acts. The possible actions open to a company are discussed in section 8.8.

However, where directors have committed a wrong against the company (for example, if the directors have stolen corporate assets) it is highly unlikely that they will initiate an action by the company against themselves! But they have perpetrated a wrong on the company and it would be unjust if the company could not pursue them and recover the money. In this case the incapacity of the company is recognised in law, which allows shareholders, including minority shareholders, to bring an action on behalf of the company. Although the shareholder is bringing the action, the authority to do so is derived from the company which has been incapacitated because the wrongdoers are in control of it. However, if there are no shareholders apart from directors, then the wrong will not be corrected unless there is a change in shareholding or an insolvency, when new shareholders or the liquidator can pursue the previous directors for their fraud against the company. If the directors have committed a criminal act, then the Crown Prosecution Service may launch an action.

2.9 WHAT LEGAL PROVISIONS APPLY TO COMPANIES?

There are many legal provisions which are applicable to companies, deriving from a number of sources – statute, the decisions of the Courts, and, increasingly, directly effective provisions of European Community law. In addition, there is a plethora of regulations that companies have to follow – for example, accounts must be prepared in accordance with certain accounting standards, quoted companies are bound by the London Stock Exchange Listing Rules, take-overs are constrained by the City Code on Take-overs and Mergers, etc.

The main provisions of company law and related regulations, apart from matters to do with corporate insolvency and certain regulations specific to the insurance, banking, investment and charity sectors, are summarised in Appendix A.

The main pieces of legislation that company directors need to be aware of are:

- The *Companies Act 1985*
  This Act is the principal codification of company law. The implications of this Act for directors are dealt with *seriatim* and especially in Chapters 8 and 9.

- The *Companies Act 1989*
  This amends certain provisions of the 1985 Act.

- The *Company Directors Disqualification Act 1986*
  Its purpose is to set out the circumstances in which a director may be disqualified; see Chapter 11.

- The *Insolvency Act 2000*
  This Act deals with insolvency, the winding up of companies, company voluntary arrangements, and administration orders. The implications of this Act for directors are dealt with in Chapter 15.

- The *Criminal Justice Act 1993*
  The implications of this Act for directors in the context of insider dealing are dealt with in Chapter 13.

- The *Financial Services and Markets Act 2000*
  This deals with companies that undertake investment business.

- The *Theft Act 1968*
  This Act deals with certain criminal offences for which the company and the officers may be liable.

- *Revenue law*
  This is a complex area and all directors are well advised to seek professional advice as to how tax law affects both them and their companies. However, a brief overview is given in Chapter 14.

- The *Employment Rights Act 1996*
  A brief overview of a director's responsibilities to employees is given in Chapter 10.

- *Other*
  There are many other obligations which the law lays upon both companies and directors. Examples are the obligations under consumer protection legislation and environmental law. In addition, some specialist businesses, for example insurance companies, are subject to further regulation. Some, but not all, of these obligations are discussed in Chapter 10.

2.10 SUMMARY

1. The constitution of a company is the Memorandum and Articles of Association. The Memorandum regulates the external affairs of the company and provides information about the registered office, the objects of the company and the shareholding. The Articles regulate the internal affairs of the company and provide information about shares, directors and meetings of the company.

2. The officers of the company are the directors, the managers, the secretary and the auditor, but particularly the directors.

3. Directors exercise power in the company on a day-to-day basis, but ultimate power lies with the general meeting of the shareholders.

4. Shareholders exercise power through the voting rights attached to their shares.

5. Companies are bound by the contracts into which they enter. They cannot rely on a lack of authority by a director or limitations in the Memorandum and Articles of Association to set aside contracts with others.

6. Companies can be wronged and may do wrong. Companies act through agents, often directors, but in general it is the company that sues or may be sued by third parties.

Part 2

The Board of Directors

Chapter 3

The Purpose of the Board

3.1 INTRODUCTION

There is no requirement in law for a company to have a board of directors. In practice, however, most companies do have a board as the prime organ of governance of the company. The board is, principally, the 'mind and will' of the company. The Articles of most companies contain a provision which states that 'the business of the company will be managed by the directors, who may exercise all such powers of the company', or words to this effect. Executive powers are therefore vested in the board as a whole. Much of the law relating to directors is designed to provide a system of checks and balances to control the potential power of directors acting in concert, that is, the board.

In practice, the board delegates executive authority to the executive directors, especially the managing director who heads the management of the business. This does not, however, negate the board's ultimate responsibility for the company's affairs. The board also, therefore, monitors what the management does and achieves, and must be prepared in the last resort to exercise its executive power by removing the managing director if necessary. In addition, the board reserves certain powers to itself, holding them separate from those delegated to the managing director.

3.2 THE PURPOSE OF A BOARD

The Institute of Directors, based on a study of good practice involving several hundred UK directors and many boards, defined the board's purpose as:

> *The key purpose of the board is to ensure the company's prosperity by collectively directing the company's affairs, whilst meeting the appropriate interests of its shareholders and relevant stakeholders.* (Institute of Directors [1999], p. 42)

It is for the board to judge, on a case-by-case basis, which stakeholders it treats as 'relevant' and which of their interests it is appropriate to meet, taking into account the law, relevant regulations and commercial considerations. This is a summary view based on the extended discussion of the role of the board in relation to shareholders and other stakeholders in Chapter 17.

Sir John Harvey-Jones [1995] put it succinctly when he said *The job of the board is all to do with creating momentum, movement, improvement and direction. If the board is not taking the company purposefully into the future, who is? The answer is, of course, no one.* Companies compete with each other in markets. Markets are difficult, capricious and challenging. It is up to the directors to point the way forward so that the company grows and is profitable.

Some economists have argued that in fact businessmen are not naturally the profit maximisers so beloved of the economic theorists but have a multiplicity of objectives. Some have stressed the desire to maximise company size; others have stressed the requirement of businessmen and of companies merely to survive. However, whilst the urge to maximise company size is undoubtedly for some companies at some times an important consideration, it is not clear that in the long run this is inconsistent with a profit-maximising objective. Similarly, whilst the board of directors has a duty to attempt to ensure the company's survival, survival is that much easier if the company is making profits.

3.3 THE TASKS OF A BOARD

The board is essentially a decision-making body. It has neither the time nor the resources to enact every decision itself and so must delegate to management a great deal of authority. However, it remains ultimately responsible for the company and any actions taken on its behalf. To ensure that the company prospers, the board must address some key tasks and ensure that they are carried out effectively.

The four key tasks of the board identified in Institute of Directors [1999] are to:

A. Establish vision, mission and values

In order to carry out this task the board must

A.1 Determine the company's vision and mission to guide and set the pace for its current operations and future development.

A.2 Determine the values to be promoted throughout the company.

A.3 Determine and review company goals.

A.4 Determine company policies.

B. Set strategy and structure

This involves

B.1 Reviewing and evaluating present and future opportunities, threats and risks in the external environment; and current and future strengths, weaknesses and risks relating to the company.

B.2 Determining strategic options, selecting those to be pursued, and deciding the means to support them.

B.3 Determining the business strategies and plans that underpin the corporate strategy.

B.4 Ensuring that the company's organisational structure and capability are appropriate for implementing the chosen strategies.

C. Delegate to management

In order properly to address this task, the board should

C.1 Delegate authority to management, and monitor and evaluate the implementation of policies, strategies and business plans.

C.2 Determine monitoring criteria.

C.3 Ensure that internal controls are effective.

C.4 Communicate with senior management.

D. Exercise accountability to shareholders and be responsible to relevant stakeholders

That is, the board should

D.1 Ensure that communications both to and from shareholders and relevant stakeholders are effective.

D.2 Understand and take into account the interests of shareholders and relevant stakeholders.

D.3 Monitor relations with shareholders and relevant stakeholders by the gathering and evaluation of appropriate information.

D.4 Promote the goodwill and support of shareholders and relevant stakeholders.

In addition, Institute of Directors [1999], pp. 41–61, contains a useful and detailed checklist of indicators of good practice which enable a director to assess whether his board of directors is effectively addressing these key tasks. Not all the indicators will be relevant in every circumstance. For example, boards of small privately owned companies will not be concerned with many issues which are peculiar to large listed companies. However, very many of the indicators are relevant to any board.

3.4 THE BOARD'S COMPLEX ROLE

In pursuing its key purpose, a board of directors faces a uniquely demanding set of responsibilities and challenges, the complexity of which can be seen in some of the seemingly contradictory pressures it faces:

- The board must simultaneously be **entrepreneurial** and drive the business forward while keeping it under **prudent** control. The role of the financial director is often crucial in securing 'managed' development.

- The board is required to be sufficiently knowledgeable about the workings of the company to be **answerable** for its actions, yet be able to stand back from the day-to-day management of the company and retain an **objective** and holistic view.

- The board must be sensitive to the pressures of **short-term** issues and yet be responsive to broader, **long-term** trends.

- The board must be knowledgeable about **'local'** issues and yet be aware of non-local (perhaps **international**) competitive and other influences, both potential and actual.

- The board is expected to be focused upon the **commercial needs** of its business whilst simultaneously expected to **act responsibly** towards its employees, business partners and society as a whole.

In sum, then, in order to carry out its tasks the board and individual directors should look both internally, to examine the component parts of the company, and externally, to examine the business in its competitive environment, and should focus simultaneously on both the short-term current performance of the business and its long-term future. It is important to reflect on these issues. How much emphasis has to be placed on different aspects of these complex and apparently contradictory issues will depend on the performance of the company and the circumstances in which it operates at any given time.

The story of Brent-Spar is an example of a board dilemma faced by the directors of Shell Group Plc in 1995. After nearly 20 years of operational use, Shell decided to scrap one of its gas and oil extraction platforms, Brent-Spar, from the North Sea. After exhaustive consultation with environmental experts it was decided to dump the large structure, some 300 feet high, under controlled conditions into a 20,000 feet deep trench in the North Atlantic. The environmental group, Greenpeace, organised a multinational campaign against this decision, based in part on data that subsequently turned out to be incorrect. The result of this campaign was a boycott of the purchase of Shell petrol in Germany, a country with a substantial 'green' vote. Shell Germany was able to exert substantial pressure on the parent board to reverse the Brent-Spar decision in the face of plummeting sales at its retail forecourts. The platform was duly moved to a Norwegian fjord for break-up and disposal. However, this break-up and disposal was not only much more expensive for the Shell Group, it was far more damaging from an environmental perspective than the original proposal. Greenpeace subsequently issued an apology to Shell. (See www.shellexpro.brentspar.com)

3.5 THE BOARD OF DIRECTORS, SHAREHOLDERS AND MANAGEMENT

3.5.1 THE DIFFERENT ROLES OF THE BOARD AND SHAREHOLDERS

The general meeting of shareholders and the board of directors are the two bodies with direct responsibility for the survival and success of the company.

The relationship between shareholders and the board is given formal expression in the company's Articles of Association. Every director should, before accepting his appointment, obtain a copy of the Articles and read it carefully to find out what the formal powers and duties of each body are. Each body may do only that which the current constitution and legislation permit it to do. Of course, how the relationship works in practice from day to day probably depends more on the business environment and history of each individual company and on the personalities of the individuals concerned than on the constitutional technicalities. Nonetheless, if one body steps outside its proper area of authority, trouble is likely to ensue and the technicalities will then matter a great deal.

The fundamental idea, discussed in Chapter 1, behind the formation of a company is that incorporation allows the owners or shareholders to limit their liability concerning the company's affairs. A company has its own legal identity, which permits it to enter into contracts with third parties, employ people, buy and sell, and be sued for wrongdoing. All such activities and any consequences of them require no involvement by the shareholders, although they may put some limits on certain actions, such as selling all or part of the company.

However, the law requires companies to have directors who take on the responsibility for the affairs of the company, its actions and transactions. The *Companies Act 1985* requires a minimum of one director for a private company and a minimum of two for a public company. In practice there is usually a larger number of directors, constituting a board. Thus it is the directors of the company, jointly and severally, who will be held to account for the company's actions. It is they who are responsible – not the owners, nor the managers, nor the employees. There is technically no limit to the liability that the directors may incur on behalf of the company and any of its employees acting for the company.

The board of directors, as a board, should not be involved in the day-to-day business of the company. The board should paint on a larger canvas. They should look to the wider strategic purposes of the company – and, in particular, they should be looking to the future of the company.

The interest of shareholders in a company is financial, namely, the returns on their investment. Ultimate power rests with them. They can, through their control of the general meetings of the company, ratify the appointment of, supervise and, if necessary, secure the dismissal of directors. The general meeting is also the guardian of the company's constitution, since it alone has power to alter the Memorandum and Articles. Shareholders empower the board of directors to direct the company on their behalf; it is to the shareholders that directors are, in a technical sense, accountable for the performance of the company.

In the case of public companies, the board's function is often directed primarily toward making strategic decisions and there will generally be a clear distinction between direction, management and ownership. In private companies a less clearcut distinction is made in practice between direction, management and ownership because the same individuals are often responsible for both direction and management, and often further complicate their status by also being major shareholders. It might be supposed that there is some lower limit of size below which it becomes irrelevant to make conscious distinctions between these functions since private companies may be very small indeed. Size itself, however, is not a satisfactory criterion; the important factor is the attitude of the individuals responsible for the company's strategy towards change and development. Any company of whatever size – if it wants to maintain an active control over its future, and not merely react passively to events – should pay proper attention to the long-term strategic function of direction and therefore, conceptually, not consolidate the roles of directors, managers and owners.

3.5.2 THE RELATIONSHIP BETWEEN DIRECTORS AND SHAREHOLDERS

The relationship between directors and shareholders is complex. The following general points are worth mentioning here. They apply to a person in his role as a director, even if that person may also be a shareholder of the company and/or a manager working for it.

a) Directors are required to show due care and skill in making decisions on behalf of the company. They must put the company's needs first, since they owe a duty to it and must not make profit for themselves or their families as a result of their having the company in their trust. These fiduciary duties (duties of trust) are described in Chapter 8.

b) In undertaking overall responsibility for the company, the directors are accountable to the shareholders for its continuing prosperity. The shareholders have the ultimate sanction under s.303 of the *Companies Act 1985*, which cannot be excluded by the Articles, of removing directors and under the Articles of Association shareholders have the power to appoint members of the board.

In practice, especially in the case of public companies, directors are normally appointed by the board and shareholders confirm appointments made by the board between annual general meetings. It is a requirement of the Listing Rules of the London Stock Exchange that a person appointed by the directors of a listed company to fill a casual vacancy, or as an additional director, must retire from office at the next annual general meeting. He will then be eligible for re-election.

The main justification for shareholders confirming or denying board appointments is that the relationship of shareholders with the company (property rights) is different from that of other parties. Shareholders lack the leverage that the contractual relationships of other parties with the company provide. Once they have subscribed the capital they forgo any detailed control over how the funds are to be used. They rank last in order for their income and take the greatest risk of irrecoverable loss of their assets. They cannot be satisfied without the company having first satisfied its creditors and then all the other parties in terms both of the amount and the security of their income. Having control over the appointment and dismissal of the company's governing body compensates them for this loss of direct control over their property.

(A caveat is necessary here. The shareholders' control over the appointment and removal of an executive director may be limited by the latter's contract as an employee of the company. The high cost of compensation on removal can act as a deterrent to shareholders exercising their powers. See section 7.6.2.)

c) A director's relationship with the shareholders may also be terminated in the marketplace in the case of public companies. Shareholders of a public company normally express their dissatisfaction, not by voting out the existing board, but by selling their shares – a process which, if continued long enough, may well lead to a bid and/or a change of directors.

d) In addition, the shareholders collectively have the power to terminate the relationship by exercising their right to liquidate the company.

e) However, directors are not mandated delegates of the shareholders. If they were, it would imply that they should forgo whatever powers of individual judgement they might have, in order to fall in with the wishes and demands of the shareholders. A director who was merely the mouthpiece of the shareholders would, by fettering his discretion in that way, be failing in his duty to act in the best interests of the company. The position of company directors is similar to that of Members of Parliament, as famously expressed by Burke:

> *Your representative owes you, not his industry only, but his judgement; and he betrays, instead of serving you, if he sacrifices it to your opinion.* (Speech to the Electors of Bristol, 3 Nov. 1774)

But are directors in some sense representatives of shareholders? Are they under some obligation to put the interests of shareholders on a higher plane than those of other parties? Only, it is suggested, to the extent that the shareholders have been equated with 'the company' to which the directors' duty is owed and to the extent that promotion of shareholder value is a key requirement. This issue is considered at length in Chapter 17.

f) Most boards now recognise the need to develop a good relationship with shareholders to promote and meet their legitimate interests. The annual report, the published accounts and the annual general meeting are tools by which shareholders may hold directors to account, though private companies can waive some procedures with the unanimous consent of the shareholders. The need to maintain a good relationship with shareholders extends both to the family company and to subsidiary companies. In both cases the mechanism may vary and will reflect the needs of the individual company and both its formal and informal reporting structures.

3.5.3 THE BOARD OF DIRECTORS AND MANAGEMENT

The board of directors has an overriding duty to act in the best interests of the company. To this end the directors, although the ultimate responsibility will still be theirs, will inevitably delegate authority of action and decision to others in the company, notably managers. Managers, given direction by the board, should seek to implement the purposes of the board, pursue the objectives and comply with the strategies determined by the board. They are involved in the day-to-day business of securing the profitable performance of their areas of responsibility within the company. They make the business work. In doing this, however, they must operate within the limits of authority given by the board.

The relationship between the board and managers is complex, dynamic and company-specific. In practice, managers will often make recommendations as to possible courses of action, with a preferred alternative, to the board. However, Harper [2000] suggests a number of areas which illustrate the differences between the responsibilities of directors and those of managers:

a) **Prosperity**. Responsibility for the long-term prosperity of the company rests with the board of directors, not the management. This responsibility is clearly identified in the definition of the purpose of the board outlined earlier in this chapter.

b) **Decision-making.** Directors have to make the important decisions which determine the future of the company and how it relates to its stakeholders and the legal/regulatory framework. Management is concerned with implementing those decisions and the policies that follow from them.

c) **Duties and responsibilities.** Directors are responsible for the health and wellbeing of the company and are required in law to apply skill and care in exercising their duty to the company (see Chapter 8). They must involve management in the exercise of this duty and must give managers sufficient authority to do their jobs, but cannot delegate the ultimate responsibilities themselves. If they are in breach of their duties or act improperly, directors may be made personally liable in law.

d) **Accountability to shareholders.** The directors are responsible to the shareholders and have the company in their trust. In that role they are held to account for the company, on behalf of the shareholders, and may be dismissed by the shareholders. Managers are not.

e) **Leadership.** While the day-to-day leadership of the company is in the hands of the managing director or chief executive, he acts on behalf of the directors. In this relationship, it is the board of directors who must provide the intrinsic leadership and direction at the top of the company, including the determination of its values and ethical position. The management must enact that leadership ethos, taking its direction from the board.

f) **Company administration.** Directors are responsible for the company's due administration. The related duties can be delegated to management, but this does not relieve the directors of ultimate responsibility for company administration.

g) **Statutory provisions.** There are numerous statutory provisions which can create offences of strict liability under which directors may face penalties if the company fails to comply (see Chapters 8, 9, 10 and 11). While the exercise of those provisions is usually delegated to management, it is the directors who may be held liable; for example, employee relations, health and safety, taxation, consumer and environmental protection are areas where directors may be liable under statute.

h) **Insolvency.** There are various provisions of the *Insolvency Act 1986*, breach of which may involve the directors in personal liability and/or criminal prosecution and/or disqualification (see section 15.3). Managers are not affected by these provisions.

3.6 RESERVED POWERS

The delegation of powers to senior management must be handled precisely as there can be no room for misunderstandings. In many companies, and the IoD recommends it as good practice, the powers of the board and managers are articulated in a statement of powers reserved to the board. This statement serves to specify the limits to the powers of the executive.

Table 3.1 is an example of a statement of reserved powers from a large quoted public company. This example is not exhaustive and, conversely, includes some matters which may not be relevant to a particular board. However, it is indicative of the matters that the board should not delegate to management. The final selection will of course depend on the type of company. A common compromise is to make some delegated powers not reserved by the board conditional – for example, a managing director may be given financial authority but only to such-and-such a stated level. There may be a degree of overlap and joint authority – for example, both the board and managers may be involved in monitoring progress, but at different levels, the board focusing on the overall progress of activities against the strategic plan and managers measuring and assessing activities within the plan.

Table 3.1 *Example of a statement of a board's reserved powers*

Statutory obligations

1.1 Approval of:

- the final dividend;
- the Annual Report and Accounts;
- circulars to shareholders, including those convening general meetings.

1.2 Consideration of:

- the interim dividend and Report;
- returns to overseas stock exchanges, if necessary.

1.3 Recommending to shareholders:

- changes to the Memorandum and Articles of Association;
- proposals relating to the appointment of auditors and approval of the audit fee.

2. Strategic and financial matters

2.1 Consideration of:

- the company's vision, mission and values;
- the company's degree of risk aversion with respect to financial, business and sovereign risks;
- strategy;
- the company's progress against plans and budgets.

2.2 Approval of:

- Treasury, financial risk management and capital policies, including funding and the issue of ordinary shares, preference shares and loan capital;
- capital expenditure, acquisitions, joint ventures and disposals in excess of the discretionary power of the managing director;
- internal accounting controls;
- significant changes in accounting policy.

3. Personnel matters

3.1 Approval of:

- the appointment and removal of the managing director, other executive directors, and the company secretary;
- the appointment and removal of other directors on the recommendation of the Nomination Committee;
- the remuneration of directors where their remuneration is not set by the Remuneration Committee;

Table 3.1 *Example of a statement of a board's reserved powers (continued)*

- the roles, duties and discretionary powers of the chairman and managing director; the arrangement of liability insurance for directors and officers;
- personnel policies, particularly in connection with health and safety matters.

4. Other matters

4.1 Approval of:

- any matter which would have a material effect on the company's financial position, liabilities, future strategy or reputation;
- contracts not in the ordinary course of the company's business; and
- the company Code of Conduct, if it has one.

4.2 Delegation of the board's powers and authority to committees of the board, such committees to be under an obligation to report back to the board.

3.7 LEADERSHIP AND DECISION-MAKING

The board should provide leadership within the company. This means that a perhaps disparate group of individuals, who are the appointed directors, need to come together to formulate a common vision and purpose for the company and ensure that the vision and purpose is implemented. Moreover, it is the responsibility of the board to set the values and standards of the company and these will become manifest in the way in which the company does business with its suppliers and customers and how it treats its employees. On a day-to-day basis, these matters are clearly management responsibilities, but the way in which these responsibilities are carried out should reflect the approach and tone set by the board.

Leadership manifests itself also in decision-taking. Boards do not simply discuss and analyse; they must ultimately make choices and decisions. The board should concern itself only with those decisions that *it* alone should make. These will be about the essential matters that will fashion the shape and destiny of the company – for example, its ethos, posture within the law, achievements, reputation, structure, commercial wellbeing and the matters subsumed under the tasks of the board. Other matters for decision should be clearly delegated. A statement of the board's reserved powers can help to define this dividing line.

It is argued in section 4.1.1 that a part of the chairman's role is to lead the board. The chairman may also exercise a leadership role externally to the company. It is usually the case that leadership within the company is given expression by the managing director. Many of the board decisions, so far as the company is concerned, will in effect be seen as made by the managing director. But it is worth remembering that company structures are not based on the principle of autocracy or dictatorship. Managing directors, by their status, ownership of shares or personality, may assume a dominating role within the company. The very title 'managing director' confers a status beyond that of other directors. The status, however, should be seen as making him only *primus inter pares*, not an autocrat.

3.8 SUMMARY

1. The key purpose of the board is to ensure the company's prosperity by collectively directing the company's affairs, whilst meeting the appropriate interests of its shareholders and relevant stakeholders. The board of directors makes collective decisions about issues that will determine the company's survival and prosperity. In doing so it must ensure that the company complies with the obligations imposed by various laws and regulations. The board also provides leadership to the company by setting its direction and pace and developing its culture and ethos.

2. The board's key tasks are to:

   a) Establish vision, mission and values.

   b) Set strategy and structure.

   c) Delegate to management.

   d) Exercise accountability to shareholders and be responsible to relevant stakeholders.

3. Directors, managers and shareholders have different roles and responsibilities:

   a) Shareholders empower the board to direct the company on their behalf.

   b) Directors have a duty to the company and are subject to potential legal liabilities that do not apply to managers. The board alone has the ultimate responsibility for corporate performance. The directors are not mandated delegates or servants of the shareholders.

c) Directors delegate, within limits, some of their powers to managers, enabling managers to control the operations of the company on a day-to-day basis.

d) In order to clarify the distinction between management and direction, it is good practice for the board to set out a statement of the powers reserved to the board.

5. Leadership in a company is the responsibility of the board.

Chapter 4

Board Members and Board Characteristics

A director is a member of the board of directors, but different directors have different roles within the board. In this chapter we examine the roles of the different board members, the roles and duties of the company secretary, and some significant differences in the characteristics of boards

4.1 BOARD MEMBERS AND THEIR ROLES

4.1.1 THE CHAIRMAN

There is no legal necessity for a board to have a chairman, though in fact most do. The chairman is appointed by the board, normally from the ranks of the members of the board, though in the case of large companies the chairman is often brought in from outside the company. Formally, the chairman is chairman of the board of directors who, under the company's Articles, also acts as chairman of the general meeting of shareholders. He is often referred to as chairman of the company but is **not** appointed as such in accordance with any stipulations of the *Companies Acts*.

The board can define the chairman's duties and responsibilities as it thinks appropriate. The chairman's role can vary from a titular or honorary position, with no real authority, to that of the most substantial figure on the board, shaping all board decisions and acting as the key 'driver' of the corporate vision, mission and values. Much depends upon the chairman's personal talents and experience, his leadership style, how the chairman uses (or is allowed to use) his power as chairman of board meetings to control the agenda, to shape the discussion and to sum up meetings. In practice the actual authority and position of chairman usually exceeds the formal legal position. This is particularly the case in larger public limited companies and quoted companies.

Tricker [1984] puts it like this:

> *There are few statutory requirements for the role [of chairman] so a range of styles is to be found. At one extreme, the chairman does no more than manage the meetings, arrange the agenda, steer the discussions and ensure that they reach a conclusion. At the other extreme is the powerful chairman who acts as a figurehead for the company, influences its strategic direction and manages the board, being concerned with its membership, committees and overall performance, as well as chairing board meetings.*

The chairman's responsibilities, relating to both internal and external roles, looking both inwards to the effectiveness of the boards and outwards to external audiences, include the following:

1. Internal

A. Board leadership

A board may be composed of outstanding individuals and yet be ineffective. It can fulfil its true potential as a board only if its members are properly led and its activities properly organised. The basic responsibility of the chairman is to exercise authority in leading the board and managing its business. Beyond this, the chairman must also ensure that the board is providing the overall leadership to guide the company.

Sir John Harvey-Jones, in the foreword to Cadbury [1990], commented:

> *If a company is successful it is due to the efforts of everyone in it, but if it fails it is because of the failure of the board. If the board fails it is the responsibility of the*

chairman, notwithstanding the collective responsibility of everyone. Despite this collective responsibility, it is on the chairman's shoulders that the competence and performance of that supreme directing body depends.

B. Board membership and composition
The chairman must

i) Monitor:

    a) the overall size of the board;

    b) the balance of age, experience and personality;

    c) the balance between executive and non-executive directors;

    d) the need for changes in board membership and the timing of any changes.

ii) Determine and regularly review each individual's role and responsibilities and how these interrelate between directors.

iii) Identify any gaps or (undesirable) overlap between individual directors' roles and responsibilities, and plan and execute the corrective action required.

iv) Initiate and lead the selection, appointment, induction, development or removal of board members or the company secretary.

v) Ensure regular and rigorous appraisal of the competence of all board members.

vi) Help the board identify and select external advisers when in-house expertise is insufficient.

vii) Lead the process of planning the succession of the managing director (see section 7.5).

An action list for deciding upon the composition of a board is provided in IoD [1999], page 33.

C. The powers, roles and responsibilities of the board and management respectively
It is the chairman's responsibility to see that the board concentrates on directing the company and does not try to manage it; monitoring progress should not spill over into intervening in the management of the business.

On the other hand, management must be effective. In practice this means that the chairman must make sure that the board properly distinguishes between the powers, roles and responsibilities of the board and management respectively.

The chairman should therefore provide guidance to the board on the following matters:

- Defining the powers and roles the board reserves to itself (see the example in section 3.6).

- Reviewing the relevance of the company's Memorandum and Articles of Association, pertinent legislation and other prescriptive guidelines.

- Specifying the powers and roles to be delegated to individual directors, including the chairman.

- Specifying the powers to be delegated to board committees and determining their terms of reference, life span, leadership and membership (see section 5.7).

- Empowering the managing director to implement the decisions of the board and other specific matters not reserved to the board itself.

D. Managing board meetings

Ultimately, the control of a board meeting is in the hands of the board members. But the chairman has the task of planning, preparing for and chairing the meetings of the board; he must therefore plan and manage these meetings.

In order to fulfil this role effectively, the chairman must

- Establish, maintain and develop meeting and reporting procedures for the board and its committees.

- Agree, with the board, policy for the frequency, purpose, conduct and duration of meetings and, especially, the setting of agenda.

- Create comprehensive agenda covering all the necessary and appropriate issues through the year, while also including important immediate issues. In particular, the chairman should try to ensure that the agenda for board meetings encourage the board to concentrate on those matters that they alone can decide. There is always a temptation for the board to stray into day-to-day operational issues. The choice of agenda items is an important source of control for the chairman (though directors have the right to add items to agenda if they wish).

- Assign tasks and objectives to individual members including, especially, the chairman, managing director, finance director and company secretary, and agree the working relationships between them.

- Define and review regularly the information needs of the board. It is essential that the chairman ensures that board members have relevant and up-to-date information on the progress of the company. In particular,

  > *It is for chairmen to make certain that their non-executive directors receive timely, relevant information tailored to their needs, that they are properly briefed on the issues arising at board meetings, and that they make an effective contribution as board members in practice.* (Cadbury [1992], para 4.8)

- Adopt efficient and timely methods for informing and briefing board members prior to meetings. Exchange of views with the other directors is a part of planning board meetings; the board meeting itself should not be the place where the chairman discovers major differences of opinion.

- Maintain proper focus on the board's key role and tasks, ensuring that all the major strategic issues affecting the company's viability, reputation and prosperity are addressed.

- Allow sufficient time for important matters to be discussed thoroughly. An effective chairman will at all times have a view of what amount of time should be spent in discussing any given item, and be firm enough to hold the board to it.

- It may well be the case that members of the board have 'hidden' agenda. In these circumstances, the chairman should ensure that discussions are not delayed or items rushed through to suit the cause of a particular director or group.

- Encourage all directors to attend all board meetings and to contribute appropriately to discussion, drawing on the full range of relevant opinions, knowledge, skills and experience.

- Draw together the pertinent points from discussions in a timely way in order to reach well-informed decisions that command consensus. Most directors will be only too well aware of discussions rambling without purpose to no conclusion. The chairman must take a view as to when to call a discussion to a halt, obtain the sense of the board, and then move on to the next topic.

- Ensure that adequate minutes are kept and that board attendance and board decisions are properly recorded.

E. Developing the effectiveness of the board as a working group

How well the board does its work, and getting the best out of the board, is largely the responsibility of the chairman. In order to improve board effectiveness it is recommended that the chairman should:

- Take appropriate action(s) – including the use of training and external specialists – to maximise the efficiency and effectiveness of board work.

- Consider the impact on board effectiveness of directors' attitudes, their interpersonal relationships and their decision-making styles. The work of a board of directors inevitably involves power, egos and personal agenda. The chairman must be skilful in addressing and mastering the associated issues if the board is to be effective.

- Identify and influence the strengths and weaknesses of individual directors where these affect the performance of the board as a whole.

- Maintain a harmonious and constructive relationship with both the managing director and the non-executive directors. The chairman can act as a bridge between different elements within the board and assist in managing group tensions. In particular, there is always a risk of division between 'insiders' and 'outsiders'; this tension is inherent in the unitary board structure. It is the job of a chairman to ensure that both inside knowledge and outside talents work in harness for the benefit of the company.

- Review regularly the degree to which the board's objectives are achieved.

- Review regularly the quality of the advice and information received by the board.

- Set and achieve objectives for continuous improvement in the quality and effectiveness of board performance, including performance in a crisis.

- Put in hand an effective system of board appraisal, whereby the board can evaluate how well it is working and what improvements might be necessary. Such a system is the subject of Chapter 6.

Effective boards do not just 'happen'. No matter how competent the individual directors, effective boards have to be fostered by the chairman.

In summary,

> *The chairman's role in securing good corporate governance is crucial. Chairmen are primarily responsible for the working of the board, for its balance of membership subject to board and shareholders' approval, for ensuring that all relevant issues are on the agenda, and for ensuring that all directors, executive and non-executive alike, are enabled and encouraged to play their full part in its activities. Chairmen should be able to stand sufficiently back from the day-to-day running of the business to ensure that their boards are in full control of the company's affairs and alert to their obligations to their shareholders.* (Cadbury [1992], para. 4.7)

2. External

A. Reporting financial results
The chairman in his/her statements to shareholders and at the annual general meeting should indicate how the company has performed and what are its future prospects.

B. Wider representational role
The chairman has a role as an ambassador for the company. Indeed he may well be tasked with the responsibility of promoting the interests of the company outside the immediate environment in which the company trades. To this end, the chairman often liaises with institutional and other shareholders and generally puts across the company's aims and policies to all those whose confidence in the business is important.

4.1.2 THE MANAGING DIRECTOR

A large body of shareholders cannot easily make decisions for the company. That is why shareholders appoint a board of directors. Similarly, at board level, it would not be appropriate to convene the board to make a decision on everything that the company does. Management has to be devolved. The board delegates all or part of its management powers to a managing director, who is the pinnacle of the management structure, including any executive directors, and is responsible for the success of the company's operations within the strategy determined by the board.

The post of managing director is not specifically recognised in statute (as distinct from that of directors) and sometimes goes by a variety of titles – 'chief executive' being the most common alternative.

The managing director has the apparent authority to commit the company in any way by virtue of holding that title. But the board is still responsible for company actions. It is therefore prudent for the board to constrain the managing director's powers, either in the Articles or in a separate document, with absolute clarity over the boundaries to delegated powers. In practice, these constraints will usually be linked to the value and type of specified transactions.

However, any constraints on the managing director's power only operate internally and will not necessarily be binding on external third parties. If the external third party is not connected to the company in any way and has entered into a transaction in good faith, and the transaction is one which it would be normal for a managing director of the company to enter into, then the transaction will be valid (see Chapter 8).

If the managing director breaks internal constraints, then it will be up to the board of directors to decide what action needs to be taken. Unlike the delegation of powers from the general meeting, delegation from the board to the managing director can be revoked at any time by the board. If the managing director commits the company outside the limits of delegated authority, the company can sue the managing director. This is the ultimate constraint on his authority. Whether or not the managing director is also the majority shareholder makes no difference. He still cannot ignore the board's authority and any restrictions the board places on the power of the managing director.

The appointment of a managing director is a major decision of the board and not just a formality and therefore should be recorded in the board minutes. It is not good practice for the board to give informal assent to a person acting as managing director. Any procedural defects by the board will not affect the person's ability to commit the company in the normal course of trading as a full managing director of the company so long as the company is holding that person out as a managing director of the company.

The role of the managing director usually includes:

- Maintaining the business in line with the board's decisions.

- Delivering the operational performance of the company.

- Taking remedial action where necessary and informing the board of changes.

- Ensuring that adequate operational planning and financial control systems are in place and closely monitoring the operating and financial results against plans and budgets, although all directors are responsible for internal controls. The managing director's role involves oversight of the various departments within the business. No other board member has this role and therefore the managing director will be the repository of information not immediately available to other members of the board. The managing director will normally form a close working relationship with the financial director of the business. Working in tandem, these two directors make a strong combination which can frequently dominate board meetings.

- Ensuring that the operating objectives and standards of performance are not only understood but 'owned' by management.

- Developing plans that reflect the longer-term corporate objectives, business strategies and priorities established by the board.

- Maintaining a dialogue with the chairman and board. The managing director will be expected to provide a report of the activities of the company. It is to the managing director that the remainder of the board look for an account of how the company is faring and how it is to progress in the near future.

In normal circumstances the managing director should be a highly influential member of the board, though the power of a managing director tends to wax and wane depending upon the success of the company. When the company is profitable, the position of the managing director will be strong. However, if the company fails to make profit over a period of time, then the managing director's position will become increasingly weakened to the point where he may be displaced by the board or by vote of the shareholders.

In private limited companies the roles of managing director and chairman are usually combined. There are many instances of companies, including Plcs, which have made excellent progress where the posts are combined, but there are often difficulties with this arrangement. Many arguments are advanced in support of the separation of roles:

- the two roles probably call for different temperaments and motivations;

- without separation, there may be confusion as to which hat is being worn in the boardroom;

- the inevitable influence of the managing director over the executive directors, added to the undoubted power of the chairman to shape and guide board discussions, is sometimes said to give too much power to one person;

- above a certain size of company, there is likely to be too much for one person to do – both jobs are extremely demanding, if they are to be done well;

- one person is more vulnerable than two, and in any case two heads are often better than one;

- succession planning is better encouraged;

- above all, under pressure, management demands invariably take precedence over governance.

For these reasons, the Combined Code [1998] recommends for listed companies that

> *There should be a clear division of responsibilities at the head of the company which will ensure a balance of power and authority, such that no one individual has unfettered powers of decision* (Principle A2).

If the two posts of chairman and managing director *are* combined, it is important in practice to distinguish between them. In particular, any individual wearing two hats should be careful to pay sufficient attention to carrying out the chairman's role effectively. More than this, if one individual holds both jobs, then, in the case of listed companies, the decision should be publicly justified, and *it is essential that there should be a strong and independent element on the board, with a recognised senior member* (Cadbury [1992], para. 4.9). In a Plc this independent element should be provided by the non-executive directors. They may provide a check on otherwise unfettered power. Hampel [1998] even suggests that the non-executive directors *should be led by a director publicly identified in the annual report* (para. 3.19). The Combined Code [1998] endorses these recommendations. (There is a full discussion of these corporate governance reports in section 17.6.) In private limited companies, where often there are no non-executive directors, whether power is unchecked or not will depend upon the character and strength of will of the directors.

The vast majority of listed companies and a growing number of unlisted companies now separate the posts of chairman and managing director.

4.1.3 EXECUTIVE DIRECTORS

'Executive' directors as such are not recognised in law. The term generally refers to individuals who have two roles – a board role and a senior management role. Although legally they are directors all of the time, the characteristics of their management role are different and additional to their role as a director.

As managers or executives they are paid employees of the company, typically acting as heads of divisions or departments and responsible to the managing director from whom they have delegated executive responsibilities for running part of the business of the company. This relationship requires them to advise and support the managing director on all relevant management matters.

In addition, however, they have full director responsibilities at board level to ensure the company's overall prosperity. As attendees at the board they will be expected to account for the performance of their area of responsibility within the business. But they should also be expected to be informed about aspects of the business other than their executive responsibilities and to bring to the board views and perspectives that go beyond narrow departmental or divisional matters. There is a danger that an executive director will carry only a specialised view into the boardroom and tend to regard other areas of the business as being matters to which he should not devote much thought or about which he should not express an opinion. An executive must recognise that his responsibilities as, say, head of sales are quite distinct from his responsibilities in the boardroom. The executive director should be there not just to press the views of a particular side of the company but to contribute to all policy decisions of the board and, if he has special skill and knowledge, present to the board this expertise in a way that the other members can understand. The only criterion for appointment to the board should be a recognisable capacity to contribute to the board's work. A directorship should not be viewed as a reward for long service as an executive with a company.

The managing director must acknowledge that these twin responsibilities and the two lines of accountability that go with them exist. The chairman should encourage the executive directors to feel free to express their opinions on board matters openly, especially at board meetings. If this is not done, board decisions may be inhibited, the perhaps valuable views of the executive directors going unheard and the managing director effectively dominating the board. Executive directors, who after all have joint and several liability for the actions of the board, should take care that the managing director does not dominate to the extent that their views are unheard or ignored.

A key executive director in all companies is the director who is responsible for finance. Finance is a crucially important matter for any company. All directors need to be kept informed on a reasonably regular basis, and at least before board meetings, of the financial state of the company. In small companies the person in charge of the finances of the company might not be a director. If that is the case, he/she should be permitted to attend board meetings to report on financial matters or a full report should be submitted to a director, usually the managing director, for delivery to the board.

The financial director should put before board members at least the following information (see also section 5.5):

- the overall performance of the company on a profit and loss basis;
- departmental performance;
- cash flow implications;
- balance sheet implications;
- changes in the company's capital structure.

Attention should be drawn to variances from budget or plan figures.

4.1.4 NON-EXECUTIVE DIRECTORS

What is a non-executive director?

Non-executive directors are directors who, broadly, do not take part in the day-to-day business of the company, confine their role to that of preparing for and attending board meetings, and are not employees of the company.

However, despite not participating on a day-to-day basis within the company, non-executive directors on a unitary board have the same legal duties, responsibilities and potential liabilities as executive directors.

It is extremely important to be clear as to what is the proper contribution of non-executive directors to a company. The overriding consideration is that they participate to the full in the board's joint deliberations. At the same time, however, they have a supervisory or monitoring role, particularly in resolving situations where the executive directors may have a conflict of interest.

The particular contributions that non-executive directors may make are:

- To widen the horizons of the board in determining strategy, by applying what they have learned from both a wider general experience and any background of relevant special skill, knowledge and experience which the board might otherwise lack.

- To take responsibility for monitoring management performance and the extent to which the management of the company is achieving the results planned when strategy was determined.

- To ensure that the board has adequate systems to safeguard the interests of the company where these may conflict with the personal interest of individual directors.

- To determine the remuneration of the executive members of the board.

- To ensure the presentation of adequate financial information, whether or not a formal audit committee exists.

- To play a key role in the appointment of the chairman and managing director.

Non-executive directors therefore are usually appointed as members of the board because they have a breadth of experience to draw upon, may also have some specialist knowledge that will help provide the board with valuable insights, are of a relatively high calibre, have appropriate personal qualities, and (sometimes) because of their shareholdings or financial connections.

Non-executive directors and 'independence'

Above all, non-executive directors should be 'independent'. This is a term often loosely used without definition. What it really means – and this is most important – is that they should bring great objectivity or impartiality to the board's deliberations. In order to be able to do this – or, perhaps, in order that the public has confidence in their impartiality – it is generally felt that non-executive directors should have no contractual relationship (other than their contract for services) with the company and should not be under the control or influence of any other director or group of directors. The Cadbury Report [1992] put it like this:

> *non-executive directors should bring an independent judgement to bear on issues of strategy, performance, resources, including key appointments, and standards of conduct.* (para 2.1), and

> the majority should be independent of management and free from any business or other relationships which could materially interfere with the exercise of their independent judgement . . . (para 2.2).

The Association of British Insurers and the National Association of Pension Funds, which together represent institutional investors with invested funds equal to about one-half of the capitalisation of the London stock market, go much further. In their joint definition of director independence (ABI and NAPF [1997]), they set out ten types of connection that in their view compromise independence. These encompass circumstances in which the non-executive director:

1. was formerly an executive of the company;

2. is paid currently or has been in the past by the company in any capacity other than as a non-executive director;

3. was selected other than by a formal process;

4. has served for more than nine years;

5. has a contractual relationship with the company, for example represents or is connected to a major supplier, customer or consultant to the company;

6. is under the control or influence of any other director or group of directors, for example being an associate of another director;

7. has a reciprocal relationship with the chairman or chief executive whereby they sit on each other's boards;

8. has share options, performance-related pay or a pension entitlement from the company; . . .*we regard it as good practice for non-executive directors not to participate in share option schemes and for their service as non-executive directors not to be pensionable by the company* (Cadbury [1992], para. 4.13);

9. represents a controlling or significant shareholder;

10. is judged by the company, for whatever reason, not to be independent.

These criteria represent a rather 'hard-line' view. Undoubtedly, not *all* non-executive directors need to be independent in this sense. After all, for example, the solicitor or accountant who comes from a company which may provide services to the company on whose board he sits as a non-executive may make a valuable contribution to the board. Many non-executive directors who are not 'independent' in the strict sense above are still able to exercise objective judgement. However, the point is that there are certain issues where independence is required, particularly matters where the interests of the executive directors and the company might diverge. It is important that at least some non-executive directors do not have interests directly at stake.

There is no objection to non-executive directors holding shares – indeed, it may help to align their interests with those of shareholders generally.

The Combined Code recommendations

The contribution of non-executives to the board is obviously potentially very important. Consequently the Combined Code [1998] requires listed companies to report compliance with, or explain non-compliance with, the following provisions:

- *The board should include non-executive directors of sufficient calibre and number for their views to carry significant weight in the board's decisions. Non-executive directors should comprise not less than one third of the board* (A.3.1).

- *The majority of non-executive directors should be independent of management and free from any business or other relationship which could materially interfere with the exercise of their independent judgement* (A.3.2).

The Combined Code recommends that for quoted companies there should be a minimum of three non-executives on the board, one of whom may be the chairman of the company provided he is not also its executive head. Additionally, two of the three non-executive directors should be independent in the sense above. The Code stipulates that non-executive directors should be appointed for fixed terms and that their re-appointment should not be automatic. The Code further recommends that non-executive directors should be selected through a formal process and that this process and their appointment should be a matter for the board as a whole. The Committee regards it as good practice for a nomination committee (composed of a majority of non-executive directors and chaired either by the chairman or by a non-executive director) to carry out the selection process of non-executive directors and to make proposals to the board. Finally, remuneration committees should be made up exclusively of non-executive directors.

The major recommendations of the Combined Code are summarised in Appendix B; see also section 17.6.

4.2 THE COMPANY SECRETARY

4.2.1 MUST A COMPANY HAVE A SECRETARY?

It is a legal requirement for every company to have a company secretary. In private companies the company secretary is usually also a director, but it is not a legal requirement. Many small companies choose to employ firms of chartered accountants or solicitors to provide secretarial services.

The company secretary as such is not a member of the board. He does, however, usually attend board meetings. The reason for attendance is that the company secretary normally prepares minutes of the meetings of the board of directors and prepares the agenda and other documentation which will be provided to directors so that they may be informed about what is to take place at board meetings.

4.2.2 WHAT DOES A COMPANY SECRETARY DO?

A company secretary has traditionally been responsible for company administration. The duties common to company secretaries include:

1. The convening of board and company meetings.

2. Advising the chairman on the agenda for board meetings.

3. Taking minutes of meetings.

4. Ensuring that the company and the board comply with the *Companies Acts*, the Memorandum and Articles of Association, and various other rules and regulations, if relevant.

5. Communicating with shareholders, dealing with share transfers, and monitoring movements in shareholdings.

6. Maintaining the registered office and filing returns with the Registrar of Companies.

7. Maintaining the statutory books of record.

8. Administering any alterations to the Memorandum or Articles of Association.

A company secretary in listed companies, because of the legal nature of the role, is frequently a solicitor or barrister who will be involved in other aspects of the company's legal work – for example, negotiating and drafting contracts, ensuring patents and copyrights are protected and dealing with employment law questions.

A close working relationship between the company secretary and the chairman of the board is generally critical to the effective running of a board. The secretary will probably be more involved in the mechanics of organising the board and the chairman more concerned with the overall management of the board.

In pursuing the above tasks an efficient company secretary can make a most important contribution to both direction and management by, first, removing from directors and managers the burden of knowing how to comply with the detailed provisions of company law and other legislation and, secondly, ensuring the efficient despatch of the board's business at the technical level.

In recent years, however, the role of the company secretary has expanded as he has become the residuary legatee for all sorts of matters that do not readily fall within the sphere of responsibility of other officers of the company. For example, the Combined Code [1998] endorses the view of the Cadbury Report [1992] that

> *The company secretary has a key role to play in ensuring that board procedures are both followed and regularly reviewed. The chairman and the board will look to the company secretary for guidance on what their responsibilities are under the rules and regulations to which they are subject and on how these responsibilities should be discharged. All directors should have access to the advice and services of the company secretary and should recognise that the chairman is entitled to strong support from the company secretary in ensuring the effective functioning of the board.* (para. 4.25)

Some company secretaries have become responsible for the compliance function within their company made necessary by the *Financial Services Act 1986*. Similarly, in quoted companies the company secretary is usually responsible for the implementation of the recommendation of the Combined Code that '*Every director should receive appropriate training on the first occasion that he or she is appointed to the board of a listed company, and subsequently as necessary.*' (Part 2, section A.1.6). Often, too, the implementation of data protection requirements under the *Data Protection Act 1998* falls to the lot of the company secretary.

The apparent authority that officers of the company have extends to the company secretary. He is an officer of the company with extensive duties and responsibilities. This is clear not only from the *Companies Acts*, but is also apparent from the role which he plays in the day-to-day business of companies. He is no longer a mere clerk. Typically, the secretary will make representations on behalf of the company and enter into contracts on its behalf which come within the day-to-day running of the company's business; so much so that he may be regarded or held out as having authority to do such things on behalf of the company.

Harvey-Jones ([1995], page 9) suggests that

> *A company secretary should have considerable personal integrity and be seen to stand for probity and right within the company. The secretary should be seen to 'side with the angels' and be prepared to state when the occasion demands that 'I fear that while what we are doing is within the letter of the law we are not within the spirit'... They have to be trusted by everyone. It is a bloody tough job.*

4.2.3 WHO CAN BE A COMPANY SECRETARY?

Anyone can be the company secretary of a private company. In a typical small company one of the directors usually is also appointed company secretary.

In the case of a listed public company, the directors must take all reasonable steps to ensure that the secretary of the company has the requisite knowledge and experience. Furthermore, to be eligible to be company secretary of a listed company, a person must:

- have been company secretary, or assistant or deputy company secretary on *22 December 1980* to the company in question; *or*

- have been the company secretary of a public company for at least three of the five years immediately preceding his appointment; *or*

- be a member of certain professional Institutes; *or*

- be a barrister, advocate or solicitor called or admitted in any part of the UK; *or*

- be a person who, either because he holds or has held any other position or because he is a member of any other body, appears to the directors capable of discharging the functions of a company secretary.

4.3 BOARD COMPOSITION

4.3.1 INTRODUCTION

The board of directors makes collective decisions about issues that will determine the company's survival and prosperity. In doing this it must ensure that the company complies with the various laws, regulations and obligations that are required of it. The board also provides leadership to the company by setting its direction and pace and developing its culture and ethics. The board alone has the ultimate responsibility for corporate performance. Even where directors are shareholders or representatives of shareholders, it is in acting as members of the board of directors that they must play their part in the stewardship of the company to which they have a duty. The board needs to be an effective group; it is not a club, nor a committee, and it should not be perceived by its members merely as a business formality.

All of the above points mean that a great deal of attention has to be paid to the composition of the board to ensure an effective working group.

Boards in the UK have a unitary structure and in some respects behave in similar ways, as they have to meet common needs. But no two companies are the same and the composition of a board should reflect an organisation's uniqueness, its particular needs and the specific context in which the company operates. There should, therefore, be a regular review of the board's composition to ensure that the required mix of attributes is available to address the future issues that are likely to face the company and the board. A full discussion of board composition is given in Harper [2000], especially Chapter 5.

In general terms, this means that boards, led by the chairman, should:

- Define the need for and timing of changes in board membership; a review of board composition needs to be regularly carried out to ensure that the correct mix of age, skill, experience and personality is available.

- Select, appoint, induct, develop and remove board members as appropriate.

- Define and review individual directors' roles and responsibilities and how these inter-relate with other directors.

- Identify, and correct where necessary, any gaps and/or undesirable overlaps between board members' roles and responsibilities.

- Determine relevant board committees, and their terms of reference, life-span, leadership and membership.

Among the many criteria the board should consider in devising the most effective board to meet the generic and specific needs of the company, three are critical: the size of the board, its configuration, and its style.

4.3.2 THE BOARD SIZE

Boards vary in size and there is no hard-and-fast rule about the size of the board. The number of individuals on the board will vary depending upon such factors as the size, age, ownership, and financial profile of the company. Maximum and minimum numbers of a board are sometimes prescribed in a company's Articles of Association and then can only be amended by the shareholders.

In general, start-ups and smaller companies are likely to have small boards, since decision-making tends to be focused around the owner-director/manager(s). If the company is relatively small and privately owned, then the board is unlikely to have institutional or major investors associated with it. Instead, the board will more likely reflect tight management and control, that is, a heavy representation by the senior management team, perhaps bolstered by external individuals who have either a stake (financial or otherwise) in the business or a recognised expertise.

As companies develop, however, it is important that the capability of the board grows. This may necessitate recruiting new executive directors with particular expertise to fulfil the changing needs of the company and the board, and non-executive directors too can make a significant contribution.

The number of members of a board can have a significant bearing on its effectiveness. A board's proper functioning requires group decision-making. It is recognised that the size of the group affects the group's dynamics: too small and the dynamics are lost; too big and the dynamics overwhelm the group's ability to make effective decisions. The size of the board can affect the opportunity for an individual to make an impact: too many members, and the meetings can become protracted and cabals can emerge; too few directors, and there may be a shortage of the necessary talents, knowledge and experience. Some companies have been known to shrink the size of their board to increase the effectiveness of decision-making. One factor is the extent to which the decision-making process requires participation, as opposed to consultation.

Boards in the UK have an average size of six directors. Boards of publicly quoted companies averaged about eight members in 1996, with the larger companies having an average of twelve directors.

4.3.3 BOARD CONFIGURATION

The board is responsible for the governance of the company and for seeing that it is properly managed. The configuration of any board will be determined by the number of directors and posts considered necessary for the board to function. Some common board posts are found in organisations of all shapes and sizes: the chairman, managing director, executive directors and non-executive directors. The overall shape of the board will tend to change to reflect the company's needs. One key consideration is the balance between the number of executive directors and non-executive directors. However, it is not only the number that is important in determining how the purpose and tasks of the board can best be met.

In an all-executive board every director has a managerial position. Many subsidiary, start-up and family companies have this structure. A potential problem of this form of structure is that the executive directors can be perceived as monitoring and supervising their own performance. Such boards perhaps tend to have relatively limited horizons and experience.

As companies evolve and develop, non-executive directors are appointed to boards for a number of reasons. It may be that the non-executive directors can provide additional expertise, knowledge or skills to supplement the executive directors. Sometimes non-executive directors are appointed as nominees of those investing in or lending money to the company. Some non-executive directors are appointed as a way of resolving succession problems in a family firm when shareholdings are split between family members. It is important to try to ensure that the non-executive directors are truly objective and impartial.

The practice of leading public companies in Australia and the USA is to have boards with a majority of non-executive directors. This structure is rarely found in UK companies but it is common in other institutions, such as mutual societies and various public sector bodies.

4.3.4 BOARD STYLE

By 'board style' is meant the way in which the board goes about its tasks. Tricker [1984] distinguishes four generic board styles:

Rubber stamp style

The directors of a rubber stamp style board have little concern for either the tasks of the board or board relationships. The meetings are formalities. Examples of this style include:

- 'letter box' companies registered in tax havens;
- companies where decisions are made by managers outside the boardroom;
- closely controlled private companies (often with one dominant individual).

Country club style

This board style focuses upon interpersonal relationships at board level. They tend to focus upon ritual, have a culture that deplores disharmony, and are frequently found in long-established companies.

Representative board style

This board style focuses upon the tasks of the board but board relationships are poor. It frequently has adversarial discussions if directors represent different stakeholder interests or if there is one or more dominant persons.

Professional board style

This style shows concern for both the board's tasks and its interpersonal relationships. There will often be tough-minded discussions among the directors, conducted with a mutual understanding and respect for each other.

4.4 EXAMPLE OF A NON-PERFORMING BOARD

THE COMPANY

GoFast International has grown rapidly during its ten years of incorporation and now operates in several countries. It provides integrated communications systems for companies and operates in a sector that is continuing to enjoy a very fast rate of growth. Turnover is £50 million per year and the company is profitable.

THE BOARD

James Wrightman, who founded the company, is chairman and managing director. He is also the majority shareholder, with Walter Cassidy, an old friend, holding the remaining 10% of the equity. Walter is a non-executive director, but has little interest in or aptitude for business and is usually happy to go along with whatever James suggests.

Nicola Frobisher has been with the company for six years, the last two as marketing director. Brendan Fisher became technical director when he was recruited by James five years ago. Neither of the executive directors have shares in the company, although from time to time the idea of some share options has been suggested. James acts as finance director, since his early discipline was finance.

BACKGROUND TO THE CURRENT SITUATION

James has been accustomed to dominating the board. His ownership of the majority of the equity, his strong personality and the influence he holds over the other directors mean that he gets his way on most issues that come before the board. This is compounded by the fact that it is James who decides what is on the agenda at the bi-monthly board meetings. Frequently he will report on something that he has either decided will be done or that he has already transacted.

Many changes are happening in the industry in which the company operates. The market is becoming ever more global and some very large competitors have emerged, often as a result of take-overs and alliances. Technology integration has blurred some of the previous product divisions so that niche operators like GoFast are having to re-evaluate their strategies and re-think what added value they can offer to customers. The executive directors know that these issues are not being adequately addressed by the board and feel frustrated that the board is not acting in its proper capacity.

THE CRISIS

A few months ago, GoFast acquired a smaller company, Compact, whose activities seemed to complement theirs. James negotiated the acquisition himself from the owner of Compact, who was an acquaintance of long standing. The purchase was presented to the board as a 'done deal' by James, who reminded his fellow directors that they had discussed the synergy that the two companies might produce at a previous board meeting. Both Nicola and Brendan remarked that the information available to the board on Compact then was quite sparse and a proposition to purchase the company was not considered at that time.

It is now apparent that the affairs of Compact are not what had been expected. There are holes in the balance sheet and it is clear that a legal dispute in which the company was engaged is likely to be found against Compact. James had not had a professional due diligence investigation of the company prior to purchase. The prospective financial write-off will be substantial, using up most of GoFast's reserves.

ADVICE SOUGHT (AT LAST!)

This matter has so shaken James that he has sought advice from a trusted and respected old friend, Bill Steady. Bill is a very experienced business-man who is chairman of two companies and a non-executive director of a third.

James explains what has happened and also that his two executive directors have formally complained that matters should have been conducted differently and that the purchase should have been a decision for the whole board to make, furnished with adequate information. They used the occasion to register a belated criticism of the way that the board's business has been conducted generally and have asked for changes to be made.

James realises that things cannot continue to be done as they have been. He asks his friend what changes he recommends should be made and how matters should be conducted in future.

BILL'S ADVICE

Bill points out to James that:

- The board of GoFast is too small and is wrongly structured: there are not enough directors for a company of this size and, in particular, there are no non-executive directors. Bill recommends a board of 7 or 8 directors, of whom 3 would be non-executive directors. At least one of the non-executives should be recruited from within the industry and should know it well.

- Too much power is concentrated in James' hands, so the board has tended to lack independent judgement and to act merely as sycophants, with the result that 'bet-the-company' decisions have been taken without adequate thought and consultation. Bill strongly recommends splitting the roles of chairman and managing director.

- Information available to the board is inadequate; there is not even a finance director. Bill urges that a finance director should be appointed as quickly as possible.

- There is no rigorous review of management or the board – for example, there is no audit or remuneration committee. Bill suggests that the (new) board should consider the desirability of these committees and, if thought useful, should utilise the talents of the non-executive directors on the committees. (These committees are discussed in section 5.7.)

- Bill suggests to his friend James that he seriously consider granting share options to the executive directors as a means of aligning their interests with those of the shareholders (himself).

4.5 SUMMARY

1. Members of the board have collective (joint and several) responsibility for the decisions of the board.

2. The tasks of a chairman include:

   a) providing board leadership;

   b) devising board composition;

   c) delineating the role and responsibilities of the board and management respectively;

   d) managing board meetings, including preparing appropriate agenda, ensuring proper information for the board, conducting board meetings effectively, and focusing on the board's key tasks;

   e) reviewing board performance;

   f) developing the effectiveness of the board;

   g) representing the company to the wider world.

3. The board delegates power to oversee the operations of the company to the managing director. The managing director has the apparent authority to commit the company in any way by virtue of holding that title.

4. Executive directors are responsible to the managing director from whom they have delegated executive responsibilities. But in addition they have wider board responsibilities.

5. Non-executive directors are expected to bring to the board wide and relevant experience, special knowledge, desirable personal qualities, and to be impartial and objective.

6. There are three types of unitary board:

    i)   the all-executive board

    ii) the majority executive board

    iii) the majority non-executive board.

7. The company secretary is responsible for company administration and usually works closely with the chairman in planning and managing board business.

8. The size of the board and configuration of the board need to be regularly reviewed to ensure that the correct mix of skill and experience is available.

9. The selection, appointment and development of board members should be considered as key processes that ought to be regularly reviewed.

Chapter 5

How the Board Operates

5.1 DECISION-MAKING

Technically, board-level decisions can be initiated only from within the board. In reality, decisions may be initiated from outside the board in the sense that events may occur inside or outside the company which force the board to take a decision. Management is not doing its job properly if it fails to bring to the board's attention the threats and opportunities which its day-to-day familiarity with the company's business allows it to identify, the various options open to the board, and (possibly) preferred options. Similarly, it is the duty of every board member to bring to his colleagues' attention the threats and opportunities which wider acquaintance with the business environment may reveal. From time to time shareholders may indicate that an issue is of major importance to the company.

The provenance of a decision is not of overwhelming importance. What matters is that the board is aware of when a decision needs to be made, allows adequate time for preparation and the provision of information prior to the decision, and then takes the decision in due time. Within the board the chairman exercises a key role in alerting the board to the need for a decision and organising discussions in such a way that a decision can be made.

If the board cannot agree a collective view, disagreements are normally resolved by a simple majority vote (not related to shareholding), with the company chairman often having a casting vote. In certain circumstances some directors may not be entitled to vote. On occasion the Articles of Association of a company may contain a special provision giving a particular director weighted voting rights.

However, boards are essentially mechanisms for generating and debating a consensus view. The board should derive its strength primarily from collegiate discussion and collective responsibility. The need to vote in a well-run board should be rare. This does not mean that there should not be disagreements at board level, but if a board is voting regularly divisions tend to become manifest and the harmonious drive forward which companies require may disappear. Indeed, if a board is split on an important issue, it is better to defer the decision for more consultation and information, rather than put it to a vote. Successful boards work easily together; unsuccessful boards are often riven with factions and rivalries.

5.2 MUST A DIRECTOR ATTEND BOARD MEETINGS?

A director has a general duty to attend board meetings, and if he consistently fails to attend he could be at risk of losing his position. A sanction for non-attendance is provided in Table A, a specimen set of Articles of Association found in the *Companies Act 1985*, which provides that a director loses his office if he misses meetings for six consecutive months without board permission *and* the directors vote to remove him.

In practical terms, though a director need not attend all board meetings, he should try to miss as few as possible. His attendance and contribution at board meetings should be an important part of the decision-making process, particularly if he possesses a special skill, say as a finance director. If this is not the case, then he should not be a board member; if it is, then he should accept the responsibility of attendance at board meetings.

5.3 CAN A DIRECTOR BE EXCLUDED FROM BOARD MEETINGS?

Generally, the board appoints directors and the shareholders of the company in general meeting approve or disapprove the appointment. A properly appointed director is entitled to attend all board meetings. A director who is wrongfully excluded could go to Court and seek an injunction restraining further exclusion. However, this scenario is unlikely to occur. It is difficult to imagine a board, or indeed a company, operating effectively if it is excluding a director against his wishes.

5.4 COLLECTIVE RESPONSIBILITIES

Directors are jointly and severally responsible for the decisions of the board and the actions of the company. If a decision has been taken by the board, then the directors are held liable for that decision together and as individuals. In general terms, therefore, members of a board should accept collective responsibility for the decisions of the board as loyal members of the board. It is not open to a director to hide behind the decision of a 'strong' managing director or to say that he personally did not agree with the board's decision. If, for example, the managing director has driven an inappropriate decision through the board, then the directors are collectively responsible and also, if necessary, individually responsible.

On the other hand, this does not mean that a director should not be prepared, if necessary, to express disagreement with colleagues, including the chairman or managing director, but it does mean that he should accept that resignation or dismissal may sometimes be the ultimate consequence of sustained protest on a matter of company policy, conscience or principle.

When a director concludes that he is unable to acquiesce in a decision of the board, some or all of the following steps should be considered:

a) making his/her dissent and its possible consequences clear to the board as a means of seeking to influence the decision;

b) asking for additional legal, accounting or other professional advice (the Combined Code [1998] recommends that the company should meet the expenses incurred);

c) asking that the decision be postponed to the next meeting to allow time for further consideration and informal discussion;

d) tabling a statement of dissent, or writing to the chairman and asking that the statement or letter be minuted;

e) calling a special board meeting to consider the matter;

f) calling a general meeting of shareholders to consider and vote on the policy of the board, or to remove the directors, or even to appoint an Inspector from the Department of Trade and Industry;

g) resigning, and perhaps advising the appropriate regulator.

If, in the extreme, a director considers that some course of action approved by the board is illegal or unethical, then he should refuse to accept the collective decision and resign. The director's fiduciary duty is to the company, not the board, and resignation may be the only way of discharging this duty. In such circumstances a director who chooses to resign may, and in the opinion of the authors should, disclose the reasons for resignation to shareholders or to the appropriate regulator, though a director should bear in mind the duty not to disclose confidential information. It would be wise in these circumstances to consult the company's legal advisers first.

5.5 INFORMATION REQUIREMENTS

The information that is presented to a board is clearly of great importance, and is relevant to the performance of a director's duty of skill and care (see section 8.5). Directors need, and are entitled to, as much complete, accurate and appropriate information as is available within the company to enable them to perform their functions. Directors therefore have a right to inspect the company's accounting records, for example, and should be able to see any records that are relevant to ascertaining whether any legal obligation has been fulfilled for which they could be liable if breached. (The duty of directors to ensure that proper accounting records are kept is discussed in Chapter 9.) If there is no steady flow of information, then directors must seek it out. Only in this way can the board director pursue the best interests of the company and fulfil his obligation as a director. Lack of information, unless it has been deliberately concealed, will not provide an adequate excuse for a director who has failed to perform his duties to the company.

The information presented to the board should be structured and should include trends and benchmarks. In addition, directors need information sufficiently in advance of a meeting to have time to study it. Regrettably, the information supplied to boards is often inadequate on all these counts.

Chairmen should always be conscious of the potential gap in knowledge of the company's performance and its affairs between the 'insiders' (the executive directors) and the 'outsiders' (the non-executive directors). It is crucial that the latter have the relevant and timely information that they need to do their job properly. Chairmen should therefore give careful attention to the information needs of non-executive directors especially. Otherwise, they will be at a disadvantage and the board will not benefit from their talents and experience.

Directors are also entitled to rely upon the information provided by management providing they have no reasonable grounds for thinking that it is misleading or wrong. They should not, however, assume automatically that information put before them is correct. It is always appropriate for directors to make enquiries concerning the source or provenance of information if there are any doubts. It may well also be proper and reasonable for directors to undertake selective health checks on financial information provided for board meetings.

Effective information is a prerequisite for risk management and is crucial to the fulfilment of the board's duty to safeguard the company's assets against fraud, mistakes, changes in the environment, and all the unwelcome surprises that a business may suffer. Turnbull [1999] gives guidance on the sort of information system that is required of listed companies and recommended, at the board's discretion, for all companies (see Appendix B).

Basic information which every director should insist on, and the circulation of which is normally the responsibility of the company secretary, is:

1. *Agenda*: there is no legal requirement to give notice of the business to be transacted at a board meeting, but it is good practice to provide directors with an agenda. In the event that a director, whether executive or non-executive, wishes items to be placed on the agenda, then he should inform the secretary of the company. The secretary, after informing and consulting with the chairman, should place the items on the agenda. Whether or not such items will be accepted will be a matter for the board at the next board meeting.

   The constructive use of the agenda, to ensure that the various proper functions of the board are performed in an appropriate manner, on an appropriate cycle, and that items appear in the best order, can make a considerable contribution to the efficiency of the board. Many chairmen find it useful to hold an 'agenda meeting' with the company secretary and managing director before the board meeting, so as to decide what should and what should not go on the agenda and in what order, and generally to discuss how the meeting should be conducted. (See section 5.6.3.)

2. *Minutes*: directors should receive minutes of the previous board meeting which they may consider prior to the next meeting. Minutes are legal documents of record which may be used as evidence in the Courts and must correctly represent board meetings. Directors should therefore review the minutes to ensure that they provide a true representation of at least the decisions of the previous board meeting. If they do not, they should be rectified at the next board meeting. (See section 5.6.4.)

3. *Financial information*: prior to the board meeting, directors should receive from the financial director (or the person responsible for the finances of the company) financial information by which the board may monitor the performance of the company. It would be a dereliction of directorial duty not to have such information on a regular basis (see section 15.3 for a discussion of the insolvency rules).

It would be good practice to insist on at least the following information:

- Financial summary of the performance of the company, especially monthly and cumulative year-to-date comparisons against budgets of orders, sales, costs, overheads, gross and net margins, cash generated or consumed.

- Financial performance of various divisions/departments.

- Selected financial and non-financial ratios, depending on the characteristics of the individual business – for example, net margins-to-working capital, tenders submitted to tenders won, turnover-to-working capital trends. Ratios, and changes in ratios, can frequently highlight actions to be taken more sharply than absolute data.

- Debtors and creditors.

- Draft balance sheet.

- A month-end cash and bank balance, together with cash flow projections.

- Inventory report.

- Performance against specific risk management targets, for example the net forward exchange position, the value of hedge contracts, etc.

- The managing director's running forecast of year-end results.

A common danger, resulting from the advent of cheap computing power, is that key financial information is obscured in a mass of data more suited to management's use than to the board's. Boards should insist on information that suits their convenience, not someone else's. The board's requirements will change as circumstances change. In recession, for example, the board may have to be very aware of cash balances; in boom times, of labour turnover or raw material prices.

4. *Non-financial information*: summaries of any quality, customer satisfaction, employee absence, etc. measures that are available. This sort of information may be very important, but is often obscured or lost in the mass of financial data with which boards are presented.

5. *Policy information*: copies of any papers relating to matters that are going to be discussed at the board meeting.

6. *The managing director's regular report*, bringing to the board's attention some of the main features or problems of the business.

5.6 REPORTING AND MEETING PROCEDURES

5.6.1 WHERE SHOULD A BOARD MEETING BE HELD?

There are no legal restrictions on where a board meeting should be held. This is a matter left to the convenience of the directors. In practice, board meetings are usually held at the head office or the main place of business of the company, though some companies hold board meetings at various company sites in rotation, thus providing an opportunity for directors to see and be seen at locations other than head office. A board meeting may be held outside the country or held by video conferencing (though there may be a risk of adverse tax consequences). There seems no reason why a meeting should not be held by telephone or even by e-mail, provided that provision for this has been put in the company's Articles of Association. The Courts do not appear to have considered this issue.

5.6.2 WHAT NOTICE SHOULD BE GIVEN BEFOREHAND?

The company's Articles and Memorandum will define who may call meetings of the board and how they should be called. They will also describe how directors can call extraordinary meetings outside of the agreed normal schedule of board meetings. The Articles may or may not state how many days' notice of the board meeting should be allowed; Table A does not lay down any specific requirement for notice of a meeting to be given. In any event, the length of notice given must be reasonable, having regard to the practice of the company and other surrounding circumstances. Notice does not have to be in writing but it is wise that it should be, particularly if there are contentious issues at stake.

Where the notice given for a board meeting is unreasonable, the meeting and any business conducted at the meeting will be 'void' in law. This means that it will be treated as if the meeting had never taken place at all. However, a director who is aggrieved must register his objection at the first possible opportunity.

In practice, an informal and short notice will probably suffice in the case of a small company where all the directors are in close touch with each other, but longer and written notice will almost certainly be necessary in the case of a large company with a number of non-executive directors. Inadequate notice, however, will not suffice in either small or large companies. One month's notice would be, in the authors' view, a reasonable minimum notice, though shorter notice may be necessary properly to deal with unforeseen circumstances.

5.6.3 BOARD AGENDA

There is no legal requirement to state what business is intended to be transacted at a board meeting. In practice, the lack of an agenda may not matter too much in the case of small companies, where a degree of flexibility is necessary and the directors are aware of the affairs of the company as a whole, though it is not recommended. However, it would be highly inappropriate for there to be no indication of the matters to be considered at board meetings of a substantial company.

In addition, background papers should be circulated in advance of the meeting, so that any decisions on important issues affecting the company may at least be informed decisions.

The prior circulation of an agenda and supporting papers is of particular value where the company has non-executive directors, whether the company is large or small. Unless a non-executive director is well informed he cannot make an effective contribution to the affairs of a company.

If a director requires clarification of information circulated with the board agenda, or additional information, he should first seek it from the company secretary prior to the board meeting.

5.6.4 BOARD MINUTES

The *Companies Act 1985* requires minutes to be kept of all directors' meetings. Furthermore, Table A requires there to be a record of the 'proceedings' at all directors' meetings. Shareholders have no right of access to board minutes.

Minutes should be a record of the actual decisions taken at a meeting rather than a record of the details of the discussions. However, in some instances directors may wish to record the reasons for their decisions. The minutes should be written with conciseness, accuracy, objectivity and the absence of any ambiguity.

Responsibility for the keeping of minutes usually falls on the company secretary, although this is not a legal requirement. In practice, any person attending a meeting can be asked to take the minutes of it and an ordinary secretary can be invited to attend for this purpose. The minutes must be entered in 'books kept for that purpose'.

There is no legal requirement that anyone should sign the board minutes, though the *Companies Act 1985* provides that a minute signed by the chairman (or purportedly by the chairman) of a meeting is evidence (but not conclusive evidence) of what has happened at that meeting. Contrary to common belief, there is no requirement for the board to confirm or adopt the minutes of a previous meeting, although it is good practice. The reason is simple: if the directors approve the minutes of a meeting in some way, it will be difficult subsequently for a director to deny his collective responsibility for any decision. A director who disagrees with the minutes should voice an objection at the first possible opportunity. However, it is up to the chairman (if he takes responsibility for the minutes) as to whether or not the objection is formally recorded. If the objection is not recorded, the dissenting director would be wise to consider some other documentary means of recording his objection and, depending on the seriousness of the matter, he may also need to seek professional advice.

The agenda, supporting reports and minutes are all official company documents. It is imperative that directors have sufficient time in advance of the meeting to read and reflect upon the documents prior to the meeting and ask any questions about them. The agenda and reports should be distributed to all board and committee members at least five days prior to a board meeting. The minutes of the last meeting should be sent as soon after the meeting as is practicable.

The Courts recognise the need for a director to be able to see minutes of board meetings as he may be called to account for matters included in them, and consequently in common law a director has the right to see the minutes, though there is no statutory right. The auditors of a company also have a statutory right of access to the board minutes. However, a company's shareholders and other persons have no such right.

5.6.5 QUORUM

A quorum is the number of people who must be present at a meeting for it to be validly held. A board meeting cannot proceed to business unless a quorum is present. How many members constitute a quorum is normally stated in the Articles of Association; otherwise, the board must decide. For their discussions to be binding, boards need to have a quorum even for *ad hoc* meetings. Where *ad hoc* or committee meetings are used to help decide issues, the decisions still need to be subsequently ratified by the full board.

5.6.6 HOW OFTEN AND REGULARLY SHOULD THE BOARD MEET?

There is no legal requirement even for large public companies to hold board meetings. However, there is a requirement for the directors to approve the accounts, so in consequence boards must meet at least once per year.

Subject to the provisions of the Articles, the directors may regulate their proceedings as they think fit. In practice, small private companies will probably hold fewer formal board meetings than larger companies. But in any event it is a good discipline even for the smallest company to establish a schedule for holding board meetings.

Most companies opt for one meeting a month, but some have quarterly or bi-monthly meetings. This schedule should be prepared very much in advance. At times of crisis, the frequency may need to be increased; further, any director has the right to call a meeting at any time.

5.6.7 THE RHYTHM OF THE BOARD

The board should be flexible and willing to discuss any subject as and when it is necessary. However, it is often helpful to bring issues forward on a regular basis, so that the board develops a natural rhythm, helping to ensure that the board discusses all relevant issues at appropriate intervals. For example, it is sensible to produce and review the business plan for the coming year at the same time of year as in previous years and on a like-for-like basis.

Suggested examples of the way board topics might be rotated are as follows:

- Management and financial accounts covering performance to date against the year's budget, together with recommendations for improvement, and the managing director's report on the trading situation, competition, overseas expansion, etc. might be discussed monthly.

- One-by-one divisional reviews might be undertaken on a quarterly basis.

- Human relations and industrial relations issues might feature on a half-yearly basis.

- Approval of plans and budgets for the coming year, the board review of its own performance as a board, the board review of the contribution of its individual directors, particularly the non-executives, and of any changes it needs to make to the mix of directors, skills and styles in the boardroom, the election or re-election of the chairman, are all matters probably best visited annually.

5.7 BOARD COMMITTEES

5.7.1 WHY DO BOARDS HAVE COMMITTEES?

Boards have a limited amount of time for meetings, and so the Articles of Association normally permit the board to delegate its functions to committees of the board. There is normally no limitation on what the board can choose to delegate to committees. There are various options:

- It can appoint a committee of directors which can make only recommendations to the board, leaving the board to make the final decisions.

- It can appoint a committee to exercise the powers of the board without further reference to it (relatively rare).

- It can appoint a committee of directors to exercise a supervisory or reporting function. The 'audit committee' is an increasingly important example of this in large companies.

Undoubtedly, the use of board committees has disadvantages. It is likely that:

- Directors will have to put in more time; committee attendance is always additional to board attendance.

- Some executive directors may feel left out or that they are only second-class board members.

- Reporting and co-ordination tasks are increased and need to be addressed.

On the other hand, the advantages are such that most companies, once they reach a certain size or degree of complexity, decide that the advantages stemming from delegating certain areas of business to a committee outweigh the disadvantages. The advantages are:

- More time is available to focus on a specific issue.

- Specialised knowledge and capability on the board is developed and utilised.

- The burden on full board meetings is reduced.

- Decision-making may be facilitated, particularly where the main board cannot agree.

- Sensitive or confidential activities may be considered in the expectation of greater confidentiality.

- Business managers may have access to an additional resource.

- Non-executive directors, who generally make up the committees, are involved more in the company's affairs.

The Cadbury [1992] and Hampel [1998] Committees recommended that boards should set up a number of key sub-committees with specific responsibilities, in particular audit, remuneration and nomination committees. These committees are committees of the board: the board agrees their terms of reference and their membership; the board retains the responsibility for committee decisions.

These committees, which are also required under the Stock Exchange Listing Rules, are discussed below.

5.7.2 AUDIT COMMITTEE

The audit committee is an important committee for both large and smaller companies and is intended to provide a link between auditor and board independent of the company's executive directors. The committee will probably have wide-ranging powers, and usually is able to seek independent professional advice. The Combined Code recommends that for listed companies this committee should include at least three non-executive directors.

In practice, the audit committee is usually required to:

- review the company's financial statements, accounting principles and the practices underlying them;
- review the scope and results and cost-effectiveness of the audit;
- liaise with the company's internal and external auditors; *and*
- monitor and review the effectiveness of internal financial controls.

The introduction of an audit committee may have extensive benefits, principally that the committee can:

- provide a check on both the company's financial controls and its auditing processes, and thereby help the board to discharge its responsibility with regard to the validity of published financial statements;
- provide a mechanism to ensure that the board focuses on key audit, accounting and internal control issues;
- provide an independent check on executive directors;
- reduce the opportunity for fraud;
- serve as a forum for consideration of any deficiencies in corporate governance that need to be addressed, particularly when there is a disagreement between the management and the auditors;
- increase public confidence in the credibility of financial statements.

Specimen terms of reference for an audit committee (for guidance only) are shown in Table 5.1.

5.7.3 REMUNERATION COMMITTEE

As a matter of good practice, in order to avoid a potential conflict of interest, executive directors should not be responsible for determining their own remuneration. The Combined Code recommends that this should be the remit of a remuneration committee made up wholly or mainly of non-executive directors. The Listing Rules of the London Stock Exchange require

Table 5.1 *Specimen terms of reference of an audit committee*

Constitution

1 The Board hereby resolves to establish a Committee of the Board to be known as the Audit Committee.

Membership

2 The Committee shall be appointed by the Board from amongst the Non-Executive Directors of the Company and shall consist of not fewer than three members. A quorum shall be two members.
3 The Chairman of the Committee shall be appointed by the Board.

Attendance at meetings

4 The Finance Director, the Head of Internal Audit, and a representative of the external auditors shall normally attend meetings. Other Board members shall also have the right of attendance. However, at least once a year the Committee shall meet with the external auditors without executive board members present.
5 The Company Secretary shall be the Secretary of the Committee.

Frequency of meetings

6 Meetings shall be held not less than twice a year. The external auditors may request a meeting if they consider that one is necessary.

Authority

7 The Committee is authorised by the Board to investigate any activity within its terms of reference. It is authorised to seek any information it requires from any employee and all employees are directed to co-operate with any request made by the Committee.
8 The Committee is authorised by the Board to obtain outside legal or other independent professional advice and to secure the attendance of outsiders with relevant experience and expertise if it considers this necessary.

Duties

9 The duties of the Committee shall be:
  a) to consider the appointment of the external auditor, the audit fee, and any questions of resignation or dismissal
  b) to discuss with the external auditors before the audit commences the nature and scope of the audit, and ensure co-ordination where more than one audit firm is involved
  c) to review the half-year and annual financial statements before submission to the Board, focusing particularly on:

Table 5.1 *Specimen terms of reference of an audit committee (continued)*

 (i)   any changes in accounting policies and practices
 (ii) major judgemental areas
 (iii) significant adjustments resulting from the audit
 (iv) the 'going concern' assumption
 (v)   compliance with accounting standards
 (vi) compliance with stock exchange and legal requirements.

d) to discuss problems and reservations arising from the interim and final audits, and any matters the auditor may wish to discuss (in the absence of management where necessary)

e) to review the external auditors' management letter and management's response

f) to review the Company's statement on internal control systems prior to endorsement by the Board

g) (where an internal audit function exists) to review the internal audit programme, ensure co-ordination between the internal and external auditors, and ensure that the internal audit function is adequately resourced and has appropriate standing with the Company

h) to consider the major findings of internal investigations and management's response

i) to consider other topics, as defined by the Board.

Reporting procedures

10 The Secretary shall circulate the minutes of meetings of the Committee to all members of the Board.

---

the annual report and accounts of a listed company to include a report to shareholders by the remuneration committee, containing various disclosures about directors' remuneration, a statement that full consideration has been given to best practice relating to remuneration policy, and a statement of compliance with the best practice provisions of the Greenbury Report (1995).

A remuneration committee avoids involving the executives in argument about each other's salaries, bonuses, pensions, share schemes, etc. In listed companies it is usually the practice to appoint an independent remuneration adviser to the committee. In smaller companies the committee is usually informal; the danger is that it is dominated by the owner/chairman/managing director.

In broad terms, remuneration committees are likely to be responsible for

- determining remuneration for senior executives in accordance with the authority delegated from the board;

- reviewing fees to non-executive directors;

- monitoring all executive benefits;

- analysing internal and external information about executive remuneration;

- commissioning external studies of the market for executives;

- ensuring that policies help the employment and motivation of high quality personnel;

- bench-marking with 'best practice' and/or competitor companies.

In practice, despite all the fine words, the role of a remuneration committee is often not to originate, but to advise and consent to proposals put forward by the managing director or others. However, having said this, there seems to be a trend for remuneration committees to arrogate more and more power and influence to themselves. They are likely to become the forum for reviewing directors' performance as well as remuneration, and to take account of the impact of their decisions on shareholders and stakeholders.

EXAMPLE

Extracts from the Report of the Remuneration and Nominations Committee on behalf of the Board of Barclays Plc (Annual Report 1998)

The Group's remuneration policy is based on the following principles:

- *To deliver improved shareholder value by ensuring that individual performance and reward reflect and reinforce the business objectives of the Group;*

- *To support the recruitment, motivation and retention of high quality senior executives;*

- *To ensure that performance is the key factor in determining individual reward taking into account internal relativities and market data of external comparator groups; and*

- *To communicate the reward structure clearly and effectively to executives and shareholders.*

In addition to a basic salary, executive Directors and senior executives may participate in a range of short and longer-term remuneration schemes designed to meet the overall objectives of the remuneration policy. The report goes on to discuss service contracts, basic salary, the annual bonus scheme, the Executive Share Award Scheme, the Executive Share Option Scheme, the SAYE Share Option Scheme, profit sharing schemes, benefits-in-kind, other long-term incentive plans, and pension arrangements.

5.7.4 NOMINATION COMMITTEE

The purpose of the nomination committee is to vet and present to the board potential new directors, especially non-executives. Such a committee is intended to improve the style and standard of contribution in boardrooms by incorporating a 'professional', methodical, semi-independent approach to the recruitment of directors, thereby reducing patronage. Non-executive directors should form a majority of this committee.

Appointment to the board should be a transparent process. Decisions should be taken, in reality as well as in form, by the whole board. We support the Cadbury Committee's endorsement of the nomination committee (Report 4.30); indeed, we believe that the use of such a committee should be accepted as best practice, with the proviso that smaller boards may prefer to fulfil the function themselves. (Hampel [1998], para. 3.20)

In the USA probably the majority of boards have a nomination committee, and the proportion is increasing; in the UK they are common.

5.7.5 FINANCE COMMITTEE

Only about one-sixth of the boards of companies listed on the London Stock Exchange have a finance committee, though rather more boards of US listed companies have them. They usually include the chairman, chief executive, finance director and one or two non-executives with financial backgrounds. They commonly consider accounts, the proposed public statements about the accounts, the funding mix, the appointment of bankers and financial advisers, and the implications of the cashflow forecasts. All these activities are so fundamental to the overall deliberations of the board as a whole that it can be argued that they are best left to the full board. (In the UK, some of these tasks are covered by the audit committee, which is one reason why there are many fewer finance committees than in the USA.)

5.7.6 PLANNING COMMITTEE

About one in seven of the larger UK companies have planning committees concerned with company-wide planning. In a large and complex business, detailed and sophisticated planning procedures necessitate very detailed subsidiary company plans and a careful aggregation into a collective corporate group plan. Such planning needs onerous explanation, exhortation and co-ordination. So the boards of large companies tend to delegate much of the detail of drawing up formats, defining and explaining contents, assisting with compilation, and illustrating how group policies affect the individual units, to a committee of the board.

5.7.7 OTHER COMMITTEES

Other committees may be set up as the board judges helpful; for example, human resources, donations, environmental compliance, health and safety, intellectual property, are all areas where a board might wish to delegate its work to a committee of the board.

5.8 SETTING UP A COMMITTEE

The values and benefits of establishing committees need to be carefully considered. There is little point in creating an elaborate board structure, including committees, if it adds no value. The operation of several committees can be a major investment of time and resource. Different committees should play different, and specific, roles. This enables their activities, membership and overall value to the board and to the business to be relatively focused. A committee with a broad or poorly defined remit of responsibilities either may not deliver useful outputs because of its lack of focus or, worst of all, may develop into an alternative or competing board.

Before establishing a committee of the board, then, it is suggested the following questions are considered:

a) What is the value of setting up the committee?

b) What is the role of the committee for the board and for the business?

c) Who should be on the committee?

d) What should be its terms of reference?

e) What should it produce or deliver?

f) To whom, and how, should it report its activities?

g) Should the committee have an 'expiry date' or 'review-by date'?

The answers to these sorts of consideration are the reason why many small companies rest content with only an audit committee and a merged remuneration/nomination committee.

5.9 SUMMARY

1. The board is essentially a decision-making body which is collectively responsible for the survival and prosperity of the company.

2. Adequate, timely and structured information should be provided by management to the board.

3. Board reporting and meeting procedures should be formalised in order to aid the efficient conduct of board business.

4. Boards often delegate some of their functions to committees. In such a case, however, the committees are committees of the board and ultimate responsibility remains with the board.

5. Key committees include

   - an audit committee;

   - a remuneration committee;

   - a nomination committee.

6. The board must take care to receive comprehensive reports from its committees.

Chapter 6

Board Appraisal

6.1 INTRODUCTION

The burden of corporate governance rests with the board. Companies periodically review the performance of important contributors to their activities – departments and managers, for example – but the key contributor to the overall performance of the organisation, the board, often escapes such a review.

Many different approaches to assessing and improving individual director and board performance have been suggested, but all have usually turned out in practice to be difficult to install. A major reason for this is that the assessment of board performance is not just about monitoring current performance; it is equally about development and improvements. The board's performance should be linked to the future aspirations for the company, so the process of board appraisal should also look at how the board deals with the futurity of events.

6.2 THE BENEFITS

The benefits to a company, and to its board, of a regular review are likely to be numerous. They include:

- Regular board appraisals can serve to clarify the individual and collective roles and responsibilities of directors. Board reviews are probably the most effective way of making performance expectations clear.

- The process of board appraisal often helps clarify whether or not the composition of the board is appropriate. No one person alone can provide all that is required on a board. Its members between them, however, should possess the required set of skills, knowledge and attributes, which means that the board should be aware of any current or future gaps with a view to filling them.

- Working relations between the board and managers are likely to be improved, simply because the appraisal process encourages greater candour in directors' dealings with the managing director and other senior managers whilst at the same time helping to assure a reasonable balance of power between the board and the managing director. Also, board appraisals show that the board is leading by example.

- The appraisal process often serves to prevent a powerful chairman or other personality from exercising control over too wide an area and evading checks and balances.

- Regular appraisals are likely to lead to a clear commitment by a board to devote more time and energy to consideration of its tasks.

- Finally, board assessments help keep the board focused on improving its effectiveness; when boards from time to time step back and ponder on what they do and how they work, the pressure is on, from *within the board*, to improve its performance.

6.3 HOW TO APPRAISE

The board is the ultimate source of authority in a company and hence there is no other governing or overseeing body within the company that is qualified to assess the board. No one in the company can evaluate the board except the board itself. Generally, therefore, the board assesses itself, or the board appoints an external expert or neutral person to assess performance, or some combination of the two is adopted.

However, effective self-appraisal is never easy; it requires board members to make judgements about themselves and about issues that probably affect all stakeholders in the company. There is a danger that self-appraisal may be self-serving. Therefore, the appraisal methodology must be effective and very robust.

It is important to remember that an evaluation of board performance is about the board's overall effectiveness, the contribution to the board made by directors, and the processes of the board itself, not about how well departments and functions are managed.

The appraisal exercise should probably be an annual process and be led by the chairman.

Assessment of the performance of a board makes sense only within the context of objectives and resources at the board's disposal. Hence, assessment of the company board might be structured in the following five stages:

- The board's ability to define its tasks and establish annual objectives.

- The resources and capabilities of the board.

- The views of individual board members.

- Consolidation of the results.

- Review of the results.

These broad headings are discussed in turn in sections 6.3.1–6.3.5 below.

6.3.1 DEFINITION OF BOARD TASKS

Every assessment should start with the board identifying its tasks. The IoD delineation of the company board's tasks are in IoD [1999] and should be regularly reviewed and approved by the company board, so that each board member understands and agrees what the tasks of the board are.

Because of the demands on the time of board members, it is unlikely that every board responsibility can be evaluated every year. The board must therefore establish priorities. So, for example, a board might choose to focus on only two or three of the tasks enumerated in Chapter 3 and more fully discussed in IoD [1999]. The choice of topics should reflect areas that the board currently feels are the most important to the company, but all tasks should be covered periodically.

However, before a board can even begin to evaluate its own performance in relation to these tasks, it must articulate the specific actions that each implies – that is, it must set detailed objectives within the broad categories of tasks against which the board collectively can eventually measure its performance. The objectives will reflect the directors' collective judgement about which aspects of which tasks need particular attention in the coming year.

For example, as part of its role in developing business strategy the board may decide that the company will seek to become the leader in a particular area of business activity, say partnering new e-commerce start-ups. The board will then specify the appraisal criteria it will use to assess whether it is helping the company achieve that goal. These criteria might include: improving the board's knowledge of start-ups and e-commerce by recruiting members with specialist expertise, facilitating a partnership with the relevant department of a local University, visiting e-commerce firms in order to meet aspiring entrepreneurs, and so on.

6.3.2 BOARD RESOURCES AND CAPABILITIES

The board needs information and knowledge, a blend of useful attributes, and needs to conduct its business efficiently. The board can refer to the checklists in IoD [1999] to identify gaps in its expertise, performance and ways of working which might then be addressed, whether through training and development, a change in the board's approach, replacement of a director or adding to the board's number.

Appraisal of the board's available resources and capabilities, therefore, would involve an appraisal of

- How the board spent its time in meetings, including at least a list of topics and issues, the date and the time spent in discussion. This information should be linked to specific tasks. Such an analysis might, for example, reveal that the board had never met with the senior executive who is the prime candidate to succeed the present marketing director.

- The administration of board business.

- The handling of big decisions, such as major capital projects.

- The use of committees.

- The skills and knowledge needed to perform the tasks, what attributes are contained within the board, and the identification of specific skills or types of experience needed to fill gaps.

- The selection, recruitment and induction of board members.

- The use of external consultants and professional advisers.

6.3.3 A SURVEY OF BOARD MEMBERS

The views of members of the board on the board's performance – that is, how nearly they met their objectives and how adequate their resources were – should be collected confidentially.

The methodology may vary, but the survey should probably comprise a mix of open-ended questions and numerically scored multiple choice items that do not change from year to year, thus allowing the board to check its assessments over time. The answers will be a mix of objective listings, subjective assessments of how well the board dealt with its key tasks, and subjective assessments of the conduct of meetings. A mass of hard data, opinion and ideas for improvement will be generated.

In appraising the effectiveness of the executive directors as members of the board, the following ways are appropriate, either individually or in combination: one-to-one appraisal with the chairman; peer group appraisal; appraisal by the nomination committee, which is normally composed of non-executive directors; and self-assessment based upon agreed goals. The appraisal of a non-executive director's contribution to the board should be conducted by the chairman. This would probably be on a one-to-one basis, but comments from the peer group are likely to be included.

The annual review of the chairman is generally performed by the nomination committee if one exists, or by the non-executive directors, either alone or as a group. The use of an independent consultant is a growing trend.

6.3.4 CONSOLIDATION OF THE RESULTS

The results, probably with the help of the chairman, should be consolidated into a single summary document showing responses, identifying strengths and weaknesses, and indicating where improvement is needed, and presented to the board in summary form. This would enable the board to discuss and review the results, generate ideas for improvement and decide appropriate action plans. Importantly, it is desirable that the report highlights areas where ratings or viewpoints diverge.

6.3.5 REVIEW OF THE RESULTS

The issues that ought to feature when considering the results of the appraisal of the board should be apparent from the preceding chapters. In brief, we suggest the following:

1. **Overall governance**. The key question is: will ultimate power over the company change during the strategic time period of the board review? If so, what would be the implications for governance and the board? For example, in a public listed company what are the prospects of a change of ownership through a friendly or hostile bid? Or in a company with a dominant shareholder, what might happen to the board if this shareholding changed hands? In a family firm, how might the balance of power change on succession? It is important to consider possible future scenarios.

2. **Relevant external factors**. This means looking at the context in which the governance of the company must operate over the period of the review. Are there any legal, political, societal or technological factors that could affect the governance of the company? Obvious examples include possible changes to company legislation in any of the countries in which the company operates, such as new regulations from the European Commission about worker representation on boards, or the imposition of new disclosure requirements in the Stock Exchange Listing Rules, or the possible effects of a change of government, or the impact of e-commerce.

3. **Strategy formulation and policy making**. The review should deal with the board's contribution to the performance roles of strategy formulation and policy making. Is adequate time devoted to this part of the board's responsibilities? Are all board members adequately informed about strategic matters? Is there a shared vision and understanding of the company's core values and competencies among all the directors? Are there any differences of view as to the strategic direction of the firm? Are the policy guidelines laid down by the board adequate for management decision-making, balancing control and freedom appropriately? What ideas do directors have for improvement?

4. **Executive supervision and accountability**. Turning to the conformance tasks of the board, do the directors adequately monitor and supervise executive management? Is the feedback of information relevant and timely? How might the process be improved? Is the board providing appropriate accountability to all those with a legitimate claim to be informed? Does this include a commitment to employees, customers,

suppliers, and the wider community? Should it? Or does the board accept a responsibility only to be accountable to the shareholders? Is this responsibility adequately fulfilled? What ideas are there for improvement?

5. **Directors' time and information**. How does the board spend its time? Are board committees as effective as they could be? This information can be extracted from an analysis of the agenda and minutes of the board and its committees, as well as by directors discussing the issue. Similarly, the board should review the nature, extent and adequacy of the information available to directors. How could board papers be improved? Can directors readily obtain additional information that they want? Do the non-executive directors have easy access to management information? Should there be regular board-level briefings to keep directors up to date? What ideas do directors have for improvement in the information provided to the board?

6. **Membership of the board**. Does the board have the balance of knowledge, skills and experience that will be needed for the planned future of the company? What is the age profile of directors? How many directors will retire over the review's time horizon? Is there a reserve list of potential non-executive directors who could be considered for board appointment? Have senior executives with potential for board appointment been identified?

The board may need new skills and knowledge. If, for example, the company is moving into new technologies or markets, if it is developing new strategic alliances or acquisitions, if its plans call for alternative financing strategies such as the use of derivatives, it is essential that the board includes members able to understand the issues and, in due course, monitor executive management's performance.

7. **Director development and training**. As much concern should be given to director development and training as is given to management development and training, but it seldom is. Directors all too readily assume that, having reached the board, they must have the experience to perform as directors. But governance, the work of the board, is not the same as management. It calls for additional knowledge and different skills. The development needs of each director therefore need to be reviewed. This could involve a carefully developed induction or updating programme on the company and its work, a new experience such as chairing one of the board committees, or it might be achieved through participation in external director-level educational programmes.

8. **Board structure**. Is the size of the board appropriate for the task that needs to be done? There may be a case for additional members; on the other hand, the board may have grown too big. Is the structure of the board satisfactory? Is the balance between executive and non-executive members appropriate? This issue will be interwoven with the board style and the way the members work together. Are sufficient of the non-executive directors genuinely independent, or are their relationships with the company such that they could affect the exercise of their judgement? Are the posts of chairman of the board and managing director separated? Should they be?

9. **Board style**. The review should consider how the directors work together, how the board's work has evolved in recent years, and reflect on the effects of any changes in its members. Is this a genuinely professional board or are there elements of the 'rubber stamp', the 'representative board' or the 'country club'? (See section 4.3.4.) What changes might be necessary to meet different circumstances in the future?

10. **Board development**. The board might prefer to review any lessons for board development arising out of the appraisal process as part of an 'away day' rather than as an agenda item for a regular board meeting, in order to encourage open discussion and the exercise of imagination. The discussion should be focused on how to develop the board. This could include planned changes to board size, structure or membership, new sources and forms of information, different uses of directors' time (such as new board committees), alternative formats for the board meetings, or asking some directors to commit different amounts of time to their board duties.

11. **Action plans and projects**. It is most important that the board agrees, and is committed to, the procedures, plans and projects that will enable the lessons of the appraisal process to be implemented. The results of the annual board appraisal thus become a part of a continuing learning and relearning process by the board.

6.4 BOARD APPRAISAL IN A CONTEXT OF CHANGE

It is important that the board appraisal is not merely backwards-looking, but relates to likely future changes in the business and the business environment. All boards have to cope with change, whether it is internal change in the board itself or the company or external change in the trading environment or the wider environment.

The growth of the company will be largely dependent upon the ability of the board to cope with change, deal with the unpredictable as well as the predictable, constantly develop to meet new demands, and maintain momentum and enthusiasm over time and not become complacent. Some examples of possible new challenges and opportunities are:

- Undertaking a new business development strategy to lead the company into a new market, or focus on a different distribution channel, or launch a new product, or set up a joint venture with a foreign company, or float on the stock market, none of which has been experienced by the organisation before.

- Making decisions to close plants, switch production to a new technology, resist a hostile take-over bid, change the managing director.

In sum, then, the board appraisal process should also consider how the board copes with change and whether it has the necessary resources to do this effectively. The appraisal process should ask, for example:

- Does the board simply note changes in the external environment and then determine whether and how it should react? Or, does the board try to anticipate what might happen and be proactive in taking decisions to try to achieve some advantage over its competitors?

- Has the board used outside expertise to complement its existing knowledge and skills base? Is the board effective at identifying the need for consultancy and selecting and managing consultants?

- Has the board taken on new members who have different experience, skills or knowledge deliberately to contribute to expected future changes?

- Are new members involved at an appropriate stage? Are succession issues thought through and planned so that progress and performance are not impeded?

- Is the board able to motivate and enthuse those key individuals and organisations with an interest in the company's future success?

6.5 ROLE OF THE CHAIRMAN AND EXTERNAL ADVICE

The starting point for the process of board appraisal is the identification of the appraiser. The natural candidate is the chairman. In many cases, certainly if there has been no previous appraisal system or even acknowledgement that appraisal of the performance of the board is useful, there will need to be some significant changes in the culture of the board, and perhaps even in its membership. The chairman will need to be the champion of the change. He would have to 'buy in' to the concept and exercise great patience and diligence in pursuing the process. Certainly, simply imposing an appraisal process on directors could be disastrous for the board.

It is likely that the chairman's task would be made less onerous by the judicious use of external advisers. A major consideration is the degree of openness the board has to learning and development. If the board is reluctant to change, an outside intervention can be useful. In addition, the use of external advisers tends to help to promote confidentiality and objectivity and provide a mechanism for feedback. There is always the risk that the candour of discussions will be damaged unless confidentiality is assured. Finally, once an effective board appraisal process is in place, third-party assessors can be used to re-examine it regularly to see how it might be improved and prevent the process from degenerating into an annoying 'tick-box' ritual merely to be tolerated.

Issues that outsiders might help the chairman with include:

Purpose: the chairman needs to have a clear vision of what will be gained from implementing the appraisal process and how the board will get there. This vision must be articulated to the board and the directors must understand the reasoning of the chairman.

Planning: the chairman probably will need help in planning the process of appraisal.

Communication: it is essential that the purpose and the process of the appraisal system are communicated to the individual board members. The greater the part board members explicitly play in the discussions of board effectiveness, the more likely is it that they become enthusiastic participants.

6.6 USE OF *STANDARDS FOR THE BOARD*

Standards for the Board (IoD [1999]) provides a sound foundation to underpin the process of company board appraisal. *Standards* is a reference document, not a list of mandatory instructions, which each board may tailor to its own circumstances. Interpretation will depend upon the size and type of the company as well as the circumstances it faces. The relevance and importance of the individual standards to a particular board will be decided by that board. Nevertheless *Standards* will help the board maintain a firm and clear view as to what its tasks are and what is good practice in its activities. The standards are presented mostly in the form of checklists. This is particularly appropriate for assessment purposes.

When reviewing progress during the past year and deciding on objectives for the coming year (stage 1 of the assessment process), the list of company key board tasks in *Standards* is a reasonable starting point. How the board has performed should be related therefore to one or more of its key tasks – that is, establishing the company's mission, vision and values; setting the company's strategy and structure; supervising, controlling and monitoring management; exercising accountability to shareholders and being responsible to relevant stakeholders.

Each of the four key tasks in *Standards* can be disaggregated into a number of subsidiary, more detailed, elements, and each of these in turn is capable of further disaggregation. It is recommended that each individual director starts at the broad level represented by the four key tasks, and that where he detects weaknesses or ambiguities in the performance of the board he proceeds to the more detailed sub-tasks.

For example, a key task of a company board is to establish the company's vision, mission and values. Each director therefore might begin by asking himself if the company has a vision and a mission, and if so what they are; how the board determines the company's values; seek examples of how the board determines company goals; and seek examples of how the board determines company policies.

Suppose the board had decided at the previous year's assessment meeting that for the forthcoming year attention was to be focused on the company's corporate values. In this case the questionnaire to be completed by each director at the end of the current year could ask, for example, has the board made the values consistent with, and supportive of, the achievement of the vision and mission? Are the values explicit, unambiguous and feasible? How does the board champion the values? Are the values influenced by the views of the employees? How does the board know the values are sensitive to the interests of shareholders and any relevant stakeholders? How are the company values embedded in the company's culture? Is there a process of regular review of company values, their appropriateness and the degree of support they have?

Similarly, another key task of the board is to set strategy. The appraisal process might concentrate on the exploration by each director of the board's performance in relation to this task of the board by dividing it into four sub-tasks:

- Review and evaluate present and future opportunities, threats and risks in the external environment; and current and future strengths, weaknesses and risks relating to the company.

- Determine strategic options, select those to be pursued, and decide the means to implement and support them.

- Determine the business strategies and plans that underpin the corporate strategy.

- Ensure that the company's organisational structure and capability are appropriate for implementing the chosen strategies.

Any one of the areas covered by these tasks can be investigated further and in more detail along the lines suggested by the additional sub-set of questions in *Standards*. For example, in discussing the board's role in setting strategy the individual responses may suggest a weakness to do with ensuring that the organisational structure of the company is appropriate. This, in turn, might lead to a general board discussion about

- How the board ensures that the company's organisational structure supports the corporate and business strategies, enables all employees' skills/motivation to flourish, has an appropriate degree of hierarchy, promotes effective two-way communications, ensures decisions are made in practice by the appropriate people.

- How the board ensures that the company's culture encourages the questioning of convention, encourages enterprise and innovation, helps develop individuals and teams, encourages training that adds value to the business, and encourages continuous learning at work.

- How the board supports and when necessary champions change, encourages employees to communicate widely and be well informed, insists on efficient and effective business systems, and promotes short- and long-term performance-related rewards such that individuals and teams are motivated to achieve desired goals.

These examples illustrate that it is not difficult to derive a schema from *Standards* which a board might use in its questionnaires. Of course, not every board task performance can be investigated every year, but each year a part of the schema might be tackled, depending on priorities.

6.7 SUMMARY

1. A regular process of board evaluation has many benefits. The responsibility for this process normally rests with the chairman, often aided by an external consultant.

2. The success of a company depends upon its ability to adapt the organisation to the fast-changing environment. This adaptation should be driven by the board.

3. Developing an effective board depends on a process of appraisal linked to a process of continual development.

4. Appraisal involves
   - defining board tasks and objectives;
   - measuring board resources and capabilities;
   - consultation with board members;
   - consolidation and review of the results.

5. Boards should regularly monitor future performance against the appraisal findings.

Part 3

The Individual Director

Chapter 7

The Selection, Appointment and Removal of Directors

7.1 THE PERSONAL ATTRIBUTES AND KNOWLEDGE REQUIRED OF DIRECTORS

A board works only intermittently and delegates to management most of the day-to-day activities of running the business. And, although it is essential that board members are prepared to collaborate with colleagues on the board, it is equally important that they maintain their independence and avoid the 'group think' that leads to poor collective decisions. A board therefore does not fit the usual model of a team found in organisations. However, a proper balance of personal attributes exhibited by the directors will help to ensure that it can work as an effective group. Effective boards will have a balance of well-chosen, competent directors who, with the chairman's leadership and guidance, provide a cohesive working group to shape the destiny of the company, safeguard its interests and ensure its profitable performance.

The research, described in Dulewicz [1994] and [1995], underlying IoD [1999] identified a number of desirable personal attributes of directors, which were classified into six categories relating to specific aspects of company direction. They are relevant to a director's role, whether as chairman, managing director, executive or non-executive director.

The categories are:

1. Strategic perception

2. Decision-making

3. Analysis and the use of information

4. Communication

5. Interaction with others

6. Achievement of results.

Other characteristics which are found to be useful attributes for directors to have are:

7. Courage/strength of character

8. Common sense

9. Tenacity

10. Diplomacy/tact

11. Wisdom

12. Intellect.

These attributes are fully described in IoD [1999]. Many of these attributes are components of leadership, by which is meant the ability to conduct the company's affairs, govern, guide and motivate others. The board of directors leads the company and whether it does this well or badly depends in part upon the personal attributes of its members. Of course, it is unlikely that any one individual will have all the personal attributes listed, but each of those deemed necessary for a particular board should be possessed by at least one director. Ideally, there should be a balance of individuals, whose strengths and weaknesses are complementary.

Personalities are important too. For example, boards composed entirely of thrusting, action-orientated people are unlikely to spend sufficient time addressing issues that will affect the company's long-run future. Someone must be reflective and provide the original thinking and ideas.

Each board will have to choose its membership in its own way but should take characteristics such as those mentioned into account in order to build an effective working group.

Additionally, directors need to know – or know how to find out – everything that is relevant to their responsibilities. Ignorance is no excuse. However, each company and each board is unique; it is therefore impossible to produce a comprehensive and definitive list of all the elements of knowledge and understanding that a director should possess. Nevertheless, some key areas of directors' knowledge and understanding are provided in IoD [1999], pp. 72–8. The areas of knowledge which are recommended result from experience with the IoD Company Direction Programme, but in addition many focus groups of experienced directors and academics contributed to defining a minimum set of the knowledge and techniques required by company directors.

The cognitive skills required by good practice with respect to the identified subject areas, based on the taxonomy in Bloom [1956], may be said to be:

- Knowledge; that is, the ability to recognise and recall a piece of information.

- Comprehension; that is, the ability to make use of information in a specific way.

- Application; that is, the ability to select an appropriate known principle in a new situation, to restructure data in a suitable form, and to apply the principle.

- Analysis; that is, the ability to split a concept into its constituent elements.

- Synthesis; that is, the ability to arrange and combine elements, ideas, etc. in such a way as to make up a new pattern or structure.

- Evaluation; that is, the ability to judge the extent to which evidence satisfies specified criteria.

The list in IoD [1999] is illustrative rather than comprehensive, covering the main areas expected to be found in a boardroom, although the breadth and depth of these requirements will vary according to the circumstances and demands faced by a particular board. Not all function-specific and specialist knowledge (which may or may not be sought from outside the board) has been included. Neither have the areas of knowledge and understanding required principally of a management role rather than that of a director – these are addressed in Management Charter Initiative [1998].

7.2 SELECTION OF DIRECTORS

7.2.1 THE SELECTION PROCESS

The costs involved in the appointment process, as well as the ongoing costs of an appointment, may be very large. It is therefore essential that the selection process is as professional as possible.

The formal process relating to the appointment of directors is not difficult. Finding the right person to be a director is harder. Because of the many differences between companies, the requirements will vary from company to company. Remember that the appointed person will change the balance of board membership. It is vital to give ample consideration to the kind of person wanted and the contribution   required. The resulting profile for the new director may be complex. In addition, over recent years the appointment process has tended to become more formal, reflecting the need to be able to provide an objective measure for legal reasons of why a candidate was appointed or, more importantly, not appointed. In practice the process can nowadays be very complex and involve executive search firms, often known as 'headhunters', psychometric testing and expert interviews.

Some companies have nomination committees with the remit to look at the appointment of non-executive directors (see section 5.7.4). Such a committee, usually chaired by the chairman, attempts to avoid the patronage which otherwise might operate in some companies, whereby a network of individuals sit on each other's boards, and attempts to ensure that any non-executive appointment adds value to the company. Whether there is a nomination committee or not, the appointment process should involve the board. This applies whether the appointment is an executive or non-executive appointment.

An example of a simplified appointment process is set out below.

Identification of a board capability gap
The first question is: What does the board need? The answer depends upon what roles the new person is to fulfil as a board member and what

personal qualities and attributes would be appropriate. The chairman or the nominations committee should identify present gaps in the board and start to build up a picture of the sort of person that the board is looking for, perhaps, for example, someone with international experience, e-commerce experience, or great analytical skills.

Develop a personal specification
Look at the knowledge, skills and personal attributes required of a director. Add these and any others that are high on the list of priorities to the specification. Bear in mind the roles of directors (see section 4.1).

Develop a search plan
The search should be planned carefully, perhaps using both personal contacts and professional recruitment consultants.

Get to know the person
Cultivate a relationship; personal contact and knowledge of the candidate are essential. If the potential new director is from outside the company, take up references other than those offered. Try to establish if the person will fit into the board.

Discuss terms
Discuss relevant details with the prospective candidate.

Appoint
Make the appointment. Directors' contracts are discussed in section 7.3.3 below.

7.2.2 SELECTING THE CHAIRMAN

The role of a chairman is discussed in section 4.1.1. The key criterion for a chairman should be an ability to run and control the meetings of the board of directors. This ability will be based on a sense of what is important to the meeting; knowing when decisions can be taken rapidly and the agenda moved on; sensing when a subject demands and warrants debate; spotting when arguments are becoming repetitive and being able to end debate. The chairman should have an ability to introduce subjects, to control debates, to ensure arguments are fairly represented and an ability to sum up discussions. Above all, in so far as the chairman is able, he should seek to ensure that the company moves forward by way of consensus. Warring boards do not as a rule produce successful companies.

The chairman will also chair general meetings of the company and this will require presence and communication skills.

The chairman should also be capable of presenting the company to the external world: he should be the principal ambassador of the company. As such he should have a standing in the circles in which the company operates.

7.2.3 SELECTING THE MANAGING DIRECTOR

The managing director is responsible for the overall performance of the company and management team. It is apparent from section 4.1.2 that the managing director should be a person with drive, leadership and a strong sense of direction. He must be capable of decisive action, when necessary. His overriding interest has to be the success of the company. He will need to be able to motivate and pass judgement on the executives of the company. At all times the managing director must be capable of presenting a clear vision of the company and must demonstrate initiative and support.

7.2.4 SELECTING EXECUTIVE DIRECTORS

Generally, executive directors will spring from the ranks of senior management – but by no means always. Executive directors, as well as being board members, will be responsible for certain activities in the company – basically for ensuring that the company remains profitable within their areas of responsibility.

Their skills will be in leading key areas of the business and presenting in a coherent manner at board meetings performance reviews of the areas of business for which they are responsible. That being said, their presence on the board should not be related solely to their particular business interest. Even when a person has won his spurs by accepting a high level of responsibility as an executive or manager, it does not necessarily follow that the person will be able to fulfil effectively the rather different role of director.

For this, executives must possess a number of additional characteristics and personal qualities, some of which are discussed in section 7.1 of this chapter. Beyond this, however, they must be able to contribute to the board's affairs across a broad spectrum of matters, rather than seeing things from a specialist's viewpoint. They must be capable of looking beyond the confines of their own particular discipline or background and have the breadth of vision and thinking necessary to help the board address policy and strategic issues as well as all the operational matters. They must be capable of contributing to the wide-ranging debates that will occur in the boardroom.

The main areas of knowledge relevant to company direction are discussed in IoD [1999]. In these areas, the basic capability needs to be already resident in the executive director, but specific knowledge can and should be acquired before or soon after appointment.

Whether an executive director is selected from within the same company or group, or recruited from outside, some education and training in the role of the director and how the board works will probably be necessary. However, as with all training, selecting the right person first, with all the attributes for the job, is an essential prerequisite.

7.2.5 SELECTING NON-EXECUTIVE DIRECTORS

It is the non-executive directors who provide the variable element in achieving a well-balanced and competent board. The board should constitute an integrated group to ensure the company's profitable performance and safeguard its interests. So the selection of each non-executive director should be done with care, taking account of the strengths and weaknesses of the other directors and the major issues likely to be addressed by the board in the years ahead. The chairman, or a nomination committee of the board, will usually take the lead in the selection process, often with professional outside help.

Before the selection process begins, it is important to determine what roles the new person is to fulfil as a board member and what personal qualities and attributes would be appropriate (see section 4.1.4).

Non-executive directors should bring attributes to the company beyond those of executive directors. The particular background, experience and any special disciplines that would be appropriate to a particular appointment will naturally depend on the qualities of the other directors of the board and the particular business concerned. Not being involved on a day-to-day basis with the company may in itself ensure that a different perspective is brought to the meetings of the board, but that alone is rarely sufficient. Experience of a larger, unrelated but relevant, enterprise, with knowledge of company matters and board competence gained in another environment, is often needed. A sharp business mind, with an ability to focus on the matters in hand without historical or day-to-day distractions, is essential. Selecting someone with a sound track record is usually wise, since opinions at the board table will benefit from the weight of that experience. Numeracy and an ability to gain an adequate understanding of the company's finances, management, employees, special capabilities and markets should also be sought. Do not seek to appoint as non-executive directors persons who have sonorous title only; no one is any longer impressed. That is not to say a military background may not be of value, say, to a company in the defence industry; but employ the person for his expertise. What the non-executive can do for the company in the future is more important than what he has done for another company in the past.

Essentially, a non-executive director should provide an independent and impartial view of the board's considerations and decisions while also identifying strongly with the company's affairs. It is essential therefore to look for strength of character and an ability to stand back from the issue being considered, combined with pragmatism and an ability to compromise. This calls for personal qualities of courage, integrity, common sense, good judgement, tenacity, diplomacy, and an ability to listen carefully and to communicate with clarity, objectivity and brevity.

Many chairmen use their non-executive directors to provide personal counsel and a different perspective on matters of concern before they are raised at board meetings. In such cases, the appropriate experience, knowledge and personal qualities will be looked for.

Finally, the board's total effectiveness can benefit from outside contacts and opinions. Companies will therefore often seek non-executive directors who have a suitable network of experienced contacts.

7.3 APPOINTMENT OF DIRECTORS

7.3.1 APPOINTMENT

Private limited companies must have at least one director and public limited companies at least two. The question of who is eligible to be a director is discussed in Chapter 8.

The first directors of a company are appointed by the subscribers to the Memorandum, since those named on the form accompanying the Memorandum are deemed, on registration of the company, to have been appointed. Thereafter, subsequent appointments must be made in accordance with the stipulations of the Articles of Association of the company. This will usually mean that they are appointed by their fellow directors.

There is no statutory obligation for shareholders to appoint directors. In practice, however, the Articles permit directors to be appointed by the shareholders in general meeting. Directors of a Plc who are appointed during the course of the year must be confirmed in office at the next AGM. The directors of a Plc retire in rotation and may submit themselves for re-election.

The Table A provisions of the *Companies Act 1985* are that:

- directors are appointed by the general meeting on a simple majority vote;

- directors are recommended to the general meeting by the directors or by any member, the member having given appropriate notice to the company of the intention to propose a person as director;

- one-third of the directors retire by rotation, excluding the managing director, but may be re-appointed;

- subject to any stated maximum number of directors, the board of directors can appoint directors to fill casual vacancies or as an additional director, but the appointed person must stand down for election at the next annual general meeting.

Many companies will have changed Table A to give the board of directors increased powers regarding the appointment of directors. For example, common extra provisions are:

- the board of directors may appoint any directors, not just directors *pro tem.*;

- the holder of a certain class of shares may appoint a nominee director;

- the directors are required to hold a certain number of shares in the company.

Further, it is important to give consideration to the termination of a director's employment. For reasons discussed in section 7.6.2 below, it is recommended that companies include a clause in directors' contracts of employment which brings the contract to an end should the person cease to be a director of the company.

7.3.2 WHAT ARE THE FORMALITIES?

An individual appointed as a director at the time the company is first formed must be named on Form 10 (Situation of Registered Office) and, if being appointed a director of an existing company, must be named on Form 288 (Notice of Change of Directors or Secretaries or in their Particulars). He must sign one or the other form to indicate consent to being a director of the company. The information on these forms includes the individual's name and address, occupation, nationality, date of birth, and any other directorships he holds. If the company is listed on the Stock Exchange, the appointment must be notified to the Stock Exchange (as must any significant change in the holding of an executive office).

7.3.3 EMPLOYMENT AND SERVICE CONTRACTS

Directors' contracts

Directors may be employees and directors; alternatively, as is the case with non-executive directors, they are not employees but have a contract for services. An executive director is entitled to have a written contract as an employee and may also have a service contract as a director. Normally, the employment status of directors is dealt with under a service agreement alone.

Executive directors are employees of the company whether there is a written contract or not. Their dismissal is governed by normal employment law and therefore certain important rights arise, namely:

- the right after one year not to be dismissed unfairly and/or the right after two years to redundancy payment;
- the right to participate in company pension schemes;
- on winding up, the right to priority in remuneration.

These are important rights, particularly as the right not to be dismissed unfairly gives access to Employment Tribunals, where a dismissed employee may test his rights with little or no fear of having to bear the costs if the action fails.

The service contract of a director will probably include:

- duties and responsibilities;
- the obligation to comply with any decision of the board;
- the duration;
- the notice period;
- remuneration and benefits;
- termination and dismissal;

- working hours (usually there is a clause to exclude the director from the requirements of the *Working Time Regulations 1998* and enable him to work beyond normal working hours whenever necessary);

- holidays;

- sickness;

- a requirement to devote the whole of the director's time and attention to the company's business;

- a requirement not to be engaged or interested in any other business without the express authority of the board;

- a requirement not to compete with the company after ceasing to be a director (usually limited to a period of time and/or a geographical area).

Four contentious issues usually included in directors' contracts are worthy of special mention. These are:

- length of contracts and notice periods;

- enticement of employees;

- confidentiality;

- restrictions on employment.

The length of contracts and notice periods

Despite the shareholders' nominal control over the appointment and removal of a director, executive directors are often protected by their contracts of employment. The high cost of compensation on removal may make it expensive for shareholders to exercise their powers and can therefore act as a deterrent to dismissal.

It is for this reason that any arrangement, whether formal or informal, which would enable a director's employment to continue beyond five years in such a way that it could not be ended by the company or only by notice in specified circumstances requires the express approval of the company in general meeting (s.319, *Companies Act 1985*). A term included in a service contract which does not comply with this provision is void and the agreement will be treated simply as one that the company is entitled to terminate at reasonable notice. These provisions also extend to contracts for service, e.g. non-executive director contracts.

In addition, good practice, as laid down in the various Codes of corporate governance, is now inconsistent with long service contracts and/or long notice periods. The notice periods granted to directors became in the 1980s a matter for scandal. Such were the notice periods to which directors were seemingly entitled – for example, three years and more – that it could actually pay a director to be dismissed! In general, opinion has now moved firmly against the desirability of long notice periods. The Cadbury Report [1992] recommended that shareholder approval of directors' contracts that exceeded three years should be sought. The Greenbury Study Group [1995] went much further, and advocated that:

- notice periods for service contracts should not exceed one year, although two years may be acceptable in some cases; if it is necessary to offer a three-year period to attract a director, any renewal of that contract should specify a shorter period;

- where the director leaves because of unsatisfactory performance the compensation commitments may be different and the reasons for leaving should be considered by the remuneration committee as a factor in determining compensation;

- payment of compensation in instalments should be considered so as to give the company the option of reducing or stopping the payment if a former director mitigates his loss by obtaining new employment.

The Combined Code [1998] recommends '. . .*setting notice or contract periods at, or reducing them to, one year or less*' (paragraph B.1.7).

In practice, however, surveys show that these recommendations are widely ignored by listed companies. For example, most directors of listed companies are still on two- or three-year fixed or rolling contracts.

However, all this being said, it may sometimes be in the interest of a smaller company to grant a long notice period. For example, in an entrepreneur company where the degree of board autonomy is low, the appointment of a director on a long service contract may have the effect of increasing the autonomy of the board. The relative security of a long contract, which makes it difficult to remove a director, may enable that director to stand up for the best interests of the company where they conflict with the personal interests of the entrepreneur or the holding company. In these circumstances there is a case for arguing that the principles of the Code recommendations on service contracts and compensation may not apply.

Enticement of employees

The staff of a business is often its major asset, and companies may devote considerable expense to the training and development of employees. Consequently directors' contracts often include a clause designed to prevent their taking colleagues with them if they join another company. A typical non-enticement clause might read thus:

> *The director shall not at any time either while he continues to be in the service of the company or for a period of one year afterwards entice away from the company or any of its associated companies any of their officers or employees.*

How effective is such a restriction? It must be said immediately that Court actions arising out of enticement are rare. Unless a director has been blatant in allowing written solicitations to fall into the hands of his previous employer it may be extremely difficult to prove the case. If a person leaves the company to join a director who has recently left, both parties will be in the defence camp and evidence will be hard to come by.

The Courts have presented conflicting views on the standing of 'enticement'. On the one hand the Courts have stated that staff are not 'an asset of the company like apples and pears or other stock in trade' (*Hanover Insurance Brokers Ltd v Shapiro* {19}) and have struck down restrictive covenants. In a more recent case, however, a restrictive covenant on enticement was enforced against an ex-managing director when he attempted to poach senior employees from his former company (*Alliance Paper Group Plc v Prestwich* {1}). A distinguishing feature of this latter case was that the ex-managing director attempted to circumvent the restriction by insisting that staff with whom he had discussions about joining him sign a declaration that they had met with a 'Mr Crowther'. 'Mr Crowther' was in fact a teddy bear which had been present at the meetings!

As in most areas of employment law, the message on enticement is not clear. Take advice before acting.

Confidential information

Directors' employment contracts normally include a clause to the effect that a director will treat as confidential any information that the director obtains because of his board position, both whilst a director and thereafter. (See section 13.11, on insider dealing.)

In general the Courts will support this sort of restriction and protect confidential information or 'trade secrets'. But in order to obtain that protection a company must demonstrate that:

- employees were told the information was confidential;
- the information has fallen into the hands of a company/person capable of damaging the company;
- the company has suffered loss.

The Courts have emphasised that it is not possible to remove from the mind of a person the information that is there. But the Courts will prevent a person using it if the above considerations are met.

Generally speaking, an action for breach of confidential information is difficult to prove.

Restrictions on employment

Limiting the scope of activities of departing employees is now a regular feature of directors' and other employees' contracts. A typical clause could read:

> *Since the director is likely to obtain in the course of his employment with the company confidential information of the company, he hereby agrees with the company that he will be bound by the following restrictions, namely: he will not for a period of six months after the lawful termination of this Agreement without the consent of the company at any place within the United Kingdom be engaged or interested in or carry on or be concerned in carrying on (whether by himself or jointly or as servant, officer, agent, manager, trustee or otherwise) any concern which is or is about to be engaged or interested in the provision of goods or services in competition with the goods or services provided by the company at any time during the six months preceding the termination of this Agreement being goods or services similar to those with which the director's activities with the company have been associated and to which any secret or confidential information obtained by him in the service of the company is relevant.*

> *The director shall not for a period of six months after the lawful termination of this Agreement (in any manner or for any cause) directly or indirectly at any place within the United Kingdom canvass or solicit the custom in respect of goods or services with which the director has been concerned hereunder of*

any person, firm or company who at any time during the six months immediately preceding the termination of this Agreement was a specific prospect or customer of the company or its distributors or sales agents or the like.

Such a covenant is generally considered to be the most 'daunting' in the employment contract. What does it mean?

Firstly, it refers to 'lawful termination' of the contract. In most contracts there will be a notice requirement on both the employee and employer. Frequently if an employee wishes to leave, the notice period will be waived. But an employer may insist on the notice period and the period being served at home, that is, 'garden leave'. Is such garden leave enforceable? It depends on the length of garden leave and how reasonable it is for the company to seek to enforce it.

Can the company prevent employees from working for competitors for a period of time or in a specific geographical area? It depends on the facts of the case. Generally it may be said that the Courts do not like these clauses, for they may result in forced unemployment. Further, having endured unemployment, job prospects could be severely limited. Set against these considerations, a company may be held to be entitled to protect itself for a limited period from the competition of companies benefiting from the know-how and experience of one of its key employees. In general, it may be said that such clauses will only be enforceable if they are reasonable to the needs of the company; this means that the time limits and the geographical restraints imposed must also be reasonable.

No clear-cut answer can be given as to the force these covenants nowadays have. In general, they will always be tested strictly as against the employer seeking to enforce them. They will be struck down if they fail the 'reasonableness' test. But this is not to say they will not be enforced. A recent review of the law (*Scully UK Ltd v Lee* {41}) suggests that:

- Restrictive covenants are void unless they can be justified and are reasonably in the interest of the party seeking protection and not against the public interest.

- Restrictions on competition from former employees will be valid if they protect confidential information.

- If these conditions are met, then the restrictions must be reasonable in both content and breadth.

The Courts will probably enforce a restraint preventing a former employee from taking business from existing clients of the company and seeking business from 'hot' prospects.

7.4 DEVELOPING BOARD MEMBERS

7.4.1 INDUCTION AND INCLUSION

An effective induction is essential for all new directors if they are to play their proper role within a reasonably short time-scale. An executive director will need to become familiar with his particular executive role in the company, as well as learning about how the company is managed generally. During the first six months or so of an executive director's appointment, executive duties will inevitably place a premium on his time. For this reason alone, it is important that the chairman sets aside a series of short, well-planned meetings with the new member during this period, to ensure that he becomes an effective, well-informed board member. New directors taking up a board position for the first time can find it quite daunting to be expected to make a contribution across all aspects of the business when in fact their primary experience often relates to one specific function only. The new director should be familiarised with the company's strategic objectives and the main issues that have been absorbing the board's time during the preceding year or so. He will also need to be aware of the issues likely to be facing the board in the future.

Just as important is an induction by the chairman into the style of the board, how issues are dealt with both inside and outside the boardroom and the way that reports and information are dealt with. All board members share the responsibility for bringing the new member up to speed as quickly as possible.

The company secretary can also play a useful part in this familiarisation process. It is most important that new directors familiarise themselves with the company's Memorandum and Articles of Association, where the secretary can act as a useful guide.

Similarly, newly appointed non-executive directors should spend time with the chairman and company secretary as part of a properly arranged induction programme. The non-executive director should also undertake some planned visits to see the facilities and employees of the business at first hand and to spend time with the executive directors to understand their work.

7.4.2 DEVELOPING DIRECTORS

All directors should be actively encouraged to take time out to gain a thorough understanding of their duties and responsibilities and the board's role with respect to the company and the many groups with an interest in its objectives and operations. In addition, every director should understand his specific role and function as part of the board and be familiar with the roles and functions of the other directors, in particular those of the chairman and managing director. Directors should be encouraged to gain a degree of familiarity with the special contribution that each of the other executive directors, because of their particular experience, background and work specialities, can make.

Appropriate reading and attendance at selected seminars can help to bring depth to such understanding. Familiarity with a company balance sheet and profit and loss account, sources and methods of finance, cashflow and other financial parameters is essential for every director. Hence any director who is uncertain of any of these matters should take the time to undertake some structured learning through a course of lectures or workshops and/or reading or other learning media. This is a prerequisite for any person who is being appointed a director for the first time. Where the appointment is the result of promotion, a proper course of study should ideally be undertaken before the appointment is taken up. Directors need to develop personal attributes, acquire knowledge appropriate to their role and be constantly aware of the changing environment in which they and their company operate.

No matter how experienced a director is, he can never be too highly qualified or too experienced to ignore the need continually to enhance his professional competence. It is essential that directors do not allow their skills and knowledge to become obsolete which, in times of rapid and substantial changes in technology, legislation, knowledge, competitive pressures and social priorities, they can all too easily become. It is good practice, therefore, for directors throughout their careers to undertake systematic maintenance, improvement and broadening of knowledge, experience and skills, and the development of personal qualities helpful in the execution of their professional duties – in other words, continuing professional development.

An important part of every executive director's development is to loosen the power and rights that he is seen to have as a manager, delegating these to others more, while raising his perceived strength as a director, concerned with policy, strategy, the security of the company, resource provision and motivation. This is a broadening process for each executive director, which at the same time helps to weld the board into an effective group to address the broader policy and strategic issues, away from the narrower confines of specialist management.

7.5 SUCCESSION PLANNING

If a company is to succeed it will be necessary for serious consideration to be given to how and when key directorships are to be filled when the holders retire. It is necessary for senior management morale that the company is seen to be providing opportunities for promotion to the board. But, equally, it will sometimes be appropriate to bring in fresh ideas and vision from outside the company. This can be particularly important if the existing board has failed to deliver expected growth and profits.

Succession planning is a matter given close scrutiny by the financial markets and directors should be well aware of the importance attached to it. Sometimes the most appropriate way of ensuring a smooth transition is to bring in or promote a director with the express intention that he is being groomed for succession. In this regard, the positions of the chairman and the managing director are crucial. The appointment of a new chairman and/ or managing director to a quoted company will be a matter of major significance to the markets and may well have a significant effect on share values.

The loss of an entrepreneur owner or family director often puts the future ownership and survival of the company in jeopardy. In these cases the succession of the company may be decided by the entrepreneur or the wider family and the board has no input. The failure properly to plan succession is one of the most frequent causes of the demise of family companies, with only a small minority of European family companies reaching the third generation. The succession problem in family companies is discussed in section 16.8.

7.6 DISAGREEMENTS ON THE BOARD AND RESIGNATION

7.6.1 RESIGNATION

Whilst it should be the objective of all boards to work harmoniously, it is inevitable that disagreements will arise. Such disagreements can often be dealt with by reasoned debate and the acceptance of a majority decision. A board decision is, even when not unanimous, still a decision of the board as a whole and a director has a duty to stand by it, once taken. However, if disagreements cannot be contained, then the director in disagreement may well have to consider his position and in the final analysis, if matters cannot be resolved, resign. It is the right of all companies to proceed by way of majority voting, and the director should weigh his views against what is the majority view. But resignation may be the only course that can honourably be followed.

The first step, however, should be to have the disagreement discussed and minuted. If a director feels particularly strongly about a point, he should raise the matter at a board meeting. If no meeting is scheduled he should call one, circulating his views in advance to the other directors. But there is no compulsion on the other directors to attend such a meeting, which may therefore lack a quorum and be unable to conduct any business.

If a director considers that his colleagues are acting contrary to the interests of the company, he may reasonably seek, if he can obtain the support of a sufficient number of shareholders, to call an Extraordinary General Meeting. If he cannot then carry the EGM, he would have little option but to resign. It should be remembered, however, that resignation is something of a 'nuclear deterrent'; the threat may be more valuable than the use.

A director may consider a board decision or policy to be not merely commercially unwise but unethical or, indeed, unlawful. In such a circumstance, if he cannot dissuade his colleagues from such action, his first duty to the company lies in taking the lead in remedying the irregularity or illegality. Directors caught up in such a situation may feel they ought to resign, but they may also feel that they should continue in office to ensure that the irregularity or illegality has been eliminated. This can be a very uncomfortable position to be in. But in attempting to square the circle they have a number of possible allies, including:

- *Professional advisers.* A director should recognise that there may be a time when he may need, and have to pay for, independent professional advice. The Combined Code [1998] recommends that directors should, in the furtherance of their duties, be able to obtain independent professional advice at the company's expense. Failure to take advice in appropriate circumstances has been found by Department of Trade appointed inspectors to be a breach of directors' duties.

- *The company's auditors* on issues relating to disclosure and the truth and fairness of published financial information.

- *The shareholders.* Shareholders have a number of rights, particularly when their interests are being unfairly prejudiced.

- *The Department of Trade and Industry,* which has wide powers to order investigations of a company's affairs.

- In the case of quoted companies, the *London Stock Exchange.*

Unfortunately the distinction between what is commercially unwise and what is unlawful is not always clear. Conduct that starts out as commercially unwise may slip almost imperceptibly into conduct that is unlawful and, in particular, may become 'wrongful trading' under the provisions of the *Insolvency Act 1986* (see section 15.3). A director will not avoid liability under this Act by resigning unless he resigns before the 'time' from which wrongful trading starts (for example, before the questionable decision is taken). Waiting for the results of the decision to become apparent may be leaving it too late.

If a director wishes to make public his misgivings about a company, he must take care to avoid making a defamatory statement. If only for this reason, he would be well advised to take legal advice at an early stage. Once a director has resigned he may find it impossible to use information acquired when a director to influence shareholders, even if the information is not defamatory, because the Court may grant the company, represented by the remaining directors, an injunction to restrain the publication of information the former director received in confidence as a member of the board.

7.6.2 REMOVAL FROM OFFICE

In general, a director may be removed under any relevant provision in the company's Articles. In addition, under ss.303 and 304 of the *Companies Act 1985*, a director can be removed by a resolution of members in general meeting passed by a simple majority. Under the *Act* the ability of a general meeting to remove a director in this way cannot be taken away. The director concerned is entitled to require that his written views are communicated to the members, provided that they are not defamatory, either by inclusion with the notice of meeting sent out to members or by having them read out at the meeting, and he is also entitled to speak at the meeting. In the case of subsidiary companies, the Articles may provide that the majority shareholder (i.e. the holding company) may appoint and remove directors by notice in writing given to the subsidiary company.

The criteria for the removal of a director which may be specified in a company's Articles include:

- Where the director is prohibited from holding the position of director by law, for example if the director has been disqualified or is bankrupt. It is a criminal offence to be a director in such cases.

- When a director is over 70 years of age he must retire at the next general meeting unless the general meeting agrees to the director continuing in office.

- Where a director is removed by the general meeting by ordinary resolution.

- Where the director is seriously mentally ill and has been admitted to hospital under the *Mental Health Act 1983* or a Court order has been made for the director's detention or for the director's affairs to be looked after.

- Where the director resigns.

- Where the director has absented himself from board meetings for six months without permission and the directors resolve that he should vacate the office.

- Where an executive director's service contract is terminated.

- Where the board of directors, by a stated majority, resolve that a director should vacate the office.

Termination of employment does not bring to an end a directorship. To effect the dismissal of a director, it will usually require a vote of the shareholders. It is necessary if there is to be a shareholders' meeting for the requisite notice period of 21 days to be given. There is thus an uneasy period between dismissal as an employee and termination as a director. In order to avoid this problem it is wise to include a clause in a director's contract to the effect that if the contract of employment is terminated then he automatically vacates the office of director of the company. However, if there is no written service contract and the Articles do not state that the board of directors can remove individual directors, then only the general meeting can remove the director by a simple majority.

This problem is usually obviated by a deal being made which avoids the necessity of calling a shareholders' meeting. However, if no compromise is reached and the director insists on the shareholders' meeting being called, then the prudent company should:

- warn the director that he has no further power to bind the company in contract;

- warn the director that if he does so he will be personally responsible;

- inform suppliers and customers that the director is no longer an employee and his authority to enter into contracts has been removed.

7.6.3 COMPENSATION AND TERMINATION PAYMENTS

The contract of employment as an executive director will normally be subject to notice, and if a director is dismissed without notice and/or unfairly the company will be liable for compensation.

The amount of compensation will be subject to negotiation. The following factors are likely to weigh in the negotiation:

- the extent of any non-performance of duties and any loss that he has caused the company which could make the director liable for damages to the company;

- any misuse of corporate property that has taken place which could give rise to potential action by the company;

- whether the director owns any shares in the company which he may wish to sell;

- whether there are any loans from the director to the company which may need to be settled;

- the company's cashflow position;

- the desire of either party to avoid publicity;

- the need to impose a restrictive covenant on the director to prevent him working for a rival company in the area;

- the presence of a restrictive covenant in the director's contract which the leaving director may want relaxed;

- the need to move quickly so as to prevent valuable corporate information, or people, being lost to the company.

Payment by a company to a director of compensation for loss of office (except a *bona fide* payment in settlement of a claim for breach of contract and pension payments) requires the prior approval of the company in general meeting. So too do *ex gratia* payments on termination of office.

In addition, there are important tax implications to bear in mind in deciding the form, manner and timing of termination payments (see Chapter 14). Payments pursuant to restrictive covenants are subject to both income tax and National Insurance Contributions (NIC). It makes no difference whether or not the covenants are enforceable or whether the payments were made during, or at the termination of, the employment. Other inducement payments such as 'golden handcuffs', 'golden handshakes' and 'golden good-byes' are likewise generally taxable and subject to NIC. However, payments made as compensation for loss of office and not arising out of any contractual term are not subject to taxation.

7.6.4 RETIREMENT

It is normal for the Articles of public (but not private) limited companies to provide for directors to retire by rotation, and to be eligible for re-election.

Beyond this provision, a director's tenure will be governed by the Articles and his contract of employment; normally, they provide for removal on the grounds set out in section 7.6.2 above. If a director retires voluntarily, he may do so forthwith if the company agrees to waive his notice requirement.

7.7 SUMMARY

1. Directors need a wide range of attributes and therefore selecting the right person to become a director takes time and effort. Selection of new board members should be based upon an analysis of current gaps in knowledge and attributes around the board table.

2. The attributes needed in executive and non-executive directors are different. Executive directors are managers as well as directors and therefore need executive skills. Non-executive directors should be chosen for their experience and their independence.

3. If possible, the company should have both a chairman and a managing director. Listed companies should not combine the two roles in one person.

4. All contracts of employment are important, but the contracts of senior staff and directors are especially important. Most service contracts contain restrictive covenants limiting job changes for directors. Such covenants are not popular with the Courts but they may be enforceable.

5. There are many far-reaching rights and obligations which arise out of employment law. Directors should keep themselves broadly aware of developments and take professional advice if unsure of their position.

6. As with other personnel, company directors need induction into the company and training in their role.

7. The continuing professional development of directors individually and the board collectively is most important if the board is to grow with the business and the external environment in which it operates.

8. An effective company must have a succession policy. Timing may be of the essence in replacing key directors.

9. Resignation, removal and compensation are as much part of a director's working life as of that of any other employee of the company.

Chapter 8

A Director's Legal Status, Duties and Potential Liabilities

8.1 WHAT IS A DIRECTOR?

8.1.1 WHO IS A DIRECTOR?

Companies have legal personality and can therefore enter into legal relationships, but they need human agents to activate these relationships. They have legal requirements imposed on them and therefore need properly designated officers upon whom a duty to ensure their compliance can be imposed. In brief, companies need persons to represent their mind and will. This representation usually falls upon the directors.

But who counts as a director? Company law defines a director as 'any person occupying the position of director, by whatever name called' (*Companies Act 1985*, s.741(1)). Even though it is an offence not to comply with the formalities of registration of directors' appointments, directors are recognised by their functions and by the authority and power they in fact exercise rather than by the formalities of registration. It follows therefore that a number of people who have not formally been appointed as directors or have not been registered as directors but who carry out the duties of a director and act as a director may have the legal status of directors.

Companies often award senior executives just below board level the title of 'director' – 'associate director', 'divisional director', 'business development director', 'director of research', etc. These are merely courtesy titles that have no standing in law. The title is usually given in an attempt to enhance the status of the individual concerned either within the company or in dealings with other companies. However, great care is necessary when granting or accepting such titles. In one sense such 'directors', without a seat on the board and without access to the information that they need as directing officers of the company, are not directors. Yet in certain circumstances such persons could be held to be holding themselves out as, or even acting as, board directors, and may not wholly escape the responsibilities which go with that office. They may not indeed have those responsibilities, but if the company was faced by a legal penalty, 'courtesy directors' might have some difficulty in denying that they are directors within the meaning of the relevant legislation. In addition, such 'courtesy directors' may commit the company to contracts beyond their powers. Such contracts are likely to be enforceable against the company.

A number of tests will serve to identify persons as directors:

- Have they been appointed as a director?
- Have they completed a Form 288 and registered it at Companies House?
- Do they appear as such in the register of directors at Companies House?
- Do they appear in the company books as directors?
- Do they have a contract stating they are directors?
- Are they held out by the company as being directors?
- Do they act as directors?

Members of the board of a company are directors. The following are directors:

- Chairman
- Managing director
- Executive directors

- Non-executive directors

- 'Shadow' directors

- Nominee directors

- Alternate directors

Directors are not automatically employees or members (shareholders) of a company, though, subject to any provision in the Articles of Association, they may be; if they are executive directors, they are.

8.1.2 ELIGIBILITY

There are remarkably few restrictions under the general law about who can be a director. The auditor of a company may not also be its director, nor may the secretary of a private company if by doing so he would be the company's only director. Undischarged bankrupts are also prohibited from being company directors. Most importantly, persons who are currently disqualified may not be appointed as directors.

Directors of public companies and of their subsidiaries are required by statute to retire at the next annual general meeting after they attain the age of 70 and are under a duty to notify the company when that age is attained. No one, in principle, may be appointed to the position of director if over the age of 70, though he may be appointed or re-appointed if a general meeting agrees. The restriction may also be removed by an appropriate provision in the company's Articles.

A company's Articles of Association may restrict eligibility further than provided for by the general law. Most companies will exclude minors, persons of unsound mind, and persons who have made any arrangement or compromise with their creditors from being a director, though they are all eligible in law to be directors.

It is quite common to stipulate in the Articles that each director must hold a certain number of shares in the company.

There is no nationality requirement for a director of a UK company.

Finally, there is no restriction on the number of directorships an individual may hold (though the particulars must be filed with the Registrar of Companies). An individual is not barred even from being a director of a competitor. But his contract and a general duty of fidelity impose an obligation to act in the company's best interests, not to risk a conflict of interest, and not to use confidential information about the company for the benefit of anyone other than the company (including himself). It is hard, therefore, to see how an individual can simultaneously be a director of two competing companies and do justice to each of them.

8.1.3 'SHADOW DIRECTORS'

A 'shadow director' is a person or company (with the exception of a professional adviser) 'in accordance with whose instructions or directions the directors of a company are accustomed to act' (*Companies Act 1985*, s.741(2) and (3)). Such a person does not become a shadow director if only a single or a small group of directors act in accordance with his directions or instructions; to be a shadow director he must, *de facto*, direct and instruct the whole board. Also, the board must act on his instructions on more than one occasion, over a period of time, and regularly.

However, the Courts have recently tended to widen the classification of shadow director. In a recent case (*Secretary of State for Trade and Industry v Deverell and another* {42}), where disqualification orders were made against two individuals on the ground that they were shadow directors of an insolvent company, it was held on appeal that the definition of 'shadow director' was not to be strictly construed, that it encompassed those with 'real influence over the affairs of the company' (though not necessarily over the whole area of the company's activities), and that whether or not any particular communication from an alleged shadow director constituted 'direction or instruction' had to be ascertained on a case-by-case basis.

Who, then, could be at risk of being classed as a shadow director? Such a person could be a powerful shareholder, a disqualified director, even a bank (though banks are fully aware of the dangers of being categorised as a shadow director and usually take care to ensure that their advice is expressed appropriately), or a board of a parent company where a 'hands on' policy is operated in relation to the management of a subsidiary.

The provisions of the *Companies Act 1985*, the *Insolvency Act 1986* and the *Company Directors Disqualification Act 1986* apply to a shadow director as well as to the other directors. It is not possible to evade responsibility and liability by not being formally appointed a director if you come within the definition of shadow director.

In general, it is highly unsatisfactory for a board to be in a position where an individual comes to exercise such a position of authority within the company that, although he is not an appointed member of the board, he is, *de facto*, a member of the board.

8.1.4 NOMINEE DIRECTORS

A 'nominee director' is usually understood to mean a director who is appointed to the board of a company on the 'nomination', that is, the request, of a particular party outside of the company.

Common situations where such an appointment is made are:

- Where a joint venture company is set up by two companies and the Articles of Association of the joint venture company or other agreement provide for the appointment of such directors.

- Where an investor in a company wishes to maintain some control over his investment.

The formalities for such an appointment are the same as those for the other categories of director. Equally, the powers and the responsibilities of a nominee director are the same as for other directors.

The position of nominee directors is a sensitive one in that it is often difficult to avoid conflicts of interest. A director's duties are owed to his company. The nominee must, strictly, exercise his judgement in the best interests of the company without any orders on how to vote or act from the nominator. He is a representative, not a delegate. He may hold directorships of more than one company, but this must not lead to any conflict of interest (see sections 8.6.4 and 8.6.5 below). The nominee director must not put the interests of the nominator before those of the company. If he does, the individual director concerned would be at risk of being liable to the company of which he was a nominee director for any damage arising out of such a conflict of interest suffered by the company.

The nominee director is liable for disqualification if he fails to observe the fiduciary and statutory duties of a director. In *Official Receiver v Voss* {27} an individual who was a nominee director of 1,313 companies was found to be 'unfit' and disqualified from acting as a director for twelve years.

8.1.5 ALTERNATE DIRECTORS

It is sometimes convenient, provided the board agrees, for a director to appoint someone to be his alternate or proxy at board meetings – for example, if he is abroad for an extended period of time.

An alternate director is taken in law to be a full director of the company and is personally responsible for all his actions while acting as a director and subject to all the legal obligations attaching to the office. An alternate is not regarded as somebody else's agent. In the absence of the director who made the appointment, an alternate will be entitled to do all that the former can do. Therefore, the alternate is, in the usual way, entitled to notice of board meetings and notice of committee meetings where the appointing director is a member. However, the alternate is entitled to attend and to vote at board meetings only when the director who made the appointment is *absent*.

It is therefore necessary to register the alternate as a director of the company in the statutory books of the company and at the Registrar of Companies, and the appointment also has to be disclosed in the company's annual accounts. A director may act as an alternate for one or more of his colleagues on the board, and in such circumstances would have an additional vote or votes to exercise on his behalf in addition to that cast in his personal capacity. The rules of appointment will depend upon the Articles of Association of the company.

It is comparatively rare for such appointments to be made. Alternates are most commonly employed where a financial institution which has made an investment in a company and which has a seat on the board reserves the right to send alternates to board meetings. Clearly the choice of an alternate requires the exercise of great care.

8.1.6 PERSONS ASSOCIATED WITH A DIRECTOR

The *Companies Acts* and other laws may impose obligations on persons associated with a director or impose obligations on the director in respect of those persons. Such persons are said to be 'connected'. These types of obligation apply in many different contexts but in each different context it is not necessarily the same type of person who is considered to be connected to the director.

Who is a connected person? Examples are:

- A wife or husband.

- Children (even if illegitimate) or stepchildren until they reach eighteen years of age.

- A company with which the director is 'associated'. Broadly speaking he is associated with a company if he and other persons connected to him either are interested in at least 20% of the equity share capital or are able to exercise or control at least 20% of the voting power at any general meeting.

- Any person who is a trustee where the beneficiaries of the trust include a director or connected persons, or where the trustees have a power under the trust which may be exercised for the benefit of the director or any connected persons.

However, none of these is a 'connected person' if he is also a director of the company.

Examples of legal restrictions imposed by statute include:

- Companies are restricted in making loans or entering into similar transactions with directors or 'connected persons'.

- A director must notify the company of which he is a director of his interests in shares or debentures of the company or subsidiaries of the company. For these purposes, interests of the director's spouse or minor children are treated as those of the director.

- It is an offence for a director or the spouse or minor child of a director to deal in options over shares or debentures of the director's company which are listed on a stock exchange or options over listed shares or debentures of members of that company's group.

- In the context of take-overs, a large number of obligations are imposed on 'concert parties' (see section 13.10). Persons act in concert where, pursuant to an agreement or understanding (which need not be formal), they actively co-operate through the acquisition by any of them of shares in a company to obtain or consolidate control of a company. Directors, their close relatives and related trusts (among others) will be *presumed* to be acting in concert unless the contrary is established.

- Where a company acts preferentially towards some creditors prior to a liquidation or administration order, the Court can make an order restoring the position if the company was influenced in giving the preference by a desire to enhance the position of the recipient in the event of the company going into insolvent liquidation. This intention is *presumed* where the recipient of the preference is a person connected with the company.

8.2 DIRECTORS' AUTHORITY AND POWERS

An individual director's powers are limited both by the powers of the company itself and by the powers of the board. A director who exceeds either limitation is in breach of his duty to the company and may be liable to compensate the company if it suffers a consequential loss. Acts of a director which are beyond the objects of the company as stated in the Memorandum and acts where a director exceeds the powers of the board or his own authority as a member of the board are discussed in the succeeding sections.

8.2.1 THE COMPANY'S CAPACITY

A company's capacity for action is defined in the objects clause of its Memorandum of Association. In principle, any transaction which a company undertakes outside its objects is void. However, a person dealing with a company in good faith is entitled, in the absence of some indication to the contrary, to assume that the company has complied with all matters of internal procedure necessary for it to enter a valid contract (see *Royal British Bank v Turquand* {39}). This ruling has been further enlarged under the *Companies Act 1985*, which (in a clear reference to the objects clause in the Memorandum of Association) states that:

> *The validity of an act done by a company shall not be called into question on the grounds of lack of capacity by reason of anything in the company's memorandum.* (s.35(1))

However, if a company lacks capacity for some other reason (e.g. a statutory prohibition) the validity of the act may still be called into question.

8.2.2 A DIRECTOR'S CAPACITY

Table A provides that 'the business of the company shall be managed by the directors, who may exercise all the powers of the company' (Regulation 70). Generally speaking, the directors do not have the power to act individually on behalf of the company or to bind the company; they must act collectively as a board (though the board can delegate powers to committees and can appoint one of its members to be managing director). But, for practical reasons, some person, usually a director of the company, has to serve as the representative of the board when the company contracts with others. For this reason the Articles invariably entitle the board to delegate powers to individual directors as the board thinks appropriate, and in practice individual directors carry out many of a company's activities.

Where a director acts within his delegated authority, the company is bound under the normal rules of agent and principal. If the director exceeds his powers as given him by the board or the Articles, the law usually allows third parties to enforce contracts against the company. The position is clearly set out in the *Companies Act 1985*:

> *In favour of a person dealing with a company in good faith, the power of the board of directors to bind the company, or authorise others to do so, shall be deemed to be free of any limitation under the company's constitution.* (s.35A (1))

There is no automatic presumption that a person shall be deemed to have taken notice of any matter merely because of its being disclosed in any document kept by the Registrar of Companies or made available by the company for public inspection (s.711(A)) – though a party dealing with the company should still make such enquiries as ought reasonably to be made.

What happens, though, if a director ignores internal constraints? The company may have restricted the managing director so that he cannot enter into contracts of more than (say) £50,000 without the prior approval of the board of directors. But what if the managing director then enters the company into a contract for £100,000? The answer is that an individual director who acts without the board having delegated the requisite authority can be liable for breach of duty to the company, though, so far as third parties are concerned, the managing director is regarded as 'held out' as having the authority to bind the company regardless of the actual extent of his delegated powers. It follows, therefore, that in this circumstance the company is nonetheless bound by the contract even if the board did not authorise it. This is because the managing director was acting within the normal authority for a person in that position. The other party to the contract, having had no actual notice of any constraint on that individual's powers and acting in good faith, can assume that the officer is properly authorised to bind the company. The managing director may be dismissed for breach of contract. But this is a matter between the company and its managing director. It does not affect the binding relationship created between the company and the third party by the managing director.

> *When there are persons conducting the affairs of the company in a manner which appears to be perfectly consonant with the Articles of Association then those so dealing with them externally are not to be apprised by any irregularities which may take place in the internal management of the company.* (Wilmer LJ, *Freeman and Lockyer v Buckhurst Park Properties (Mangal) Ltd.* {17})

'Dealing with' is widely defined as being 'a party to any transaction or other act to which the company is a party' (s.35A (2)). It is up to the company to rebut a presumption of good faith; mere proof that the third party has knowledge of a director's lack of capacity is not sufficient by itself to rebut it and a third party is not bound to enquire about any limits on the company's or directors' capacity (s.35B).

There is no exhaustive list of the types of transaction into which a director or officer of the company has the implied or apparent authority to enter the company. It will depend upon:

- The ordinary course of business in that particular sector – for example, the normal course of business concerning subcontracting may be different in the construction industry compared to other businesses.

- The role of the director and current business practice in that sector for those holding the position of director; for example, the normal authority of a purchasing director in a hotel business may be different from the normal authority of an equity trading director in a bank.

Taken as a whole, the position appears to be that a company will be bound by a transaction authorised by the board or entered into by a director and probably by a transaction entered into by a 'courtesy' or 'local' director or other employee having the apparent authority to enter into contracts of the type in question, whatever the state of the actual authority of the individual concerned. That is, a director can bind the company to any contract that would normally be within the powers of a director of the relevant type and is in the ordinary course of the company's business. The company will be bound even if the director has not been delegated power to enter that type of contract by the board. The conferral of a title, or a course of previous dealings with an individual which have not been challenged, is sufficient for a third party reasonably to infer that the director has the authority to bind the company. Procedural defects on the appointment of a director do not affect the validity of the acts of the director, as long as there has been some form of appointment, even by mere acquiescence of the board.

However, directors should be aware that if they exceed their authority, the company may seek redress against them.

Board members should know what actual authority the board has delegated to the managing director as well as the extent of their own delegated authority. A director's actual implied authority may be apparent from the title that he holds and the normal authority that this confers in his business sector. 'Sales director', 'marketing director', 'finance director' or any other executive label attached to the function of director will normally confer some actual implied authority. Of necessity the authority will vary from company to company and from sector to sector. It is unusual for non-executive directors to have any actual implied authority to commit the company. Actual implied authority should be constrained by internal company rules approved by the board which detail how far any such implied authority extends.

8.2.3 THE DUTY TO ACT WITHIN YOUR POWERS

The board of directors should always ensure that they do not do anything that is outside the capacity of the company as laid down in the Memorandum of Association. Additionally, no director should do anything that goes beyond the powers conferred upon him as a director by the company's Articles of Association unless the shareholders expressly approve it, or will subsequently ratify it.

Directors should be aware of three possible consequences if the board of directors exceeds its powers in connection with a transaction:

1. The transaction may be voidable at the company's instance if it is with a director or an associated person, unless

    i)   restitution is no longer possible; *or*

    ii) the company is indemnified for any loss or damage resulting from the transaction; *or*

    iii) rights are acquired *bona fide* for value (and without actual notice of the directors exceeding their powers) by a person who is not party to the transaction and would be affected by the avoidance; *or*

    iv) the transaction is ratified by the company in general meeting.

    In practice, however, it is very likely that the company will have to accept the consequences of the transaction.

2. Any director who authorised the transaction will be in breach of his or her duties to the company and may be personally liable to the company for any loss. It may be possible for the shareholders *ex post* to ratify the act itself, but a separate special resolution is required if, in addition to ratification of the act, the directors concerned are to be relieved from liability to the company for that act.

3. The directors may also be personally liable to a third party if the third party suffers loss. This may be a remote possibility, but, as noted in section 8.2.2 above, third parties who act in good faith will be able to assume that the powers of the board of directors to bind the company are free from any limitation under the Articles.

8.2.4 CAN A DIRECTOR DELEGATE HIS POWERS?

An individual director may delegate his powers. However, where powers are delegated, the director still remains responsible for their exercise and will still have a duty of care to the company. Therefore, it is always good practice to confirm in writing what is delegated to a manager or other members of staff. A director should also obtain the consent of the board or at least inform it before delegating powers.

8.3 CONTROL OF ABUSE OF POWERS

A director's duties relate to the company as a whole and therefore, *prima facie*, are enforceable by the company as a whole. The underlying rule, enunciated in *Foss v Harbottle* {16}, is that a duty owed to the company can be enforced only by the company and not by individual shareholders. Moreover, if the breach of duty were capable of being ratified by the shareholders, the approval of a bare majority will often suffice, and the Court will not ordinarily intervene.

This rule rests upon acceptance of the directors' power of management and the principle of majority shareholder rule. However, it can have harsh consequences for minority shareholders, particularly if, as is often the case, the majority of shareholders are also directors. As proceedings on behalf of the company are normally instigated by the directors as the company's agents, most of the cases relating to breach of directors' duties have been brought only after control of the company has changed hands or by liquidators of insolvent companies after the directors' powers have lapsed.

Consequently there is a degree of legal protection given to minority shareholders. In the first place, the *Companies Act 1985* gives a shareholder the right to restrain by injunction an act which is beyond the directors' power (s35A(4)). But the injunction must be sought before the company has entered into any legal commitment to a third party and the shareholder wishing to bring proceedings will have to persuade the Court that it is appropriate for him as a shareholder (as opposed to the company itself) to bring the proceedings and that the rule in *Foss v Harbottle* should not apply.

Secondly, an individual shareholder is able to take proceedings against the persons who controlled the company on certain grounds (see *Edwards v Halliwell* {15}), namely, that the act complained of:

1. was *ultra vires* or unlawful; *or*

2. should have been sanctioned by extraordinary or special resolution, and was not; *or*

3. secured for those controlling the company an advantage at the expense of the minority (a 'fraud on the minority'); *or*

4. infringed the rights of an individual shareholder in his capacity as a member of the company.

If a shareholder brings an action under the first three of the exceptions, the action must be brought on behalf of the company. It is a derivative action, in which the shareholder's standing in the case is derived from that of the company and any wrong is remedied on behalf of the company.

Generally speaking, a shareholder's action on the ground of fraud on a minority is difficult to initiate and win. In such cases the Courts have imposed strict rules before they have been prepared to set aside the principle of majority rule and allow an individual to act on the company's behalf. It is necessary for a shareholder to show that there has been a 'fraud', although it has been held that the directors' negligent use of their powers (resulting in their benefiting at the expense of the company) would fall within this exception. It is also necessary to show that the 'wrongdoers' are in control of the company so that the action cannot be brought in the company's name. It has been held that this exception may also apply where the wrongdoers are not actually the majority shareholders but are the directors; the Court will allow the exception to apply in such circumstances if the interests of justice would otherwise be defeated (*Prudential Assurance Co Ltd v Newman Industries Ltd* {31}).

In the case of infringement of shareholder rights, the shareholder may bring the action on his own behalf or on behalf of all the shareholders who are similarly affected. In the case of such a representative action, there must have been a fundamental wrong done to the shareholder which cannot be ratified by the majority of shareholders – for example, an attempt to remove the shareholder's right to vote. In other circumstances, such an action is unlikely to succeed.

In addition to a shareholder's ability to bring an action under the exceptions from the Foss v Harbottle rule, s.459(1) of the *Companies Act 1985* gives aggrieved shareholders the right to seek redress where the conduct of the majority is 'unfairly prejudicial' to the minority. It was recently decided that majority shareholders also could invoke this provision (*re Legal Costs Negotiators Limited* {24}). The Secretary of State may also petition the Court on the ground of unfairly prejudicial conduct.

The Courts have interpreted 'unfair prejudice' very widely. It has generally been taken to mean a visible departure from the fair dealing and fair play that shareholders are entitled to expect. There has been no need to show that the persons in control of the company acted in the conscious knowledge that an action was unfair to the shareholder or that they acted in bad faith, though it does generally require more than mere mismanagement of the company's affairs. Recently, however, the Court has found that s.459 of the Act is more restrictive than previously thought (*O'Neill and another v Phillip and others* {28}) in that it is not possible to rely merely on general notions of unfairness or on the reasonable expectations of the shareholder and s.459 is not automatically applicable where there has been a breakdown in trust between the parties.

The Court, if satisfied that the petition is well founded, has the widest discretion to make orders as it thinks fit. In particular, it may regulate the company's affairs in the future or order it not to do something that the petitioner has complained of or to do something that the petitioner has claimed it has omitted to do. It may also provide for the purchase of the shares of any members by other members or by the company itself, and in practice a buy-out of the minority shares is the most common result. Most importantly for directors, the Court can authorise civil proceedings to be brought in the name of the company by such person as it may direct – for example, for breach of duty against a director where the company itself refuses to act.

There is an alternative remedy to those mentioned above open to shareholders. Under the *Insolvency Act 1986* s.122(1)(g), a shareholder may petition the Court to order that the company be wound up. The Act provides that the Court shall make a winding-up order if it is of the opinion that the shareholder is entitled to relief either by winding up the company or otherwise and that it would be just and equitable that the company should be wound up. An order will not be granted, however, if the Court is of the opinion that some other remedy is available to the shareholder and that he has acted unreasonably in seeking a winding-up order instead of pursuing that other remedy. A winding-up petition should therefore be used by shareholders only as a last resort.

Proceedings may be brought against a shadow director, a retired director, the estate of a deceased director, and a bankrupt director, as well as current members of the board.

Directors should note that, at the time of writing, it seems likely that, as a result of the review of company law that was instigated by the Department of Trade and Industry in March 1998, there will be a reform of the remedies available to minority shareholders. The suggested reforms include a reform of the personal rights of shareholders under the company constitution, of the 'unfair prejudice' remedy, of the law on derivative actions, and the inclusion of a provision in a company's Articles to facilitate the resolution of disputes. How extensive these reforms will be is at present unclear.

8.4 TO WHOM ARE DIRECTORS RESPONSIBLE?

The duties of directors have evolved over a number of years; they have arisen out of case law, and case law does not always produce clarity. It has been suggested that the Combined Code [1998] and the Turnbull Report [1999] should together be treated as a code of best practice against which to assess a director's performance of his fiduciary duties. Certainly, because of the linkage between these documents and the Listing Rules, directors of listed public companies must pay great attention to them and, in effect, treat them as possessing quasi-legal status. (A summary of the Combined Code and the Turnbull Report is given in Appendix B.) Alternatively, the Law Commission and the Scottish Law Commission [1999] have recommended that the duty of care and skill and the principal fiduciary duties of directors should be set out in statute. The proper relationship between company law and non-statutory standards of corporate behaviour is currently being considered as part of the government's proposed reform of company law.

The present situation, however, is that the law regarding directors' duties is set out in different parts of the law. A director is treated for some purposes as an agent of the company, sometimes as a trustee of the assets of the company, and sometimes as an employee of the company. The responsibilities and duties of directors are not defined in any single statute, nor even completely stated in statute at all. The *Companies Act 1985* lays down general provisions about appointment, removal, qualifications, duties and responsibilities. More specific requirements are imposed on directors elsewhere in the Act, and in other associated legislation, in particular in the *Insolvency Act 1986* and the *Company Directors Disqualification Act 1986*. In addition, the decisions of generations of judges have created and interpreted the common law from which are derived many of the most important features of directors' duties.

The fundamental principle is that company directors owe duties to the company of which they are a director. These are general duties, applicable in all circumstances, arising from the relationship between the directors and the company, and they are owed by each director individually. Where a director breaches any of these duties, the company can take action to recover its property, seek damages from the director as compensation for any loss incurred, or seek any profits that the director has gained.

The consequential question of how the company is to enforce directors' duties when the directors control the company is taken up in section 8.3 above. Where the company does not seek redress for a breach of duty, in some circumstances the director's actions may be ratified by the shareholders (see section 8.9).

In certain circumstances, directors owe duties to a wider audience than the company or its members. In particular, directors should give consideration to:

- The interests of employees where to do so is in the best interest of the company, as required by s.309 of the *Companies Act 1985*, and as required by employment law (see Chapter 10).

- The interests of the company's creditors. Certain provisions of the *Insolvency Act 1986* lay a duty upon directors to take every reasonable step to minimise any loss to creditors as soon as it becomes reasonably apparent that the company cannot avoid insolvent liquidation. This duty is discussed in Chapter 15.

- The interests of other stakeholders. Directors are obliged under many statutes and regulations to ensure that their company pays regard to the interests of various parties who are affected by the company's operations. The relevant legislation and the associated obligations are discussed briefly in Chapter 10.

This chapter is concerned with the following types of general direct duties:

- First, a director has a strict duty to act only within his powers as a director. This is discussed in section 8.2.3 above.

- Secondly, a director has a 'duty of care'; this is to do with the degree of care, diligence and skill which a company director is required to exercise in order not to be considered to have undertaken his legitimate duties negligently.

- Thirdly, there are a number of fiduciary duties which restrict the acts that a director can properly do in connection with the management of the company.

There are, in addition, direct statutory duties placed on directors (e.g. in relation to the disclosure of shareholdings). These duties are treated in Chapters 9 and 13.

8.5 THE DUTY OF CARE AND SKILL

8.5.1 THE PRINCIPLES

In the performance of their work company directors are required to display a certain standard of skill and exercise reasonable care. The classic exposition of the duty of care and skill expected of a director was provided by Romer J in *Re City Equitable Fire Insurance Company Ltd* {9}, which established three basic principles:

1. A director need not be an expert and need display only the skills he reasonably can be expected to possess. He cannot be expected to exercise a level of skill he does not have.

2. A director is entitled, in the absence of grounds for suspicion, to rely on fellow directors and officers of the company to perform duties that properly may be delegated.

3. A director is not bound to give continuous attention to the affairs of his company. He is not bound to attend board meetings, for example, but should do so, since continued absence could be considered a breach of duty.

8.5.2 DEGREE OF CARE AND SKILL

It appears, then, that the level of skill required of a director is subjective. He is not expected to possess any particular skills, but must diligently apply any skills he actually has. The honest incompetent would therefore be exonerated on the basis that he could do no better. But if, for example, the director is a chartered accountant, then he would bear a weightier responsibility with respect to financial matters than someone with no accounting skills or knowledge.

However, in recent years the standard of care and skill that directors must bring to their duties and the manner in which these duties are to be performed have been significantly extended, mainly in director disqualification cases and 'wrongful trading' cases under the *Insolvency Act 1986* (see Chapters 11 and 15, respectively). In determining whether a director is 'unfit' to be a director, and therefore ought properly to be disqualified from so acting, the *Company Directors Disqualification Act 1986* requires the Court to have regard to *A misfeasance or breach of any fiduciary or other duty by the director in relation to the company* (Part I, Schedule I); this clearly includes a breach of the duty of care and skill. This enables the Courts to use disqualification as a means of raising standards among directors generally. Similarly, under s.214 of the *Insolvency Act 1986* in relation to wrongful trading, a director of a company is expected to have (and to exercise):

- the general knowledge, skill and experience that may reasonably be expected of a person carrying out that director's specific duties in relation to the company, *and*

- the general knowledge, skill and experience that the director has, if higher.

This test is now considered to have general application to the standards of care and skill expected of a director in the performance of his duties, whether or not his company becomes insolvent or goes into liquidation (see *Re D'Jan of London* {11} and *Norman v Theodore Goddard* {25}). Thus a director must comply with both an objective standard (i.e. one expected of a person in his position) and, if his skill level is higher, a subjective standard (i.e. one expected of him personally).

Courts are thus able to distinguish between directors according to their functions – finance director, marketing director, non-executive director, and so on. The test is quite severe – the minimum standard can be raised to accommodate any special skills the director has, but the incompetent who fails to attain the standard of what can reasonably be expected of the reasonably diligent director will fail the test. Additionally, and importantly, the basic standard to be met is flexible; what can reasonably be expected of a director of a large, quoted company may be different from that which can reasonably be expected of a director of a small private company.

In the case of *Dorchester Finance Co. Ltd and another v Stebbing and others* {13}, two non-executive directors left management of the company's affairs to a third executive director. The non-executive directors of the company signed blank cheques which were diverted to the personal use of the executive director, causing the company to lose £400,000. The company brought an action against all three directors, alleging negligence in the management of the company and seeking damages. The non-executives both alleged that they had relied on the auditors and the fact that the relevant accounts were not qualified. However, the Court held that the non-executives were liable to the company in negligence because they had fallen below the minimum standard of care and skill which no director, whatever his background or skills, should fall below. Further, no distinction was to be drawn between the executive and non-executive directors, the test of negligence being dependent upon the directors' knowledge and experience (the non-executives were both accountants by profession).

In the case of *Re Barings Plc* {3} a director was disqualified on the ground of 'unfitness' because he showed *not so much discrete failures of management as a general failure to manage: they amount not so much to bad management as to non-management. As such, they demonstrate . . . a high degree of incompetence* (Jonathan Parker J).

8.5.3 RELIANCE ON OTHERS

A director is entitled, in the absence of grounds for suspicion, to rely on fellow directors and officers of the company to perform duties that properly may be delegated. The same holds true for reliance on a properly constituted committee of the board. Likewise, the default of one director does not necessarily impose liability on the others. The absence of suspicious circumstances proved sufficient justification in one case (*Huckerby v Elliott* {21}) where a director failed to enquire of his fellow directors whether a gaming licence had been obtained but had no grounds to suspect otherwise.

> The business of life could not go on if people could not trust those who are put in a position of trust for the express purpose of attending to details of management.
>
> (Halsbury LJ, *Dovey v Corey* {14})

Some degree of delegation is probably essential if a company's business is to be carried on efficiently. But sensible reliance on the expertise of others is one thing, and careless disregard of a director's duties is another. Directors may delegate certain tasks, but they are still under a duty to supervise the performance of the delegated tasks. Overall responsibility is not delegable. The board and individual directors cannot ignore their responsibility to govern:

> . . .just as the duty of an individual director . . . [d]oes not mean that he may not delegate, neither does it mean that, having delegated a particular function, he is no longer under any duty in relation to the discharge of that function, notwithstanding that the person to whom the function has been delegated may appear both trustworthy and capable of discharging the function.
>
> (Jonathan Parker J, *Re Barings Plc* {3})

In the case of a company that goes into liquidation, directors cannot avoid personal liability by saying they took no part in the management of the business. The argument here is that, no matter what a director did in fact know or not know, in assessing liability a Court should consider what information about the company's financial position the director *ought* to have known. On the one hand, a director is not entitled to hide behind ignorance of the company's affairs which is of his own making or is due to his own failure to make further necessary enquiries. On the other hand, directors are not required to have omniscience. What each director is expected to do is to take a diligent and intelligent interest in the information either available to him or which he might with fairness demand from the executives or other employees and agents of the company. Directors seem increasingly to be expected to monitor and supervise the activities of managers and others, at least to such an extent as to uncover unauthorised actions. It seems that a director must ask questions and seek answers in a proactive way. You may be held liable where you should have been aware of a wrong even if you were in fact unaware of it. Ignorance therefore may not be a sufficient defence, particularly in the case of an insolvency.

8.5.4 ATTENTION TO THE BUSINESS

The size and nature of the company's business will determine the matters to which a director can give personal attention. In order, therefore, to ascertain the degree of attention that should be expected of a particular director, it is necessary to consider the company's business. Romer J expressed it thus:

> *The position of a director of a company carrying on a small retail business is very different from that of a director of a railway company. The duties of a bank director may differ widely from those of an insurance director, and the duties of a director of one insurance company may differ from those of a director of another. In one company, for instance, matters may normally be attended to by the manager or other members of the staff that in another company are attended to by the directors themselves. The larger the business carried on by the company the more numerous, and the more important, the matters that must of necessity be left to the managers, the accountants and the rest of the staff. The manner in which the work of the company is to be distributed between the board of directors and the staff is in truth a business matter to be decided on business lines. (Re City Equitable Fire Insurance Company Ltd {9})*

A traditional perspective is that a director is not bound to give continuous attention to the affairs of his company. His duties are of an intermittent nature. However, this view now no longer commands universal support. It has been held recently (*Re Barings Plc* {3}) that directors have a continuing, not intermittent, duty to keep themselves abreast of the company's business, though the extent of this duty will depend upon the nature of the business.

8.5.5 CONCLUSION

The duty of care and skill is applicable to all directors with a minimum threshold, though the height of the bar above that may be higher in the case of an executive director, whose service contract normally stipulates that he devotes himself full-time to the company, than in the case of a non-executive director, who may be privy to less timely information. Even so, as a non-executive director you must take seriously the duty of care you owe as a director. If you do not and are in breach of the duty, it may not be a defence to say that you did not take part in management or relied on others. Information provided by executives should be assessed critically and queried if it does not stand up to scrutiny. Non-executive directors may be held liable if, at the least, they have not satisfied themselves that a system of internal control is in place and operating effectively. Even protesting about the actions of executive directors may not be enough if you continue to participate in a management system you know to be unsatisfactory. In general, it appears that the Courts are prepared to whittle down the distinction between executive and non-executive directors with respect to the duty of care and skill.

The basic minimum standard of care and skill expected of a director is a flexible threshold. It is impossible to give an exhaustive list of the duties of care and skill of a director of a company because the range of companies of which people are directors and the practical duties of directors vary enormously. The extent of the duty, and the question whether it has been discharged, therefore depends upon the facts of each particular case. However, it is clear that the Courts, aided by statute, are gradually raising the standard of competence expected of directors. The Courts are basing their tougher approach partly on the objective test of reasonableness that the *Insolvency Act 1986* has imposed in order to assess whether a director can be made liable for wrongful trading. A desire to raise the baseline of competence of directors can also be seen in 'disqualification' cases brought under the *Company Directors Disqualification Act 1986*. The result is that the level of skill a director has to possess, the degree of diligence he must show, and the attention to the business required of him, have all been raised in recent years.

8.6 FIDUCIARY DUTIES

The word fiduciary derives from the Latin word 'fides', which means faith or trust. Directors must, then, act in a faithful or trustful manner towards or on behalf of the company. These duties owe their origins to a historical mix whereby a director was regarded as both a trustee of the company's assets and an agent of the company. Fiduciary duties are now supplemented by a host of statutory provisions.

The fiduciary duties are:

8.6.1 TO ACT IN GOOD FAITH IN THE INTERESTS OF THE COMPANY

Directors must act 'bona fide *in what they consider – not what a Court may consider – is in the interest of the company, and not for any collateral purpose*' (Greene LJ, *Re Smith and Fawcett Ltd* {46}). They should act in good faith, and should not have a personal motive in making decisions.

The duty to act *bona fide* in the best interests of the company is a subjective duty. But, most importantly, it is left to directors to decide where the best interests of the company lie. The Courts will interfere only if no reasonable director would have concluded that a particular transaction was in the best interest of the company. Directors can therefore be in breach of this duty, and the transaction in question can be set aside by a Court, without any conscious dishonesty on their part. In one case an agreement to pay the widow of a deceased general manager a pension was held to be not binding as it was not reasonably incidental to the company's business and not *bona fide* in the company's interest, even though the director acted in good faith on the advice of a solicitor (*Re Roith (W & M) Ltd* {38}).

The obligations on directors are particularly serious if the company is in a precarious financial situation, when the directors must ignore the interests of, say, a holding company and focus on the creditors of the subsidiary. Once a company is insolvent, or the directors are aware that there is no reasonable prospect that the company will avoid going into insolvent liquidation, the interests of the creditors override the interests of the shareholders as the creditors have a prior claim on the assets of the company. Nominee directors must consider the interests of *all* of the creditors, not just any debts owed to whoever is the director's nominator. The directors of a subsidiary should ignore any requests from a holding company, say, to transfer money over. Otherwise they will be personally liable.

EXAMPLE

Henry is the sole shareholder and director of two small companies – a building company, Buildco Ltd, and an import-export trading company, ImExco Ltd. ImExco is profitable; Buildco barely so. Henry wants to buy a sports car. He wants ImExco to buy the car so that the high costs of running it can be set off against ImExco's trading profits. However, ImExco does not have sufficient funds for the purchase. The bank will not accept ImExco's security for a bank loan but will accept Buildco's guarantee. Henry therefore wants Buildco to guarantee the bank loan for the purchase of ImExco's car.

Henry must be able, if asked, to explain why he believes the use of the car by one company and the guarantee given by the other company are in the interests of both companies concerned. He should bear in mind that, as far as ImExco is concerned, the bank has asked for additional security. If Henry's actions are ever examined critically in the future, this

> may be interpreted as meaning that the bank believes that the extra cost of running an exotic sports car rather than a conventional executive saloon is rather extravagant. On the other hand, Henry might be able to justify the additional cost – for example, he might think that a distinctive and noticeable car would bring valuable publicity for the company. Is this a reasonable belief? More pointedly, will it seem reasonable if the company becomes insolvent in the future? Similarly, wearing his hat as a director of Buildco, Henry must ask himself whether it is in Buildco's interests to give the bank guarantee. Buildco's creditors may suffer if ImExco defaults, the guarantee is called in and the assets of Buildco are depleted as a result.
>
> Whatever Henry decides to do, it would be prudent to record the reasons for the decisions with great care.

In attempting to satisfy the obligation to act *bona fide* in the best interests of the company, directors are faced by two difficulties. First, like Henry in the example above, they often wear a multitude of hats and therefore may be subject to conflicting demands. Secondly, a company's best interests are sometimes hard to define.

Examples of where conflicting demands could occur demonstrate the difficulty for some directors, particularly nominee directors. Nominees will be expected to represent the interests of the person or company who appointed them; that is why they are on the board. But what if that conflicts with the best interests of the company?

For instance, directors of a subsidiary company could be required to act in a way that is in the best interests of the holding company but which is detrimental to the subsidiary's interests. The board of the subsidiary may, say, wish to make a capital commitment to ensure that the factory is safe, but the holding company will not allow the capital expenditure. What do you do as a board of directors when you believe that the holding company is risking the safety of your products or your staff? You may well consider resignation.

Again, venture capital support usually requires a great deal of involvement in the running of the company, a seat on the board being a common requirement. It is usually in the best interests of the company that the nominator's interests are reflected in the decisions of the company – financial support may depend upon it – but this is not always the case. To give another example, suppose you are a nominee director on the board of a company.

The company that has nominated you has invested loan capital into the company which is secured by a fixed and floating charge on the assets of the company. The company is in financial difficulties but is not insolvent. However, you are concerned that the security that protects your nominator may be in jeopardy and you advise it to enforce the security. Have you broken your duty to the company?

In all the above cases the subsidiary company directors or nominated director owe their duty to the subsidiary or other company to which they have been nominated in priority to the interests of any other group companies or persons. They are entitled to give due consideration to the view that benefiting the group and its component companies could also benefit their own company. But it is not sufficient for directors to look only at the benefit to the group as a whole as regards the benefit of any particular action, for:

> Each company in the group is a separate legal entity and the directors of a particular company are not entitled to sacrifice their interests of that company. . . The proper test, I think, in the absence of actual separate consideration, must be whether an intelligent and honest man in the position of a director of the company concerned, could, in the whole of the existing circumstances, have reasonably believed that the transactions were for the benefit of the company.

(Pennycuick J, *Charterbridge Corporation Ltd v Lloyds Bank Ltd* {8})

Similarly, it is not unknown for a board to be dominated by an outstanding personality, probably the major shareholder, and for the dominant individual to be using and disposing of the assets of the company as if they were his own private property. This may include the purchase of luxury items and the use of the company's assets for the individual's own private use. What should the other directors of this company do? They must object and take the objection to the point of resignation if necessary, otherwise they will be endorsing unlawful acts.

Directors should be aware that, in acting *bona fide* for the company, the interests of the company are not identical with the interests of the shareholders collectively. A company also owes a duty to its creditors, present and future, not to dissipate its assets and to keep them available for the repayment of its debts. Similarly, directors must have regard to the interests of the company's employees in general. Also, many statutes (for example, the *Health & Safety at Work etc Act 1974*) impose duties upon the company and its directors – the performance of which may not be in the strict commercial interest of the company – which must be obeyed.

If there is a legal dispute, however, judges are generally reluctant to intervene. The Courts recognise that what is in the interests of a company is not always clear-cut and is often a matter of opinion. Also, the test is what the directors consider to be the best interests of the company, not the Court. The Court will not be concerned with the commercial merits of a particular decision. The Court will intervene only if it concludes that the breach of good faith or the collateral purpose is clear-cut, or the directors have refused or neglected to take into account matters which they should properly have taken into account, or that no reasonable director would have considered the action taken was in the interests of the company.

Acting for a collateral purpose may not always be against the interests of a company and it may be possible for the shareholders to ratify an act that is in breach of the *bona fide* rule. Further, where a director is negligent or in breach of trust or duty, the Court may excuse the director provided he acted honestly and reasonably and the Court considers he ought fairly to be excused.

8.6.2 PROPER PURPOSE

The specific powers that directors possess and the manner in which they can be exercised are determined by the company's Memorandum and Articles of Association, relevant shareholders' resolutions and board minutes. These powers must be used for the purposes intended or for the benefit of the company. Acting honestly, a director will have performed his duty if he reasonably believes that a transaction about to be approved is for the benefit of the company; but that will not be enough if the transaction is based on an improper use of the director's powers.

An improper use may not necessarily be one that benefits the director in any way. For example, even though the directors may consider that it is in the best interests of the company to issue more shares in order to block a take-over bid, this has been held to be an improper use of the directors' powers and therefore a breach of duty. In this case, therefore, the issue of shares was overturned.

> It must be unconstitutional for directors to use their fiduciary power over shares for the purpose of destroying a majority or creating a new majority.
>
> (Wilberforce LJ, *Howard Smith Ltd v Ampol Petroleum Ltd* {20})

In certain circumstances an improper use of powers can be ratified after the event by the members in a general meeting.

8.6.3 NOT TO MAKE SECRET PROFITS

If a director makes a personal profit arising out of his relationship with the company without it being disclosed to the company, even if he is acting honestly and in the interest of the company, that profit belongs to the company and the director is under a duty to account for it to the company. This principle has been extended by the Courts to profits arising from the directors' making use of information or a corporate opportunity.

If, for example, a director uses company time to make money for himself, then the company may well be entitled to such profit as he makes. Equally, if he sets up another business without the permission of the company and makes a profit, then the company may well be in a position to claim that profit.

It makes no difference that the profit is one that the company could not itself have made if the director had not deployed his own resources to making it, nor that he acted in good faith, nor that the company benefited as well as the director, and neither need the director's profit be at the company's expense. All that is required is simply that what was done resulted in a profit to the director concerned, which was not disclosed to and permitted by the company, and which related to the company's affairs in such a way that it could be said to have been done in the course of the director's management or by virtue of his opportunities or special knowledge as a director.

EXAMPLE

The directors of a cinema-owning company (Regal) wanted their company to acquire two cinemas for later sale, using a subsidiary company to make the purchase. Since Regal did not have enough capital to make the purchase, the directors themselves bought shares in the subsidiary company. They later sold the shares for a profit. They had to pay their personal profit to the company (*Regal (Hastings) Ltd v Gulliver & Others* {36}), since their profit arose only through knowledge they had gained as directors of Regal.

In *Guinness Plc v Saunders* {18}, where a director entered into a contract for his own personal benefit and made a secret profit, the company successfully pursued an action for repayment of the director's profit to the company.

Even if a director leaves a company, opportunities that were made known to the director while a director of the company, and which the company could have had an interest in, cannot be pursued without a risk of the company being successful in extracting all the profits of the venture from the former director.

A director can benefit from a situation where he is in possession of information which he can use for personal gain only if he has disclosed to the company the profit and the circumstances in which it was obtained and in addition his retention of that profit is sanctioned by an ordinary resolution. This should be recorded in the minutes of the general meeting. If, however, the profit has been obtained through misapplication of the company's property or involves dishonest conduct by the director, it is not capable of ratification.

8.6.4 TO AVOID CONFLICTS OF INTEREST

Directors must not let their personal interests conflict with their duty to the company. Directors may put themselves in a position where there is a potential conflict between their personal interests and their duties to the company, but they must always prefer the company's interest to their own. Unless the shareholders or the Articles of Association permit it, a director must account to the company for the benefit of any transactions in which he has an interest. This is the case even if the director took no part in, or was even unaware of, the decision in question.

A conflict of interest will arise where the director deliberately exploits the assets of the company – particularly information gained through the company – for his own benefit, even where the company cannot or chooses not to exploit the information itself. A conflict of interest may arise solely through the company itself entering into a transaction with another company in which the director has an interest. There will also be a conflict of interest where the director receives favours (e.g. a commission) for exercising his directorial powers.

It is sometimes difficult to identify the potential for a conflict of interest. There is no clear-cut set of circumstances which can define when conflicts arise. But the law suggests an objective test: a conflict could arise where *the reasonable man looking at the relevant facts and circumstances of the particular case would think that there was a real sensible possibility of conflict* (Upjohn LJ, *Boardman v Phipps* {4}). If you have any doubts, the prudent course is to err on the side of disclosure.

The 'no conflict' rule might be expected to prohibit a person from being a director of competing companies. However, it has been held by the Courts to be proper providing approval is obtained from the directors of both companies. But a director must not fetter his discretion to act in the best interests of the company by, for example, a contract with a third party. Care must be taken not to subordinate the interests of one company to those of the other. Shareholders may seek protection from the Court when they consider the company's affairs to have been conducted by a director in an unfairly prejudicial manner (see section 8.3 above). In addition, whatever the legal niceties, being a director of a competing company, or even a shareholder, is not generally considered to be good practice. For example, in 2000 public and press outcry led to the Director-General of the BBC selling the shares he held in a competing broadcaster.

There are also statutory provisions governing the most common areas where a conflict of interest in contractual matters is likely to arise between a director and the company. These are directors' service contracts (see section 7.3.3), substantial property transactions involving directors (see section 9.6), and loans from a company to its directors (see section 9.7).

EXAMPLE

The company has had to turn down a contract because its order book is full. Can a director take it on personally?

If the board decides to turn down the opportunity, a director may take the contract on personally, provided that he discloses all the information which is relevant about the contract to the board first, the board turns down the opportunity in good faith, and the director's service contract does not insist on his full-time commitment to the company. It is recommended in such circumstances that the board minutes its reasons for rejecting the opportunity, to show that the decision was taken in good faith, just in case this is challenged at a later date.

8.6.5 TO DECLARE AN INTEREST

If a director has an interest, then he must disclose that interest to the board. The *Companies Act 1985* (s.317) requires that the director should declare the nature of the interest at the first board meeting where the question of entering into a contract in which he has an interest is considered. Failure to do so is a criminal offence for which a fine can be imposed. The director may be liable to reward any profits made and the contract or transaction may be voided by the company (see *Guinness Plc v Saunders* {18}).

Where the interest arises only after a contract has been proposed or made, the director should declare the interest at the next board meeting, whether or not that contract is to be considered.

A contract in this context includes any transaction or arrangement, including loan and guarantee transactions, whether or not constituting a formal contract. Further, the interests of 'connected persons' are deemed to be the interests of the director.

The Articles of Association normally permit conflicting interests only if they are disclosed to the company. For example, a non-executive director may have an interest in a business that has a trading relationship with the company. It is usual for the Articles of Association to provide that in such a case the director must declare his interest to the board and must not vote in any proceedings concerning the contract (although he may be included in the quorum). The company can also authorise the transaction in advance or ratify the transaction subsequently in general meeting.

8.7 JOINT AND SEVERAL LIABILITY

Directors of a company are jointly and severally liable in circumstances in which directors' liability arises. This means that they are liable both together as a group and individually.

This is the case even where the directors do not share the effort equally. For example, many companies are directed by a husband-and-wife team where one of the spouses will take no significant role in the direction or management. (Often, the appointment of the inactive spouse is made for the administrative convenience of having a second person who can sign documents as a director, though there is no need for this as a matter of law. Private companies need have no more than one director.) In such a case, in principle, both spouses together, each individually, one spouse alone, or none, is liable.

The manner in which a Court might distribute liability will be a function of the issue in dispute. In an insolvency, for instance, it might be that the whole board could be held liable or an individual director – perhaps the finance director if he had withheld or manipulated information. If a sole director remains in the country after the precipitous departure of his colleagues, liability may well fall on his shoulders alone.

8.8 CONSEQUENCES OF A BREACH OF DUTY: ACTIONS OPEN TO THE COMPANY

The duty of care and skill, the fiduciary duties and the duty not to exceed proper powers have been supplemented by a substantial number of statutory provisions. Many of these statutory provisions impose financial and criminal liability on directors who breach the requirements of these statutes. For example, if the director's conduct involves criminal activity, then the director may be subject to criminal prosecution in addition to any steps taken by the company. This section, however, is concerned only with possible remedies by the company.

Faced by a breach of duty by a director, a company can do one or more of the following:

1. Ratify the action of the director in general meeting, where the director concerned can vote in favour of the ratification if he is also a shareholder. However, some actions are not capable of ratification. In these cases it may be possible for shareholders to pursue an action on behalf of the company against the director concerned.

2. Obtain an injunction to prevent the director from carrying out, or continuing with, the breach of duty.

3. Seek rescission of any contracts improperly entered into, though if a third party has entered into the contract in good faith his claim will almost certainly be upheld as against the company.

4. Seek restitution for loss of company property as long as there are no intervening third parties who have acted in good faith who now have the property.

5. Pursue the director in question for damages to indemnify the company for any loss suffered as a result of the breach of duty.

6. Sue the director for negligent performance.

7. If secret profits have been made, pursue the director to account to the company and to hand over the profits. This profit can be recovered even

if it would have been impossible for the company to make the profit itself – for example, through trading in its own shares.

8. Dismiss the director at a company meeting as breach of duty will be regarded as breach of the terms of a service contract.

If the company will not take action – perhaps because the company is under the control of a wrongdoer – then shareholders may bring a derivative action on behalf of the company. Actions open to shareholders in this circumstance are discussed in section 8.3.

8.9 RATIFICATION

Some breaches of duty by a director may be ratified by an ordinary resolution of the shareholders. The effect is to make the wrongful act no longer wrongful, so that no action by, for example, a minority shareholder can arise. Generally, a shareholder has no remedy if he thinks that a company is being improperly prevented from suing a director, provided that the majority of shareholders have ratified the act in question after full disclosure of the facts of the case.

Examples of ratifiable acts are: failing to disclose an interest in a contract and making a secret profit (without damaging the company); and a transaction involving a failure in care and skill.

However, many acts are not ratifiable. Any act that is unlawful or beyond the powers of the company may not be ratified by the shareholders. For example, fraudulent acts are not ratifiable and an unauthorised return of capital or payment of dividends out of capital cannot be subsequently ratified even if all shareholders agree.

8.10 DUTIES OF EXECUTIVE AND NON-EXECUTIVE DIRECTORS

The application of the duties of directors applies equally to executive and non-executive directors. Executive directors may have additional responsibilities placed upon them as a result of the contract of employment that they will have entered into, either written or unwritten. A common example is that there are clauses in an executive director's contract that require the director to work exclusively for the company. However, the duties that apply to directors make no distinction between executive and non-executive directors. That said, the duties themselves contain subjective elements and it is possible that the Courts will recognise that it is unreasonable to expect every director to have equal knowledge and experience of every aspect of the company's activities.

8.11 SUMMARY

1. If you have consented to be a director and your name is on the company's register of directors at Companies House, then you are a director.

2. You may also be a director if you and the company hold you out as a director – even though the formalities have not been complied with.

3. Generally, directors may commit the company in contract and the company will be bound.

4. A director has a duty to exercise such care and skill as a reasonable person in his position would exercise and in addition such care and skill as a person of his actual knowledge and experience would exercise. In short, directors must be proactive in their direction of the company.

5. Directors must exercise the fiduciary duties

   • to act in good faith;

   • to act for proper purpose;

   • not to make secret profits;

   • to avoid conflicts of interest;

   • to declare an interest.

6. Directors must act within their due powers.

7. The liability of directors is joint and several – together and separately.

8. In order to ensure that all your duties are fulfilled, you should:

   • be methodical in the way you make decisions;

   • record the reasons for decisions at the time they are made;

   • take advice as soon as you suspect you need it; not to do so is often a false economy.

Chapter 9

Disclosure of Information and Other Legal Requirements of Directors

9.1 INTRODUCTION

Matters to do with the formation of companies, the formalities of registration, the consequences of incorporation and the limited liability of shareholders are dealt with in the *Companies Acts*. But, once in existence, there is a need for a company to be governed properly. In attempting to ensure that proper governance is achieved, statute and common law seek to ensure both fair dealing by directors and the appointment of suitable officers. Fair dealing is largely dealt with by the provisions covering directors' fiduciary duties (the subject of Chapter 8), the creation of statutory rights for creditors (see Chapter 15), and the creation of statutory rights for certain stakeholders (see Chapter 10). Matters relating to the appointment of directors and other officers of the company have been discussed in Chapter 7.

However, in addition, the means chosen to ensure that companies are governed properly include:

- disclosure: companies are required to make public a great deal of information about their affairs;

- requirements that such information must not be false or misleading;

- rules regulating transactions between a director and the company;

- requirements that a company's capital is maintained.

Many elements of these requirements create duties and corresponding liabilities for directors, either directly, when the law imposes a duty (for example, to prepare a company's accounts) and a corresponding liability to penalties on the directors alone, or indirectly, when the duty is placed on the company and the directors are required to ensure that it is complied with and penalties for non-compliance may be imposed on the company and directors jointly and severally or on either party alone.

9.2 DISCLOSURE

Many of the provisions of the *Companies Act 1985* are designed to protect the interests of the shareholders and stakeholders by forcing directors to release certain information about the company. Companies and their directors must comply with these disclosure requirements. However, shareholders' rights to information about a company are limited to those provided for in the Act; other stakeholders have only minimal rights in law to information about a company.

Companies are required to disclose information by:

- including information, particularly the company's name, address and registration number, on stationery and certain other printed material issued by the company;

- making returns to the Registrar of Companies which are available for public inspection;

- making documents available for inspection at the company's registered office or elsewhere (these documents are listed in section 9.2.3);

- circulating information to shareholders in reports and accounts and to prospective investors in prospectuses or listing particulars.

The company secretary will probably prepare and process these documents, but the responsibility for meeting the disclosure requirements falls on the board, whose members may face financial liabilities or penalties for any incorrect or misleading statement or default (including the risk of being disqualified from acting as a director – see Chapter 11).

9.2.1 INFORMATION ON DOCUMENTS

Table 9.1 lists the information that companies must include on documents.

Table 9.1 *Information required on documents*

Information	Documents
Company name	All company letters, notices, cheques, invoices, receipts, etc. The name must be displayed conspicuously outside every office and place of business of the company. If a company carries on business under a name other than its corporate name, it must state on business letters, orders, invoices and receipts, the corporate name and an address for the effective service of documents and display a notice of its name and address at premises to which customers or suppliers have access.
Company's registration details	All business letters and order forms.
Identity of directors	If the name of any director appears in any form (other than in the text or as a signatory) on any business letters on which the company's name appears, the names of all the directors and 'shadow directors' must be shown

9.2.2 RETURNS TO THE REGISTRAR

For companies registered in Great Britain, documents relating to the following matters must be filed with the Registrar of Companies:

- appointment and resignation of directors and the company secretary;
- changes to the company's Registered Office;

- special and extraordinary resolutions of general meetings of shareholders;
- changes to the Memorandum and Articles of Association;
- alterations to share capital;
- allotments of shares;
- charges on company property;
- changes to the company's accounting reference date;
- accounts and the directors' report;
- the statutory annual return;
- removal of auditors before the end of their term of office;
- purchase of a company's own shares;
- winding up.

The Department of Trade and Industry is becoming increasingly stringent in enforcing these filing obligations and has a policy of prosecuting defaulters.

9.2.3 INFORMATION AVAILABLE FOR INSPECTION

The following documents must be available for inspection by shareholders and the public:

- a register of members;
- a register of debenture holders (if any);
- a register of directors and secretaries, which must contain details of all present and some past directorships of companies incorporated in Great Britain;
- a register of directors' interests in the shares of the company;
- a register of charges.

These documents are to be kept at the company's Registered Office or at a place notified to the Registrar.

Directors' service contracts must be available for inspection by shareholders at the company's Registered Office or its principal place of business or where the register of members is kept, if different.

In the case of quoted companies, the London Stock Exchange requires that each director's service agreement must be available at the Registered Office or at the office of the company for inspection by any person during normal business hours on each business day and at the place of the Annual General Meeting for at least 15 minutes prior to and during the meeting. Details must include full particulars of directors' remuneration, including benefits as well as salary, and details of any arrangements necessary to enable investors to estimate the possible liability of the company upon early termination of the contract. The extent of disclosure of information regarding the grant to and exercise by directors of options under share option schemes is the subject of non-mandatory guidelines issued by the Accounting Standards Board and certain recommendations contained in the Combined Code.

9.3 THE COMPANY'S ACCOUNTS

Directors are not required to be technical experts in accounting or to know the statutory requirements in detail, but the responsibility for compliance with the requirements of the *Companies Acts* on accounts rests squarely on directors' shoulders and every director should therefore be aware of at least the broad outline of the requirements.

9.3.1 WHY DO COMPANIES HAVE TO PRODUCE ACCOUNTS?

The purpose of making the company's annual accounts available is primarily to provide an account of the stewardship of the directors during that year to assist shareholders and debenture holders in the informed exercise of their rights. So far as shareholders are concerned, this is interpreted as meaning *to enable them to question the past management of the company, to exercise voting rights, if so advised, and to influence future policy and management* (*Caparo Industries Plc v Dickman* {6}).

9.3.2 WHAT ACCOUNTING RECORDS MUST A COMPANY KEEP?

The general duty

All companies are under a duty to keep accounting records. The accounting records must be such as will reveal, at any time, a reasonably accurate picture of the company's financial position and must be kept in a way which enables the directors to ensure the preparation of annual accounts in accordance with the *Companies Acts'* requirements. The *Companies Acts* also prescribe the formats in which the balance sheet and the profit and loss account must be set out.

It is the duty of the directors under the *Companies Act*s:

- to ensure that proper and accessible accounting records are kept by the company;

- to prepare and approve annual accounts which comply with the Act;

- to ensure that the company sends copies to parties entitled to receive them;

- to lay the annual accounts before members in general meeting (unless, in the case of a private company, a valid election has been made to dispense with this);

- to deliver the annual accounts to the Registrar of Companies.

If the directors' report fails to comply with the Act's requirements about preparation and content, every person who was a director immediately before the end of the period for laying and delivering accounts and reports for the financial year in question is guilty of an offence, unless he can prove that he took all reasonable steps for securing compliance with the requirements. If annual accounts are approved which do not comply with the Act's requirements, every director who is party to their approval and who knows that they do not comply with the Act, or is reckless as to whether they comply, is guilty of a criminal offence unless he can show that the default was excusable in the circumstances in which the company's business was carried on. A director would be reckless if he was either indifferent to and gave no thought as to whether the accounts complied or was aware of the possibility that they did not comply but nevertheless persisted in approving them. Every director of the company at the time the accounts are approved is taken to be 'a party to' their approval unless he shows that he took all reasonable steps to prevent their being approved. The Court may also order the directors to prepare and publish corrected accounts. It may also order the directors who were party to the approval of defective accounts to bear or contribute to the costs of the application and the expenses that the company incurs as a result of having to make and publish the correction.

Management accounts

The Institute of Chartered Accountants in England and Wales recommends as best practice that:

In addition to the statutory requirement to keep proper accounting records, the directors have an overriding responsibility to ensure that they have adequate information to enable them to discharge their duty to manage the company's business.

(Institute of Chartered Accountants [1997])

The nature and extent of the accounting and management information needed to exercise this degree of control is discussed in section 5.5, and will depend upon the company's business. But it will certainly involve far more records and transactions than the statutory minimum prescribes, and will encompass, for example, cash, debtors and creditors, stock and work in progress, capital expenditure, and major contracts. In order to restrict the possibility of actions for wrongful trading, directors will constantly need to be aware of the company's financial position. The board should be satisfied that the accounting records provide them with sufficient regular and prompt information to enable them to draw conclusions on these matters.

Directors must also be aware of a company's prospects. It may therefore be prudent to prepare a business plan against which the subsequent performance of the business can be measured. The need for, extent and frequency of the preparation of management accounts, and the level of management to which they are presented, will depend upon the size, scope and nature of the business. However, the directors' report on the financial statement must contain an indication of the likely future developments in the business of the company and its subsidiaries (*Companies Act 1985*, s.234 and Schedule 7), and a business plan is likely to be helpful in this respect.

Other records

There are many other requirements to be taken into account. Various payroll records must be kept, and tax and VAT legislation impose further requirements with which the company must comply. Companies also need to comply with the provisions of the *Data Protection Act 1998*, particularly in relation to the keeping and supply of information about employees. Specialised types of business may also be subject to special requirements – regarding personal data kept by the company, for example, an 'investment business' has to comply with various record-keeping requirements laid down in the *Financial Services Act 1986*.

9.3.3 ACCOUNTING PRINCIPLES

Directors must also observe certain 'Accounting Principles'. These are that:

- in preparing the accounts, the company is to be treated as carrying on business as a going concern (if this is indeed the case);

- accounting policies must be applied consistently within the same accounts and from one financial year to the next;

- the accounts must be prepared on an accruals basis, not on the basis of receipts and payments;

- the amount or value of any item must be determined on a prudent basis, taking account only of profits realised before the end of the financial year and of all liabilities and losses which have arisen or are likely to arise in respect of the year in question even if the directors only became aware of them after the end of the financial year but before the accounts were signed.

Any departure from these principles must be noted, with reasons, in the accounts.

In addition, there are rules for accountants – known as Statements of Standard Accounting Practice (SSAPs) and Financial Reporting Standards (FRSs) – which set out methods of accounting and disclosure for application to all accounts intended to give a true and fair view. Directors should be aware of the SSAPs and FRSs which are relevant to their business. Except for small and medium-sized companies (see section 9.3.5), accounts must state whether they conform with the current SSAPs and FRSs and give particulars of any material departure from those standards and the reasons for them. These accounting standards now have a degree of legal backing and need to be observed.

9.3.4 GROUPS

The directors of UK holding companies are required to produce consolidated accounts for the parent company and its subsidiary undertakings.

9.3.5 EXCEPTIONS FOR SMALL AND MEDIUM-SIZED COMPANIES AND GROUPS

Small and medium-sized private companies and groups (though there are exceptions) may file modified accounts with the Registrar of Companies. In the case of small companies, the accounts required to be filed may be very much shortened – no profit or loss account, no directors' report and shortened balance sheet and notes. In addition, private companies which are not part of a group and which are small may be exempt from the need to have an audit and be entitled to have a 'compilation report' prepared by a reporting accountant.

Small and medium-sized companies and groups are those which satisfy at least any two of the following conditions:

- annual turnover does not exceed £2.8m (small company); £11.2m (medium company); £2.8m net in aggregate or £3.36m gross in aggregate (small group); £11.2 net in aggregate or £13.44m gross (medium group);

- balance sheet total (i.e. all assets without deduction of liabilities) does not exceed £1.4m (small company); £5.6m (medium company); £1.4m net in aggregate or £1.68m gross in aggregate (small group); £5.6m net in aggregate or £6.72m gross in aggregate (medium group);

- average number of employees does not exceed 50 (small company); 250 (medium company); 50 in aggregate (small group); 250 in aggregate (medium group).

A parent company of a small or medium-sized group need not prepare group accounts provided the auditors state in a report attached to the accounts that in their opinion the company is entitled to the exemption.

9.3.6 DIRECTORS' REPORT

Directors of every company are required to prepare a report for each financial year. Failure to prepare a report or to include all necessary information can lead to the imposition of fines upon directors. The report must include:

- a fair review of the development of the business of the company and its subsidiary undertakings during the financial year and of their position at the end of it;

- the amounts which the board of directors recommends to be paid as dividends;

- the names of all persons who at any time during the financial year in question were directors, and their shareholdings and other interests;

- the principal activities of the company and its subsidiary undertakings, any changes in them and in asset values;

- details of charitable and political gifts made by the company;

- details of acquisitions of the company's own shares or charges on them;

- if the company has more than 250 employees, a statement describing the company's policy as to the employment of the disabled and a statement as to the action relating to the involvement of employees in the affairs, policy and performance of the company;

- a statement relating to the company's policy and practice concerning the payment of creditors.

9.3.7 STOCK EXCHANGE DISCLOSURE REQUIREMENTS

Companies listed, or applying for a full listing, on the London Stock Exchange must satisfy the basic conditions for listing and comply with the relevant Listing Rules (set out in London Stock Exchange [1999]), which require the circulation to shareholders of information not necessarily required by the *Companies Act 1985*. Similar provisions apply to companies seeking admission to the Alternative Investment Market (AIM) of the London Stock Exchange.

Subject to Stock Exchange rules and to detailed conditions set out in law, public companies with Stock Exchange listing may provide shareholders with a summary financial statement (instead of full annual accounts and directors' and auditors' reports) in cases where they are not prohibited from doing so by any provision in their Memorandum and Articles of Association. Copies of the full report and accounts must still be filed with the Registrar of Companies and be sent to any shareholder who wishes to receive them.

9.3.8 APPROVAL OF ANNUAL ACCOUNTS AND DIRECTORS' REPORT

A company's annual accounts must be approved by the board of directors and signed on the balance sheet by a director. The directors' report must be approved by the board and signed on its behalf by a director, normally the chairman. Copies of both documents which are laid before the general meeting or otherwise published must carry the names of the persons who signed them.

9.3.9 LAYING AND FILING OF ACCOUNTS AND REPORTS

Except when a private company has validly elected to dispense with the laying of accounts and reports before a general meeting, when different provisions apply, the directors must lay the annual accounts for each financial year, together with the directors' report and the auditor's report, before the company in general meeting within ten months (private companies), seven months (unlisted public companies), or (under the Listing Rules) six months (listed public companies) of the end of the company's financial year. They must also deliver the same documents to the Registrar of Companies within the same period.

If accounts are not laid or delivered within the prescribed time, or if they fail to comply with the requirements on laying and delivering in some other way, every director in office immediately before the end of the period is guilty of an offence, unless he can prove he took all reasonable steps for securing compliance with the requirements. If accounts are filed late, the Court, on the application of the Registrar or any member or creditor of the company, may order the directors to make good the default within a specified time and to pay all costs of and incidental to the application. The Registrar may recover a civil penalty for late delivery of the accounts from the company. The amount of the penalty depends on the status of the company, and on how late the accounts are, and ranges from £100 for a private company's accounts being less than three months late to £5,000 for a public company's which are more than a year overdue.

Failure to comply with filing requirements is also one of the easiest routes to being disqualified from acting as a director (see Chapter 11).

9.3.10 WHAT IF PROPER ACCOUNTING RECORDS ARE NOT KEPT?

On trial on indictment *all* the directors can be imprisoned for a maximum of two years and/or given an unlimited fine. On summary trial a director can be imprisoned for a maximum of six months and/or given a fine of up to £5,000. It is a defence, however, if directors can show that they took all reasonable steps to prevent the accounts being approved.

A company's auditors are placed under a specific duty to carry out such investigations as will enable them to form an opinion as to whether a company has kept proper accounting records (see section 9.4.3). If they cannot come to such an opinion, or their opinion has to be qualified in some way, this will be mentioned in their audit report attached to the accounts. This will certainly concern the company's bankers and may be noticed by the Department of Trade and Industry, Customs and Excise, and the Inland Revenue. The consequences could then be serious.

Directors should be aware that the extent of a director's responsibility for a failure by his company to comply with the company law provision in respect of company records is a factor that could later be taken into account by a Court assessing whether the director is 'unfit' to be a director and should, therefore, be disqualified (see section 11.4).

The *Companies Act 1989* allows for the voluntary revision of annual accounts or the directors' report where it appears that the accounts or report did not comply with the requirements of the 1985 Act. It also permits the Secretary of State to require the revision of defective accounts.

9.3.11 FOR HOW LONG MUST ACCOUNTING RECORDS BE KEPT?

Company law requires a private company to keep its accounting records for three years from the date when they are prepared and a public company for six years. However, there are a number of other considerations. For example, all companies registered for VAT must keep certain records for at least six years. A similar period is recommended for records related to tax generally, since the Inland Revenue can assess a company for tax for six years after a chargeable period.

9.4 THE COMPANY AUDITOR

9.4.1 MUST THERE BE AN AUDITOR?

On incorporation of a company an auditor must be appointed either by the directors or by the shareholders before the first general meeting of the company at which the accounts are laid. The auditor holds office only until the end of the first general meeting at which the company's accounts are presented, and he may then be re-appointed. He then holds office until the next such meeting. If, for any reason, the company ceases to have an auditor between meetings, the directors (or if they fail to do so, the shareholders) may appoint a new auditor.

If a private company has elected to dispense with the laying of accounts before the company in general meeting, auditors must be appointed in general meeting within 28 days from the date on which copies of the annual accounts are sent to members. A private company may also elect to dispense with the annual appointment of auditors by following a defined statutory procedure.

If for any reason a company has no auditor, the Secretary of State for Trade and Industry must be notified within a week, and he may then appoint an auditor himself.

9.4.2 HOW IS AN AUDITOR APPOINTED?

An existing auditor is re-appointed by an ordinary resolution of the company's shareholders. The auditor will normally send the company a letter of engagement defining the extent of the auditor's responsibilities in an attempt to minimise the risk of any misunderstanding in the work that he may carry out. The letter will usually cover the following issues:

- The responsibilities of the directors and the auditor respectively in relation to the audit and any irregularities or fraud.

- The need for the directors to confirm in writing any oral representations made to the auditor during the course of the audit.

- The nature and scope of any other service to be supplied by the auditor, for example, accounting, taxation or consultancy services.

- The basis on which fees are to be calculated.

The board should confirm the company's agreement to the engagement letter in writing.

9.4.3 WHAT DOES AN AUDITOR DO?

It is not the auditor's job to prepare the accounts (although in practice the board often requests him to do so).The obligation to prepare accounts is that of the directors. The directors are responsible for giving a 'true and fair' view. The auditor has only to report to shareholders whether the financial statements have been properly prepared in accordance with the *Companies Act 1985* and whether or not in their opinion these give a 'true and fair' view. The auditor is also obliged to state by exception in his audit report if proper accounting records have not been kept, or if the information in the directors' report is not consistent with the accounts and other similar matters. He has to disclose certain information such as loans to directors and directors' remuneration if the accounts do not do so.

Most importantly, auditors are not responsible for the prevention or detection of irregularities or fraud. These responsibilities belong to the board of directors. However, if the auditors discover irregularities or frauds, they should not ignore them.

In order to help him perform his job properly, the auditor has the right to attend and be heard at general meetings, the right of access to the company and the right to require information and explanations from the company's officers. There are sanctions on directors and other officers who make false statements to auditors.

In practice, the auditor will assess the reasonableness and reliability of the company's accounting system and test samples of important transactions. He will concentrate on high-risk areas and significant or unusual transactions. The auditor obtains evidence by observing the way in which the operations are carried out and by inspecting invoices, statements, purchase orders and the like. He will seek independent confirmation from third parties, such as debtors, creditors and banks, where appropriate. The auditor will review the financial statements, concentrating on such matters as the valuation of stocks, provisions for doubtful debts and disclosure of contingent liabilities. At the end of the audit the auditor will discuss any concerns with at least the finance director and, if everything is satisfactory, sign an unqualified audit report.

9.4.4 WHO MAY BE A COMPANY'S AUDITOR?

Only a 'registered auditor' is able to audit companies incorporated in the UK, that is, an accountancy practice which has been registered by one of the major professional accounting Institutes as eligible to accept audit appointments.

Certain persons who are connected in some way with a company are prohibited by law from being the company's auditor. These include: a director of the company, the company secretary, and an employee of the company. Any person who acts as an auditor knowing that he is disqualified from appointment commits a criminal offence.

9.4.5 CHANGING THE AUDITOR

A company can change its auditor, but it is not easy to do so without the auditor's consent. The idea is to guard against companies changing their auditor for other than good reasons.

Auditors can be changed only by resolution of the general meeting of the company. But special notice is required for such a resolution and a copy of this resolution has to be sent to the proposed new auditor and also to the retiring or resigning auditor who is not proposed for reappointment. The retiring auditor not proposed for reappointment is entitled to make written representations to the company and require the company to circulate these to shareholders or, if this is not done, require them to be read out at general meeting.

When an auditor ceases to hold office for any reason he must deposit at the company's registered office a statement of any circumstances connected to his ceasing to hold office which he considers should be brought to the attention of members or creditors of the company. The company must then send a copy of the statement to members within 14 days. Even if the auditor considers there are no circumstances which should be brought to the attention of members, he must deposit a statement that there are none. In any event the company must send a copy of the auditors' notice of resignation to the Registrar of Companies within 14 days. In addition, as a matter of professional etiquette, the new auditor will write to the outgoing auditor to ask whether there is any reason why he should not accept the appointment.

If a company does adopt a resolution to remove an auditor before his term of office expires, the company must give notice on the prescribed form to the Registrar of Companies within 14 days.

9.4.6 THE BENEFITS OF AN AUDIT

The audit can be of great value to a board. First, the board receives a second opinion on the financial statements. Secondly, because of his experience, his technical expertise and his independence from his clients, an auditor is well placed to advise on aspects of financial reporting which go beyond his required role of giving an opinion on financial statements. He is likely to be able, for instance, to advise on accounting policies most suited to the business and on the best accounting practice.

Further, in the course of the audit the auditor will have the opportunity to look into the company's business in depth. He can often usefully comment on such matters as, for example, the quality of the staff, the effectiveness of the accounting department, or the accuracy of the management information system. This sort of advice may be of great benefit to the board of directors. However, the audit firm often has a consultancy arm, and in recent years there has been concern that partnerships in effect subsidise their audit fees in the expectation of winning expensive consultancy assignments. The board should be aware of this business possibility.

9.5 FINANCIAL SERVICES AND MARKETS ACT 2000

The regulatory arrangements established under a number of different statutes were harmonised in the *Financial Services and Markets Act 2000*. Businesses regulated under the Act include commercial banks, building societies, investment banks and securities firms, insurance companies, friendly societies, investment and pension advisers.

The Act provides a framework within which a regulator for the financial services industry, the Financial Services Authority (FSA), operates. Under the Act the FSA has created a scheme of compensation to consumers who suffer loss because of the inability of a financial intermediary to meet its liabilities. The speedy resolution of disputes between the public and financial intermediaries is facilitated by a new ombudsman.

It has been stressed that, although the company is a separate person, directors may well have personal liability for actions and events arising from the company's activities. A clear example of such liability may arise out of a purchase of shares. Under the Act, if an investor acquires securities and suffers loss through false or misleading information in a prospectus, then he may proceed against the persons responsible for such false or misleading inform-ation. Such a person is likely to be a director – and in such circumstances extreme diligence is required before the publication of a prospectus. The Act also gives the FSA the power to impose financial penalties on those who abuse investment markets, by insider dealing or market price manipulation, for example.

The FSA is empowered by the Act to take over the role of UK listing authority; it will exercise substantially the same powers as previously exercised by the London Stock Exchange.

9.6 SUBSTANTIAL PROPERTY TRANSACTIONS

In general a company must not enter into a contract with one of its directors under which the director acquires from or transfers to the company 'non-cash assets' **unless** the transaction is first approved by a resolution of the company in a general meeting. This prohibition also applies to shadow directors and to persons connected with a director. A non-cash asset is defined as any property or interest in property other than cash.

The provisions apply to cases where the non-cash assets exceed either £100,000 or 10% of the company's asset value, whichever is the lower, subject to a *de minimis* rule of £2,000.

Such limitations exist to prevent companies benefiting directors by acquiring directors' assets at inflated values or, alternatively, selling company assets to them at an under value.

There are even stricter requirements in relation to listed companies, which involve full disclosure to members, and often approval is sought by resolution.

Any director or group of directors who are in breach of these requirements must, if there is a profit, account for it to the company and, if necessary, reimburse the company personally against any losses incurred. Where shareholder approval in advance was not obtained for a transaction, the shareholders can ratify the transaction if they wish.

9.7 LOAN TRANSACTIONS BETWEEN A DIRECTOR AND THE COMPANY

There are complex statutory provisions in an area where conflicts of interest commonly arise, namely, loans by a company to a director. Other areas where conflicts of interest frequently arise – namely, contracts between a director and a company, and dealings by directors in their company's shares – are discussed in Chapters 8 and 13 respectively. If contemplating any transaction in these areas, directors are strongly advised to seek professional advice.

9.7.1 GENERAL RULE

There are rules prohibiting loans and similar transactions in favour of directors set out in the *Companies Acts*. These prohibitions generally refer to directors of companies and directors of any holding companies. They also extend to 'shadow' directors and any 'connected' person. A 'connected person' is a person whom the law regards as capable of being influenced by a director and the more important examples of a 'connected person' are listed in section 8.1.6.

The general rule applicable to all companies is that a company must *not* make a loan to a director of the company or of its holding company. It follows, therefore, that in general a director cannot lawfully borrow money from his company. Neither can a company avoid the prohibition on loans by giving a guarantee or indemnity or by providing security in connection with a loan made by a third party to a director.

There are exceptions to this general prohibition, but they are minor (see section 9.7.6 below).

The exact rules are very complex. What follows is general guidance only; if there is any doubt in your own circumstances, the recommendation is: seek professional advice.

9.7.2 WHAT IS A LOAN?

The expression 'loan' is not defined in the *Companies Act 1985*. However, it was interpreted in a case brought under the *Companies Act 1948*, where it was held that the definition of a 'loan' was a *sum of money lent for a time to be returned in money or money's worth* (*Champagne Perrier – Jouet S.A. v H.H. Finch Ltd* {7}), and this is very close to the man-in-the-street's definition.

9.7.3 FURTHER RESTRICTIONS ON PUBLIC COMPANIES

There is a distinction in law between what is termed 'relevant' and 'non-relevant' companies. A 'relevant' company is either a public company or a company that belongs to a group which contains a public company. All other companies are 'non-relevant' companies.

Relevant companies are subject to more stringent requirements than non-relevant companies. Relevant companies must not:

● make (or take part in an arrangement to make) a loan, or a quasi-loan, to a director or a person connected with a director; *or*

● enter into a credit transaction as creditor for a director or a person connected with a director; *or*

● enter into any guarantee or provide any security in connection with a loan, quasi-loan or credit transaction for a director or a person connected with a director; *or*

● enter into any guarantee or provide any security to a person who has made a loan to a director.

Furthermore, although there is an exception in respect of small loans (see section 9.7.6), this exception does not apply to loans from relevant companies to a director's connected person. Nor does it apply to guarantees, etc. given by public companies of the liabilities of directors or their connected persons.

9.7.4 'QUASI-LOANS'

A 'quasi-loan' is an arrangement under which the company meets some of a director's financial obligations on the understanding that the director will reimburse the company later. The value of a quasi-loan is the amount, or maximum amount, that the person receiving it is liable to reimburse. Companies may not, as a general principle, make quasi-loans to directors or to connected persons nor enter into any guarantee nor provide security in connection with such quasi-loans.

A common example of a quasi-loan arises where a director uses a company credit card to buy personal goods, and he does so on the understanding that the company will settle the liability and he will reimburse the company at a later date. The law treats a quasi-loan as a transaction in which a director is interested, and therefore the director must disclose his interest to the board. This applies to directors of both public and private companies.

Where a public company is a member of a group, it is not prohibited either from making a loan or quasi-loan to another member of that group or from entering into a guarantee or providing security for any such quasi-loan, by reason only that a director of one of the group companies is associated with another group company.

Various ways of indirectly achieving a company loan, etc. are also prohibited. For example, it might be thought that a director could just take out a loan from his bank and then subsequently the company could purchase the bank's rights under the loan. Or, say, a director's father might guarantee a bank loan to the director and subsequently the company could arrange with the father and the bank for the father to be released from the guarantee and for the company to assume the associated liability. But companies cannot arrange to have assigned to them, or to assume responsibility for, any rights or obligations or liabilities under loans or quasi-loans or credit transactions where the transaction concerned would have been unlawful for the company to enter into.

9.7.5 'CREDIT TRANSACTIONS'

A 'credit transaction' is any transaction where a creditor:

- supplies any goods or sells any land under a hire purchase agreement; *or*

- leases or hires any land or goods in return for periodical payments; *or*

- disposes of land, or supplies goods or services (basically, anything other than goods or land) on the understanding that the payment is to be deferred.

Directors of private companies are not affected by the rules regarding credit transactions.

A public company can enter into credit transactions with a director only if the total amount of such transactions does not exceed £10,000 and is prohibited from entering into a credit transaction for the benefit of its directors, its holding company's directors or a 'connected' person in excess of this amount. The value of this type of transaction is the price that could usually be obtained for the goods, land or services that the transaction relates to if they had been supplied in the ordinary course of the company's business and on the same terms (apart from price). If the value of the transaction cannot be ascertained, then it will be assumed to be in excess of £100,000, and the procedures for a 'substantial property transaction' will need to be followed (see section 9.6 above).

The only circumstances in which a public company may enter into credit transactions with a director for *any* amount are where the value of, and the terms of, the credit transaction offered by the company to the director are no more favourable than the value and terms the company would have offered to someone of the same financial standing unconnected with the company, and the transaction is in the ordinary course of business.

9.7.6 EXCEPTIONS

The exceptions to the above general prohibitions may be summarised as follows:

a) Loans for any purpose

A company may make a loan to a director provided the total of such transactions does not exceed £5,000. Any loans to 'connected persons' have also to be taken into account in determining whether a director is within this limit.

Money-lending companies are permitted to make or guarantee loans or quasi-loans for any purpose provided that the loan, quasi-loan or guarantee is made in the ordinary course of business and the terms are no more favourable than those the company might reasonably offer to persons of the same financial standing but unconnected with the company. But if the money-lending company is a relevant company and is not a banking company, it may not enter into any transaction if the aggregate of the amounts exceeds £100,000.

b) Loans for house purchase

Any money-lending company including a banking company is permitted to make or guarantee loans of up to £100,000 for the purchase or improvement of a director's only or main residence if the company ordinarily makes loans for this purpose to its employees on no less favourable terms.

c) Short-term quasi-loans

As noted above, companies may not, as a general principle, make quasi-loans to directors or to connected persons nor enter into any guarantee nor provide security in connection with such quasi-loans. The only exception is when a quasi-loan is made to a director (but not to a connected person) on terms that it must be reimbursed within two months of its being incurred and that the amount outstanding on all quasi-loans to that director at any time does not exceed £5,000. The total amount of quasi-loans will include such loans made by the company or by any of its subsidiaries to the director concerned, or, if the director is also a director of the company's holding company, by any fellow subsidiary.

d) Minor and business credit transactions

Relevant companies are not permitted to enter into credit transactions for the benefit of directors or connected persons nor to enter into any guarantee or provide security in connection with any such transactions unless:

- The aggregate of the amounts owing by any one director and/or the persons connected with that director is no more than £10,000; or

- The transaction has been made in the ordinary course of the company's business and its terms are no more favourable than those which the company might reasonably offer to persons of the same financial standing but unconnected with the company.

e) Transactions for the purposes of the company

Companies are permitted to make a loan or guarantee a loan for the purposes of providing a director with funds to meet expenditure incurred or to be incurred by him for the purposes of the company or to enable the director properly to perform his duties. Similarly, the use by a director of a company credit card exclusively for company business would not constitute a quasi-loan. However, the transaction must be given prior approval by the company in general meeting, or made on the condition that, unless so approved at or before the next AGM, the liability will be discharged within six months of the AGM.

Relevant companies may enter into transactions totalling no more than £20,000 in relation to each director for this purpose. Transactions with persons connected with the director are aggregated for the purpose of determining whether £20,000 is exceeded.

f) Transactions within a group of companies

The prohibition on relevant companies making, guaranteeing or providing security for loans and quasi-loans to persons connected with a director does not prevent a relevant company doing these things to, or for the benefit of, a company in the same group by reason only that a director or one member of the group is associated with another member.

Any of the prohibited transactions undertaken by a company in favour of its holding company are excepted from the general prohibition (accordingly a holding company is not to be treated as a shadow director for this purpose).

Table 9.2 summarises the exceptions to the general prohibition on loans and similar transactions to directors.

9.7.7 LIMITS ON TRANSACTIONS

The limits cited above apply to individual directors, not to the company. Each amount is defined to embrace all the transactions permitted by the relevant exception. For example, it is the total of all transactions entered into for a director of a relevant company for the purposes of the company that must not exceed £20,000, not each individual transaction within a larger total. Where relevant, the indebtedness of connected persons is also included

Table 9.2 *Permitted loans and other credit transactions*

Exemption	Description	Conditions
Group transactions	Loans, quasi-loans and provision of guarantees or security for loans between companies within a group	Permitted
Directors' expenses	Provision of funds in advance to meet expenditure the director has incurred or is about to incur in the normal conduct of his duties	Permitted, provided: (i) prior approval is obtained from members in general meeting, *or* (ii) any money advanced does not exceed £20,000 (relevant companies only).
Transactions in the 'normal' course of business	Loans, quasi-loans and provision of guarantees where such activities are within the normal course of the company's business	Permitted, provided: (i) the terms and the amount offered are not more favourable than those which would be offered to a person of similar standing in the normal course of business, *and* (ii) the amount concerned does not exceed £100,000 (relevant companies only).
Loans to fund purchase of and/or improvements to a director's main residence	Loans, quasi-loans and provision of guarantees where such activities are within the normal course of the company's business	Permitted, provided: (i) the aggregate amount of the loan does not exceed £100,000, *and* (ii) such loans are available to employees and the terms offered are not more favourable
Short-term quasi-loans	An arrangement where the company pays an amount for the director pending reimbursement (e.g. use of a company credit card where the director reimburses 'personal' expenditure)	Permitted, provided: (i) the company is reimbursed within 2 months of the expenditure being incurred, *and* (ii) the aggregate amount does not exceed £5,000.

Table 9.2 *Permitted loans and other credit transactions (continued)*

Exemption	Description	Conditions
Loans of small amounts	Loans of an amount not exceeding £5,000 for any purpose	Permitted Permitted in the case of private companies.
Minor and ordinary business transactions	Entering into a credit transaction or providing a guarantee for such a transaction where the goods or services are supplied to the director	Permitted in the case of public companies provided the aggregate amount does not exceed £10,000. Where the credit transaction is in the normal course of business and the terms and level of credit offered are not more favourable than would be offered to a person in the normal course of business, there is no upper limit.

for determining whether a particular sum falls within the limit. Where a director is a director of a holding company and the director, or persons connected with him or her, enters into a transaction with a subsidiary, the value of the transaction with the subsidiary is added to transactions with the holding company for the purposes of the prohibitions and relevant exceptions.

9.7.8 DISCLOSURE OF TRANSACTIONS WITH DIRECTORS

The *Companies Act 1985* requires that the notes to a company's accounts must disclose details of the following transactions entered into by the company or any of its subsidiaries:

- loans and similar transactions (including guarantees) for the benefit of directors and connected persons mentioned above;

- any agreement to enter into any of the above transactions for the benefit of a director and/or persons connected with that director;

- any other transaction or arrangement with the company in which a director has, directly or indirectly, a material interest.

These disclosure requirements apply to all persons who at any time during the period covered by the accounts were directors of the company producing the accounts or directors of any holding company it may have. Disclosure is required even if the transaction or arrangement was entered into at a time when they were not directors.

The only exceptions to the disclosure requirements are:

- credit transactions and related arrangements where the total involved (less any repayments) did not, at any time of the financial year, exceed an aggregate of £5,000 for any one director and the persons connected with that director;

- transactions and arrangements where any one director has a direct or indirect material interest such that the aggregate value of all such transactions and arrangements in which the director had a material interest did not at any time during the financial period exceed £5,000 or 1% of net assets of the company if that is less than £5,000, except that, whatever the value of the net assets, there is no requirement to make disclosure where the aggregate value is less than £1,000. For the purpose of these limits transactions or arrangements made in previous financial years (after deducting repayments) must be taken into account.

The disclosure requirements do not apply in relation to:

- the accounts of banking companies and their holding companies in relation to loans and similar transactions for the benefit of directors and connected persons – different provisions apply;

- transactions and arrangements between one company and another company in which a director of the first company or of its subsidiary or holding company is interested only by virtue of his being a director of that other company;

- a contract of service between a company and one of its directors or one of its holding company's directors or a contract of service between one of the company's directors and a subsidiary of the company.

9.7.9 DISCLOSURE OF TRANSACTIONS WITH OTHER OFFICERS OF THE COMPANY

Disclosure must be made in the accounts of loans and similar transactions entered into by the company or any of its subsidiaries for the benefit of officers of the company who are not directors.

Details must be disclosed of the aggregate amounts outstanding, if more than £2,500, at the end of the period as in the case of directors, and the number of officers for whose benefit the transactions within each of the categories were made. The provisions do not apply in relation to a transaction entered into by a banking company for any of its officers or for any of the officers of its holding company. Different requirements apply to banking companies.

9.7.10 WHAT HAPPENS IF A DIRECTOR BREAKS THE RULES ABOUT LOANS, QUASI-LOANS AND CREDIT TRANSACTIONS?

There may be serious consequences. First, the transaction is voidable unless it is no longer possible for the cash or property involved to be restored to the company or a third party would be damaged.

Secondly, the director and connected person who benefits from the transaction will be liable to account to the company for any gain made as a result and to indemnify the company for any loss or damage it may suffer. In addition, any director who authorised the illegal transaction, as well as the director in whose favour the illegal loan or other transaction was made, may be liable to account to the company for any gain made and to indemnify the company against its loss. Liability of a director who authorised the transaction may be avoided only if he can show that at the time the transaction was entered into he did not know the relevant circumstances constituting the contravention. A director of a public company may also incur criminal liability if he authorises or permits the company to enter into such a transaction knowing or having reasonable cause to believe that the company was thereby committing an offence. Conviction on indictment carries with it a maximum prison sentence of two years and/or an unlimited fine. Summary conviction carries with it a maximum prison sentence of six months and/or a fine up to a maximum of £5,000. The company, too, will be guilty of an offence unless it did not know the relevant circumstances.

9.8 CAPITAL AND THE MAINTENANCE OF CAPITAL

The capital of a business is the amount that would be due, on winding up, to its proprietors after the lawful claims of all the other parties associated with the business have been met. The doctrine of maintenance of capital is very important for limited companies. The basic principle is to protect shareholders and creditors by ensuring that capital provided to the company cannot be dissipated or extracted except by trading or other business activities. A company must neither return to shareholders any part of the paid up capital as if it were a distribution of profits, nor arbitrarily diminish the fund from which creditors legitimately expect to be paid. If a company issues shares, for example, the board must ensure that the company obtains a proper consideration for them – at least nominal value – and cannot hand back any of the fund so acquired of its members except by a repayment of capital permitted by law.

A company and its directors must also make a clear distinction between what funds are distributable and what are not. This distinction underlies many of the legal provisions relating to a company's capital. Directors may be held liable to the company if it appears that they have paid a dividend without having sufficient realised reserves to do so (see section 13.5.3).

9.8.1 MINIMUM CAPITAL

To be a public company, a company must have an allotted share capital with a nominal value of at least £50,000 paid up to at least 25% plus any premium related to the shares issued. If the net assets of a public company fall to one-half or less of the amount of its called-up share capital, the directors must, not later than 28 days after the fact becomes known to a director, duly convene an extraordinary general meeting of the company to consider what to do, and such meeting must be held within 56 days after the day on which the fact becomes known to the directors.

9.8.2 PAYMENT FOR SHARES IN COMPANIES

Any shares allotted by a company must be paid up (in respect of the nominal value and the premium) in money or money's worth (which can include goodwill and know-how). In the case of a public company there are some restrictions as to what counts as a non-cash consideration.

It is lawful for a company, if authorised by the company's Articles, to buy its own shares or to issue redeemable ordinary shares. The *Companies Act 1985* lays down an extensive code covering the exercise of these rights to protect creditors and shareholders. Private companies generally have wider powers to purchase their own shares or to issue redeemable shares than public companies. In particular, a private company may use capital to redeem or purchase its own shares to the extent that it cannot do so out of distributable profits or the proceeds of a new issue. However, this procedure is subject to a number of procedural requirements, principally to safeguard creditors. The directors must first make a statutory declaration as to the company's solvency and viability over the coming year, confirmed by reference to reports from the auditors. The members must then approve the scheme by special resolution (the shares which are to be redeemed or purchased under the resolution may not be voted). Directors who have signed the statutory declaration can be liable personally if the company is wound up within a year of the purchase of its own shares. It is an offence (punishable by two years' imprisonment or an unlimited fine or both on indictment) for directors to make the statutory declaration without having reasonable grounds for the opinion expressed in it.

The power to acquire its own equity is of particular value to a private company by providing a way of buying out a shareholder whether on retirement or because of dissatisfaction or a dispute. There are provisions in the *Income and Corporation Taxes Act 1988* which alleviate some of the adverse tax consequences of such a purchase of unquoted shares of trading companies.

9.9 INDEMNIFICATION OF DIRECTORS, EXEMPTION FROM LIABILITY AND RELIEF

The law, quite properly, does not make it easy for directors to be indemnified by their company if they have failed in any duty owed to it. Not all breaches of duty by a director may be ratified by an ordinary resolution of the members (see section 8.9). A company cannot make an agreement with its directors or any other officer (including its auditors) to indemnify them against, or exempt them from, any liability arising from any negligence, default, breach of duty or breach of trust in relation to the company. Any provision purporting to have this effect, whether in the Articles or in any contract with the company, is void. A company may make a prior agreement to indemnify a director against any liability to a third party arising from his directorship only if the breach of the duty to the third party is not, at the same time, a breach of the director's duty to the company. A company may, however, make an agreement to indemnify a director for the costs of a successful defence of a civil or criminal action against him.

A company may also purchase and maintain insurance for a director against liability for negligence, default, breach of duty or breach of trust in relation to the company (see section 12.16).

Even if a director is found in breach of duty or trust, he may escape personal liability if the Court so decides. Relief can be granted only if the Court finds that:

- the director has acted honestly; *and*
- the director has acted reasonably; *and*
- having regard to all the circumstances, he ought fairly to be excused.

It is important to note that *all* the conditions must be satisfied; failure on any one count will disqualify the director for relief. For example, a director will not obtain relief if he acts honestly but fails to obtain legal advice where a reasonable person would have done so. Relief is less likely to be granted if the director concerned receives substantial remuneration. In any event relief is available only in respect of actions brought by or on behalf of the company against its directors for breach of duty to the company and in respect of penal proceedings for the enforcement of the *Companies Acts*.

9.10 SUMMARY

1. Due and proper disclosure of required information to the Registrar of Companies is of major importance.

2. The company's letterheads and other literature must be correct.

3. Maintaining and producing proper company accounts goes to the heart of board responsibility.

4. To deal with the company of which you are a director, and in particular to take loans from the company, is a matter fraught with danger. Your company cannot avoid the general prohibition on loans by giving a guarantee or indemnity, or by providing security, in connection with a loan a third party makes to you. Any loans to 'connected persons' have also to be taken into account in determining whether you are within the limits. Directors should seek external professional advice before taking a loan, quasi-loan or credit facility from the company.

5. There are strict disclosure requirements relating to loans and similar transactions.

6. A director should:

a) Always bear in mind that the interests of the company are not necessarily the same as his personal interests; if there is a difference, the company's interests have priority.

b) Identify problem situations when or before they become too pressing, and take professional advice as soon as it is thought help may be needed, not after the event.

c) Be disciplined when taking decisions – in particular, consider all the options, think whose interests must be considered, think how the decision may be explained if the need arises, and record the reasons why a decision was taken.

d) Consider taking out the appropriate directors' and officers' indemnity insurance.

Chapter 10

Directors, Employees and Other Parties

10.1 OVERVIEW

There are a number of areas, broadly concerning stakeholders affected by the processes or results of the company's operations, where legislation imposes sanctions if statutory requirements are infringed. Directors have an indirect duty. The company is required to act in a particular way for the benefit of third parties or in the general public interest and an obligation is placed on the directors to ensure that it does so. They will be personally liable for an offence committed by the company not only if they initiated or participated in the commission of the offence but also where their negligence led to the commission by the company.

Statutes frequently refer to a wide range of employees of the company, but in practice the intention is to hold **directors** personally liable for the actions of the company,

> . . .to fix with criminal liability only those who are in a position of real authority, the decision-makers within the company who have both the power and responsibility to decide corporate strategy. It is to catch those responsible for putting proper procedures in place; it is not meant to strike at underlings.

(Simon Brown J, *R v Boal* {32})

There are many statutes which apply to all companies and many other sector-specific statutes. In addition there are myriad regulations, made by government under powers in various Acts, which are as legally binding on companies and directors as the main Act from which they sprang. However, there are five main areas where statute has imposed obligations on the company and, both directly and indirectly, on directors. These are the areas of:

a) employee rights;

b) health and safety;

c) customer rights;

d) human rights;

e) the environment.

10.2 DUTIES TO EMPLOYEES

10.2.1 INTRODUCTION

The majority of directors and managers recognise that providing security and good working conditions to employees makes sound commercial sense in that it promotes harmonious employee relations and increased productivity. Many companies have adopted staff motivation and training schemes – for example, 'Investors in People' and 'Building Better Business' – in recognition of the benefits such initiatives provide to the company. In addition, however, employment protection legislation extends the rights of employees far beyond the bounds of the contractual relationship by which employees sell their labour to companies in exchange for wages and other benefits. A substantial and complex body of law confers an array of rights and obligations.

Broadly, directors must act in the best interests of the company in their treatment of employees. Specifically, this means that:

a) an employment contract must be provided to each employee and the terms of the contract must be observed (section 10.2.3);

b) there must be no discrimination at work, neither sexual, racial nor on grounds of disability (section 10.2.6);

c) employees' statutory rights must be observed (see sections 10.2.4, 10.2.5 and 10.2.8);

d) companies must ensure that the place of work and methods of work are safe and healthy (section 10.3);

e) when an undertaking is transferred to a new owner, employee rights must be protected (section 10.2.7);

f) appropriate insurance cover must be in place (section 10.3.5);

g) illegal immigrants must not be employed (section 10.3.6);

h) employees must be of a legal age (section 10.3.7).

A breach of the legislative requirements in these areas may result in claims against the company which may result in damages and also injure the company's reputation. An aggrieved employee may claim against the company and also the director if there is negligence on the part of the director against the employee. In addition, where the directors are considered by the shareholders to have acted in a negligent manner in breaching the requirements of employment legislation, the company may make a claim against them for failure to act in the best interests of the company and to attend diligently to its affairs. The claim will be for the amount of any damages imposed on the company for the breach.

Furthermore, in common law 'vicarious liability' applies to companies if employees in the course of their work injure third parties, which means that the company may be liable for such acts even if the directors did not know that the acts had occurred.

The board of directors needs therefore to address employee rights and associated matters, communicate the company's policy and procedures to employees, and monitor the application of the policy and procedures. This is likely to be an easier task for directors of large companies, who may have lawyers and personnel specialists in-house, than for directors of smaller companies who are unlikely to have such resources within the company. Directors of small companies should consult outside specialists, such as the

Advisory, Conciliation and Arbitration Service (ACAS) and the Department of Employment Advisory Service.

This section touches only briefly on employment rights, and even the best informed director would be wise to act in this area only after taking advice from experts within or outside the company.

10.2.2 THE DUTY TO EMPLOYEES

Company directors are under a legal duty to have regard to the interests of their employees (*Companies Act 1985* s.309). This obligation is particularly important when a business is sold or closed down. In such an event the directors are permitted, if the Articles of Association give them the power, to make provisions for employees out of distributable profits even where it might be considered counter to the interest of the company (s.719 *Companies Act 1985*).

Probably this means that directors must consider the interests of employees in judging what is in the best interests of the company, not that they must consider the interests of employees in such a way that, where they think it appropriate, they must override the interests of the company. The duty is seen as an extension to the fiduciary duties owed by directors to the company and is therefore enforceable only by the company and not by the employees.

10.2.3 CONTRACTS OF EMPLOYMENT

The *Employment Rights Act 1996* requires employers to provide a written statement of the basic terms and conditions of employment to all employees who will be working for eight or more hours a week and be employed for more than a month. There are minimum statutory requirements for notice of termination, statutory sick pay, maternity pay and redundancy payments, etc. The statement of basic terms must include details of the company's disciplinary and grievance procedures.

Employment contracts of some employees – directors, for example – normally contain terms in excess of the statutory minimum. But care must be taken since such provisions generally cut both ways, increasing both the employee's benefits and the restrictions on him. Section 7.3.3 discusses directors' employment contracts, particularly with regard to restrictive covenants, such as prohibiting the director from working for competitors for a given period of time.

The directors have a duty to ensure that terms in the contract are observed and adhered to by the company.

It is unlawful to change the terms of an employment contract without the consent of the employee; it cannot be imposed unilaterally by the employer. If directors were to terminate the employee's contract and offer a new contract with new terms, they would be in breach of the employee's existing contract. The likely result would be a claim for damages for wrongful or unfair dismissal. However, a change, if it is not in breach of the law, can be made at any time if both parties agree. A written statement incorporating full details of the change must be supplied to each employee concerned within a month of the change (although failing to do this will not necessarily invalidate the change).

10.2.4 DISMISSAL

Directors may dismiss an employee from working for the company where there is a valid and sufficient reason to cause dismissal. But the *Employment Rights Act 1996* gives employees the right not to be dismissed 'unfairly'.

An employer may dismiss an employee for reasons relating to capability, qualifications, conduct, redundancy, a statutory requirement, or any other substantial reason. In practice the most common reason for dismissal is the employee's conduct, and for dismissal to be considered fair the conduct must be sufficient to warrant dismissal. For example, unauthorised use of a restricted computer file was considered gross misconduct and the resulting dismissal was deemed to have been fair (see *Denco Ltd v Joinson*{10}).

However, even where there is a valid reason for dismissing an employee, the directors must be careful to ensure that no inappropriate or unreasonable action is taken in the period leading up to dismissal. For example, where an employee's work performance has been consistently poor, he must be made aware of the problem and be given an opportunity to improve before dismissal is considered; thereafter, disciplinary procedures should be reasonable and employees should be allowed rights of hearing and representation.

In practice, in order to ensure that each case is treated consistently, it is advisable for directors to implement a formal disciplinary procedure with clear rules and steps to be taken. Adherence to such a procedure will greatly help the defence against a claim of unfair dismissal.

An employee (including a director) who has been employed for at least one year and considers himself to have been unfairly dismissed may apply to an Employment Tribunal for adjudication. The complainant is subject only to his own costs if he loses his case (unlike the County Court or the High Court). The Tribunal may order a basic award (linked to age and number of years employed) plus compensation (up to £50,000) or reinstatement, though the latter is rare.

There are a number of circumstances where dismissal is automatically unfair. For example, dismissal will be unfair if:

a) it is consequent upon a refusal to permit return from maternity leave;

b) it occurs because the employee attempts to assert a statutory employment right;

c) it occurs as a result of the employee taking action on health and safety grounds in a situation of imminent danger;

d) it follows a transfer of undertaking, except where it could not be avoided for reasons of economic, technical or organisational change;

e) it occurs because the employee refuses to work on Sundays;

f) it occurs due to membership or non-membership of a trade union;

g) it results from an employee 'blowing the whistle', in good faith and for no personal gain, on wrongdoing at work. A criminal offence, failure to comply with a legal obligation, a miscarriage of justice, health and safety hazards, a risk to the environment, and deliberate concealment of any of these matters, are examples of 'wrongdoing'. Any 'gagging clause' in an employment contract is unenforceable. It is wise to establish and communicate to employees the procedure to follow and channels of communication through which to make authorised disclosures;

h) it is a case of 'constructive' dismissal where, although the employee terminated the employment contract, the employer allegedly gave him no choice but to do so.

In addition to a claim for unfair dismissal, an employee may also pursue a civil claim for *wrongful dismissal* in the Courts where, for example, the employer terminated the employee's contract with insufficient notice or payment in lieu of notice.

10.2.5 REDUNDANCY

Employees may be treated as redundant only if work has ceased or diminished or is expected to cease or diminish. To qualify for redundancy payments an employee must have been employed for at least two years. He waives the right if he refuses suitable alternative employment.

Where an employer proposes to dismiss more than 20 employees within a period of 90 days or less, the employer must consult with appropriate representatives of the employees concerned.

The amount payable for redundancy is calculated by multiplying a week's average wage (with a ceiling of £230) by a figure reckoned by relating age to years in employment. The statutory ceiling is presently £6,900. However, in many cases employers will pay above this sum in order to induce voluntary redundancy.

10.2.6 DISCRIMINATION

Discrimination, victimisation and harassment, direct or indirect, against any person on the grounds of sex, race, disability or 'spent' convictions is unlawful. At the time of writing, discrimination on the ground of age is under review by the Department for Education and Employment.

Where an aggrieved employee considers he has been treated in a discriminatory manner, he is entitled, for a period of up to three months after the alleged discriminatory event, to take his case to an Employment Tribunal for consideration.

Directors must be aware of the requirements of the following legislation to avoid any employee claims of discrimination: the *Equal Pay Act 1970*, the *Rehabilitation of Offenders Act 1974*, the *Sex Discrimination Act 1975*, the *Race Relations Act 1976*, the *Employment Act 1990*, and the *Disability Discrimination Act 1995*.

In addition, directors should be aware of the following statutory bodies:

a) The Equal Opportunities Commission has the power to seek out information and to enforce the provisions of the *Sex Discrimination Act 1975*.

b) The Commission for Racial Equality has the authority to direct formal investigations into race relations, issue non-discrimination notices, apply for an injunction for failure to comply, and take action in connection with discriminatory advertising.

c) The Disability Rights Commission is able to enforce the provisions of the *Disability Discrimination Act 1995* and has powers similar to the other two Commissions.

Prudent directors will ensure that their companies have formal policies addressing issues of discrimination so as to ensure that an employee or prospective employee cannot be considered to have been treated in a different manner to that in which any other employee is treated. Aggrieved employees should be clear about how to make a complaint and the manner in which it will be dealt with. A formal policy on discrimination communicated to employees will probably also serve as a deterrent against employees practising discrimination in the workplace. The Commissions publish relevant codes of practice, which may serve as a basis for a company's policy on discrimination.

10.2.7 TRANSFER OF UNDERTAKINGS AND EMPLOYMENT RIGHTS

When a business or part of a business is acquired by another company, employees enjoy a degree of protection under the *Transfer of Undertakings Regulations 1987*.

The directors must ensure that employees are provided with details of the transfer, the reasons for it and the implications for the employees (for instance, relocation details). Directors must also ensure that the employees' rights are protected as follows:

a) by ensuring that the terms and conditions of employment with the new employer are the same as they were with the old (with the exception of pension scheme rights);

b) by ensuring that there are no dismissals as a result of the transfer except where they can be proven necessary on technical, economic or organisational grounds;

c) by notifying the employees' trade union or other representative about the transfer;

d) by ensuring that any existing trade union is recognised by the new employer.

Failure to observe these conditions is likely to lead to a claim of unfair dismissal.

10.2.8 OTHER STATUTORY RIGHTS

There are many other statutes primarily designed to protect employees' rights. Directors must ensure that all employees' contracts of employment and the company's internal procedures, such as the records of hours worked by each employee and provisions for taking rest breaks, comply with regulations made under these statutes.

For example:

a) The *National Minimum Wage Regulations 1999* require employers to pay not less than the minimum wage to all workers with contracts of employment, as well as some temporary workers.

b) *Statutory maternity rights.* Dismissal of a woman for a reason connected with her pregnancy would normally be considered unfair. Pregnant women are entitled, among other things, to:

- time off for ante-natal care;

- protection from dismissal on maternity-related grounds;

- return to work after their maternity absence;

- maternity leave of 18 weeks regardless of length of service and extended maternity leave of up to 50 weeks after one year's employment. During this time the employees' non-wage contractual benefits must be maintained;

- maternity benefit.

c) *Working Time Regulations 1998.* Most categories of employees have the right, amongst other things, to work on average (over a reference period of 17 weeks) no more than 48 hours per week. By written agreement individuals may opt out of the 48-hour week. Most directors will probably be expected 'voluntarily' to sign such an agreement! There are additional rights to do with rest breaks and paid annual leave.

d) *Statutory sick pay.* Eligible employees are entitled to receive statutory sick pay for periods of absence due to sickness exceeding 3 days and up to 28 weeks. The company can normally recover a part of the sick pay paid by deducting it from its National Insurance contributions.

e) *Statutory notice periods.* All employees are entitled to a minimum period of notice, specified in the employment contract, which increases according to the employee's length of service.

10.2.9 DATA PROTECTION

The *Data Protection Act 1998*, which came into force on 1 March 2000, both limited the activities of employers in holding information concerning their employees and gave rights to employees to know about information relating to them held by an employer.

The main points of the Act are:

- Personal data should be processed in accordance with the rights of employees.

- Employees have the right to
  - know why the data are being collected, for what purpose, and to whom they will be disclosed;
  - inspect the files and see all data about them;
  - know the identity of any third-party sources;
  - be told the reasons behind any decision based on the data – the logic behind the decision-making.

- Protection is extended to paper records as well as computer records.

- 'Data' covers expressions of opinion.

- Employers may not process 'sensitive personal data', e.g. data concerning ethnic or racial origins, political opinions, religious beliefs, trade union membership, physical or mental health and data relating to offences.

Contravention is a criminal offence punishable by a fine; in addition the Courts have the power to order compensation by way of damages.

10.2.10 STAKEHOLDER PENSIONS

Stakeholder pension schemes are low-cost pensions meant for people who do not have the appropriate pension options available to save for their retirement. In particular, this means people who cannot join an occupational pension scheme.

The *Welfare Reform and Pensions Act 1999* obliges many employers to offer their employees access to a stakeholder pension scheme. Directors should check if their companies must provide access to a stakeholder pension, and then see which employees the access requirement applies to.

The conditions for being exempt are:

- The company employs fewer than five people (including directors). If there are five or more employees, and fewer than five of them meet the conditions to have access to a stakeholder pension scheme, the company must provide these (four or fewer) employees with access to a stakeholder pension scheme.

- The company offers an occupational pension scheme.

- The company offers employees access to a personal pension scheme which meets the following conditions:

  - it is available to all employees who should have access to a stakeholder pension scheme (except those under 18);

  - the company contributes an amount equal to at least 3% of the employee's basic pay to the personal pension;

  - the scheme has no penalties for members who stop contributing or who transfer their pension.

Directors should check with the providers of existing occupational or group personal pension schemes whether these schemes meet the conditions for being exempt.

However, even exempt employers can still give their employees access to a stakeholder pensions scheme if they want to. On the other hand, employees do not have to join the pension scheme, and the employer does not have to make contributions to employees' stakeholder pensions if he does not wish to.

Companies do not have to provide access to a stakeholder pension scheme for any employee:

- who has worked for the company for less than three months in a row;

- who is a member of the company's occupational pension scheme;

- who cannot join the occupational scheme because they are under 18 or they are within five years of the scheme's normal pension age;

- who could have joined the company occupational pension scheme but decided not to;

- whose earnings have not reached the National Insurance lower earnings limit for at least three months in a row; or

- who cannot join a stakeholder pension scheme because of Inland Revenue restrictions (for example, the employee does not normally live in the UK).

Directors, unless their company is exempt, must arrange access to a stakeholder pension scheme for those employees who enjoy access rights. Each such employee can then decide whether to join the scheme or not. Employees must have been given access to a stakeholder pension scheme no later than 8 October 2001.

Directors need to take the following steps:

- Consult your qualifying employees and any organisations that represent them (such as trade unions and staff associations).

- Choose a registered stakeholder pension scheme or schemes from the list of registered pension schemes held by the Occupational Pensions Regulatory Authority (Opra).

- Discuss your choice of scheme (or schemes) with those of your employees who qualify for access to the stakeholder pension scheme, and provide them with sufficient information so that they can decide whether to sign up to the designated stakeholder pension scheme. The scheme provider may give you their own literature or leaflets for you to pass on to your employees. The law states that the designated scheme provider must be given 'reasonable access' to employees, perhaps by visiting the workplace.

- Make the final decision about which scheme to designate.

  Directors should take care when giving employees help and extra information about the benefits of saving for their retirement. Directors must **not** advise employees; for example, a director must not tell employees that they should or should not sign up for a stakeholder pension, or that they must join the designated scheme. There may be another pension option that suits the individual better. The choice is up to the individual. The Financial Services Authority strictly controls who can give financial advice, and what advice they can give.

- Arrange to deduct contributions from employees' pay for those who have chosen to pay into the designated stakeholder pension scheme.

- Send employee contributions (and any employer contributions) to the stakeholder pension scheme provider within the given time limits.

- Record the payments you make to the stakeholder pension scheme provider.

A stakeholder pension scheme cannot charge more than 1% a year on the value of each member's funds, will accept contributions of as little as £20, will accept transfers into, or out of, the scheme without imposing any extra charge, and will either have trustees or be run by scheme managers authorised by the Financial Services Authority.

Directors should set up systems which ensure that, for example, if the company has taken on a fifth employee after 8 July 2001, the company becomes exempt, the company or Opra changes the designated stakeholder pension scheme, the correct procedures are complied with.

Directors need to make sure that the company payroll system can cope with changes or a stop in contributions and that the employee's payment has been calculated correctly and sent to the scheme provider.

If Opra finds that an employer who is not exempt is not offering employees access to a stakeholder pension scheme, it will make the employer aware of their legal responsibilities and has the power to impose penalties (up to a maximum fine of £50,000) on employers who deliberately ignore their responsibility. Opra may fine companies that do not set up a record of the payments made, keep the record up to date and send the record to the scheme provider. Stakeholder pension scheme providers must check that all the payments they receive are on time and for the agreed amount, and must report to Opra late payments, payments that are not made or reduced payments that are not explained. Opra will then investigate why the scheme provider did not receive the agreed payment. Companies that make late or incorrect payments are liable to a fine.

10.3 HEALTH AND SAFETY AT WORK

Employers have a common law duty to ensure the safety of their employees. Further, the *Health and Safety at Work etc. Act 1974* and regulations made under this Act lay upon all employers a general duty to employees to ensure their safety and health at work.

Health and Safety inspectors have powers under the Act to enter and inspect premises and to bring prosecutions. They can issue prohibition notices to stop dangerous practices, with immediate effect. They can seize, render harmless or destroy any article or substance that may cause imminent danger or serious personal injury.

Directors have a responsibility to ensure that the company's insurance policy covers the cost of civil penalties under the Act and indemnifies the company against the costs of a successful defence of a criminal charge.

10.3.1 GENERAL DUTY

In general terms, the Act requires all employers to provide employees with safe conditions of work and to enable them to perform their work safely. The directors, as the directing mind of the company, must ensure that these statutory duties are observed by the company. Virtually every aspect of the workplace which has an effect on the welfare of employees – the physical design of the workplace, the provision of safety appliances, training and instructions on the use of equipment, procedures for the storage of hazardous substances, and the provision of welfare facilities – is covered by the Act.

Directors should be aware of at least the following considerations:

a) A company cannot delegate responsibility for the health and safety of its employees to other people.

b) Employers must consult their employees on specified health and safety matters either directly with employees, via 'employee elected represent- atives', or via 'safety representatives' appointed by a recognised trade union. These representatives must be given appropriate training, paid time off and facilities to enable them to carry out their functions.

c) Companies have an obligation to ensure the health and safety of all those involved in the construction, repair, maintenance and cleaning of premises.

d) Employers must provide physical safety devices in certain circumstances. Instructions or a code of practice alone would not be considered sufficient.

e) Employers are required to conduct and record in writing (where there are five or more employees) a specific assessment of risks relating to fire and the arrangements that have been made in terms of fire exits, fire fighting and fire detection equipment and procedures for evacuation.

f) Lifting equipment must be properly maintained and it must be operated properly in terms of safe and suitable working loads. Directors need therefore to ensure that relevant work tasks are assessed carefully.

g) If the safety of work equipment depends on the installation, then the equipment must be thoroughly inspected and checked before use.

h) Companies must ensure, as far as is practical, that third parties are not exposed to risks to their health and safety caused by negligence of an employee.

10.3.2 LIABILITY FOR HEALTH AND SAFETY BREACHES

It is most important that directors observe health and safety provisions on behalf of the company. A breach of duty in this respect may constitute a criminal offence and negligence in civil law. Directors may be prosecuted personally where they commissioned the offence or where it can be proven to be caused by their negligence.

Examples of situations in which both the company and its directors may be liable are:

a) Failure by junior managers to take reasonable precautions for the health and safety at work of employees, even where head office is not aware of the offending actions. This is illustrated in *R v Gateway Foodmarkets Limited* {34}, in which it was held that the company was liable for a breach of the Act where an employee died by falling down a lift shaft. The lift had not been adequately maintained. When the fault occurred, employees, without the knowledge of head office, repaired it themselves without calling in a lift engineer.

b) Corporate manslaughter, where it can be proven that a controlling officer had knowledge of the risks being taken which resulted in death.

10.3.3 HEALTH AND SAFETY POLICY

Directors should be aware that where there are five or more employees the company has a statutory obligation to prepare and review periodically a formal written statement of the company's health and safety policy. The policy must contain the following information:

a) A general statement of the company's policy on health and safety.

b) The name of the senior manager responsible for safety and details of how responsibility is allocated to individuals for particular aspects of health and safety.

c) A statement of practical arrangements and procedures for implementing the policy, such as fire prevention, evacuation, first aid, accident recording, maintenance of equipment and reporting faults, etc.

It is not enough merely to prepare this statement. Directors must ensure that arrangements are made to communicate the policy to employees by means of notice boards, posters, training, etc. and that activities are monitored on an ongoing basis to ensure that work practices comply with the policy.

10.3.4 RISK ASSESSMENT

Under Regulations made pursuant to the Act directors are required to conduct a formal assessment of the conditions and arrangements in the workplace to determine whether there are any risks to employees that need to be addressed by the health and safety policy. Arrangements for protective or preventative measures to reduce any risks identified by the assessment must be implemented. Failure to conduct a risk assessment is an offence.

The assessment of risk involves examining the workplace, considering and implementing appropriate precautions, identifying the need for safety equipment, identifying the need for training, writing a statement of safe working procedures, implementing safety measures and procedures, and controlling, monitoring and reviewing performance under the safety constraints.

Items that would typically be covered in the assessment include the following:

a) the physical characteristics of the workplace – for example, carpets, lighting, ventilation, heating, the layout of work areas, access routes and obstructions, etc;

b) fire fighting equipment and evacuation procedures;

c) first aid provisions and facilities;

d) arrangements for maintenance and servicing of equipment;

e) the smoking policy and arrangements for smokers;

f) arrangements for visitors to the premises;

g) procedures for the storage, transportation, use and disposal of hazardous substances.

Where five or more persons are employed, the findings of the risk assessment must be recorded in writing.

10.3.5 EMPLOYERS' LIABILITY INSURANCE

The *Employers' Liability (Compulsory Insurance) Act 1969*, as amended by later Regulations requires employers to effect insurance to cover employees for illness, bodily injury or disease caused during, or arising as a result of, their employment.

Typically, an employer would be covered for legal liability arising from:

a) negligence in failing to use reasonable care and skill in providing safe equipment, a safe system of work and a safe place of work;

b) breaches of the *Health & Safety at Work etc Act 1974*; and

c) employees' negligence causing injury to fellow employees.

It is a criminal offence not to take out insurance and display the policy in the work premises. The policy must be effected to indemnify the employer for a minimum of £5 million for a single occurrence. The insurer will cover the employee's claim even where the employer has failed to comply with health and safety requirements or has not kept proper records. Inappropriately high policy 'excesses' are also prohibited.

The directors are responsible for maintaining the insurance policy and they must ensure that they select an approved policy with an authorised insurer. It may even be the case that directors who failed to ensure the company had taken out proper employee insurance could be personally liable to an employee unable to recover from the uninsured company.

10.3.6 EMPLOYMENT OF IMMIGRANT WORKERS

It is a criminal offence to employ any person who is not entitled to work in the UK (the *Asylum and Immigration Act 1996*). Non-compliance can result in action against both the company and the directors where they have connived in the offence or if it has been committed as a result of their negligence. The penalty for an offence is a fine of up to £5,000.

Prudent directors obtain and keep copies of documents which are acceptable evidence of an employee's right to work – for example, a birth certificate, NI card or P45 form from previous employment.

10.3.7 EMPLOYMENT OF CHILDREN AND YOUNG PERSONS

Employment of children and young persons is restricted by the *Children and Young Persons Act 1933*, as amended by later Regulations, and directors must ensure that the company does not contravene the provisions prohibiting employment of a child under 13 years of age, employment of young persons at night time, beyond certain hours on school days and weekends and without breaks, etc. The *Working Time Regulations 1998* state a 'permitted list' of occupations suitable for 13-year-olds. Any breach of these restrictions renders the employer liable to a fine.

Further requirements are imposed by the *Health and Safety (Young Persons) Regulations 1997* which specifically state the employer's duty to ensure that young persons employed by them are protected at work from any risks to their health or safety which arise from their lack of experience, unawareness of existing risks or their lack of maturity. Furthermore, provisions in the *Management of Health and Safety at Work Regulations 1992* require employers to assess the health and safety risks to young workers before they commence employment and to notify parents of school-age children of the outcome of the assessment, together with details of the control measures introduced.

10.4 DUTIES TO THE CUSTOMER

There is a substantial amount of legislation, the intent of which is to protect the customer, of which directors need to be aware.

10.4.1 HEALTH AND SAFETY REQUIREMENTS

The *Health and Safety at Work etc. Act 1974* imposes on the company a duty to ensure that the health and safety of others, apart from employees, who are affected by the company's operations are not at risk. Action may be taken against both the company and the directors for a breach of this duty.

10.4.2 PRODUCT SAFETY

All products placed on the market for consumer use, unless specifically exempt, must be safe for the consumer to use (the *General Product Safety Regulations 1994*). Information about any risks from the use of a product and any precautions that may be necessary must accompany the product. The producing company is required to investigate genuine complaints and carry out tests to ensure that any risks presented by their product are known and controlled. This may necessitate, for example, recalling or withdrawing batches from the market where goods are not safe. Contravention of the regulations is an offence and may attract a penalty of up to £5,000, three months' imprisonment, or both.

The *Consumer Protection Act 1987* imposes liability on a supplier of a product for damage caused, wholly or partly, by a defect in their product. The

Secretary of State has the power to warn the public, to prohibit the supply and sale of, and to suspend the production of, unsafe products.

Directors must ensure that products that their companies sell, though not dangerous, meet certain minimum standards of quality. Much legislation – particularly the *Consumer Credit Act 1974*, the *Sale of Goods Act 1979*, the *Supply of Goods and Services Act 1982* and the *Sale and Supply of Goods Act 1994* – seeks to prevent the sale of goods which are defective, sub-standard and not of a reasonable quality.

10.4.3 TRADE DESCRIPTIONS

The *Trade Descriptions Act 1968* and the *Consumer Protection Act 1987* make it a criminal offence falsely to describe goods in the course of a trade or business – for example, in advertising the goods, on the packaging, or in descriptions of fitness for purpose, etc. This applies both to goods 'off-the-shelf' and to custom-made goods. The directors, as well as the company, may be personally liable for the offence if it was committed with their knowledge or consent or was due to their negligence. The penalty for making a false trade description may be a fine of up to £2,000 or two years' imprisonment or both.

A prudent board of directors will institute procedures to monitor all advertisements to ensure that any statements made are correct, to withdraw all sales and technical literature as soon as it becomes out of date, and to ensure that employees are giving correct information to customers.

It is also an offence to give a false indication of the price of goods or services and, if the offence was committed with the consent or connivance of directors or was caused by their neglect, the directors will be personally liable for the offence, and punishable by imposition of a fine. It is therefore important that the board ensures that the company has effective procedures to check that advertised prices and any statements about discounts and price reductions are correct.

10.4.4 UNFAIR TRADING PRACTICES

The *Fair Trading Act 1973* is largely concerned with protecting the interests of consumers against unfair trading practices and is regulated by the Office of Fair Trading and the Consumer Protection Advisory Committee. These regulatory bodies investigate whether trade practices are fair with regard to the terms and conditions of supply, the promotion of goods and services, the sales methods used, the packaging, and the methods of securing payment.

The Secretary of State may issue an order against an offending person or company, and breach of the order is a criminal offence.

The *Competition Act 1998* bans any anti-competitive agreements and outlaws abuses of a dominant market position, thereby extending consumer protection still further. The Director General of Fair Trading polices this legislation and has the power to impose stiff financial penalties of up to 10% of turnover. Prudent directors will therefore review existing agreements with customers, suppliers and competitors for compliance with this recent Act.

10.4.5 CONTRACT TERMS

The *Unfair Terms in Consumer Contracts Regulations 1994* require consumer contracts to be fair and invalidate any unfair terms in such contracts provided they have not been individually negotiated.

10.4.6 MARKETING

It is an offence to send unsolicited direct marketing faxes to an individual. Companies not wishing to receive unsolicited direct marketing telephone calls can register with opt-out schemes.

10.5 HUMAN RIGHTS AND SURVEILLANCE

The *Human Rights Act 1998* came into force on 2 October 2000. The Act brings into domestic law the European Convention on Human Rights. The effect of this law on employment and company matters is at this stage unclear.

All public authorities have to act compatibly with the Convention rights. The Act therefore directly applies to public sector bodies and what are known as 'hybrid bodies' (private sector bodies carrying out a public function, e.g. a privatised utility).

What will be the impact in the private sector? The Act is not directly enforceable against private sector employees. However, the principles of the Act will pervade all aspects of UK law. Thus, in disputes, the issue will have to be raised as to whether an action of an employer conforms with the principles which were set out originally in the Convention and are now given force by the *Human Rights Act 1998*.

The key rights which will be important to employers and employees are:

- Prohibition of slavery, servitude, forced or compulsory labour.
- The right to a fair trial in public before an impartial tribunal.
- The right to respect for private and family life, home and correspondence.
- The right to freedom of thought, conscience and religion.
- The right to freedom of expression.
- Freedom of peaceful assembly.
- The right to enjoy other freedoms without discrimination.

Employers should consider their employment manuals and disciplinary procedures in the context of these rights. It would be wise to take expert advice.

Pursuant to the *Regulation of Investigatory Powers Act 2000* there has been enacted, following a lengthy consultation, the *Lawful Business Practice Regulations 2000*. Under these Regulations, employers may monitor or record all communications transmitted over their telecommunications networks without consent for the following purposes:

- Establishing the existence of facts.
- Ascertaining compliance with regulatory or self-regulatory practices or procedures.
- Ascertaining or demonstrating standards which are achieved or ought to be achieved by persons using the system.
- Preventing or detecting crime.
- Investigating or detecting unauthorised use of the business's telecommunications system.
- Ensuring the effective operation of the system.

The Regulations also authorise businesses to monitor (but not record) communications for the following purposes:

- To check whether or not communications are relevant to the business.
- To monitor calls to confidential, counselling helplines run free of charge.

10.6 DUTIES REGARDING THE ENVIRONMENT

Directors are under increasing pressure to demonstrate to shareholders, investors, pressure groups, customers and employees their concern for the environment and the practical steps that the company is taking to avoid damaging the environment. Failure to protect the environment is likely to attract adverse publicity, damage shareholder relations, discourage investors and possibly affect sales. Further, in response to increasing public concern about the extent of the damage to the environment caused by industry, there is extensive 'green legislation' imposing strict regulations. The main provisions are contained in the *Water Act 1989*, the *Town and Country Planning Act 1990*, the *Environment Protection Act 1990* and the *Environment Act 1995*. This legislation covers such issues as emissions into the air, water quality and effluent, solid waste (including toxic and radioactive waste), dust emissions, noise pollution, litter, disposal of waste, environmental labelling, and other issues.

The Environment Agency has the statutory power to regulate and control pollution, inspect premises and impose bans where it finds that operating methods or controls need to be changed to prevent or minimise pollution.

A company has a civil liability for environmental damage, but in addition legislation imposes criminal liability where statutory requirements have been infringed. It is established that the company may be responsible for damage to the environment even if it is not aware of the damage. At the same time, directors should be aware that they may be held personally liable for offences committed by the company where they were perpetrated with their consent or connivance or resulted from their negligence.

10.6.1 THE REQUIREMENTS

Some of the legal requirements that companies must observe, mainly under the *Environment Protection Act 1990*, are listed below. This list is not exhaustive and directors should always consult with experts if there is any doubt.

a) Directors must obtain authorisation before the company commences operations to operate certain specified processes which have an inherent risk of harm to the environment, and carry out operations in accordance with the conditions under which authorisation is granted.

b) The company may be required in a planning application for a new industrial development to assess and report on the likely impact of its operations on the environment.

c) Directors must ensure that emission limits are monitored and adhered to. Similarly, they must be able to demonstrate that they have used the 'best practicable environmental option' for controlling pollution.

d) Adequate arrangements for disposal of waste products (including paper waste) must be made. The Landfill Tax, levied on waste dumped in landfill sites, penalises companies not attempting to recycle or recover any of their waste.

e) The Act re-defined 'statutory nuisance' as an offence, and this includes smoke, dust, steam, gas, fumes or other effluents from industrial or trade premises which are either prejudicial to health or a nuisance.

f) The *Environment Act 1995* requires companies to assess existing and potential levels of pollution and identify options which will be implemented where the need to prevent, minimise, remedy or mitigate pollution is identified.

g) Companies must apply for a permit before certain regulated activities can be carried out. In granting a permit, consideration will be given to whether:

- preventative measures are in place to safeguard against pollution;

- any significant pollution is caused;

- waste production is minimised;

- energy is used efficiently;

- measures are in place to prevent accidents and limit their consequences;

- there are recovery procedures.

The permit conditions must be complied with on an ongoing basis and prudent directors will therefore implement control policies and procedures to ensure these requirements are met.

10.6.2 THE SANCTIONS

Where authorisation to operate is required and has not been obtained, or a company breaches the conditions of authorisation, the Environment Agency or a Local Authority Environmental Health Officer has the authority to issue enforcement notices requiring immediate remedial action to be taken and/ or prohibition notices suspending authorisation until remedial action has been taken.

Depending on the nature of the pollution, a fine will be imposed for breach of an enforcement or prohibition notice. In addition, the company is liable for criminal proceedings and the Court may issue a compensation order under the *Powers of Criminal Courts Act 1973*.

Action may be taken against the directors as well as, or instead of, the company for the offence. For example, the *Environmental Protection Act 1990* states that

> *Where an offence under any provision of this Act committed by a body corporate is proved to have been committed with the consent or connivance of, or to have been attributable to any neglect on the part of, any director, manager, secretary or other similar officer of the body corporate or a person who was purporting to act in any such capacity, he as well as the body corporate shall be guilty of that offence and shall be liable to be proceeded against and punished accordingly.* (s.157)

Similar wording is commonly found in other statutes. For example, s.217 of the *Water Resources Act 1991* states

> *. . .whether or not the company is prosecuted for an offence, its directors can be, and they can be imprisoned for up to five years, depending on the offence.*

Many environmental offences – e.g. the unlicensed depositing of waste, the unlawful discharge of trade effluent, the illegal storage of substances – are punishable by summary conviction, with up to two years' imprisonment and/ or an unlimited fine. In addition, the director may be liable for disqualification as a director under the *Company Directors Disqualification Act 1996*.

10.6.3 ENVIRONMENTAL POLICY STATEMENTS AND MANAGEMENT SYSTEMS

There is no legal requirement for a company to have an environmental policy, but increasing pressure from regulators, investors, shareholders, customers, pressure groups and the media is forcing many companies to develop an environmental policy. Government has expressed dissatisfaction at the number of companies without such a policy and has warned that unless companies voluntarily adopt environmental policies and report on their progress under the policies, a mandatory standard may be imposed. In addition, some representative bodies have called for government intervention at least to ensure consistency in the measurement of environmental perform-ance, so that the performance of companies may be more easily compared.

Furthermore, many organisations insist, as a condition of supply, that suppliers have an environmental policy. For these reasons, directors' duties in relation to the environment are often no longer limited to the legal minimum.

Ultimately, the board is responsible for formulating, developing, implementing and monitoring an environmental policy. Directors must carefully consider the most suitable policy for their business, bearing in mind the nature of the business and the potential impact on the environment. It may be that an integrated environmental management system encompassing environmental policy, the organisation of personnel and management, details of statutory requirements, clear objectives and targets, operational controls, record systems, audits and reviews is appropriate.

The environmental management system may be independently assessed and, if successful, the company may achieve ISO 14001 certification and/or obtain registration under the Eco-Management and Audit Scheme of the EC.

10.6.4 INSURANCE

Public liability policies normally either exclude pollution cover entirely or exclude cases of gradual pollution over a period of time. Directors need to ensure that pollution risks are identified and that appropriate pollution cover is arranged. This may necessitate the need for a pollution audit as a condition of cover and for a 'tailor-made' policy for the company or site.

10.6.5 PACKAGING

In brief, the *Packaging (Essential Requirements) Regulations 1998* require that:

a) packaging is reduced to the minimum possible, subject to safety and hygiene requirements and the specific needs of the packed product and the consumer;

b) packaging is recoverable;

c) packaging is re-usable;

d) packaging materials contain minimal amounts of noxious or hazardous substances;

e) depending on the type of packaging, maximum levels of heavy metals are not exceeded.

The regulations are enforced by the local Trading Standards Officers, who can require a company to provide technical documents in order to check compliance. Directors should note that a breach of these regulations may lead to both a civil penalty on the company and, where the offence is found to have been committed with the consent, connivance or neglect of a director, a criminal penalty on the director personally.

10.7 DIRECTORS' POTENTIAL LIABILITIES

As the company's officers are its mind and will, directors must ensure that both they and the company comply with their legal obligations. These are, for good reason, wide-ranging and complex; they are also the subject of considerable public attention.

A company can commit an unlawful act only through the agency of natural persons – directors or employees. The liability of both the company and its human agents differs depending on whether the unlawful act concerned is a civil tort (a breach of duty which entitles a wronged person to sue for damages) or a criminal offence, and on how it is treated. Liability also differs according to the degree of criminal intention which is required to be proved to establish whether an offence has been committed.

It might be thought that the Articles of Association of the company could absolve or exempt the directors from liability. However, the *Companies Act 1985* makes any Article void in so far as it exempts a director from liability for negligence, default, breach of duty or breach of trust in relation to the company. The company may, however, insure the director against such a liability (see section 9.9).

The range of liabilities that can be imposed on directors can be grouped into the following categories:

- statutory financial liability
- parallel criminal liability
- civil tortious liability
- civil contractual liability.

10.7.1 STATUTORY FINANCIAL LIABILITY

Various statutes make a director of a company liable to compensate the company or another party for some action or inaction. For example, if prohibited loans are made to a director, the directors responsible are liable to recompense the company (see section 9.7.10).

Perhaps the most important areas of potential financial liability imposed on directors by statute are fraudulent and wrongful trading. For instance, a liquidator of an insolvent company can apply, under the *Insolvency Act 1986*, s.214, to the Court for an order that the directors should contribute towards the assets of the company, thereby increasing the assets that the liquidator has available to distribute to the creditors of the company. The liquidator has to prove that the company has traded while insolvent and that the director knew or ought to have concluded that the company could not avoid going into insolvent liquidation (see section 15.3).

EXAMPLE

The case of *Re Produce Marketing Consortium Ltd. Numbers 1 and 2* {29} is an example of wrongful trading. Produce Marketing Consortium Ltd (PMC) imported fruit and charged a commission on the gross sale price of the fruit. From 1981 the company traded at a loss. The company had a bank overdraft limit of £75,000 which was guaranteed up to £50,000 by one of the two directors and additionally secured by a charge on all the company's assets. By mid-1986 PMC was regularly exceeding the bank overdraft and company cheques were being returned unpaid. The auditor's reports for 1984/85 and 1985/86 (prepared, late, in February 1987) stated that the company was insolvent and could only continue because of the bank's support.

The auditors informed the directors that they were in danger of being made personally liable for the company's debts if they continued to trade. The directors ignored this warning, the company continued to trade and, under pressure from the bank, reduced its overdraft by increasing its indebtedness to its principal supplier of fruit. Eventually the company went into liquidation in October 1987.

The liquidator sought to make the directors personally liable to contribute nearly £108,000, being the amount that the company's debts increased between the statutory last date for preparation of the 1984/85 accounts (though in fact they were prepared six months late) and the date of liquidation, under the wrongful trading provisions. It appears that there was no deliberate wrongdoing in this case, just false optimism and a desperate desire to keep going. Nevertheless, the Court ordered the two directors to contribute £75,000 between them to the assets of PMC and to pay the costs of the action brought by the liquidator.

10.7.2 PARALLEL CRIMINAL LIABILITY

There are numerous statutes and regulations made by government under statutory powers which, in relation to offences committed by a company, impose parallel criminal liability on a director to whose actions or neglect the offence is attributable or who consents to or connives at the offence. Most statutes protecting consumers, employees, investors or the environment contain a provision to this effect. The potential sanctions vary; it will usually be a fine, but it can include imprisonment.

Most of the statutes creating offences of strict liability also provide for statutory defences based on the concepts of 'due diligence' or 'act or default of another person'. However, it may not be easy for a company, and therefore for its board, to escape liability by invoking these defences if the issue involved is of sufficient importance.

> In one case (*Tesco Supermarkets Ltd v Nattrass* {48}), Tesco admitted contravention of the *Trade Descriptions Act 1968* but was able successfully to contest liability by demonstrating that there was a relevant company policy created by the board and an adequate and appropriate system to ensure that the policy was put into practice. The Court ruled the contravention was not the act of the company nor the directors but the act of an individual store manager. By contrast, British Steel was found liable (*R v British Steel* {33}) under the *Health & Safety at Work etc. Act 1974* for failing to conduct its undertaking in such a way as to ensure, so far as reasonably practicable, that all persons not in employment (in this case subcontractors) were not exposed to risks to their health and safety (a worker was killed in an accident). The Court of Appeal rejected arguments that the company could escape liability on the basis that the company at 'directing mind' level was not involved in the offence, since British Steel had not displaced the burden of proving that it had done all that was reasonably practicable to delegate supervision of the work in question. The Court suggested that health and safety cases imposed a higher burden than cases of consumer protection.

It is well established that a company can commit a criminal offence requiring proof of criminal intention. The intention is evidenced by its 'controlling officers', including senior managers as well as directors, participating in the commission of the offence. The state of mind of such officers, who may also be guilty of the offence, is imputed to the company. However, the circumstances in which a company and its directors may be criminally liable for failing to take action are not entirely clear. For example, in determining whether the company has the required state of criminal recklessness for manslaughter to be established, the Court has to be satisfied that the 'controlling mind' is identified and is proved to have unlawfully caused the death. This is not an easy task. There appear to have been very few prosecutions of a company for manslaughter in the history of English law.

EXAMPLE 1

In December 1994, OLL Ltd became the first company in English legal history to be convicted of the crime of manslaughter (*R v Kite, Stoddart and OLL Ltd* [35]). The conviction arose from the death by drowning of four teenagers off Lyme Regis while on a canoe trip organised by OLL Ltd. The managing director of OLL Ltd became the first director to be given an immediate custodial sentence for a manslaughter conviction arising from the operation of a business. In this case the risks to which the teenagers were exposed were so serious and obvious that the 'gross negligence' required to convict the company was proved. Furthermore, there were only two persons with directorial and managerial control over the company's affairs; it was therefore relatively straightforward to establish who were the controlling minds of the company.

EXAMPLE 2

In 1990, as a result of the loss of 187 lives when the cross-Channel ferry *The Herald of Free Enterprise* capsized off Zeebrugge, manslaughter charges were brought against the operating company together with seven of its directors and employees (*Re P & O European Ferries (Dover) Ltd.* {30}). In the event the charges were not proven. In this case, where there was a board of directors running a large operation with very many employees, it proved impossible to establish a direct link between the action or inaction of any person who could be considered as having a 'controlling interest' and the tragic deaths that could have given rise to a finding of manslaughter. The board was responsible for the policies and practices of the company, but the connection between the board's actions and the deaths was judged not to be close enough to establish guilt under this serious offence.

In March 1996 the Law Commission published a report, 'Legislating the Criminal Code: Involuntary Manslaughter', recommending that there should be a new statutory offence of 'corporate killing' and that the need to prove the existence of a 'controlling mind' should be done away with. At the time of writing this has not reached the statute book.

A director can also fall foul of the criminal law without the company being liable. Directors of companies can be made criminally liable for breaches of various provisions of the *Companies Act 1985*, the *Insolvency Act 1986* and the *Criminal Justice Act 1993*. These include the following:

a) Insider dealing (*Criminal Justice Act 1993*); see section 13.11.

b) Failure to inform the auditors of a relevant written resolution of the general meeting (*Companies Act 1985*, s.381B).

c) Failure to deliver the company's annual return to the Registrar of Companies (*Companies Act 1985*, s.363); see section 9.3.

A prudent director will read relevant publications or attend seminars or lectures in order to update himself on the latest regulations and laws that affect his company. The company secretary should take steps to keep the board abreast of relevant changes in the appropriate industrial sector and should ensure that directors are aware of any occasions when they might be in danger of breaking the law.

10.7.3 CIVIL LIABILITY

Generally, it is the company that sues or is sued for civil wrongs. The directors generally do not have personal liability even though the wrongful act was done on their authority.

However, there are two sets of circumstances where a director may be personally liable: where a tort has been committed and where a contract is broken.

a) Torts

Unlawful acts which entitle a person suffering loss or damage to sue are known as 'torts'. Both the company itself and the directors who authorised the tortious action may be involved in the commission of a tort and therefore may be liable jointly.

Generally, for a director to be liable for a corporate tort some measure of direct participation in the commission of the tort, authorising, directing or procuring it is required, or it results from the director's own negligence. The bare fact that an individual is a director is not, without more, sufficient to make him liable for a tort. Apart from cases where a director himself orders an employee to take action which results in damage to himself or another person, many corporate torts result from a director's omission (for example, negligence). It is safest to assume that directors who fail to ensure that the company acts with due diligence towards third parties may thereby expose themselves to an action from a third party injured through a corporate default. (Additionally, of course, a director may also be liable to the company because his negligence may be a breach of the duties of care and skill, or be in breach of a service contract.)

Areas of potential tortious liability where directors have been made liable with the company are:

a) negligence (the most common area of tortious liability);

b) deceit;

c) defamation;

d) breach of consumer protection;

e) negligent misstatements in a prospectus (in addition, the *Financial Services Act 1986* provides that if directors issue misleading or incorrect listing particulars then they may be liable to pay compensation to any person who has suffered loss as a result).

Directors of smaller companies are probably at greatest risk of committing a tort, since such directors are more likely to be involved in the day-to-day decisions that could give rise to a civil wrong.

Contracts

Directors are not normally liable on contracts made between the company and third parties. They are not liable even if the company breaks the contract due to negligence by the directors. However, there are some circumstances where the director may be personally liable:

● Where the name of the company is not mentioned on cheques, invoices, etc.

- Where the director does not make it clear that he is contracting as an agent of the company and not on his own behalf.

- Where the director makes fraudulent or negligent misrepresentations in the course of negotiating a contract.

- Where the company fails to perform a contract guaranteed by the director.

Directors need to ensure that, when they act for the company in contractual matters, it is clear to the other party that they are not acting in a personal capacity but as an authorised officer of the company, otherwise they will risk being personally liable on the contract. This status will usually be evidenced by the title that they use and the format for the signature of the contract ('for and on behalf of XYZ Ltd.'). Directors should be careful to ensure that the company name is accurately described on any cheque or order and includes at the end of the name 'limited', in the case of a private company, or 'public limited company', in the case of a public company, or their permitted abbreviations, Ltd or Plc respectively. In the interests of clarity, prudent directors write all business correspondence only on the company's headed letter paper. Where large or unusual contracts are concerned it is wise to take professional advice.

EXAMPLE

The following is the sort of situation to avoid. Suppose that Mr A did not know that Mr B was a company director (perhaps because negotiations took place outside the working environment) and Mr B verbally ordered some goods which Mr A delivered. Mr A could easily think that he had entered into a contract with Mr B, not with a company. In the event of the company not paying for the goods, Mr A would have a good case for holding Mr B personally liable for payment. Mr B would ordinarily be entitled to be indemnified by the company, but this would be of no concern to Mr A.

The most frequent type of contract where the director may be personally liable is the provision of a personal guarantee to the company's bank. In circumstances of financial difficulty or insolvency, there is an obvious temptation for directors to ensure that the company loan from the bank is cleared prior to any liquidation of the company, so that their personal guarantees are not called upon. But this is not treating all creditors equally and may subsequently be set aside if it constitutes a preference (see section 15.3).

10.8 SUMMARY

1. The law has imposed obligations on companies in five key areas:

a) employee rights;

b) health and safety at work;

c) consumer/customer rights;

d) human rights;

e) the environment.

Breaches in these areas usually result in action being taken against the company; there may also be an action against a director personally.

2. Employment rights:

a) Under the Companies Act 1985, directors are to have regard to the interest of employees.

b) Employee rights have been significantly extended in the areas of

   i)   Dismissal;

   ii)   Redundancy;

   iii) Discrimination on grounds of sex, race or disability;

   iv)   Transfer of undertakings;

   v)   Minimum wages;

   vi)   Maternity rights;

   vii) Working hours.

This legislation is complex and professional advice should be sought before action is taken in these areas.

3 Health and safety:

a) Employees are entitled by law to safe conditions at work.

b) All companies employing more than five people must have a health and safety policy which must be communicated to employees.

c) Breaches of health and safety requirements may result in liability for both the company and the directors.

4. Consumer protection:

a) Producers, suppliers and importers are liable for damage caused wholly or in part by defects in their products.

b) It is a criminal offence to describe goods falsely.

c) The law places constraints on the sale of defective or sub-standard goods and services.

5. Human rights

Employers must be sure that their actions towards employees conform with the principles set out in the *Human Rights Act 1998*.

6. The environment

There is now a considerable body of law to protect the environment. Tight regulations control what may be built, put into the atmosphere and taken out of, or put into, protected waters, for example.

7. Directors' potential liabilities

Directors may be liable for:

a) statutory financial liability – for example, if guilty of fraudulent trading;

b) parallel criminal liability, where the responsible director is held liable for an offence committed by the company;

c) civil tortious liability in the event a director and/or a company commits an unlawful act which enables an aggrieved person to sue;

d) contractual liability. Normally the company will be liable for contractual obligations but a director may make himself liable – for example, as a guarantor.

The penalties for breach of your duties as a director can be severe. A summary of the principal *personal* liabilities and possible sanctions is in Appendix C.

Chapter 11

Disqualification of Directors

11.1 WHAT DOES DISQUALIFICATION MEAN?

A director's office is automatically vacated if he is disqualified by the Court under the *Company Directors Disqualification Act 1986* (CDDA). The terms of a disqualification order prohibit an individual from being, without leave of the Court, a company director, a liquidator or administrator of a company, a receiver or manager of its property, or in any way, directly or indirectly (for example, via a nominee), being concerned in or taking part in the promotion, formation or management of a company. The Courts have tended to interpret this latter 'management' restriction quite widely.

The maximum period of disqualification under the CDDA is fifteen years, although most disqualifications are for five years or less; for example, conviction of an offence based upon persistent default in making returns carries a five-year maximum disqualification. Breach of a disqualification order is a serious criminal offence with custodial sentences (see section 11.6 below).

The number of directors disqualified has risen dramatically in recent years, from 374 in 1994 to 1540 in 1999. This increase is due to a combination of factors – a general increase in the degree of scrutiny of directors' actions, tougher action by Courts, and more vigorous action by government, particularly the initiation in 1998 of a telephone and e-mail hotline for 'whistle-blowers' and the publication of disqualified directors' names on the Companies House website. Directors who are in breach of their duties face an increasingly real threat of disqualification.

11.2 DOES THE LEGISLATION APPLY TO ALL DIRECTORS?

The law applies to any person occupying the position of a director, whatever title he is given. Shadow directors may also be disqualified, but only on the grounds of 'unfitness' in the context of an insolvent company (see *Re Sykes (Butchers) Ltd* {47}, *Secretary of State for Trade and Industry v Richardson* {43}, *Re Richborough Furniture Ltd* {37}, *Secretary of State for Trade and Industry v Deverell and another* {42}). You will need to be aware of your responsibilities to avoid disqualification, even if, for example, you are a non-executive director or an alternate director, or even if you do not have the title of director at all, but are regarded as one in law.

11.3 WHAT ARE THE GROUNDS FOR DISQUALIFICATION?

There are three grounds for disqualification – 'general misconduct', 'unfitness', and 'wrongful trading'. These are discussed in turn.

11.3.1 'GENERAL MISCONDUCT IN CONNECTION WITH COMPANIES'

A director can be disqualified if:

a) he is convicted of an indictable offence (for example, insider dealing or an offence under the *Health and Safety at Work etc Act 1974*) in connection with the promotion, formation, management, liquidation or striking off of a company or with the receivership or management of the property of a company (a maximum of 5 years' disqualification if made by a Court of summary jurisdiction; in any other case a maximum of 15 years' disqualification) (s.2 CDDA); *or*

b) he has been persistently in default in delivering any sort of document or notice to the Registrar of Companies as required under the *Companies Act 1985* (a maximum of 5 years' disqualification; three convictions in the five preceding years are conclusive proof of persistent default, but proof does not depend on previous convictions having been obtained) (s.3 CDDA); *or*

c) on a winding up, he appears to have been guilty of fraudulent trading under s.458 of the *Companies Act 1985 – even if he has not been convicted for that* – or he is found to have acted fraudulently or in breach of his duties to the company (a maximum of 15 years' disqualification) (s.4 CDDA).

11.3.2 'UNFITNESS'

The Court *must* make a disqualification order where, on the application of the Secretary of State, it is satisfied that the person about whom the application is made:

a) is or has been a director (or shadow director) of a company that has become insolvent; *and*

b) his conduct as a director makes the individual 'unfit' to be concerned in the 'management' of a company.

This applies even if the individual ceases to be a director before the company becomes insolvent. Further, and this is a very powerful factor, the individual's conduct as a director of *other* companies apart from the company in question may be taken into account.

Additionally, the Secretary of State may apply to the High Court for a disqualification order if he considers it is in the public interest to do so. There is no requirement for the company to be insolvent. The Court may make a disqualification order if it is satisfied that the conduct of the director makes him unfit to be concerned in the management of the company.

The minimum period of disqualification for unfitness is 2 years and the maximum period is 15 years.

11.3.3 'WRONGFUL TRADING'

This is an important ground for disqualification of a director of a company in insolvent liquidation. The *Insolvency Act 1986, s.214*, imposes upon directors a duty to consider the interests of creditors. In particular, a director is obliged to take steps to minimise the potential loss to creditors if the director knew or ought to have concluded that an insolvent liquidation was unavoidable. Failure to do this is known as 'wrongful trading'.

Liability for wrongful trading is discussed in section 15.3.3. A Court may disqualify a director from being a director whenever it determines that he should be personally liable to contribute to a company's assets because of fraudulent or wrongful trading, *even if no application for disqualification is made.*

11.4 WHAT DETERMINES IF A PERSON IS 'UNFIT' TO BE A DIRECTOR?

By far the most frequently used provision to disqualify directors is that to do with 'unfitness' (s.6 CDDA). Approximately 90% of these cases arise in circumstances of insolvency. It is clear that one of the consequences of insolvency may well be disqualification as a director.

The CDDA sets out two lists of matters that a Court must consider when it has to decide whether a person's conduct renders him unfit to be a director. The first list sets out those matters that apply regardless of whether or not the company is insolvent. The second sets out additional matters that apply where the company has become insolvent.

The first list requires the Court to consider:

a) Any misfeasance or breach of any fiduciary or other duty by the director in relation to the company, for example failure to exercise due care and skill (see section 8.5).

b) Any misapplication or retention by the director of any money or other property of the company.

c) The extent of the director's responsibility for the company entering into any transaction liable to be set aside as intended to defraud creditors.

d) The extent of the director's responsibility for any failure by the company to comply with the duty to prepare annual accounts and to make the statutory returns to Companies House.

The second list, which applies when the company has become insolvent, requires the Court to consider:

a) The extent of the director's responsibility for the causes of the company becoming insolvent.

b) The extent of the director's responsibility for any failure by the company to supply any goods or services that have been paid for.

c) The extent of the director's responsibility for the company entering into any transaction or giving any preference that is liable to be set aside in a winding up. In *Verby Print for Advertising Ltd, Fine and another v Secretary of State for Trade and Industry* {49}, for example, two directors were disqualified for two years for not paying Crown debts and for paying the bank in preference to other creditors in order to release themselves from their personal guarantees prior to insolvent liquidation.

d) The extent of the director's responsibility for a failure to act lawfully during an insolvency – for example, non-compliance with the duties to call and attend a creditors' meeting, to provide the company's statement of affairs in an administration, to deliver up company property and to co-operate with a liquidator.

These are daunting lists. The Department of Trade and Industry has issued guidance that receivers and liquidators should not take a pedantic view of isolated technical failures – for example, the occasional lapse in filing annual returns – but should form an objective view of the director's conduct. However, in the final analysis the judgement rests with a Court. There is therefore always an uncomfortable degree of risk.

11.5 DISQUALIFICATION PROCEDURES

Ultimately, it will be the Court that determines whether a director should be disqualified. The procedure for this varies depending upon the grounds for disqualification in question.

The *Insolvency Act 2000* has improved the efficiency and effectiveness of the procedure for disqualifying unfit company directors. Basically, the Secretary of State is allowed to accept undertakings which would have the same legal effects as a disqualification order made by a Court. The key points of the legislation are:

a) Where a decision is made to apply for a disqualification order on the ground of unfit conduct, the Secretary of State may offer the director the opportunity to resolve the matter by giving an undertaking not to be involved in the promotion, formation or management of a company or any other activities precluded by the disqualification order, subject always to the leave of the Court.

b) Unfit directors would be able to consent to a period of disqualification without the need for involvement by a Court.

c) The undertaking would be registered at Companies House, and its breach would carry the same penalties and sanctions as a breach of a disqualification order (see section 11.6).

11.5.1 GENERAL MISCONDUCT

An application for a disqualification order against a person on one of the grounds coming under the category of general misconduct can be made by either:

- the Secretary of State for Trade and Industry or the Official Receiver; *or*

- the liquidator, or any past or present member or creditor of any company in relation to which that person is alleged to have committed an offence or other default.

Note that the person need only be *alleged* to have committed an offence or other default.

11.5.2 UNFITNESS

The Official Receiver, a liquidator, an administrator, or an administrative receiver are obliged to make reports on the conduct of directors and former directors to the Secretary of State for Trade and Industry where they consider the director's conduct makes him unfit. If these persons take the view that a particular director is, in their opinion, unfit to be a director, they must give details of the conduct that makes it appear that the conditions of the legislation are fulfilled, as above. Where a report is made, the Secretary of State may decide to make an application (or direct the Official Receiver to do so) to the Court for a disqualification order.

The approach adopted by the Courts when considering 'unfitness' is broadly that the primary purpose of disqualification is not to punish the individual but to protect the public. However, even a marked lack of competence, rather than dishonesty, has been held to be sufficient to justify disqualification.

EXAMPLES

For example, in the case of *Sevenoaks Stationers (Retail) Ltd* {44} a chartered accountant was a director of five companies which became insolvent with unpaid debts of £559,000. The main reason for the failures was the lack of financial controls. It was alleged that accounting records were inadequate, there were no audited accounts for any of the companies, preferential payments were made to some creditors even though the company was insolvent, the company traded while insolvent, and there were unpaid Crown debts of £120,000. On appeal, the original disqualification period was reduced from seven years to five years.

> His trouble is not dishonesty, but incompetence or negligence in a very marked degree and that is enough to render him unfit *(Dillon LJ)*.

Similarly, in *Re Barings Plc* {3} a director was disqualified on the ground of 'unfitness' because he showed

> not so much discrete failures of management as a general failure to manage: they amount not so much to bad management as to non-management. As such, they demonstrate . . .a high degree of incompetence (Jonathan Parker J).

11.5.3 PARTICIPATION IN WRONGFUL TRADING

No formal application is necessary for a disqualification order in these situations. The Court that is considering the issue of fraudulent or wrongful trading will also consider whether to make a disqualification order.

11.6 THE CONSEQUENCES OF IGNORING A DISQUALIFICATION ORDER

The consequences can be severe. First, if a person breaks a disqualification order he is liable either to imprisonment for up to two years and/or an unlimited fine, on conviction on indictment, or to imprisonment for up to six months and/or a fine not exceeding £5,000, on summary conviction.

Secondly, he can be made personally liable for all the debts and other liabilities of the company of which he is unlawfully a director incurred while he was involved in its 'management'. The law may regard a person as being 'involved' in the management of a company even if not a director of it.

11.7 SUMMARY

1. The *Company Directors Disqualification Act 1986* significantly enlarges the range of penalties that may be inflicted upon directors so as to include disqualification.

2. The *Company Directors Disqualification Act 1986* sets out the circumstances in which a director may be disqualified from being a director, in particular for

a) general misconduct: the commission of an indictable offence in relation to the company, or failure to deliver accounts;

b) unfitness arising out of an insolvency.

3. Directors should be particularly aware that disqualification may result from fraudulent trading and wrongful trading.

4. An individual is barred automatically from being a company director in certain circumstances, including if he is disqualified after a company investigation.

Chapter 12

Directors' Remuneration

12.1 REMUNERATION POLICY

Directors may receive two sorts of remuneration: fees paid for the office of director and a salary or other remuneration in return for the additional duties that are performed as an executive of the company. The executive director's total remuneration package will be identified in a contract, either written or unwritten. The non-executive director will get just a fee as a director.

Executive directors thus face a dilemma when their contracts are subject to discussion and agreement since they wear two hats – they are directors of the company but also hold employee contracts, the approval of which is part of the board's responsibilities. This is why, although fees paid for the office of director are at the discretion of the general meeting, the Cadbury Report [1992] stated that executive directors' remuneration should be subject to the recommendation of a remuneration subcommittee of the board, comprised mainly of non-executive directors. The Greenbury Study Group [1995], reporting after a period during which there was great public concern about executive reward, especially in the industries that were privatised in the 1990s, and when there were also many examples of very large pay-offs to directors who were leaving companies (often for unsavoury reasons), made a number of recommendations to the same effect. The Cadbury and Greenbury Reports are endorsed in the Combined Code [1998]. Companies quoted on the Stock Exchange have to disclose in their annual reports the extent to which they comply with the Combined Code provisions.

The recommendations of the various Codes with respect to directors' remuneration are discussed in section 17.6.

It is good practice to have a written remuneration policy, even if only a very brief description. Most companies do not have a written policy. A common practice is that the chairman undertakes individual negotiation. This may be appropriate for many companies, but there may come a time when a more structured approach is required.

The statement in the 1998 Annual Report of Pearson Plc is an example of good practice:

> The Company's executive remuneration policy aims to attract, retain and motivate high calibre senior executives through pay and other arrangements which are competitive and represent best practice. The philosophy that guides the Company's policy is to help employees own shares and to ensure that the rewards for the most senior executives follow from, and are consistent with, the overall system of compensation that applies to Pearson's employees. Within a framework of linking reward to performance, the philosophy also seeks to align the interests of directors and senior management with the interests of shareholders by creating an overall compensation system to enable the Company to attract and retain the highest calibre executives worldwide by giving significant rewards but only for outstanding achievement.

> *The main components of the Company's remuneration policy are base salary, an annual bonus plan, long-term incentives, pension benefits and other market specific benefits. (Details of each of these are given).*

> *All executive directors have agreements which can be terminated by the Company on 12 months' notice.*

It is worth noting that there have been many attempts to investigate the effect of remuneration on company or share performance in the UK and the USA. On the whole, particularly in the UK, there is only a very weak statistical link between various measures of director remuneration and measures of either corporate profitability or the stock market performance of companies' shares.

12.2 ENTITLEMENT TO REMUNERATION AND EXPENSES

Directors have no automatic entitlement either to remuneration for their services or to reimbursement of expenses. Such remuneration as they may receive is usually determined by the board – often the Articles will provide for this – and sometimes, though rarely, determined by ordinary resolution of the company. It is all a matter of what is considered best for the particular company involved.

Non-executive directors normally receive directors' fees, as distinct to remuneration, under a contract for services. The Articles of Association often contain a clause to the effect that 'the directors shall be entitled to such remuneration as the company may by ordinary resolution determine'. The disadvantage of this arrangement is that the shareholders must agree to any increase. Where a director is to be employed under a service contract, the remuneration (which will probably include director's fees) will be governed by the terms of that contract, and these terms should be approved by the board. In practice, a director, in considering his remuneration, will not be concerned solely with the salary payable but also with the entire package.

Even when there is no provision in the Articles, a director who has no service contract may be able to recover on a '*quantum meruit*' basis for work done for the company. Where a director has a service contract (for example, a non-executive directorship) with his company, this will mean that he is not employed by the company. The terms of that contract will govern his remuneration.

A company may pay directors a pension provided that the power to do so is included in the Articles. However, even if the board of directors is expressly authorised in this way to pay a pension, payment may still be unlawful if the directors act in breach of their fiduciary duties towards the company, for example, by paying a pension to a director's wife. They must act *bona fide* in what they consider to be the interests of the company. The same applies to any *ex gratia* payment.

In practice, pension arrangements which have been made prospectively or during the director's tenure of office and can be demonstrated to be deferred remuneration or to have some form of incentive effect will normally be lawful, so long as the company is generally authorised to make them. It will normally be more difficult to show that arrangements made retrospectively on or after a director's resignation, retirement or death are made under a proper exercise of those duties. Similar considerations apply to lump sum *ex gratia* payments to retiring directors.

Non-executive directors as such are not automatically entitled to a company pension. In any event, it is normally not desirable for non-executive directors of a company to be reliant for their future financial security on pension arrangements provided by that company; such reliance is hard to reconcile with the independence of judgement which non-executive directors are expected to bring to bear on the company's affairs.

If expenses incurred in attending board and general meetings are to be reimbursed, it is best that written guidelines as to the nature and size of expenses are adopted.

12.3 WHAT COUNTS AS DIRECTORS' REMUNERATION?

The remuneration which has to be disclosed in the annual accounts for a particular year is the aggregate amount of emoluments paid to, or receivable by, a director in respect of that year. The aggregate of such emoluments includes:

- salary, fees and bonuses;
- expenses (if they are chargeable to tax);
- the estimated money value of any non-cash benefits;
- pension contributions;
- in the case of listed companies, the capital gains made by the exercise of any options;
- any money paid under any long-term incentive scheme;
- the value of any other net assets received.

It is likely that any payment made to a director will have to be disclosed as an emolument, unless the director can show clearly that the payment was not in respect of services as a director or in connection with the management of the company.

12.4 SETTING REMUNERATION

Setting the remuneration of directors can be a difficult business. How your remuneration as a director is in fact determined will probably depend on the particular circumstances of your appointment, and whether you are to be a non-executive director or are to be an employee as well as a director.

In most private companies the matter is usually determined in accordance with the wishes of the majority of shareholders. The most important determinants of the salary of directors in private companies should be how the company has performed and what is the going rate in the marketplace. Directors may also be 'incentivised' by the prospects of bonus payments, and the possibility at some date in the future of realising the value of shares which they may own in the company.

So far as public companies are concerned, this matter has been subject to much debate. The Combined Code [1998], as has been indicated above, states that *boards of directors should set up remuneration committees of independent non-executive directors to make recommendations [about directors' remuneration] to the board.* The work of such a committee is discussed in section 5.7.3.

If you are an owner-director of the company, your remuneration is a simple matter. The company of which you are a director and shareholder is a corporate entity and separate from its shareholders, and you should therefore not treat any of the company's assets as your own. Subject to tax considerations and the cash requirements of the business, however, you may take as much out of the business you own as you legally can.

The important point is not to pay yourself more than the company can afford. Recent cases show that the courts are likely to hold that payments, for instance as salary, to directors who are also shareholders are illegal distributions out of capital where the company does not have sufficient distributable profit to make the payment. Such distributions would be *ultra vires* and recoverable from shareholders/directors, even if they had consented to them, to the extent that the company did not have sufficient distributable profits to pay a dividend of an equivalent amount (see the discussion in section 13.5).

12.4.1 WHAT REMUNERATION MUST BE DISCLOSED?

You are under a legal duty to give your company information about your remuneration so that the information can be disclosed in its financial statements. If you fail to do so, you are liable to a fine. The remuneration you disclose should include all amounts you are paid for being a director of the company, whether you are paid by it, by a subsidiary or by some third party. You cannot avoid disclosure by setting up a company in, say, the Cayman Islands to receive the remuneration on your behalf; that would need to be disclosed as well.

The *Companies Act 1985* does not, however, require your company's financial statements to show the remuneration you have disclosed to the company individually, unless you are the chairman or paid more than him, or you are the sole director. All that is required is that the notes to your company's profit and loss account show the total amount of *all* the directors' emoluments as directors which are received by them during the financial year in question. The note must split the amounts received between remuneration as directors and otherwise.

Listed companies must also set out in the accounts the total attributed to the highest paid director.

Every company must keep at its registered office or principal place of business a copy of each director's service contract and make such contracts available for inspection by shareholders.

12.4.2 WHAT OTHER INFORMATION HAS TO BE SHOWN?

If your company is part of a group of companies and the total directors' emoluments shown in the financial statements exceed £200,000, the company (except those that are entitled to file abbreviated accounts for a small company) must disclose the following additional information:

- the remuneration bands into which the emoluments of *all* directors fall;
- the chairman's emoluments;
- the highest paid director's emoluments, unless he is the chairman;
- where directors have waived their rights to emoluments, the number of directors and amount of emoluments waived.

In all these cases emoluments do *not* include pension contributions.

None of this disclosure is required in respect of directors who work wholly or mainly outside the UK.

12.5 SHARE INCENTIVES AND SHARE OPTIONS

There are a host of special schemes and provisions intended to facilitate or encourage pay structures related to the performance of the company. The detailed rules are often very restrictive for anti-avoidance reasons and it will not always be possible to introduce a particular scheme in a particular company; even where it is possible, the disadvantages of complying with the restrictions may outweigh the potential benefits. Generally, the motivational benefits of performance-related pay and share ownership arrangements are unlikely to be achieved unless the arrangements are closely tailored to the circumstances of the company and employees concerned; coming within the rules for tax relief is a less important consideration.

As a second general rule, there is no point in providing employees with shares if there is no mechanism in place for them to dispose of the shares at a fair value when the time comes. This alone rules out share and option schemes in many private companies unless they have an Employee Share Ownership Plan (see section 12.6) or similar arrangement.

Approved *profit sharing schemes* and approved *savings-related share option schemes* are required to be open to all employees (or at least 80% of employees in the case of a registered profit-related pay scheme) on similar terms, except to those who have been employed for less than a certain period or have a material interest. Only 'full time' directors may participate in these schemes, which in practice means those working at least 25 hours per week for the company. Employees are awarded free shares up to the value of £3,000 per year or up to 10% of salary up to a maximum of £8,000, whichever is the greater. The shares must be left in a trust for two years but can be taken out after three years free of tax and National Insurance. Some 900 companies have an approved profit sharing scheme with about 1.25 million participants, and 1,200 companies have a savings-related option scheme with approximately 1.75 million participants. It is to be noted, however, that such schemes are now being phased out.

Approved *company share option plans* may be restricted to particular employees and directors (although the 'full-time' requirement still applies). The option is to acquire shares at the market price and the total value of shares held under the option and any other approved option (excluding SAYE scheme options) must not exceed £30,000. There is no tax or National Insurance charged on the gain made when the option is granted or exercised, provided that the options are held for at least three years and there is a gap of at least three years between each tax-relieved exercise. The benefit of the option is taxed only at the time of disposal of the shares obtained by exercising the option. This type of option is a common performance incentive for directors and those senior executives for whom the movement in the share price over a period of years is the best performance indicator. Approximately 3,750 companies have a company share option plan, with about 450,000 employees holding options.

In any event, directors and employees who have, or (except in the case of a profit-related pay scheme) within the previous 12 months have had, a 'material interest' in the company (or a company which controls it) are generally excluded from participating in any of the above types of registered or approved scheme. The exception (in the case of approved share schemes) is if it is a close company or would be a close company but for the exception for certain listed companies. For the purpose of executive share options, a 'material interest' is an interest (as defined) in 10% or more of the share capital and for the other schemes it is 25% or more.

Besides the statutory restrictions on the above schemes, it may be necessary to comply with rules laid down by the London Stock Exchange and by the Investment Committees of the National Association of Pension Funds and Association of British Insurers concerning, in particular, any requirement for shareholder approval and the total number of shares and options which may be given to employees. Exceptions to the limits may sometimes be negotiated in individual cases.

The laws and regulations in this area are complex and are frequently changed. Specialist advice should be sought prior to the adoption of any scheme.

12.6 EMPLOYEE SHARE OWNERSHIP PLANS AND TRUSTS

'Employee Share Ownership Plan' (ESOP) is a term used to describe a versatile type of arrangement based on a Trust for the benefit of the employees, which has one or both of the functions of distributing shares to employees and providing a market in those shares. ESOPs are particularly useful in unquoted companies and where the intention is to transfer a substantial proportion of the shares into the hands of the employees, whether in connection with a buy-out or otherwise. Inland Revenue approval is not required.

The Trust may obtain the shares by purchase or gift from the proprietors, by purchase from employees or on the open market, or by subscription for new shares. The Trust may borrow the initial funds to buy the shares and repay the borrowings over a period out of contributions from the company. The shares may be sold to the employees or given to them as remuneration directly or via an approved profit sharing scheme.

Employee Share Ownership Trusts (ESOTs) are ESOP Trusts which, if they meet certain statutory conditions (including the exclusion of beneficiaries with a material interest), qualify for tax relief. In particular, the company is given a statutory right to deduct contributions to the Trust as an expense for corporation tax. This legislation was introduced in 1989 and has been frequently amended since with a view to making ESOTs more flexible vehicles.

12.7 ALL-EMPLOYEE SHARE PLAN (AESOP)

From April 2000 employers have been able to allocate shares to their employees. Employers may use any or all of three methods of allocation:

- the provision of shares up to a value of £3,000 per annum free of tax and National Insurance;

- the purchase of shares by employees from pre-tax salary up to a maximum of £1,500 per annum (so-called 'partnership shares') free of tax and National Insurance;

- the provision of up to two free matching shares for each share purchased by an employee.

Employers have until April 2002 to transfer existing approved profit sharing schemes into the new all-employee share plan. Tax breaks on the former will be discontinued thereafter.

Employers offering free shares have to do so on similar terms to each employee. Employees are not subject to income tax or National Insurance if their shares are held for five years or more. Any gains in the value of a participant's shares, while they are in the plan, are not subject to capital gains tax. The company is entitled to deductions in calculating its profits for corporation tax purposes on the market value of any free or matching shares, the gross salary allocated by employees to buy partnership shares, and the costs of setting up and administering the plan.

12.8 PHANTOM OPTIONS

'Phantom option' is a term commonly used to describe a cash bonus calculated according to a pre-set formula designed to achieve the same net result in cash terms for the employee as the granting of a share option. Phantom options thus have most of the performance incentive effects of share options (except for the extra cachet of potential participation in the ownership of the company) but differ in their tax effects and, more importantly, can be used in situations where share options cannot be used or are inappropriate. Such a situation might be, for example, where the employee has already received the maximum permitted approved options or where there is no ready market in the shares.

12.9 ENTERPRISE MANAGEMENT INCENTIVES

The government has legislated in the Finance Act 2000 for a new Enterprise Management Incentive (EMI) scheme. This scheme is targeted at the higher risk group of small companies with growth potential and is intended to help them offer competitive remuneration packages. Quoted companies are excluded from the scheme.

The scheme will include the following elements:

- Only 'qualifying' companies will be eligible to participate in the scheme – this is likely to mean companies with less than £15 million of gross assets and to exclude financial services and certain other service companies.

- The scheme will be available only to 'key individuals' in a company – i.e. individuals who can make a critical contribution to the success of the company.

- Key individuals will be allowed to take tax-advantaged share options, up to a maximum of £3 million worth of shares in total.

- A tax charge will arise only when the shares are disposed of and the charge will be to capital gains tax; capital gains tax relief will date from when the option was granted rather than from when it was exercised.

- The scheme will be free-standing.

12.10 COMPENSATION FOR LOSS OF OFFICE, AND *EX-GRATIA* PAYMENTS

Directors may receive compensation for loss of office, and *ex gratia* payments. Compensation for loss of office may arise by way of either redundancy or payment for termination of a contract by way of damages for settlement of any claim.

Any such sums paid must be set out in the accounts of the company. The first £30,000 of any such payment may be tax-free, but great care must be taken in the way the payment is described in order to attract this exemption. (The description must, of course, reflect the facts!)

12.11 VAT ON DIRECTORS' FEES

In general, the fees of executive directors do not attract VAT. The rewards of a non-executive director on a contract for services should include VAT if the individual's income from all sources for services (as opposed to employment) is sufficient (as it probably will be) to make him liable to registration or if he has registered voluntarily.

12.12 DIVIDENDS VERSUS SALARY

Most executive directors and employees require a basic salary on which they and their families can live and out of which reasonable expenses can be met. However, if payments are warranted above this level, then it will be possible to make payments by way of additional salary, bonus or dividends.

The most advantageous option to be followed will be reached by analysing the tax implications of each alternative. It is to be noted that if a company decides that it is in its best interests to spread share ownership in the company, then dividend payment may not be so much a choice as a requirement, if the performance of the company allows. Employees need to be rewarded and involved in the continued prosperity of the company.

Further, the role of minority shareholders is not to be ignored in these calculations. If directors decide to take high emoluments, rather than distribute profits in dividends, then this may have an unfair effect on minority shareholders. Indeed, it may lead to an action against the company, though such an action would be likely to succeed only if a substantial imbalance as between emoluments and dividends was sustained, unreasonable and unwarranted.

12.13 EXPENSES AND BENEFITS-IN-KIND

All directors should have expenses legitimately incurred for the purposes of the business reimbursed. Directors may also be paid all hotel, travelling and other expenses properly incurred in attending directors' meetings.

Any benefit-in-kind which a director receives will count for tax purposes as part of his income and as such be taxed. The most important benefit-in-kind which has become subject to taxation is the company car. However, what was until recently fully accepted as a company 'perk' for directors is now at best only a marginal benefit. Indeed, directors are advised carefully to weigh up whether they should take the car or take a car allowance, if it is on offer. It may well be tax efficient to pursue the latter course.

12.14 SUBSCRIPTIONS

Directors' subscriptions to such bodies as the IoD will normally be paid by the company. Given the advantages of membership, for example office space, dining facilities and the library, it will not be difficult for any company to set such membership payments as a legitimate business expenditure. Membership subscriptions are benefits-in-kind for individual directors, but they will not be subject to tax if the body is on the Revenue's list (the IoD is), membership is relevant to the director's employment and the director makes a claim.

Likewise, if the individual member, if he himself has paid the subscription, can show that the body is on the Revenue's list and membership is relevant to employment, then he can deduct the membership costs from income for taxation purposes.

12.15 PENSIONS

12.15.1 INTRODUCTION

This is an area where long-term financial planning is vital. The range of choices and the complexity of the rules and the calculations involved make professional advice essential when taking decisions about the company's or a director's own pension affairs.

12.15.2 TAX ADVANTAGES

The basic tax treatment for approved schemes is that the contributions (within certain limits) are tax deductible for employee and employer, and the income and capital gains on pension fund investments receive favourable tax treatment. However, pension benefits are taxable as earned income when paid. Commuted (lump sum) benefits are permitted on a tax-free basis within limits imposed by statute.

For unapproved funded schemes almost the opposite applies: the employees get no tax relief on their own or their employer's contributions (thus the employer's contributions are subject to Income Tax and NIC as a benefit of the employment), there is no exemption for the income and gains of the fund and the pension benefits are taxed. Unapproved unfunded pensions are simply taxed as income. Unapproved schemes are now usually used only to 'top-up' approved schemes for highly paid directors and employees whose benefits under approved schemes are affected by the statutory limit on pensionable earnings.

12.15.3 APPROVED SCHEMES

Approval and monitoring of approved funds is carried out by the Pension Schemes Office of the Inland Revenue (PSO). The PSO works in co-operation with the Occupational Pensions Board, which has a supervisory role over the relationship between the state pension scheme and occupational and personal schemes, particularly the contracting-out arrangements.

There are several types of approved scheme which the employer can provide. The main ones are:

● Final salary scheme: the pension benefits are determined by reference to the employee's final salary and the rates of employee and employer contributions are set (and adjusted as necessary over time) at whatever level is required to fund the promised benefits. The funding risk is in effect borne by the employer because invariably the company pension fund will pay a fixed percentage of final salary. This sort of scheme can be contracted out of the State scheme.

- Money purchase scheme: the contribution rates, for both employee and employer, are fixed at the outset. Such schemes can be contracted out of the State scheme.

- Simplified money purchase scheme: a 'no frills' version of the above with standard documentation designed by the PSO with smaller employers in mind.

- Small self-administered pension scheme: a scheme (usually on a money purchase basis) for a maximum of twelve members, who are usually all or mostly the Trustees of the scheme and its shareholding directors. It is, however, necessary for one of the Trustees to be a reputable professional person with pensions experience approved by the Revenue. A scheme of this type therefore provides much greater flexibility over investment policy. In particular, up to 50% of the fund can be invested in the shares or assets of or loans to the company (up to 25% during the first two years of the scheme's existence). Such schemes are particularly suitable for the controlling shareholders of private companies, providing a means of lessening their reliance for their retirement security on the uncertain capital gain they hope to realise on selling their shares when they retire.

12.15.4 PENSION CHOICE

An employer cannot make it a condition of employment that an employee join the company's occupational scheme. A director or employee basically has the right:

- not to join the employer's scheme;

- to join that scheme and top up (within approvable limits) his entitlement with Additional Voluntary Contributions (AVCs) to the employer's scheme or free-standing AVCs to a scheme provided by an approved institution;

- to join a stakeholder pension scheme;

- to join a scheme provided by a third party for employees in a particular industry or occupation – if such a scheme exists for the industry in question;

- to set up one or more personal pension schemes. These are money purchase schemes provided by insurance companies and other approved institutions such as banks and building societies, to which the employer can, but is not compelled to, contribute.

The only option open to the self-employed is a personal pension and this will often be the most suitable for those who change job frequently or have several directorships and/or employments concurrently or are non-executive directors.

12.15.5 MAXIMUM PENSION

The maximum pension that may be provided under an employer's exempt approved scheme (after, normally, 10 years' service) is two-thirds of final remuneration. This is, however, subject to an overriding statutory limit on relevant earnings of £90,600 for 1999/2000 and price index-linked for the future. This means that the maximum pension per year under such a scheme cannot exceed £60,400, i.e. two-thirds of the statutory limit.

The limit on the amount which may be taken tax-free as a lump sum is either one and one-half times the statutory limit or, for employees who joined a scheme after 31 May 1989, two and one-quarter times the initial amount of pension payable. Further limits apply to spouses' and other benefits. There is a stricter definition of final remuneration for those who have been controlling directors at any time in the ten years prior to retirement date.

12.15.6 CONTRIBUTION

There is no limit on employers' contributions (except that they must not lead to over-funding of a scheme) but large contributions of a one-off or catching up nature have to be spread over several years for corporation tax deduction purposes.

An individual's total contributions to all approved schemes of his employer in the year are subject to a limit of 15% of remuneration. For personal pension schemes the limit is 17.5% of net relevant earnings for those aged 35 or under, rising on a sliding scale to 40% for those aged 61 or over.

Benefits-in-kind are relevant earnings for the purposes of the limits on both contributions and benefits but many occupational schemes include only basic salary in pensionable pay.

12.16 LEGAL EXPENSES PAID OR REIMBURSED BY THE COMPANY

If a director is charged with an offence or sued for damages and lawyers become involved, then the matter will become expensive. Can the company meet such expenses?

If there is a direct company interest, then it is legitimate for the company to pay such expenses. If the case is personal and has no connection with the company, then normally the company cannot meet the legal expenses. However, it may well be possible to stretch a point so that the company may assist – for example, if the employment of first-class lawyers, who would not otherwise be involved, resulted in the director being able to devote more time to work.

Whatever, if the company does make such payments then the law is that such payments, even if it is a very direct company interest, constitute a benefit-in-kind to the director and as such are a taxable benefit.

12.17 'KEY MAN' INSURANCE

'Key man' insurance refers to an insurance policy, either whole life or fixed term, to cover the life of an individual director whose contribution to the company is thought to be vital.

This is an option which boards should consider carefully. Whilst it may be objectionable for a board to single out an individual on a board as a 'key man', it may well be the case that the company's bank or a participating venture capitalist, having invested in the company, insists on it.

The board should check the tax implications of such insurance as, depending on the terms, it may be that the premium is deductible by the company as an expense with any receipts as revenues and therefore taxable, or it may be non-deductible with any proceeds non-taxable as capital receipts.

12.18 DIRECTORS' LIABILITY INSURANCE

At present the law deters individual shareholder action and derivative actions against directors. Nor did the various corporate governance Reports tackle the issue of making directors and officers more responsible for the actions of the company, not even in an insolvency situation when the unsecured creditors and independent shareholders may feel aggrieved at the actions of the board.

Nevertheless, there is an increasing tendency to see directors as the gate-keepers of liability for the corporate entity. Shareholders, creditors, insolvency practitioners, and the State, through the Health and Safety Executive and other regulatory arms, are more and more attempting to make directors and officers personally accountable for the actions of the company. For this reason many directors are concluding that it is prudent to insure against potential actions against them.

Companies can insure against most forms of civil action that may be taken against their directors (and other officers), indemnifying them against liability arising from acts comprising negligence, default, and breach of duty or trust committed by the directors whilst performing their duties as directors. However, liability in a number of civil cases, including claims arising from dishonesty, fraud, slander, libel, pollution, breach of professional duty and claims based on the director gaining a profit or advantage to which he was not legally entitled, and all claims of criminal liability, will usually be uninsurable.

The company can pay the premiums on behalf of its directors and officers. Directors should check the company's Memorandum and Articles of Association before the company takes out such insurance, to ensure it is within the company's objects and the directors' powers to do so. The fact that the company has purchased such insurance must be mentioned in the directors' report.

Despite the cost, it is recommended that directors arrange appropriate cover. Even a relatively small claim in commercial terms can be ruinous if it has to be borne personally by a director, not least because of the associated legal costs.

12.19 SUMMARY

1. The remuneration of directors is best dealt with through a remuneration committee of the board, and this is a requirement for listed companies.

2. Remuneration includes all the emoluments of a director, including, for example, benefits-in-kind and pension contributions.

3. A director's performance may be rewarded by participation in profit related share schemes and share options.

4. It is still highly advantageous from a taxation point of view to invest bonuses or a part of wages in pension schemes.

5. In privately owned companies Employee Share Ownership Plans and Trusts can provide a market for the shares of directors and other employees.

6. Directors wishing to make pension or share option arrangements should seek specialist professional advice.

Chapter 13

Directors and Shares

13.1 DIRECTORS' POWERS TO ISSUE SHARES

Directors must not exercise any power of the company to allot shares unless they are authorised to do so by the company in a general meeting of the company or by the Articles of the company. Subscribers' shares taken on formation, shares allotted under an employees' share scheme, and shares issued on the exercise of conversion or subscription rights are exempt from these restrictions.

A simple but important matter that directors must check before any issue of shares is made is this: has the company sufficient nominal share capital as specified in its Memorandum? If not, the capital will have to be increased before the issue is made.

Under the Articles of most private companies directors have the power to refuse to register the transfer of shares without giving any reason. This power is important in private companies as it prevents shareholders disposing of shares to persons who are hostile to the interests of the company. A shareholding director who is dismissed or is forced out of the company may seek to disrupt the company by selling his shares to a competitor of the company. Directors, charged with protecting the best interests of the company, are therefore given the power to prevent such occurrences.

13.2 DIRECTORS' SHAREHOLDINGS

It is a myth to suggest that directors *must* be shareholders. It is perhaps desirable that they do hold a shareholding stake in the company, but it is not a necessity. That being said, it may be an Article of the company that directors must be shareholders. If the director fails to take the shares up within a reasonable period, then he can be forced to resign.

Directors should not use their special knowledge to deal in their company's shares; if they do so, they are likely to be criminally liable (see section 13.11). Since dealings by directors in their company's shares may be concealed, for instance behind nominees, there are a number of statutory provisions which seek to monitor and control them:

- On appointment, a director must notify the company in writing of any interest of his in shares or debentures of the company or any other company in the group.

- Subsequently he must notify the company of any dealing or change in such interests (including entering into a contract to sell any such interest).

- The company must keep a register of directors' interests and record any changes in the register.

- Where the company has allotted shares or debentures to a director or granted him an option to subscribe for shares or debentures, the director is not required to notify the company but the company is obliged to enter the resulting interests in the register without notification from the director.

- Where the director's interests are in shares or debentures which are listed on a recognised stock exchange, the company must notify that exchange of the interests recorded on the register.

- In addition, any director holding 3% or more of the nominal value of a listed company's voting share capital must comply with separate disclosure requirements (see section 13.10).

These obligations of disclosure and notification extend to the interests of a director's spouse and minor children. 'Interest' is very widely defined. For example, a person is taken to be interested in shares or debentures of the company which are held by him as a trustee (other than as a bare trustee) or by a body corporate of which he controls one-third or more of the voting power at general meetings.

The obligation to notify arises when the director knows that he has a notifiable interest or when he learns of the existence of the facts that cause an interest to be notifiable. Directors who fail to notify their company of the above matters commit an offence and are liable on trial on indictment to be imprisoned for a maximum of two years and/or given an unlimited fine. On summary trial they can be imprisoned for a maximum of six months and/or given a fine limited to £2,000. An offence is also committed if a director makes a false statement in giving his notification.

It is an offence for directors to buy options to deal in shares or debentures quoted on a stock exchange of 'their' company or a member of 'their' company's group. They may buy an option to subscribe for shares directly from the company.

13.3 FINANCIAL ASSISTANCE FOR THE ACQUISITION OF A COMPANY'S SHARES

It is in general unlawful for a public company to give financial assistance for the acquisition of its own shares or those of its holding company. Any transaction that could be seen as having this effect should be approached with caution.

However, public companies may give such assistance if:

- the giving of the assistance is in good faith, in the interests of the company and is an incidental part of some larger purpose of the company; *or*

- the company's business includes the lending of money and the loan is in the ordinary course of that business; *or*

- the assistance is given in good faith in the interests of the company for the purposes of an employees' share scheme; *and*

- such financial assistance as set out in the last two cases is financed out of distributable profits or does not thereby reduce the company's net assets.

In contrast, a private company may in general provide financial assistance for the purchase of its shares for any purpose, but the assistance must be approved by a special resolution of the company and of every holding company. The assistance must come out of distributable profits or not reduce the company's net assets and there are detailed rules governing the exercise of this power, on the filing of statutory declarations by the directors as to the company's solvency, and the auditors' reports to be annexed to such declarations.

13.4 PAYMENT FOR SHARES IN PUBLIC COMPANIES

Generally, directors may pay for shares in money or money's worth, including goodwill, know-how and past or future services. However, in Plcs it is permissible to allot shares for future performance only if that performance is to take place within five years and there is an independent valuation of the consideration or money's worth.

If a director is offered shares without a requirement to pay for them by money or in money's worth, extreme caution is advised; to accept shares in such circumstances may be an offence.

13.5 DISTRIBUTIONS AND DIVIDENDS

There is no requirement in law to pay dividends. It is a matter for the directors and the shareholders to decide.

A final dividend, though not an interim dividend, must be ratified by the shareholders in general meeting. A company may declare a dividend by a resolution of the company – but it must not exceed the amount recommended by the directors. The dividend will be paid in accordance with the amounts paid up on the shares. A company may not make a distribution except out of profits available for the purpose. The company may make a distribution out of accumulated realised profits, i.e. out of reserves, but such a distribution should only be undertaken with care. Directors who pay directly or indirectly an unlawful dividend are jointly and severally liable to repay the amount – even if it has been approved by the shareholders.

Public companies and investment and insurance companies are subject to tighter restrictions.

Subject to the statutory provisions, a company's rules about the declaration and payment of dividends are laid down in its Articles.

13.5.1 PRIVATE COMPANIES

The principles of distribution of profits are summarised below:

- Profits and losses must be 'accumulated' over the years. The brought-forward balance must be positive before the company can pay a dividend.

- Only 'realised' profits can be distributed. Whether a profit is 'realised' or 'unrealised' has to be determined in accordance with generally accepted accounting principles. For example, in general, a revaluation of property does not give rise to a 'realised' profit.

- In calculating the accumulated realised profit or loss, account must be taken of any distributions or capitalisation already made and any losses written off in a capital reduction or reorganisation.

- The directors can then make a distribution only where it is in the company's best interests generally.

13.5.2 PUBLIC COMPANIES

The principles that apply to private companies apply equally to public companies, but there are additional requirements, principally that accumulated unrealised losses must be made good.

There are further special provisions that relate to investment and insurance companies.

13.5.3 WHAT HAPPENS IF A DIVIDEND IS PAID UNLAWFULLY?

A shareholder is liable to repay a dividend to his company if he knew, or had reasonable grounds to know, that it was paid unlawfully. Furthermore, the directors may be held liable to the company if it appears that they have paid a dividend without having sufficient realised reserves to do so.

In September 1999 four former directors of Queens Moat Houses Plc were ordered by the High Court to repay £28 million (plus £14 million of interest) of unlawfully paid dividends (*Bairstow v Queens Moat Houses* {2}). The judge ruled that the hotel group's 1991 accounts had not given a true and fair view and that there had been insufficient distributable reserves to pay a dividend to ordinary shareholders.

13.6 DUTIES IN RESPECT OF SHAREHOLDERS

There is a great deal of extensive and complex law relating to directors' obligations to shareholders.

A director should be aware that:

a) He may become personally liable as the agent of an individual shareholder if he undertakes to act on the shareholder's behalf – for instance, by offering to find a buyer for the shareholder's shares.

b) He may also be liable for making a negligent misstatement as to, for example, the financial strength of the company to anyone who might reasonably be expected to rely on the statement for business purposes.

b) If a director makes an incorrect statement of fact with the intention of misleading people or enticing them to give credit to or invest funds in the company, he may well incur a criminal liability for fraud as well as a civil liability for deceit.

d) In addition, the *Financial Services Act 1986* contains three important criminal offences. These are:

i) Knowingly or recklessly making a false or misleading statement or dishonestly concealing facts about an investment for the purpose of inducing someone (or being reckless as to whether someone is induced) to enter into (or refrain from entering into) an 'investment agreement' (which has a very wide meaning) or to exercise (or to refrain from exercising) any rights conferred by an investment.

ii) Manipulating the market, i.e. deliberately creating a false or misleading impression as to the market in, or price or value of, investments, if it is to induce others to deal in (or refrain from dealing in) those investments.

iii) Soliciting investors or potential investors or advertising investments when not authorised to do so.

In other words, directors should consider carefully before their company makes any approaches to other persons which could be seen as an invitation to invest or to dispose of securities. Issues of shares, merger proposals or bid defences are all examples of situations in which directors may become responsible for the accuracy of the contents of documents. Any failure in this area may expose both the company and the directors to civil liability and criminal penalties both under statute and at common law.

13.7 SHAREHOLDERS' PRE-EMPTION RIGHTS

Under the *Companies Act 1985* holders of ordinary shares are in effect given the right to maintain their proportion of a company's shares when further equity shares or rights to subscribe for or to convert into such shares are offered for cash. Unless the shares are offered under an employees' share scheme or are allotted wholly or partly for a non-cash consideration, companies must first offer them to existing shareholders *pro rata* to their existing holdings.

Shareholders can modify these rights by special resolution and in the case of a private company the rights can be excluded in the Memorandum or Articles of Association.

13.8 TAKE-OVERS AND MERGERS

A prudent board will always bear in mind the possibility that its company may be the subject of a bid and should have a contingency plan for managing such an event – for example, by assigning responsibility for different actions to different individuals. It is better to work out this sort of detail in advance, in order to leave the board free to consider the issues of principle that a bid raises.

The main rules governing take-overs and mergers of public companies are not all statutory – the City Code on Take-overs and Mergers and the London Stock Exchange's requirements are important and should be faithfully observed. The City Code lays down, first, that no relevant information should be withheld from shareholders of a target company and, secondly, that all shareholders of the same class should be treated equally. They should be given sufficient information and advice to enable them to reach a properly informed decision and sufficient time within which to make such a decision. Where the board of the target company (or the offeror company in the case of a reverse take-over) knows of an offer or a pending offer, it should, in the interest of shareholders, seek competent independent advice at an early stage. Indeed, this latter step must be the safest and best course in any take-over bid or amalgamation situation, and a mechanism for doing it should form part of the contingency plan referred to above.

13.9 PURCHASE AND REDEMPTION OF A COMPANY'S OWN SHARES

Companies can buy their own shares and issue redeemable shares. However, because such actions could result in a diminution of funds available to creditors of the company, such transactions are subject to stringent statutory requirements and authority as set out in the Articles of the company. Generally speaking, private companies have wider powers in these areas than public companies.

All companies can issue redeemable ordinary shares provided at the time of issue there are other issued shares which are not redeemable and they have all been paid up. Redeemable shares have attached to them a date on which they must be repaid. There is thus a certainty as to when money will be received back. Most companies do not make such issues unless the circumstances demand such action. It may be a convenient way in which to raise funds from sources who demand something more than interest and capital repayment on a loan.

The purchase of its own shares by a public company must be made out of distributable profits. Private companies may use capital in addition to distributable profits to redeem or purchase their own shares, provided the Articles of the company so allow, subject to the directors making a statutory declaration (accompanied by a report of the auditors that the amount of capital to be paid is properly determined and that they know of nothing to suggest that the contents of the declaration are unreasonable) that the company is able to meet its debts and that the company will in the following year be able to carry on business as a going concern. Directors should note that false statutory declarations may result in imprisonment or substantial fines. And if the company is wound up within a year of the purchase of its own shares, then the directors may be personally liable (s.76(2)(b) *Insolvency Act 1986*).

The payment must be approved by a special resolution of the company passed within one week of the directors' statutory declaration, and within one further week the company must publicise the details. Any creditor may seek to set aside the special resolution.

Purchase of shares may be of particular value to private limited companies in buying out disaffected shareholders.

These are dangerous waters for the director. Serious consequences can arise if the wrong steps are taken. Failure to follow the correct procedures can result in very costly rectification indeed. No director should contemplate or sanction such actions as set out above without detailed professional advice.

13.10 'DAWN RAIDS' AND 'CONCERT PARTIES'

If a company seeks to acquire a public company it is very likely that it will wish initially to build up a substantial stake in the latter's shares before a full bid is launched. Such a circumstance – a pre-emptive strike – has become known as a 'dawn raid'.

Such raids are now subject to restriction by the *Companies Act 1985* and the City Code on Take-Overs and Mergers. Part VI of the *Companies Act 1985* is designed to reveal the build-up of secret stakes in public companies, whether listed or not. Under the Act a person with 'material interests' in shares representing in aggregate 3% or more of the nominal share capital must within two days notify the company of that interest.

An 'interest' in shares includes: ownership, beneficial ownership, contract for purchase, options to purchase, and any other arrangement which will result in exercise of, or control the exercise of, voting power. It should be noted that the shares in which a person is taken as having an interest include shares in which his/her family has an interest and the shares of any company in which he is either a director (including a shadow director) or controls more than one-third of the voting power.

The Act also deals with 'concert parties', in which a group of persons join together to act in obtaining shares in a company and accept restrictions on the retention or disposal of the shares or on the use of those shares (for example, as to how the votes will be exercised) but each individually may not cause an interest to be notified. The *Companies Act* requires each person in such circumstances to be attributed with the interests of all others. Thus if the 3% rule is broken by all in total, then each must act as if 3% of the company shares were in his hands and notify the company accordingly.

Public companies can serve a notice on persons interested in their shares to disclose their identity and, if they do not declare such interests, apply to the Courts to freeze the voting powers, dividend entitlements and transferability of shares. The same effect can be secured without reference to the Court by including in a company's Articles a power to remove the rights from any shares where there has been a failure to disclose identity.

Every public company must keep a register of all interests disclosed to it and failure to do so can result in the directors being liable to a fine.

13.11 INSIDER DEALING

13.11.1 WHAT IS INSIDER DEALING?

Put simply, insider dealing means consciously using information which is not available to the public to make a profit or avoid a loss by dealing in listed securities at a price which would have been materially altered by the publication of that information.

The confidence of the users of any market is vitally important for its success and this is no less the position with the Stock Exchange. Prices of securities should reflect their market value undistorted by any special knowledge of one party dealing in them. It is therefore illegal for individuals to deal on their own account either directly or through a professional intermediary on a regulated market (i.e. most stock markets in the developed world), or in certain cases off-market, in securities of any company if they have, by virtue of their position or employment, confidential unpublished price-sensitive information relating to those securities. Unpublished price-sensitive inform- ation is information of a specific nature relating to or of concern to a company that is not generally known to those persons who are accustomed to deal or would be likely to deal in that company's securities, but would, if it were generally known, be likely materially to affect the price of that company's securities. This is commonly referred to as 'inside information'.

The value of inside information in the case of a listed company is usually short-lived, because the company must in any event notify the Stock Exchange of any information that is necessary for shareholders and the public to appraise the company's position and to avoid a false market in its securities being created. The information may nonetheless be extremely valuable.

Dealing in securities means both personally dealing and/or arranging for someone else to deal. The prohibition also extends to individuals who have knowingly obtained, directly or indirectly, information from insiders. Insiders with confidential unpublished price-sensitive information are also prohibited from encouraging others to deal in the relevant securities and, generally, from passing on such information.

A person has inside information if it is inside information and he knows it, or he has it or he knows that he has it from an inside source (i.e. a director or employee or shareholder or issuer of securities) or through having access through employment or office, or the direct or indirect source is an insider. Thus directors may be at risk, but so too may be wives, husbands, partners, employees and office cleaners; and if you get inside information from any of the above and trade, then you, too, will be guilty of insider dealing.

13.11.2 WHAT ARE THE SANCTIONS?

The offence of insider dealing is laid down in the *Criminal Justice Act 1993*. It is punishable by imprisonment of up to seven years and/or an unlimited fine. In addition, section 177 (11) of the *Financial Services Act 1986* provides that a person who is convicted of an offence involving insider dealing following an investigation ordered by the Secretary of State may be ordered to pay the cost of the whole or part of the investigation. Not surprisingly, persons who are most likely to have such information are directors and therefore they, or any person connected with them, must take great care when dealing in securities regarding which they may be alleged to possess inside information.

In addition the *Financial Services and Markets Act 2000* gives the Financial Services Authority the power to impose civil penalties for insider dealing.

The law is concerned only with dealings in securities that are traded on the Stock Exchange or on the over-the-counter market. Do not assume, however, that because you are a director of a private company, whose shares cannot be traded, that you need not be aware of these rules. The rules apply not only to directors but to any individual. For example, the rules may apply to you if your company has a business relationship with a company in whose shares you wish to deal.

13.11.3 HOW DOES A PERSON COMMIT AN OFFENCE?

There are a variety of ways in which an offence can be committed. These can be divided into four headings:

- Dealing as an insider.
- Counselling or procuring insider dealing.
- Communicating inside information.
- Acting as a 'tippee'.

First, you commit an offence if you deal on a regulated market in a company's securities, either on your own behalf or on someone else's behalf, if you have inside price-sensitive information on the securities.

Secondly, you commit an offence if you pass inside information to anyone you know (or have reasonable cause to believe) would use it to counsel or procure other people to deal in price-affected securities in relation to the inside information.

Thirdly, you commit an offence if you pass inside information to anyone you know (or have reasonable cause to believe) would use it to deal in those securities. This would apply, however, only if it would have been reasonable to have expected you not to disclose that information except in the course of your duties.

Fourthly, you commit an offence if you are a 'tippee' and deal in a company's securities knowing that you have inside information. You will be a 'tippee' if you get inside information, and know that it is inside information, from someone who in the previous six months has been connected with the company in question, and obtained the inside information there which he ought to have treated as confidential.

13.11.4 TO WHOM DO THE RULES APPLY?

The rules apply to any person who is 'connected' with the company whose securities are in question. You will be connected with a company if:

- you are a director of it;
- you are an officer or employee of the company with access to inside information that you ought to keep confidential;
- you, your employer, or the company that you are a director of have a professional or business relationship with the company that gives you access to inside information that you ought to keep confidential;
- you are connected with a subsidiary, fellow subsidiary or the holding company of the company in question;
- you are a 'tippee'.

13.11.5 IS THERE ANY DEFENCE?

A person may have a defence to the charge of insider dealing thus, that he:

- acted without a view to making a profit or avoiding a loss, even though he knew that he possessed inside information, because he would have dealt in the securities in any event – for example, in order to meet an urgent personal financial problem;

- did not expect any person, because of the disclosure, to deal in the securities;

- did not expect the dealing to result in a profit or avoidance of loss attributable to the fact the information was price sensitive;

- believed reasonably that the information had been distributed widely;

- would have done what he did if he had not had the information;

- acted in good faith as a market maker (dealer in stocks and shares);

- acted in connection with, and with a view to facilitating, an acquisition or disposal.

13.11.6 INVESTIGATIONS

The Secretary of State for Trade and Industry may launch an investigation into suspected insider dealings. Such investigations are facilitated by the fact that share dealings can easily be tracked on data files held at Stock Exchanges.

13.11.7 STOCK EXCHANGE CODE

A model Code of Conduct has been drawn up by the Stock Exchange relating to dealing in securities. The Code states that a director or employee must not deal in any securities of the listed company thus:

- during a close period (two months preceding the publication of results);

- if he possesses price sensitive information;

- without advising the chairman and receiving clearance;

and in addition directors should seek to prohibit dealings with connected persons.

The rules are tough and the outcome if caught can be condign, i.e. a criminal record. In addition, the *Financial Services and Markets Act 2000* has created a new insider dealing watchdog, the Financial Services Authority, and gives the Stock Exchange the power to impose unlimited fines on directors and their companies for breaches of the Listing Rules and the Code of Conduct. Prosecution may become more common, as the burden of proof in prosecutions will change from 'beyond reasonable doubt' to 'on the balance of probability'.

13.11.8 CONCLUSION

It must be said that there have been remarkably few charges relating to insider dealings, and only one person has been jailed for this offence. However, it seems likely that the very recent changes will lead to a tougher regulatory regime. In any event, conscientious directors should exercise extreme care and diligence before dealing in their own company's shares as they are extremely vulnerable to allegations that they knew an event was about to happen, or had happened but was known only to them, and that knowledge of the event either assisted in the making of a profit on a share transaction or in the minimising of a loss. When buying or selling their own company's shares a wise director should always ask himself if he has inside information which is material to the price of the shares and which would affect the decision of the prudent buyer or seller in agreeing to the sale and to the terms. If he has, then completing the transaction will involve a legal risk. It is desirable that directors hold equity in their own companies, but it is probably unwise for them to deal on short-term considerations. Company secretaries need to be vigilant in reminding directors when they can and cannot trade in the company's shares; in the case of listed companies this may be only a few months of the year. If in doubt – seek advice.

13.12 SUMMARY

1. Directors must allot shares in conformity with the Articles of the company.

2. Directors in private companies can refuse to register a transfer of shares.

3. Directors must be transparent concerning their interests in their company's shares.

4. Generally, companies should not assist directors to buy shares.

5. Directors recommend the payment of dividends to be approved or not by the shareholders in general meeting.

6. Strict care should be taken over the purchase by a company of its own shares; take advice before acting.

7. Public companies, basically, are entitled to know the persons or groups with a substantial share stake in the company.

8. Insider dealing is a criminal offence.

9. Directors, by virtue of their position, have information about their companies' financial situation and future plans well in advance of the public. Even if not true, directors will always be regarded as having more information than has been published. If you deal in your own company's shares, then you must take extreme care if you are not to contravene the insider dealing rules.

10. A prudent board should have a policy for the dissemination of information to ensure that price-sensitive information is made public in a timely and appropriate way and is kept strictly confidential otherwise.

Chapter 14

Taxation

14.1 INTRODUCTION

This chapter gives a brief outline of the main provisions affecting both companies and individual directors and some of the areas where decisions have to be made. It does not purport to be comprehensive. The rules and law governing both personal and company taxation are highly complex and cannot be covered in full in a brief chapter. This *Guide* is therefore not a substitute for taking proper professional advice and, since tax is a continually changing field, the up-to-date position should always be checked. This chapter is based on the law in operation during 2000/2001 and includes the provisions of the *Finance Act 2000*.

There are five main taxes affecting companies:

- corporation tax, which is charged on the profits and gains of the company;

- value added tax, which the company may be obliged to charge on the sales it makes to third parties;

- income tax, which is charged on the wages and salaries of the company's employees and directors and collected by the company on behalf of the Inland Revenue;

- employees' national insurance contributions (NIC);

- employer's NIC.

The main types of tax which affect directors personally are:

- income tax;

- capital gains tax, charged on any capital gains made by a director;

- NIC, which is a quasi-tax.

Taxes on companies are discussed first, followed by taxes on directors individually.

14.2 CORPORATION TAX

14.2.1 THE GENERAL RULES

Corporation tax is a tax payable by a company on its profits. Profits include all sources of income (other than dividends from other UK companies) and capital gains.

Trading profit can be defined broadly as the difference between the value of sales and the expenses incurred for the purposes of the company's business. However, not all expenses may be deducted from the sales figure in order to arrive at the profit on which tax is levied – in particular, entertainment expenses, some directors' personal expenses, legal costs relating to capital expenditure, and depreciation (but see capital allowances, below) are not allowable as deductions. The major expenses which are allowable are therefore:

a) the cost of goods sold, that is, the cost of purchases of inputs used in the production of a good or in the provision of a service;

b) rent, rates, heat, light and insurance for the business premises;

c) wages and employer's NIC for all employees;

d) vehicle and distribution expenses;

e) other overheads, advertising, office supplies, training and recruitment costs, etc.

The tax legislation concerning allowable deductions is complicated; this is an area where professional advice should be sought if there is any doubt as to the deductability of a particular item.

Capital gains arise when a company purchases an asset (other than an asset which it intends to sell in the normal course of its business) and then sells that asset at a later date for a higher price than it cost. The more common assets which may give rise to a capital gain are machinery, land, buildings, and equity investments in other companies.

Certain expenses may be deducted when calculating the amount of the gain, for example the legal costs involved in purchasing or selling the asset and capital improvement expenditure (but not repairs). In addition, the gain may be reduced by an indexation allowance, which is calculated on the original cost of the asset and is a broad-brush attempt to provide relief from tax on that part of the gain produced by inflation rather than by 'real' capital appreciation. Tax on capital gains may, subject to certain conditions, be deferred if the gain, or part of the gain, is reinvested in another asset.

A limited company's taxable gains are included in the corporation tax computation and taxed at the corporation tax rate, though, historically, surpluses have often been subject to different tax rates depending on how they are classified. However, the distinction between profit and capital gain is important in the tax treatment of losses.

14.2.2 CAPITAL ALLOWANCES

The cost of capital assets is treated differently from that of other costs as far as deductibility for tax is concerned. Expenditure on, for example, rent, rates and wages is allowable against the profits in the accounting period in which the expense was incurred. This is not so in the case of capital assets purchased by the company; the cost of capital items can be offset against profit by only a portion of the cost of the asset per year. The amount that may be offset is called a capital allowance. The capital allowance varies between types of asset, but for the majority of normal business assets – vehicles, plant, machinery, computers and so on – the rate is currently 25% of the unused balance each year.

Table 14.1 *An example of the calculation of capital allowances*

Suppose a new machine costs £100,000. The costs allowed against the company's annual profit are:

Year	Capital allowance	Costs allowed (@25%)
Year 1	£100,000	£25,000
Year 2	£75,000 (£100,000 less £25,000)	£18,750
Year 3	£56,250 (£75,000 less £18,750)	£14,062

and so on.

The company's accountant or tax adviser should always be consulted if significant capital expenditure is planned, since capital allowances may be used to minimise or at least delay tax liability.

14.2.3 THE TREATMENT OF LOSSES

A company may incur trading losses or capital losses and may claim tax relief in respect of them in the following ways.

Trading losses may be:

- Set off against the profits of the company from all other sources in the same accounting period.

- Carried back and offset against the profits of the company from all other sources in the twelve months prior to the accounting period in which the loss was incurred, provided that the trade was carried on in that earlier twelve-month period. Where a trade has ceased, the period of carry-back for losses incurred in the last twelve months of trading is extended to three years.

- Carried forward against the profits from the **same** trade. Care should be taken when a loss-making company radically re-structures. If the Revenue is able to argue successfully that the extent of the re-structuring is such that the company has effectively ceased its original trade and commenced a new one, the accumulated unrelieved tax losses of the old trade will not be available for offset against the profits that might be made in the new trade.

Capital losses may be offset only against capital gains of the same or of a future accounting period.

14.2.4 THE CALCULATION OF CORPORATION TAX

In the majority of cases the amount of corporation tax due is simply the taxable profit, after deducting all allowable items of expenditure and adjusting for depreciation and capital allowances, multiplied by the corporation tax rate.

Rates of tax

There are currently three corporation tax rates, with the rate used depending on the amount of the taxable profits for the period. The starting rate of 10% applies to companies with an annual taxable profit of less than £10,000. The small companies rate, which is currently 20%, applies to companies with an annual taxable profit of less than £300,000. The full rate, currently 30%, applies to companies with taxable profits greater than £300,000. Where taxable profits lie between £300,000 and £1.5 million, tax is calculated at the full rate and then reduced by a formula to give marginal relief. The effect of marginal relief is that the marginal rate of tax on profits between £300,000 and £1.5 million is 32.5%. There is an important tax planning point here: a company forecasting profits to be between £300,000 and £1.5 million should consider, for instance, bringing forward capital investment plans to reduce the amount of taxable profits charged at 32.5%.

Corporation tax rates are set for financial years ending on 31 March. Where a company does not have a 31 March year-end and therefore its accounting period straddles two financial years, the profit of the accounting period is time-apportioned to determine how much profit needs to be charged at each rate.

Payment of tax

For accounting periods ending before 1 July 1999, corporation tax is collected under the Pay and File system. Under this system the company makes its own calculation of the corporation tax liable, and must pay it to the Inland Revenue no later than nine months and one day after the end of the accounting period. A statutory return with supporting accounts and calculations must be submitted within twelve months of the end of the accounting period. Once the Revenue has agreed the amount of tax payable, it will issue a corporation tax assessment and additional tax may become due or repayable, depending on how the payment by the nine-month date compares with the final assessment of tax due.

For accounting periods ending on or after 1 July 1999, the obligation to calculate and pay corporation tax rests solely with the company itself and the Revenue does not issue final assessments of tax due. For companies with taxable profits greater than £1.5 million, corporation tax is payable in four equal quarterly instalments on the basis of the anticipated liability for the current accounting period. The instalments start in the seventh month after the company's accounting year-end. Companies with taxable profits below £1.5 million are not required to pay their corporation tax by instalments and must pay the total liability within nine months and a day of the end of their accounting period. (At the time of writing, this system is being phased in. For the next few years some tax will still be payable nine months and a day after the end of the accounting period.)

Under both systems the Revenue has the power to levy interest and penalties if returns are not submitted by the due date or if tax is paid late.

Groups of companies

In principle, groups of companies are assessed in the same way as a single company. Each company within the group prepares its own tax computation, based on the results in its own accounts. However, if there is a company in the group which has either made losses in the period or has overpaid corporation tax, then the losses or overpayment may be transferred to another company in the group and used against that company's profit or tax liability. There are certain conditions to be met between the two companies regarding share ownership and accounting periods. Transferring losses within a group is known as *group relief*.

14.2.5 DIVIDENDS AND ADVANCE CORPORATION TAX

Profits are distributed to shareholders in a company by means of a dividend. Prior to 6 April 1999, when a company paid a dividend it was obliged to pay some of its corporation tax liability in advance. This payment was called Advance Corporation Tax (ACT) and was generally payable fourteen days after a quarterly return period. The ACT was recoverable by deducting it from the corporation tax due for the accounting period in which the dividend was paid ('mainstream corporation tax'), subject to a maximum set-off. If the full amount of ACT could not be offset against the mainstream payment of corporation tax, there were provisions to carry the surplus ACT back to be set against the mainstream corporation tax of earlier accounting periods or forwards for offset against the mainstream corporation tax of future accounting periods.

ACT was abolished with effect from 6 April 1999. However, some companies may have surplus ACT carried forward from prior accounting periods and a system of 'shadow' ACT applies to ensure that companies may recover their surplus ACT.

14.3 VALUE ADDED TAX (VAT)

VAT is collected and controlled by HM Customs and Excise, a government body quite separate from the Inland Revenue. A company is obliged by law to register for VAT if the supplies made by the company are subject to VAT (some goods and services are not subject to VAT), and such turnover has exceeded a prescribed amount (the VAT threshold) in the preceding 12 months or is expected to exceed this amount within the forthcoming 30 days. The company must charge VAT on all those sales made which are subject to the tax. Note that 'supplies subject to VAT' includes zero-rated supplies.

Companies registered for VAT are allotted a VAT registration number by HM Customs and Excise and must print this number on all sales invoices.

Revenue from the sale of goods or services is categorised into three types:

1. standard-rated – the rate is currently 17.5% on the selling price;

2. zero-rated – VAT is charged at 0%;

3. exempt – VAT is not relevant and not applied.

If the supplies are all standard-rated, then the company must add VAT (known colloquially as output tax) at 17.5% to all the sales invoices and may reclaim VAT on anything purchased which carries VAT (input tax). If the supplies are zero-rated, then VAT is added to all the sales invoices at 0% and shown on the invoice, and the company may reclaim VAT on anything purchased to which VAT has been added. If the supplies are exempt, then VAT must not be charged on any sales made, and the company cannot reclaim any VAT which has been charged on purchases. If all the supplies are exempt, the company will be unable to register for VAT. In situations where some of the sales made are standard or zero-rated and some are exempt, the company must separate the input tax on purchases which relate to the standard or zero-rated items and only reclaim VAT on those expenses. In this situation HM Customs and Excise will often agree to reclaim a proportionate percentage of the input tax.

It is important to distinguish between supplies which are exempt and supplies which are zero-rated. Conversely, in certain cases, where for instance all sales are zero-rated, a company may wish to register for VAT voluntarily, even if the level of turnover is below the threshold. It would be able to reclaim the input tax paid on items purchased and would therefore benefit.

A VAT return – a statement of inputs and outputs and the relevant tax totals – must be made to HM Customs and Excise quarterly, together with payment of the VAT due (output tax less input tax). Refunds – typically, where a company makes zero-rated supplies and reclaims all its input tax – are paid automatically into the company bank account upon submission and acceptance of the VAT return.

14.3.1 SMALL COMPANY ARRANGEMENT

Smaller companies may arrange to pay VAT 'on account' each month and at the end of the year submit an annual return and settle the balance of VAT due.

Additionally, small companies can operate under a cash accounting arrangement. If a company has to pay over the 'output' tax charged on sales invoices before it has actually been paid by the customer, cashflow can suffer. A smaller company is allowed therefore to pay only the net difference between the VAT amount actually received from its customers and the VAT actually paid by the company to its suppliers during the VAT period.

14.3.2 SCALE CHARGES

If a company provides motor vehicles for use by employees on non-business mileage, additional VAT must be paid each period. The amounts vary, according to the type of vehicle, and advice should be sought.

14.3.3 VAT INSPECTIONS

Inspectors from HM Customs and Excise make regular visits to VAT-registered businesses to inspect the accounting records and check that the information shown on the VAT returns is accurate. This is normal procedure and directors should co-operate with the inspection.

14.4 PENALTY REGIMES AND DIRECTORS' RESPONSIBILITY FOR COMPANY TAX DEBTS

In the case of VAT, PAYE and NIC (National Insurance Contributions), corporation tax and income tax on profits from self-employment, there are financial civil penalties where the taxpayer/employer is late or inaccurate in returning and paying the tax due. Interest is generally payable on any under or late payments. Most of these penalties are in effect automatic and cannot be mitigated.

There may be criminal penalties in addition. In practice, however, the Inland Revenue, except in extreme cases of tax evasion, rarely tries to prove an offence to be criminal ('beyond all reasonable doubt') rather than civil ('on the balance of probabilities'), since substantial civil penalties are easily obtained.

It is particularly important for directors to note that many statutory provisions defining tax offences impute to certain directors and officers of the company parallel liability for the same offence as the company and therefore directors may be made personally liable for the tax and penalties due by the company. The formula for non-payment of NIC, for example, is that any director is liable where the offence was committed with the consent or connivance of, or was attributable in part to the neglect of, the director concerned. Whilst a director may succeed in showing that an NIC offence was not committed with any consent, connivance or neglect on his part so far as the NIC due in respect of other directors and employees, it will be much more difficult to show the same in respect of NIC on his own earnings.

Similarly, directors should be aware that they may be personally liable if they have signed an underdeclaration on their company's VAT return.

The moral is that timely and accurate tax compliance is now essential for any business; any failure in this area is likely to be expensive for the company in the first instance and could give rise to substantial personal liabilities for any director who has not taken reasonable steps to prevent such offences from occurring or, once detected, from continuing.

14.5 DIRECTORS' PERSONAL TAXATION

14.5.1 DOMICILE AND RESIDENCE

This section is limited to the tax provisions affecting UK resident directors of UK resident companies.

Liability to tax depends on your country of residence, ordinary residence and domicile. Broadly, residence normally requires you to be in the country at some time in the tax year; ordinary residence means habitual residence;

and domicile is the country which the tax authorities accept that you regard as your permanent home.

If you are resident, ordinarily resident and domiciled in the UK, you are normally subject to UK tax on your world-wide income. For visitors to the UK, the tax treatment depends on whether they are viewed as being resident or non-resident in the UK. If they are deemed to be non-resident, they are liable to income tax only on income that arises in the UK. If they are regarded as resident in the UK, then in addition they will be liable to tax on any overseas income remitted to the UK. Visitors are regarded as resident for a tax year if they spend more than 183 days in the tax year in the UK or if they average 91 days or more a year in the UK for four consecutive tax years.

The UK law on domicile and residence is complex. Further information is given in HM Inland Revenue [1999].

14.5.2 INCOME TAX AND PAYE

As office-holders, directors are liable to income tax under Schedule E and to Class 1 National Insurance Contributions on their remuneration from the company whether or not they are also employees. Income tax and employees' NIC must be deducted at source under the Pay-As-You-Earn system and the employer becomes liable for the employer's NIC at the same time. Thus, although the rules are not identical in a number of respects, directors are generally taxed in the same way as other employees.

14.5.3 NATIONAL INSURANCE CONTRIBUTIONS

Earnings for Class 1 NIC purposes are not the same as emoluments for PAYE income tax purposes. In particular, most benefits-in-kind are subject to income tax but not subject to NIC, although since April 2000 most benefits have been subject to Class 1A NIC, payable by the employer only. Conversely, pension contributions paid by the director or employee are deducted for income tax but not NIC. In addition, lower rates of NIC apply to the tranche of earnings between the upper and lower earnings limits if the employee is contracted out of the State Earnings Related Pension Scheme. Despite government efforts to align the rules, there are still several lesser differences relating to expenses and benefits, termination payments, timing of when earnings become subject to NIC and PAYE, etc.

One effect of this is that the pattern of NIC payments by directors can result in considerable fluctuations in the director's monthly net pay over the year. In practice, however, where remuneration for the year is reasonably predictable, the authorities may agree to NIC being spread smoothly over the period up to the date when the upper limit is reached.

Directors in employment have an annual earnings period. The annual lower and upper earnings limits apply (£3,484 and £27,820 respectively in 2000/ 2001) for the purposes of determining which NIC rates apply to which tranches of earnings and indeed whether NIC are payable at all; at present no employee's contributions are payable on the tranche above the upper limit.

All earnings from the same employer, whether in respect of a directorship or otherwise, must be aggregated.

Further, any earnings from other employers who 'in respect of those employments carry on business in association' with that employer must also be included in the aggregate, but only if it is practical to do so with regard to employer's contributions.

The NIC rules for directors, which are very complex, are described in complete detail in various Inland Revenue publications, particularly HM Inland Revenue [2000].

14.5.4 DEADLINES

The responsibility for assessing the tax due under the various taxes in the first instance and for filing the appropriate returns falls on the taxpayer or employer. If the taxpayer elects for the Inland Revenue to calculate his tax, he must submit his return by 30 September following the tax year. He has until the following 31 January if he is calculating the tax himself.

14.5.5 INTEREST RELIEF ON INVESTMENT IN SHARES

There are only two situations in which directors and employees may obtain income tax relief on interest paid on borrowings used to buy ordinary shares in, or to make loans to, the company. These are:

- where the company is a close company (see section 14.7) and the individual has a material interest in it or works for the greater part of his time in the actual management or conduct of it and its associated companies;

- where the company is employee-controlled at the time the interest is paid and the shares were bought or the loan made within twelve months of the company first becoming employee-controlled.

14.6 CAPITAL GAINS TAX

Capital gains tax (CGT) taxes the capital gains of individuals and trustees. The capital gains of companies are chargeable to corporation tax rather than CGT, though some of the CGT rules apply in calculating the gain.

CGT applies on the disposal of chargeable assets. All types of property are chargeable unless specifically exempted. The main exemptions are: an individual's main residence, private motor vehicles and gifts to charities.

Gains or losses are calculated on individual assets disposed of in the tax year by deducting the original cost, improvement expenditure and the incidental costs of acquisition and disposal from the sales proceeds. For assets acquired before 31 March 1982, the original cost of an asset is generally taken as its market value at that date. An indexation allowance provides some relief from the effects of inflation by further reducing the amount of any gain (but cannot be used to create or increase a capital loss). For individuals and trustees the indexation allowance is frozen at April 1998 and taper relief applies thereafter. Taper relief reduces the amount of the gain according to the number of complete years that the asset has been held after April 1998.

The gains and losses on individual assets are aggregated for the tax year, with losses being netted off against gains. For individuals the first £7,200 of gains in 2000/2001 is exempt. Any excess, if not reduced by capital losses carried forward, is taxed at 10% to the extent that an individual's tax income is below the starting rate limit of £1,520, thereafter at 20% to the extent of any unused part of an individual's basic rate band (i.e. up to £28,000 of taxable income for 1999/2000) and at 40% on the remainder. If a net capital loss is incurred in the tax year it may be carried forward indefinitely to set off against capital gains of future years.

Some useful planning points to consider are:

1. Disposals between husband and wife are not chargeable. The acquiring spouse effectively 'stands in the shoes' of the disposing spouse for the calculation of any gain or loss on a subsequent chargeable disposal of the asset. This means that it should always be possible to avoid the situation where one spouse incurs CGT whilst the other has an unused annual exemption or losses carried forward.

2. No CGT applies on death. The estate beneficiaries are treated as acquiring the assets at the market value on the date of death.

3. Unlike indexation allowance, taper relief is applied *after* the deduction of losses brought forward. Care should be taken to avoid using a carried forward loss to reduce a gain that would otherwise have been taxed at a very low rate because of taper relief.

A number of other important reliefs can apply, such as retirement relief (see Chapter 16) and replacement of business assets. The subject is complex and in view of the large sums that can be involved, especially in the case of business interests, professional tax planning advice is essential before entering into a transaction.

14.7 CLOSE COMPANIES

Most private companies are so-called 'close' companies. A few public companies are also close companies.

The exact definition is complex, but broadly a company is 'close' if it is:

- controlled by five or fewer participators; *or*

- controlled by participators who are directors, irrespective of number; *or*

- one where five or fewer participators, or any number of participator-directors, together have the rights to over one-half of the assets on a winding up of the company.

A listed company will, nevertheless, not be close if shares with at least 35% of the votes are publicly held and principal members (those who individually control at least 5% each) control less than 85% of the votes in total.

There are wide definitions of 'participator', 'associates' (whose interests must be aggregated with those of the participator with whom they are associated) and 'control' for this purpose.

Loans by a close company to participators and their associates are subject to a special tax charge equivalent to Advance Corporation Tax, which is repayable if and when the loan is repaid.

There are also detailed rules extending the definition of what is a distribution and preventing use of a close company to make tax-free gifts by making certain transfers of value made by such a company liable to Inheritance Tax.

14.8 'ONE PERSON' COMPANIES

A company may be incorporated with only one shareholder, allowing an individual to create a 'one person company', being the sole member and director. The company, however, still must have a separate secretary.

The advantage of incorporation is that the director's company can contract with various client companies for the provision of his services as a director and deductions can be more easily obtainable for travel and other expenses at the company level under Schedule D Income Tax. Care is needed in drafting the contracts (which should be in writing) to ensure that they reflect the facts of the situation; otherwise they may be open to challenge by the Revenue on the basis that the company is not the real contracting party but merely the agent of the director in respect of a contract which is really between the director personally and the client. It is also advisable to ensure that any contract of employment between the company and the director's spouse is set out in writing and provides for remuneration at a rate which is reasonable in relation to the actual duties performed by the spouse.

NIC and tax under PAYE must be deducted in the normal way when the company passes on its income to the director as remuneration. The advantages of such an arrangement are much less significant under present tax rates and tax rules than they once were. After April 2000 full rates of NIC are payable and a deduction for the cost of employing a spouse will almost certainly be refused. In addition, company legal and tax compliance costs and the degree of exposure to personal liability involved in operating through a company are much greater than they once were.

14.9 ENTERPRISE INVESTMENT SCHEME

Under the Enterprise Investment Scheme, relief is available for an individual who qualifies for relief on his investment in eligible shares in a qualifying company carrying on a qualifying business. To be eligible a person must subscribe for the shares on his own behalf and not be connected with the company at any time in the period beginning two years before the issue of the shares and ending five years afterwards.

A 'qualifying' company carrying on a qualifying business is a trading company not quoted on the Stock Exchange (though it may be quoted on the Alternative Investment Market) carrying on business wholly or mainly in the UK, the business activities of which are not specifically excluded.

The meaning of 'connected' is wide and includes the situation where a person (or his associate(s)) is a director or employee of the company or any subsidiary (see section 8.1.6). However, directors and their associates are not necessarily connected if the only money they are entitled to receive from the company or any subsidiary is travel expenses incurred while carrying out their duties as a director, normal dividends and reasonable remuneration for services in the course of a trade.

14.10 SUMMARY

1. Companies, no less than individuals, have to meet their taxation and National Insurance obligations. Directors should, at all times, act prudently so far as company taxation issues are concerned.

2. Directors may find themselves personally liable if companies fail to make due payments to the Inland Revenue or HM Customs and Excise.

3. Directors must always ensure that the financial affairs of the company are under competent control.

4. Directors are responsible for the assessment and settlement of their own personal tax liabilities.

Chapter 15

Insolvency

15.1 INTRODUCTION

When a company is insolvent (or approaching insolvency) the directors' paramount duty is to the interests of creditors, not shareholders. This is because the *Insolvency Act 1986* imposes various duties and requirements on the directors designed to protect the interests of the company's creditors.

A company is insolvent *either* when it is not able to pay debts as they fall due *or* the company has an excess of liabilities over assets. So, even if its assets exceed its liabilities, the company will still be insolvent if it has no cash.

It is vital for directors correctly to assess when a company is in financial difficulty, since the personal consequences of failing to do so may be catastrophic. These consequences are discussed below.

15.2 THE COMPANY IS IN FINANCIAL DIFFICULTIES. WHAT CAN YOU DO?

15.2.1 SEEK ADVICE AND TELL INTERESTED PARTIES

First, if you suspect your company may be, or may become, insolvent, or that a particular decision may cast doubt on the company's prospects of solvency in the future, you should immediately call a board meeting to acquaint all the directors with your suspicions.

The board should seek and obtain independent professional advice. In the first instance, your auditor or accountant should be able to help. In practice, unless the financial difficulties have arisen suddenly, they will probably be aware of the company's situation from their normal work. They may help prepare accurate and up-to-date financial information and management accounts for the board. If the company is experiencing cash flow problems, short-term profit forecasts and cash flow projections are vital. Frequently, when companies experience financial difficulties, administration of such matters is neglected under pressure to save the business. In the long term, it may be necessary to ascertain the parts of a business's activities that are profitable and those that are not, probably with a view to closing down or selling the unprofitable parts. Your professional advisers need adequate financial data if they are to help you make an informed decision.

It is also important that you contact your company's bankers and keep them informed of the situation. Frequently, financial difficulties arise because of temporary cash flow problems. However, a well-presented case to the bank, supported by your professional advisers, may enable you to obtain an increased loan facility and therefore some vital breathing space.

There may be a good chance of an acceptable rescue plan which preserves the company, or a substantial part of it, in its existing form. However, you must not forget that, if there is a real risk that the company might become insolvent, leaving creditors unpaid, and if you continue to trade and incur debts, you may later be held personally liable for those debts.

15.2.2 WHAT ARE THE ALTERNATIVES?

It may be that, after investigating the financial position of your company thoroughly and taking advice, you conclude that it is insolvent and cannot trade its way out of the situation. There are several options in this event, though it is not practicable to give more than an outline of them here. Some of these options are commercial in nature, others relate to the procedures established for insolvent companies by law.

Some possible courses of action, starting with those which will least affect the company, are:

- an injection of capital into the company (see section 15.2.3);

- arrangements with the company's creditors (see section 15.2.4);

- the reconstruction or amalgamation of the company (see section 15.2.5);

- an 'administration order' (see section 15.2.6);

- receivership (see section 15.2.7);

- voluntary winding up (see section 15.2.8);

- compulsory winding up (see section 15.2.8).

15.2.3 ADDITIONAL CAPITAL

Very often a company finds itself in difficulties because of cash flow problems even though, technically, it is profitable and assets exceed liabilities. In such circumstances the best course of action may be to obtain external finance. The terms upon which such capital is offered should be considered in close consultation with your professional advisers. For example, if the provider of new capital wants an equity share in the company, then you need to place a value on the company, and this is not easy in circumstances of financial difficulty.

15.2.4 AN ARRANGEMENT WITH THE COMPANY'S CREDITORS

Again, where a company's financial difficulties stem from temporary cash flow difficulties, it would be wise to contact the company's creditors and try to negotiate deferred payment of outstanding accounts. This is likely to involve 'eating some humble pie', and it is important not to tell any lies, but it may give the company some vital time. Creditors often judge that it is in their own best interest to give the company help by accepting deferred settlement of their invoices. Much will depend upon the relationship; as in many matters, mutual trust is most important.

Informal arrangements are preferable but, if all else fails, the *Insolvency Act 1986* has introduced a method of compromise with creditors known as a company voluntary arrangement (CVA) which is conducted under the supervision of an insolvency practitioner. The *Insolvency Act 2000* allows the introduction of an optional moratorium in the CVA procedure for small companies. It is suggested that such a stay on creditor action would give the directors of a company a breathing time in which to agree a rescue proposal with creditors. The company's creditors, however, have to agree the terms of the arrangement, and they may not. This may not be a sufficient course of action anyway, depending upon how close your company is to insolvency.

15.2.5 A RECONSTRUCTION

Internal reorganisation of the company may be advisable. *The Companies Act 1985* (ss.425–427) provides a procedure under which a company, its creditors, its members, the liquidator (in a winding up) or the administrator may put forward proposals for an arrangement which then has to be approved by the Court. Alternatively, s.110 of the *Insolvency Act 1986* gives power to a company to reconstruct by means of a voluntary liquidation and for the liquidator to seek the sanction of shareholders to the transfer of the assets of the company to a new company in exchange for shares or other securities of the new company. A similar process may be employed by a receiver. The receiver sells the assets under his control to a new company set up for the purpose and the shares in the new company are then held by nominees of the receiver in trust for the old company. The new company can be sold more easily than the assets separately and this is often a huge advantage.

15.2.6 ADMINISTRATION

The company, the directors, the shareholders of the company or creditors can each petition the Court for an administration order appointing an 'administrator' (who must be a licensed insolvency practitioner).

The Court must be satisfied that the company is, or is likely to become, unable to pay its debts, but is not in liquidation. The Court can make an order only if it considers it likely to achieve one or more of the following purposes:

- the survival of the company, and the whole or any part of the business, as a going concern;
- the approval of a voluntary arrangement with creditors;
- the sanctioning of a company reconstruction;

- a more advantageous realisation of the company's assets than there would be if the company were wound up.

The administrator must make proposals to the Court within three months that show how the purposes specified in the administration order can be achieved. In practice, commercial reasons dictate a shorter period. These proposals have to be given to the company's shareholders, creditors, and the Registrar of Companies. A meeting of creditors must be called to consider the proposals. If they are approved, the administrator will be required to manage the affairs, business and property of the company in accordance with those proposals. In order to do this, he is given power to 'do all such things as may be necessary for the management of the affairs, business and property of the company'. A long list of particular powers is given in the *Insolvency Act 1986*, s.14 and Schedule 1.

The administrator may at any time ask the Court to be discharged where it becomes clear either that the purpose of the order has been achieved or that it cannot be achieved.

Whilst an administration order is in force, the company may not be wound up, the company's secured creditors cannot take any steps to enforce their security, and no legal proceedings can be started or continued without the leave of the Court. This gives the company time in which the administrator can draw up his proposals for the company's future.

In an administration, directors may remain in office, although they can exercise their powers only in such a way as will not interfere with the administrator. They may be removed by the administrator. The administrator can also appoint directors. The administrator must report on any 'unfit' director to the Secretary of State for Trade and Industry, and this may result in a disqualification order being made (see Chapter 11).

Administrations, however, are rare, affecting only between 1% and 2% of all company failures. The reason for this is simply that they are very expensive to implement and hence are beyond the means of most insolvent companies.

15.2.7 RECEIVERSHIP

Any creditor, secured or not, may apply to the Court for appointment of the Official Receiver to wind up the company. Alternatively, an 'administrative receiver' or 'receiver' may be appointed out of Court under powers contained in a charge over a company's assets.

Frequently, not just when a company appears to be in financial difficulties, a major creditor, usually the company's bank, will trade with the company only on the condition that the company gives security for the balance owing to it. Such security is seen as protecting the creditor in the event of the company becoming insolvent. (The security will often be sought before any financial difficulties have become apparent since, if given at a time of financial difficulty, there is a risk that the security will be set aside in any subsequent liquidation as being a preference under s.239 of the *Insolvency Act 1986*.)

The security is given in a document called a 'debenture'. Debentures create either a 'floating charge', which 'floats' over all the present and future assets of the company, whatever they may be, or a 'fixed charge' which relates to specified assets only, such as a machine or the company's buildings. Under a floating charge, directors have control over the company's assets in the normal course of business, but the debenture deed specifies particular events that will end the company's right to deal with the assets subject to the charge and entitle the debenture holder to appoint a receiver. Bank debentures usually incorporate both fixed and floating charges.

Directors should know that the registration procedures for charges and the accompanying documents, the priority of floating charges and the circumstances in which a floating charge may be altered differ between Scotland on the one hand and the rest of the United Kingdom on the other hand.

A debenture will normally entitle its holder to appoint a receiver in the following circumstances:

- where the company fails to repay the monies secured by the debenture;

- any breach of the debenture terms, normally by exceeding the borrowing limits;

- at the request of the directors.

An 'administrative receiver' is a receiver of the whole, or substantially the whole, of a company's assets and is appointed by a secured creditor whose security includes a floating charge. His task is to take control of the charged assets with a view to realising all of them. On the other hand, a receiver – a person appointed over only a part of the assets, whether under a fixed or floating charge – is appointed to sell only the asset over which the creditor has a fixed charge in order to realise the debt owed to the secured creditor.

From the moment a receiver is appointed, directors will no longer have the authority to deal with the property charged under the debenture. Where there is a floating charge this will effectively divest them of any authority within the company. Directors should remember, however, that although they are divested of many of their powers as a director, their obligations – for example, to file an annual return with the Registrar of Companies – are unaffected.

A receiver, by contrast with an administrator, does not have the power to remove directors from office.

An administrative receiver is under a duty to report on any unfit director to the Secretary of State for Trade and Industry, which may result in a disqualification order being made.

Frequently, receivership leads to a company's liquidation. However, if a receiver is able to pay off the amount secured by the debenture and has given notice to the Registrar of Companies that he has ceased to act, the existing directors will continue to be directors with full powers as before.

15.2.8 LIQUIDATION OR 'WINDING UP'

Where a company is either unable or not allowed to continue trading, application may be made to the Court that it be placed in liquidation (known as 'winding up'). A company may in addition be wound up voluntarily by either the shareholders or the creditors.

Voluntary winding up

If a company is in financial difficulties, yet is solvent in that it could pay its debts in full by selling its assets, a voluntary winding up may be advantageous. This is because a voluntary winding up may be done in an orderly way and is likely to realise a higher value for assets than a forced sale.

A members' voluntary winding up is commenced when the shareholders of a company adopt a resolution for their company to be wound up. The liquidation will proceed provided that a majority of the board of directors make a statutory declaration of the company's solvency within five weeks before the adoption of the winding up resolution. Otherwise the winding up will have to proceed as a creditors' voluntary winding up. The statutory declaration has to state that the directors making it have made a full enquiry into the affairs of the company and are of the opinion that the company will be able to pay its debts in full, together with interest, within a specified period that must not exceed twelve months from the commencement of the winding up. The statutory declaration must include a statement of the company's assets and liabilities at the latest practicable date before it is made.

A director should consider very carefully whether or not to make such a declaration. If the company's debts are not paid or provided for within the period stated, the Court will presume that the directors did *not* have reasonable grounds for making it. It is a criminal offence to make the statutory declaration without having reasonable grounds for the opinion expressed in it. This is punishable with imprisonment for up to two years and/or an unlimited fine on trial on indictment or to a maximum of six months' imprisonment and/or a fine of a maximum of £2,000 on summary trial.

The shareholders will usually appoint a liquidator at the general meeting at which the winding up resolution is adopted. No notice is required to propose the appointment and the winding up commences immediately the resolution for winding up is passed. The company must immediately cease business, except so far as may be required for its beneficial winding up. The appointment of a liquidator will usually end an individual's powers as a director, although the shareholders or the liquidator may permit him to exercise some or all of his directorial powers.

The liquidator will try to realise the company's assets and distribute the proceeds to creditors and shareholders, net of his own costs. If at any time he comes to the opinion that the company will not be able to pay its debts in full within the stated period, he must call a meeting of the company's creditors and the winding up will become a creditors' voluntary winding up.

In a creditors' voluntary winding up there must be a creditors' meeting to appoint a liquidator and there are various publicity requirements that attempt to ensure that creditors are informed of the meeting. At the creditors' meeting the creditors may decide to appoint a liquidation committee to assist the liquidator and to receive reports on the progress of the liquidation.

Approximately two-thirds of insolvent liquidations are voluntary, rather than compulsory, windings-up. The process is slightly less onerous for directors and may be interpreted by creditors as a helpful decision to stop trading.

Compulsory winding up

A compulsory winding up is where the Court orders the company to be wound up on petition from any of the following: the company itself, the company's directors, the Secretary of State for Trade and Industry, a contributory (usually meaning a shareholder), a creditor, an Official Receiver (except for companies registered in Scotland), and an administrative receiver or administrator.

The grounds on which a petition may be sought are as follows:

a) The company has passed a special resolution that it be wound up by the Court.

b) It is a public company and a year or more has expired since incorporation without it obtaining a certificate relating to compliance with its share capital requirements.

c) The company does not commence business within a year of its incorporation or suspends business for a year.

d) The number of shareholders is reduced below two, except in the case of a private limited company.

e) The company is unable to pay its debts. This is the most common ground where a creditor petitions for a company's winding up. A company is deemed to be unable to pay its debts primarily where a creditor owed more than £750 has served a written demand on a prescribed form requiring the company to pay the sum due and the company fails to pay it within three weeks. A company is also deemed unable to pay its debts if the value of its assets is less than its liabilities.

f) The Court considers it just and equitable that the company should be wound up. This ground is often used in the case of small companies which are essentially a partnership in corporate form, where there is an irreconcilable difference of opinion between the 'partners'.

The procedure for a compulsory winding up usually starts by a creditor presenting a petition to the County Court (where the company's paid-up share capital does not exceed £120,000) or to the Chancery Division of the High Court. A copy of the petition is served at the company's registered office and a date will be fixed for the petition to be heard. There are various publicity requirements and in addition the creditor has to file an affidavit with the Court. A 'provisional liquidator' may be appointed before the petition is heard to preserve the company's assets. This effectively takes away the directors' powers, although they can apply to the Court to discharge the order. For obvious reasons, the application has to be made *ex parte*, which means that the company will not have an opportunity to put its side of the case. However, the Court will invariably require an undertaking from the petitioner that he will compensate the company for any loss it suffers if winding up is not subsequently ordered, since it would be unfair if such an order could be made without the company having any redress.

Creditors or shareholders may apply to the Court for someone other than the Official Receiver to be appointed as the liquidator. Insolvency practitioners, usually employees of a firm of chartered accountants, will generally accept appointment as liquidator only where the company has sufficient assets to pay their fees. However, most will be willing to attend creditors' meetings on behalf of creditors free of charge in the hope that they will be appointed liquidator. Where a company has few assets, it will not usually be worthwhile appointing a liquidator (if one could be found willing to be appointed). Where the petitioner does not seek the appointment of a person other than the Official Receiver, the Official Receiver will be appointed as provisional liquidator to take custody of the company's assets. This occurs in the majority of cases. The Official Receiver is appointed by the Secretary of State for Trade and Industry and each Court has one or more Official Receivers attached to it.

Directors' powers do not automatically cease on the appointment of a liquidator in a compulsory liquidation (unlike the position in a voluntary winding up). However, the extensive powers of a liquidator will leave the directors with little role. For example, the liquidator will take into his control all of the company's property.

The law places a duty on the company's directors, employees, company secretary and auditor to give the liquidator such information concerning the company as he reasonably requires, and also to attend upon him at such times as he may reasonably require. A director cannot escape this by resigning; it applies to those who have been officers of the company at any time. It is a criminal offence to fail to comply.

When the liquidator has realised all the company's assets and completed the distributions to creditors, he will send a summary of receipts and payments to the creditors and a final account to the Department of Trade and Industry. The liquidator must summon a final creditors' meeting when it appears to him that the winding up is complete for all practical purposes. He then notifies the Registrar of Companies that the final meeting has been held. On receipt of that notice the Registrar of Companies must complete various publicity requirements and after three months the company will be dissolved.

15.2.9 THE ORDER OF PAYMENT IN LIQUIDATION

The order in which the liabilities of a company in liquidation are settled is as follows: preferential creditors, then secured creditors, and finally unsecured creditors.

- *Preferential creditors* are the Crown or its agents (in most cases this will be the VAT due in respect of the six months prior to liquidation and any PAYE and National Insurance contributions which have been deducted from employees' wages during the previous twelve months but not passed on to the Inland Revenue) and certain amounts of holiday pay and wages.

- *Secured creditors.* These are creditors who hold a charge, mortgage or debenture over any assets of the company. If the charge is fixed, that is, attached to a particular asset, then such a creditor ranks before the preferential creditors. If the charge is floating, the creditor ranks after preferential creditors.

- *Unsecured creditors.* This group contains any creditor who is neither preferential nor secured, typically trade suppliers and any directors who have lent money to the company.

15.2.10 SCRUTINY OF DIRECTORS' ACTIONS

When a company is placed in liquidation the actions of the directors before and during liquidation will come under close scrutiny by the liquidator, often prompted by aggrieved creditors. There are potential liabilities of wrongful trading and fraudulent trading. These are serious offences and are dealt with in section 15.3. In particular, where the company is insolvent, the liquidator will be looking at the treatment of creditors, with particular regard to any evidence of preferential treatment and of the avoidance of debt.

15.2.11 STRIKING OFF

If the Registrar of Companies has reasonable cause to believe that a company is not carrying on business (for example, because it fails to file any documents or reply to correspondence), he will write to the company enquiring whether it is in operation. If he receives no reply, he will send a warning letter. If there is still no reply, he will issue a notice in the *London Gazette* (in the case of a company registered in England and Wales) and send the company a copy. The notice will state that the company will be struck off the Register (unless a reason is shown for it not to be) three months from the date of the notice, from which time it will be unincorporated and cannot trade as a company. If a company has been struck off the Register by this procedure, however, it can be restored.

It is also possible for a company to request the Registrar of Companies to strike it off the Register. Where a company has no assets or liabilities, striking off may be an alternative to a voluntary winding up, but it is at the discretion of the Registrar of Companies.

15.2.12 CAN ANOTHER COMPANY WITH THE SAME NAME AS A WOUND UP COMPANY COMMENCE TRADING?

If a company goes into insolvent liquidation, the same, or a similar, name to that of the insolvent company cannot legally be used by a new company if a director (or shadow director) of that company was a director of the insolvent company at any time during the twelve months before liquidation. The prohibition applies for five years unless the Court rules otherwise. Breach of this prohibition is a criminal offence. If a company does operate under such a prohibited name then any person involved in the 'management' (that is, direction) of that company can be made personally liable for the debts of the company.

This is intended to prevent 'phoenix' companies with similar owners, directors and name being formed by the directors of companies that have gone into insolvent liquidation. It must be admitted, however, that in practice this rule is observed much more in the breach than in the observance.

15.3 THE CONSEQUENCES OF TRADING WHILST INSOLVENT

The consequences will depend upon the circumstances. There are five principal sanctions in law against directors who, in dealing with the company's assets, act irresponsibly with regard to its creditors. These are:

1. Criminal penalties for fraudulent trading under the *Companies Act 1985*.

2. Directors may be personally liable to make contributions to the assets of the company if, in the course of a winding up, it appears that they were knowingly a party to business being carried on with the intention of defrauding creditors or for any fraudulent purpose.

3. Directors may become personally liable to make such contributions to the assets of the company as the Court thinks proper if the company trades 'wrongfully'.

4. Directors may be personally liable to contribute to the company if there has been any misfeasance.

5. Directors may be disqualified by a Court.

These are dealt with in turn below.

Directors should note that under the *Insolvency Act 1986* they may be made personally liable in circumstances where a company has become insolvent. The Act thus removes part of the protection available to directors through the existence of a separate entity – the company – and makes them in certain circumstances liable for actions undertaken by the company.

The ability to mount a successful defence against personal liability will be very much enhanced if the directors have followed the procedures discussed in section 15.2 – that is, taken immediate advice from accountants or lawyers with the necessary expertise as insolvency practitioners to determine whether any remedial measures short of liquidation are possible; informed the company's creditors of the situation; considered whether they should invite anyone with the power to do so to appoint an administrative receiver; considered whether they should apply to the Court for an administration order under Part II of the *Insolvency Act 1986*; and so on.

15.3.1 CRIMINAL LIABILITY FOR FRAUDULENT TRADING

Any person (not necessarily a director) who has been knowingly party to a company's fraudulent trading may at any time (regardless of whether the company ever goes into receivership, administration or liquidation) be prosecuted for this as a criminal offence. 'Fraudulent trading' means carrying on the business of a company with intent to defraud its (or any other person's) creditors or for any other fraudulent purpose. It is an offence which may result in imprisonment. On trial on indictment the penalties are a maximum of seven years' imprisonment and/or an unlimited fine, or on summary trial a maximum of six months' imprisonment and/or a fine of up to £2,000. A guilty director may also be disqualified from acting as a director for up to 15 years.

Actions which could be held to be fraudulent are:

a) falsifying company documents;

b) publishing, with intent to deceive, a false prospectus;

c) publishing false statements in notification of share interests;

d) making false statements to the company's auditors;

e) obtaining goods on credit when it is known that there is no reasonable prospect of repaying the debt when it falls due or within a reasonable time thereafter.

The offence of fraudulent trading is notoriously difficult to prove. It must be proved beyond all reasonable doubt that the business was carried on *with intent* to defraud creditors.

15.3.2 PERSONAL LIABILITY FOR FRAUDULENT TRADING

In addition, any person who has been knowingly party to fraudulent trading by a company which becomes insolvent may be made personally liable by the Court to contribute to the company. Liquidators have an incentive to initiate proceedings for fraudulent trading because, if their application is successful, the Courts may order 'punitive' damages as well as compensation for the appropriate trading loss.

15.3.3 PERSONAL LIABILITY FOR WRONGFUL TRADING

The *Insolvency Act 1986*, s.214, imposes upon directors a duty to consider the interests of creditors. The basic rule is that in an insolvent situation the directors are responsible to the creditors to maintain the assets of the company for the benefit of *all* the creditors *prior to* a formal insolvency. In particular, a director is obliged to take steps to minimise the potential loss to creditors if the director knew or ought to have concluded that an insolvent liquidation was unavoidable. Failure to do this is known as 'wrongful trading'.

If the directors engage in wrongful trading – by, for example, undertaking certain transactions to reduce the assets of the company – then these transactions may be set aside and the directors made personally liable if the assets cannot be recovered. There is a real risk that their assets may be seized and used to pay off creditors if they have failed to take all necessary steps to minimise the potential loss to the company's creditors. In addition, where a Court orders a director to contribute personally to the assets of an insolvent company, it may impose a disqualification order for up to 15 years.

The sorts of transactions which may lead to liability are:

a) *Transactions at an undervalue*; i.e. where the company makes a gift of its property or takes for its property a consideration less than the value of the property transferred.

b) *Transactions to the detriment of creditors*; these are transactions where a company transfers its assets in order to put them out of reach of a person who has a claim against the company.

c) *Preferential payments*; i.e. any act done by a company which has the effect of putting a creditor into a better position than that creditor would otherwise have occupied in the event of the company's insolvency. An example of a preference is granting security to an existing unsecured creditor or repaying one creditor in advance of other creditors. It would be very difficult to persuade a Court that there is no preference if the preferee is a director or a person connected with the director.

d) *Granting a floating charge*, unless given for fresh consideration.

e) *Excessive credit transactions*.

In matters of insolvency a director includes a 'shadow' director.

The conditions

In order for a director to be personally liable it is necessary for the following conditions to be satisfied:

a) the company has gone into insolvent liquidation; *and*

b) at some time before the commencement of the winding up of the company, the director knew or ought to have concluded that there was no reasonable prospect that the company would avoid going into insolvent liquidation.

A director will be judged against the facts known or ought to be known, the conclusions that ought to be reached, and the steps that ought to be taken by a reasonably diligent person having both:

a) the general knowledge, skill and experience that may reasonably be expected of a person carrying out the same functions as are carried out by that director in relation to the company; *and*

b) the knowledge, skill and experience that that director has.

The test is what a 'reasonable director' having the special skills of the director concerned would have known or done in the circumstances in question. It effectively means that the Court has to be assured that the reasonable average person would have concluded that there was no doubt that there was no reasonable prospect of avoiding liquidation. But there is a higher duty placed upon directors who possess a special skill, for example a finance director who is a chartered accountant. There is thus an element of double jeopardy: on the one hand, the incompetent director may be penalised for being unreasonably incompetent; on the other hand, the very competent director may be penalised for performing below his own high standards. The precise limits of the 'reasonable director' test will only become clear when the Courts have had the opportunity to consider a number of individual cases.

The timing problem

The liability of a director does not depend solely on the director having participated actively in wrongful trading. The crucial question is whether or not the director took the action required by the Act to minimise the potential loss to the creditors of the company, and a critical issue in determining whether or not he took such action is to decide the time from which such action should have been taken. This in turn depends upon the moment when the director knew or ought to have concluded that there was no reasonable prospect of avoiding insolvent liquidation. It is often difficult to recognise this moment except in the most obvious cases.

This means that, to minimise the risk of incurring liability, every director should ensure that he:

- is kept informed of the current financial situation of the company (especially regarding cash flow and debtors and creditors) by somebody upon whose statements he is reasonably entitled to rely;

- is aware of the key factors which could, if they changed, trigger the insolvent liquidation of the company;

- is aware of the earliest possible time of any changes which may have occurred or may be about to occur in these key factors; *and*

- as soon as he is aware on the basis of his subjective special skills or knowledge (or ought objectively to have been aware) that there is no reasonable prospect of avoiding insolvent liquidation, he should take the appropriate action required by the Act. This may mean immediately ceasing to trade, although this is not necessarily the case – it might, for instance, be possible to complete a valuable contract in such a way that no new liabilities are voluntarily incurred.

As drafted, the law undoubtedly causes problems for the director who knows or (perhaps because of his superior skill and experience) *ought to have concluded* that the reasonable consequence of a strategic decision taken or ducked by his colleagues is insolvency. It is clear that directors in such a position may not be able to escape liability if they simply keep their doubts to themselves; indeed, if they did so, they might end up by being the only directors found to be liable.

An individual director must be vigilant, not only to anticipate the time at which he ought to conclude that insolvency is likely, but also in order to mitigate his own individual potential liability. It would be prudent to take at least the following precautions:

- Satisfy yourself that the financial information supplied to the board is accurate and sufficient. Some guidance as to what information is necessary (though whether it is sufficient will depend on the circumstances) is given in section 5.5. You should, if you feel it necessary, go beyond the information supplied and investigate the basis on which it was collected.

- Seek independent help from a professional accountant. This may not be a popular step amongst your colleagues, but it may be the only practicable step open to you. The advice you receive will obviously be very relevant to any examination of what you 'ought to have concluded' if the company does go into insolvent liquidation.

- Put your fears to the board. You may have to urge that the company stops trading.

- Finally, resignation may be unavoidable. This is a risky course of action, however, for you will still *prima facie* be liable whether or not you leave the board.

These precautions may well prove very helpful to you in both avoiding insolvency and lessening the consequences to you personally if the worst happens. The Court may not make a contribution order if it is satisfied that you took '. . .*every reasonable step with a view to minimizing the potential losses to the company's creditors . . . as [you] ought to have done'* (*Insolvency Act 1986*, s.214(3)).

For more extensive treatment of the steps a board might take once financial difficulties are apparent, see section 15.2.

Case law

In applying the test as to whether the directors knew or ought to have concluded that there was no reasonable prospect that the company would avoid going into insolvent liquidation, it has been held that the facts which the directors ought to have known or ascertained and the conclusions they ought to have reached were not limited to those which they, showing reasonable diligence, would have known, ascertained or reached. They included those that a person with the general knowledge, skill and experience of someone carrying out their functions would have known, ascertained or reached.

In *Re Produce Marketing Consortium Ltd* {29}, two directors (who were the only full-time employees) were held liable for wrongful trading and ordered to contribute to the company's assets to the extent that the assets were depleted by their actions. The judge paid regard to the functions to be carried out by the director in relation to the company. It followed, therefore, that the general knowledge, skill and experience expected of a director would be much less extensive in a small company than it would be in a large company. Nevertheless, certain minimum standards had to be assumed to be attained since a company had a statutory obligation to maintain accounts showing its financial position and to prepare annual accounts. The facts which a director 'ought to know or ascertain' therefore include not only the information that was actually there, but that which, given reasonable diligence and an appropriate level of general knowledge, skill and experience, was ascertainable. 'Knew or ought to have concluded. . .' (s.214(2)) and 'took every step . . . he ought to have taken' (s.214(3)) may be taken to be based upon the conclusions which any person in the context of the range of information which should have been available to him ought to have come to. For the purposes of this test in s.214(2) the judge decided that the financial results of the company for the year ending 30 September 1985 ought to have been known at the end of July 1986, at least to the extent of the deficiency of assets over liabilities. (This is because the *Companies Act 1985* gives a private company ten months after its year end in which to file accounts with the Registrar of Companies. The company's accounts for the year ending September 1985 should, therefore, have been filed by the end of July 1986. The accounts were in fact not signed until February 1987.) With the knowledge that the directors were to be assumed to have of the company's financial position there would have been no alternative but to conclude there was no prospect of an insolvent liquidation being avoided. The directors should, therefore, have taken every step with a view to minimising the potential loss to the company's creditors from the end of July 1986 and not the date when they actually signed the preceding two years' accounts (i.e. in February 1987). The directors had continued trading for another year after July 1986 and could not, therefore, be said to have taken any steps with a view to minimising the potential loss to the company's creditors. Neither of the directors involved was intentionally dishonest. Wrongful trading can be seen here as the consequence of incompetence only.

The judgement indicates that, even in small companies, all directors should obtain regular reports on their company's financial position and monitor the company's progress. If any problems show up, the directors must ask for more information. If they do not do so, they may find themselves personally liable for the company's debts if it becomes insolvent.

The importance of directors being aware of their duties was emphasised in another wrongful trading action. In *Re DKG Contractors Ltd {12}*, Mr and Mrs G, the only directors and shareholders of DKG Contractors Ltd, were found liable for wrongful trading and ordered to contribute £417,000 to the company's assets. They were also liable under s.239 of the *Insolvency Act 1986* as they had made preferential payments of the same amount to Mr G (who was also a creditor) at a time when the company was unable to pay its debts with a view to putting him in a better position in the event of liquidation than he would otherwise have been in. The judge accepted that neither of the directors knew much about company direction, but they had made no attempt to find out what their duties as a director might be. Mrs G had only limited previous experience of bookkeeping. The judge considered that whilst neither Mr nor Mrs G had acted dishonestly, they had not acted reasonably and consequently ought not to be excused from personal liability.

EXAMPLE

Vanessa is the sole director of a company which trades as an art dealer. The company has little capital and operates on a sizeable overdraft from its bank. The overdraft is guaranteed by Vanessa's husband, James. James acts as a consultant to the company, providing advice and other services, but has not so far been paid.

A client makes a substantial claim against the company, alleging negligent misattribution of a painting. The claim is not covered by insurance. The dispute is acrimonious and the claimant has taken the matter to Court. Judgement is expected soon and Vanessa believes it likely that the company will lose. The company at the moment has cash but the probable award will make it insolvent.

First, Vanessa must ask herself: *Do I genuinely believe the company can continue to trade?* On the facts, insolvency seems likely. Vanessa might take the view that the interests of the creditors are best served by ceasing to trade now. If Vanessa simply carries on trading, the company is likely to incur fresh debts (even if its overall level of debt does not increase) which might not be paid. She might well be open to criticism for ignoring the interests of the new creditors and might be liable to a charge of wrongful trading. On the other hand, it is not certain that the case will be lost. Going into liquidation might simply throw away a viable business unnecessarily.

In deciding what to do, Vanessa must consider her duty to treat all the creditors equally. The company could use its available cash to pay off existing creditors (i.e. James and the bank). However, because of her relationship with James, Vanessa has a clear conflict of interest. Paying the debt owing to James is unlikely to be seen as satisfying a director's duty to resolve any conflicts of interest in favour of the company as a whole, rather than in favour of the director (or her husband). The same might be said of any payment to the bank, since receipts by the bank will reduce the guarantee liability of the director's husband.

The disgruntled client, if he obtains judgement, will certainly object to any payments to James and the bank, both on the grounds of conflict of interest and because (it will be alleged) Vanessa deliberately wished to prevent the client from recovering what he is owed. A payment made in favour of James or the bank is likely to raise accusations against Vanessa that in making the payment she furthered her own interests and that, in the event of liquidation, there had been a preference in favour of the bank and her husband. This would be very difficult to rebut. It is likely that the Court will make an order restoring the position prior to any payment to the bank or James. In addition Vanessa may be judged to be personally liable to the client for any loss and runs the risk of being disqualified from acting as a director on the ground of 'unfitness' (see Chapter 11).

Summary

In summary, then, where a company is insolvent the tests that may be applied to the director with regard to wrongful trading are:

a) Does the director meet the minimum standard reasonably to be expected of someone carrying out the duties of a director?

b) Has the director applied any additional knowledge, skill or experience which he has over and above the minimum standard? If he has additional knowledge, then he is expected to apply it. A finance director will be expected to have greater competence in the area of finance and accountancy than, say, a marketing director.

c) Finally, ignorance of the company's affairs is no excuse. The director has a duty to have information about the company sufficient to be able to judge the financial state of the company at any time.

15.3.4 RESTITUTION AND COMPENSATION FOR MISFEASANCE

Misfeasance does not necessarily involve dishonesty, but includes any breach of duty involving a misapplication of assets or wrongful retention of the company's monies, for instance payment of dividends out of capital, sale of assets (for example, a company car) at an undervalue, or directors making a secret profit.

If in the course of a company's winding up it appears that any director, past or present, is guilty of a misfeasance or breach of trust, the Official Receiver, liquidator, any creditor or shareholder can apply to the Court for the conduct of that director to be investigated. The Court has power, after such an investigation, to order payments to the company by way of restitution or compensation.

In *D'Jan of London Limited* {11} the Court decided that a director who signed an insurance proposal form which inaccurately stated that he had never been a director of a company which had gone into liquidation, with the result that the insurers repudiated liability for a fire at the company's premises, was negligent and thus liable (at least in part) to the company for the loss resulting from the absence of effective insurance.

15.3.5 DISQUALIFICATION

A person, whether an executive or non-executive director, who is responsible for fraudulent or wrongful trading may be disqualified from being a director of a company. Disqualification is the subject of Chapter 11.

15.4 DIFFERENTIAL LIABILITY

Given the tests which have been set out for directors to meet, it is clear that the Courts may discriminate between directors in the context of the knowledge, skill and experience available to them. Thus if a finance director deliberately manipulates the management accounts so that the other directors cannot reasonably be aware of what is going on in the company, then there will be an increased onus upon the finance director. Likewise, if a sales director misleads the board as to the sales that are being achieved, then that director may bear a responsibility over and above that of his fellow directors.

AN EXAMPLE

The board of a small private company is considering making a major investment in new capacity. However, the non-executive directors draw attention to the inadequacy of the financial information provided to the board by the finance director. As a result, the finance director produces new accounts for the next meeting; they appear correct and appropriate to the type and size of the company concerned but in fact are grossly inaccurate. The non-executives – having nothing to put them on suspicion – accept them at face value. However, executive directors, in the light of their knowledge of the company, spot inaccuracies. If the investment contemplated by the board had been taken on the basis of these inaccurate figures, there would have been no reasonable prospect of avoiding insolvent liquidation.

The likely liability of the respective categories of directors is as follows:

THE FINANCE DIRECTOR

He is in a situation where, because of special knowledge and skills, he ought to have been aware that the information was wrong and therefore that, if the proposed action were taken, there would be no reasonable prospect of avoiding insolvent liquidation. Accordingly he should have taken steps to prevent this action being taken. If the company had become insolvent, his failure to act appropriately would have resulted in liability under the *Insolvency Act 1986*.

THE OTHER EXECUTIVE DIRECTORS

A failure by the other executive directors to have the inaccurate figures corrected would be likely to lead to liability under s.214 of the Act.

THE NON-EXECUTIVE DIRECTORS

The non-executive directors ought to have called for adequate financial information as 'reasonable directors'. They did so. If they had failed to do so, the proposed action would have been taken and then there would have been no reasonable prospect of avoiding insolvent liquidation. They would almost certainly not be found liable, if insolvency had not been avoided at a later stage, due to their questioning of the financial information.

If the non-executive directors did not include directors who, because of their special knowledge, skills or experience, ought to have been aware that the figures subsequently provided were inaccurate or had not been prepared on a systematic or accurate basis, they would not be compelled to take action under the section at that time. Nevertheless, if the proposed action were taken, then there would have been a time when they knew or ought to have known that there was no reasonable prospect of avoiding insolvent liquidation. From that moment on, they must take the action required by s.214 if they are to avoid liability.

As this example shows, the *Insolvency Act 1986* creates considerable pressure on directors with specialist knowledge to do their jobs properly and for their non-specialist colleagues to ensure that they do so. That being said, it is important to emphasise that directors cannot hide behind each other – particularly, the finance director. Joint liability may well outweigh individual liability.

15.5 SUMMARY

1. When companies get into financial difficulties, there can be serious personal consequences for directors. In these circumstances it will often be prudent for directors to seek professional advice.

2. If cash flow limits are being strained, key debtors are known to be unable to pay, and creditors have launched actions against the company, then there are clear and present dangers that the company may be wrongfully trading and directors need to be very aware of the dangers facing them personally.

3. What may be done if the company is in financial difficulties?

   ● Inject more capital.

   ● Make an arrangement with creditors.

   ● Merge with another stronger company or sell off profitable parts of the business.

   ● Seek an administration order from the Court to allow an administrator time to find a way for the company to settle its financial problems or to realise the assets of the company to pay off creditors.

   ● Appoint a receiver, if there is a debenture deed on the company; banks owed money usually appoint receivers.

   ● Wind up the company either by voluntary or compulsory means.

4. If directors permit a company to continue trading when it is insolvent or there is no reasonable prospect of avoiding insolvency, then the directors may become personally liable for:

   ● Fraudulent trading – this will mean that they may be ordered to contribute to the assets of the company. In addition, fraudulent trading is a criminal act which may result in imprisonment.

   ● Wrongful trading.

5. If the company trades whilst insolvent, then the directors run a risk of being disqualified.

Part 4

Related Matters

Chapter 16

Directors and Family Companies

16.1 THE FAMILY COMPANY

A family company is a company where one individual or members of a family in combination own at least 50% of the voting shares or are significantly the largest shareholder. In addition, family members often hold most of the senior management and directorial positions. It may be that some of this share-holding is diluted over time in order to attract and motivate outside directors and managers. But, in a family company, the family *en bloc* is able to control, or at least hold great sway over, the affairs of the company.

If the family business is incorporated, and most successful family businesses are, then all that has been said previously in this *Guide* will apply to family companies. We emphasise that a family company is subject to the same laws and ought to follow the same rules of good practice as any other company.

The family company is one of the most enduring features of the corporate landscape. Indeed, the majority of businesses in the UK started as family firms, often based at the family home. Family businesses are the seedcorn of

323

our commercial life. If you have an idea and want to test it in the marketplace, it is natural to give it a try with people you are close to and trust, often your family. They will have the same self-interest as you in making a success of the venture. Family members can also usually be paid in kind rather than in cash. In time, or even initially, the family may wish to seek the advantages of working through a company and will register a company at Companies House.

Most family companies are small or medium-sized enterprises, but not all. Ford Motor Co Inc, Michelin SA, Henkel KGAA, BMW AG and J. Sainsbury Plc are examples of very large family companies.

16.2 STRENGTHS AND WEAKNESSES

Family companies are similar to each other and different from other companies in that they tend to have a distinctive character which derives from the founder and the family. This ethos is often a source of strength. In most family companies, certainly in their early periods, family members with the same values and a deep commitment to the company dominate the board. There is a single goal at which all aim. There is a clear locus of power. Opportunities can be exploited quickly and decisively, perhaps simply on the judgement and instinct of a single individual. Family companies are often prepared to take a long-term view – to build a business for future generations – and to ignore the vagaries of the market or of investor sentiment, which again may add to business performance. Finally, family firms very often command the loyalty of the families of their employees, so that employee motivation and effort are sometimes beyond the call of duty.

On the other hand, however, family firms can also face unique difficulties, and the owner/directors have to learn ways of dealing with them without damaging the inherent advantages that the family firm has. The strength of these difficulties is testified by the fact that in Britain only 24% of family companies survive to the second generation, and in Europe as a whole only 5–15% continue into the third generation in the hands of the descendants of the founder (Neubauer and Lank [1998]).

At the root of the problems is the fact that two 'businesses' are intermingled – the company and the family. Personal, family relationships can affect the running of the business, and problems within the company can spill over into family life. The situation becomes ever more complicated as the business grows and as the family shareholdings become more diffuse. If the company is successful, on the one hand the family will contain shareholders who are not involved in the management or direction of the company and on the other hand the board of directors of the company will probably include non-family members.

More specifically, there are a number of issues with regard to family companies which are worthy of special consideration. These are:

- the relationship between the family and the company;
- governance problems;
- the use of non-family directors;
- inactive and absentee owners;
- succession problems;
- remuneration and tax issues.

These are discussed in turn below. Much of what follows is based on IoD [1995], IoD [1996] and IoD [1997].

16.3 THE FAMILY OR THE BUSINESS?

The ownership structure, organisational structure and culture of family companies may vary greatly. Generally, family companies are established by an individual or a couple only. One person (usually the founder) holds or controls the majority of the equity and acts as managing director/chairman. In time, the founder's children may be given a shareholding and some or all of them may become directors of the company. Shares may also be given to children who do not work in the business. The children may marry and themselves have children. Within a fairly short period, if the company survives, the shares may be held by many individuals. Some of them may be related by blood, whilst others may be related only through marriage. By the third or fourth generation most of the owners will be neither directors nor executives of the company. The situation is even more complicated when the original founders of the company are not related. As their shareholdings devolve through their respective families, the group of shareholders becomes ever less coherent. Some may be closely related to others and have great commitment and interest in the affairs of the company. Others may feel remote from it and see it only as a financial investment.

In both cases, different shareholders in the family will often have different interests. The classic example relates to the way in which family members are to earn a living. Owner-directors will probably take a long-term view when making important company decisions. They will tend to want to plough profits back into the business and to limit borrowings. They may also be risk-averse, since the business is their livelihood and may be their children's too. Small shareholders who are also executive directors may want the company to pay generous salaries, even if the consequence is that the profits available for dividends are diminished. On the other hand, family shareholders not employed by the company may prefer to see dividends or capital growth maximised and may expect the directors to accept modest salaries. Family directors may feel under-rewarded and that they are 'carrying' the rest of the family; members of the family who are shareholders but not directors may feel the directors are taking too much out of the business and feel frustrated at their lack of directorial control. If some members of the family are denied access to benefits-in-kind, such as a company car, chauffeur, discounts on purchases, and so on, then there will be allegations of unfairness and bitter feelings. These conflicts have sometimes proved so severe that, in the end, the family owners have sold the business over the heads of the family directors.

A major problem arises if some family members wish to cash in their stake in the company. Normally, the Articles of Association of family companies, as with other private limited companies, restrict the rights of shareholders to sell their shares – usually, they can be sold only to other family members – and the value of the shares is thus obviously lessened. Buyers will want a low valuation; sellers will tend to feel that the buyers within the family are taking advantage of them.

Family members have deep and powerful emotional connections, both positive and negative, and may well have a long history together. All family members by definition have interrelationships which are 'outside' the company but may nevertheless spill over into company affairs. On the other hand, business life can intrude into the family; the single-minded entre-preneur, obsessed by the business and neglectful of family obligations, is a familiar figure.

But it is more complex than this. Family businesses often contain a built-in contradiction. Family behaviour is often influenced by deeply felt principles, or even subconscious desires – for example, the need to treat children equally, the need for elder siblings to set an example to younger siblings, the need for children to be respectful to their parents. Families tend to be inward-looking and place great value on loyalty. Change is often unwelcome since it can be perceived as threatening the stability of the family unit. By contrast, the company system is probably task-orientated, based on contractual relationships, emphasises performance and results, pays scant attention to subconscious desires, and recognises the necessity of change. The different priorities of the business and the family tend to create value conflicts and thus friction for the family members and the directors of the business. Where membership of these two groups overlaps, the tensions can be very severe indeed. When the company is successful, these potential problems may never actually materialise. But if the company runs into difficulties, then the interdependence of the family and the company, and perhaps their basic incompatibility, will ensure that the problems come to the surface.

The rational answer to these sorts of problems is to recognise the potential for conflict, address it early, and tackle any potential problems before they emerge. Always, the aim must be, as far as is possible, to disentangle family interest from the interest of the company and to balance the competing demands. In practice, this means that the family defines and articulates its relationship with the company – that is, makes a plan for the present and the future. What issues such a plan might address are discussed in section 16.9 below.

16.4 GOVERNANCE PROBLEMS

Family companies often find it difficult to adapt their governance structure as the business grows. Families tend to prefer informal meetings. After all, meetings of shareholders can easily take place without notice to suit the interest of the family – and in non-business environments. Similarly with board meetings. Informality can be an advantage, facilitating speedy reactions and decisions. However, as the business grows, there comes a point where it is not efficient simply to take business decisions around the family dinner table or to allocate tasks as they arise to whoever happens to be present. Additionally, if company and board meetings are habitually undisciplined, it may be difficult to introduce more formal and appropriate meeting arrangements if the shareholding or the board is expanded to encompass non-family members.

Allocating business tasks on a non-business basis is particularly dangerous. The result can be a mix of responsibilities among senior executives and directors that can lead to conflict in the boardroom. A natural result is that the board tends to concentrate on management issues, especially if they are the cause of internecine strife and therefore require immediate attention, and neglects strategic issues. This can be a recipe for disaster.

16.5 THE ROLE OF 'OUTSIDERS'

It is generally desirable for family companies, as they grow, to extend the directorate and perhaps even widen the shareholding to include non-family members. Sometimes outsiders are necessary because the family is just too small for the size of business. But, this apart, most dominant family managing directors, however much they feel it may diminish their power, should realise that it will almost certainly be in the interest of the company to bring in an outsider(s) and introduce other influences besides that of the family into the direction of the company.

Most probably the outside director in a family company will be a non-executive director, with all the potential advantages discussed in section 4.1.4. They may have a wealth of experience and skills lacking in the family that they can bring to bear. They may have a network of contacts that can be mobilised to the company's advantage – new customers, new sources of finance, foreign contacts, connections in the public sector, and so on. They may have knowledge beyond that of the family – for example, regarding acquisitions or a listing. They may take a relatively dispassionate view about the merits of proposed family appointments or promotions. They can serve as 'honest brokers' in disputes about unfairness in the dealings between members of the family and between family and non-family executives. It might even be that they can act as an unemotional and trusted sounding-board for sensitive issues such as the succession, or even serve as mentors to the younger family members. Their objectivity may also be the most effective way of protecting the interests of those family members who play no part as executives or directors of the company.

Suitable candidates for the job of non-executive director might be, for example, professional executives who have served as a director of a division or subsidiary of a large Plc and taken early retirement. They will not want a huge commitment, but to be able to play a role in a small company is often very appealing. In contrast, professional advisers to the company are unlikely to be a good choice as non-executive non-family directors. Their expertise is available anyway, and their appointment as a director may create a conflict of interest. Spouses and relatives with little or nothing to contribute will not serve the company well and in the long run may damage their own interests as shareholders. Similarly, retired employees and friends of the family are unlikely to be sufficiently independent and objective.

Unfortunately, however, in family companies the board is often seen as a family preserve. There tends to be a reluctance to utilise the talents and experience of non-family members in the management and direction of the company. There are many reasons for this. First, families are often reluctant to accept that they are not of the necessary calibre to run the company. To suggest that outsiders be brought in to direct 'their' company may be viewed as a criticism or even insult. Secondly, sometimes there is a failure to understand that the mere fact of their membership of the family, because of the associated conflicts of interest, limits their ability to be sufficiently objective in the boardroom. Additionally, the tasks of a board inevitably involve family questions that owner-directors are reluctant to face up to – for example, job definitions of family members, the remuneration of family members and, above all, succession. Family directors generally do not want to share confidential information, nor to discuss family matters, with outsiders. Finally, many managing directors simply do not want an independent board to whom they would be accountable.

There is, however, a common misconception. Having non-family directors on the board does not mean that the managing director or the family shareholders must surrender all power. But it does mean that the managing director must consciously keep his role as the controlling shareholder separate from his role as a board member. Having outsiders on the board does not limit the managing director's powers as the owner of the company. There may be times when, as the owner, he will overrule the board. Board members have to accept this, but they must feel that they have been listened to, that their opinions are valued, and that they are respected.

If an outsider is appointed to the board, it is necessary for the family-dominated board to consider with great care how they can best ensure the integration of the new director into the company. If this is not done effectively, then there may be disastrous consequences for the family business.

On the other hand, it may not be easy to attract and retain competent non-family directors. One reason for this is that power in a family company ultimately rests with one or several members of the family. In the final analysis, this is an inevitable restriction on the outside director. Outsiders may feel that their authority within the company will never be the same as that of family members, even if the latter are ostensibly junior to them. There is also always a danger of the board being a family cabal into which the new director is not invited. Or decisions may be taken outside the boardroom. Worse, it may even be that family power is used if necessary to ensure that family interest prevails over the company's interest. It may also be the case that the non-family director is poorly rewarded given his efforts and contribution to the company, and there may be little that he can do about it.

The onus is always with the family to behave with restraint. Power in itself is neither good nor bad: it is how it is used that matters. If the family's ownership power is used only with a view to the best interests of the company, then there will probably be little conflict with the outside director. On the other hand, if that power is used to pursue a family agenda at odds with the company agenda, then no professional outside manager or director worth his salt will stay.

16.6 ABSENT OWNERS

A common situation in family companies is where one or more majority shareholders take no part in the day-to-day management of the company and may not even be directors themselves. This situation is particularly common in the farming industry, or where the proprietors of a business have become non-resident in contemplation of a trade sale, or where the proprietors have retired (and perhaps moved overseas), appointing professional managers as directors to run the company in their absence.

Difficulties may occur between the full-time director and the absentee owner. Whilst the full-time outsider, as director of the company, has certain legal responsibilities, the company may be run entirely in accordance with the instructions of the absentee owner(s), who will normally have complete voting and financial control. Further, the absentee owners probably 'interfere' a great deal in the running of the company, as their entire family fortunes may be at stake. The result is that the full-time director can find himself in a difficult position. He has the same duties and legal responsibilities as any other director, without the freedom of action that usually goes with those burdens. For example, the controlling shareholder may, for perfectly proper commercial reasons, ensure that the company does not have cash reserves greater than are necessary to cover routine operations. No decision that requires financial backing, therefore, can be taken before the shareholder(s)' approval has been sought and obtained. In addition, a policy that requires all surplus cash to be distributed immediately may appear imprudent if the company runs into financial problems without the reserves to deal with them. It is the director who will be held responsible for excessive distributions if it results in loss to the company and its creditors.

The situation can also pose difficulties for the absentee owner. In particular, the law may regard him as a shadow director; it does not matter that he has not been formally appointed. In that event the absentee owner will be subject to all the legal duties of any other director. This is not in itself a problem, so long as the shareholder/director realises and understands the position. However, there may well be reasons (for example, to avoid a certain tax residency) why it is important that the status of a director of the company must be avoided.

16.7 INACTIVE DIRECTORS

Many family companies are owned and run by a team of family members who genuinely participate in the board's decisions and share the effort. Sometimes, however, a member of the family is appointed a director for essentially family reasons, but takes no significant role in direction.

Directors should be aware that there are a number of potential dangers in appointing a 'sleeping' director. First, any payments to that director must be justified by the contribution made to the company. The active directors cannot give away the company's money, even to a director. Secondly, from the sleeping director's point of view, he or she might well be judged equally as liable as the active directors since in law there is no distinction between an active and an inactive director. For example, the 'sleeper' might be pursued by a liquidator if imprudent handling of the company's affairs by the active directors caused loss to creditors and the inactive director had done nothing to stop it. Or, to take another example, if the 'sleeper' had helped out by acting as a signatory to cheques without understanding and approving the underlying transactions and it turns out that the payments are improper or careless, then the sleeper is likely to be judged to share liability with the active director. It may be possible to show that it was reasonable to rely on assurances from the active director, but this will not be easy. By acting as a director, an individual tells the world that he is running the company's affairs; it may be no good denying this later, if third parties have lost money.

16.8 SUCCESSION ISSUES

Generally, all the factors discussed in Chapter 7 on the selection of directors, the managing director and the chairman apply equally to family companies. Most importantly, the selection of a new managing director should be a collective decision of the board.

It is not easy to transfer a family company to the next generation, because it always raises complex and emotive problems which may harm the business as well as cause damaging splits and tensions within the family. However, the practical and psychological aspects of succession are probably less stressful and damaging if a process for managing the succession is agreed upon. A written document, drafted well in advance of retirement and in collaboration with the family and perhaps outside board members, is often a useful device to minimise potential conflicts. The willingness of family company owners to face up to and plan for their succession is probably the most important factor determining whether the business fails or survives to future generations.

16.8.1 WHOM TO CHOOSE?

The first obvious decision concerns the identity of the 'heir'. The founder must typically decide between appointing a family member as the successor managing director, appointing a 'caretaker', appointing a professional non-family director, selling the business, or doing nothing.

'Doing nothing' is by far the most likely option in practice. This may be for a whole host of reasons. Many entrepreneurs, for psychological reasons, are reluctant to 'let go' and accept that it is time to relinquish formal power. Some have a temperamental aversion to planning. They may fear a loss of identity if they retire. There may be insufficient financial provision for retirement. There may be family concerns too. It is distasteful to have to choose between children, as may be necessary when the needs of the company conflict with family feelings. Jealousy, opposition from the founder's spouse, a distaste for discussion between parents and children about the implications of the deaths of the parents, children's psychological fears about parents leaving them, all may play a part. Finally, senior managers may raise objections; often their close personal relationship with the founder is the best thing about the job and the latter's replacement is seen as a threat to job satisfaction and security. There is a minefield of complex and interrelated factors that are all operating against contemplation about the succession, let alone any kind of planned effort to manage it.

16.8.2 A FAMILY SUCCESSOR?

Families normally have a strong desire to bring children into the company, even if the children do not have the aptitude or even the desire to succeed the parent. If no child has the necessary motivation and talent to be an obvious successor, forcing the child to take over is often a great mistake, leading to both business failure and personal misery for the child. If this is the case, the only answer is to sell up or to bring in outside executives.

Treating all children equally is rarely a practical option; having several joint managing directors is often a recipe for disaster. Joint leadership is practical only if there is the relatively rare combination of a shared business vision, similar abilities and a very strong family bond.

One child may stand out, be sufficiently able and committed to command the respect and assent of the board, employees and family. But sibling rivalry may be so strong that none of the children will accept one of the others as leader.

In practice, these decisions are rarely clear-cut. It is not easy for a family to agree on a successor. How family members are perceived by the family will depend on a whole host of factors, some of them with little relevance to business skill. Assessing the business acumen of a family member is notoriously difficult. We all see our children 'through a glass darkly'. People change; a child may not be ready now, but might grow into the job in the future. Differences between the generations may serve to worsen the problem. Children may have to be promoted over the heads of their 'elders and betters', both in the family and the company. This is not easy.

By the time the third generation is reached there may be many dozens of family members who are shareholders, and there will be quite a large number of potential successors. The choice is therefore harder, and the potential for family conflict is greater. Cousins usually have less in common than siblings brought up together. The need for a formal governance system is that much the greater.

16.8.3 AN OUTSIDER?

An outsider may be brought in to lead the company. This may be the only feasible way of resolving the succession problem. The issues then are ones of trust and competence: will the family fortunes be safe in the hands of an outsider?

16.8.4 DIVIDING THE COMPANY

One solution sometimes adopted is to leave each child a different part of the original company, which then develops independently. This is possible only if the original business can be restructured and demerged.

16.8.5 SELLING THE COMPANY

Disposing of the company is often a traumatic experience. Founders tend to have a huge amount of emotional capital invested in the company. But it may be the only option that preserves family unity and financial security.

16.8.6 AN EXAMPLE

This hypothetical example is based on that given in IoD [1997] and illustrates the complexity of the succession problem. Imagine a company owned equally by a second-generation family of two brothers and a sister, and directed by a triumvirate of the two brothers and their brother-in-law. They are the only directors. The elder brother, Brother 1, is managing director. The three have worked well together, the business has grown, but now they are of an age when they are thinking about the succession. Each has children, most of whom are working in the company (marked *). Each set of parents wishes to treat their own children equally, and hence bequeaths their respective shares in the company equally to their offspring. Figure 16.1 illustrates the ownership:

Sister = Brother-in-law (33.3%)					Brother 1 (33.3%) Managing director			Brother 2 (33.3%)
C1* (6.6%)	C2* (6.6%)	C3* (6.6%)	C4 (6.6%)	C5 (6.6%)	C6* (11.1%)	C7* (11.1%)	C8 (11.1%)	C9* (33.3%)
Future MD? ↓ Future owner-director? ↓								

Figure 16.1 *Illustrative share ownership in a family company*

Each of the siblings is concerned about the future role of their own children in the company. At the same time, each wants the best for the company. The children of Brother 1 are likely to feel that their father, as managing director, has made the greatest contribution to the success of the business.

Each branch of the family will have hopes, expectations and assumptions built up over the years. There may be emotional undercurrents among the cousins – resentment, ambition, envy, and so on.

The second generation had equal shares of the company. However, the cousins now have significantly different shareholdings, ranging from 6.6% to 33% each. As luck would have it, the generally recognised successor as managing director is a child of the sister, say C3. But C3 is likely to want at least parity in terms of ownership – otherwise he will never really have the power his formal status confers.

Altogether, in this example, twelve people are involved in the succession. The permutations of possible answers to the succession problem are, for practical purposes, endless. If formal mechanisms commanding general acceptance have not previously been agreed upon, there is likely to be trouble, affecting both the business and the family.

16.9 THE FAMILY PLAN

It will never be possible to provide for every problem that may arise in the future. However, the same set of issues and problems tend to arise in all family companies and experience has shown that many of the common difficulties inherent in family businesses may be obviated by forward planning (perhaps with appropriate professional advice).

But who leads the family consultation process? Some family member has to take the lead, champion the process, and garner the enthusiasm of other family members. It may be that a trusted and respected non-executive director or family friend may be helpful. Whoever it is, he or she must understand the business, be respected by all parties, and be able to combine the roles of mentor for the children and adviser to the parents. This is not easy.

16.9.1 THE ADVANTAGES OF A FAMILY PLAN

A family plan has many advantages:

- Issues are generally easier to deal with if they have been discussed in advance. Sometimes the best decisions for a business are wrong for the family, which owns and runs it. Conversely, as owners, the family may set goals for the business that do not appear practicable or sensible in terms of business practice. The intermingled family/business issues – for example, how to provide a stable income for individual family members, how to provide job satisfaction for family members, how to involve junior generation or in-law family members in the business, how to maintain family tradition, status or craftsmanship, what should be the future strategic direction of the company – are often resolved in a family forum. In general, the more communication among the family and the more consensual planning there is, the more likely it is that an enduring balance between the best interests of the company on the one hand and the well-being of the family on the other can be struck.

- The process itself may bring benefits. Simply separating the discussions from day-to-day family and business affairs may provide an opportunity for family members to clarify their relationship to the business, and may serve as a friendly way of 'educating' recalcitrant family members to face up to the tricky personality and relationship-based emotional issues that, uncontrolled, can damage the business and family.

- The family planning process also allows the family to think about its approach to non-family members and to work out how far they are to be integrated into the organisation of the business, and what their relationship with the family is to be.

- A formal document – to which everyone has contributed and to which everyone can refer – may reduce the potential for suspicion and misunder-standings.

16.9.2 THE PROCESS

There are no hard and fast rules. But flexible and sensitive approaches along the lines indicated below are likely to be helpful.

Start the planning early

In the absence of a plan, the unexpected death of a founding managing director/owner may expose the family to large tax liabilities without the liquid assets to settle them. This is just the sort of circumstance that leads to a forced sale of the company.

The founder can gradually move from full-time managing director to part-time chairman. If managed skilfully, the process is almost imperceptible; the founder becomes used to a new role, his successor gradually grows into the job with the full confidence of the patriarch, and other family members have time to absorb the implications.

Encourage teamwork between the generations

As time goes by and succeeding generations inherit the company, the emotional factors often become more intense. Unresolved issues, grudges and jealousies left over from preceding generations fester, and end up being more difficult and complicated as time goes by. Recognising these sorts of issues and trying to find inter-generational solutions is the only rational way forward.

Develop a written succession plan

Such a plan should incorporate a step-by-step approach to dealing with the practical and psychological aspects of the succession process. The issues the family should regularly discuss and agree upon are listed in Table 16.1.

Use outside help

Non-family members of the board of directors may be able to provide useful expertise and objectivity. The company auditor, accountant, banker and lawyer may have relevant experience of succession problems.

Prepare the successor

The development of children or other family members to succeed the current owner/managing director is beyond the scope of this chapter, but is well covered in IoD [1996].

Plan for retirement

Above all, the current leader of the company should establish a target date for retirement. This should be far enough ahead for plans to be made, but not so far ahead that no one believes it. The owner/founder must prepare for retirement both emotionally and financially. The use of leisure time and any work activities must both be planned. How much time will the retired founder devote to the business? What part-time or consultancy role is possible? Almost certainly he can make a valuable input by introducing managers and directors to those individuals and organisations that are important to the success of the company.

Retire unequivocally

There is a very natural reluctance to step down. Not retiring until all energy and talent has gone, or not retiring on the previously agreed date, produces

337

confusion and demoralises successors. This does not mean that the founder ceases to play any role in the company, but it does mean that his or her new role does not include participation in the day-to-day business of the company.

16.9.3 THE ISSUES TO BE DECIDED

The issues that should be addressed by the family plan are listed in Table 16.1 as a series of questions. These questions are never easy to answer. The answers to many of them are interrelated. It is not surprising, then, that these sorts of question are often never answered and are left unresolved, even though a failure to confront them head-on usually damages the company.

Table 16.1 *Checklist for a family strategic plan*

Long-term issues	1. What are the family beliefs and values?
	2. How are they to be reflected in the company's vision, mission and values and in the day-to-day running of the business?
	3. What are the family's objectives for the business? Is the aim of the business to generate family revenue, to grow and prosper as a business, or some combination of these targets?
	4. What are the family plans for ownership of the business? To sell it eventually?
Family members in the business	5. Who will lead the business in the future? When is the decision about the successor to be made? By whom is it made? (The board of directors? The family shareholders? Or the family generally?) What are the criteria for succession? When will the transition take place?
	6. How is the succession decision to be communicated to customers, employees, the bank, and so on?
	7. What are the retirement plans of other family members active in the business? How can the family help them to achieve them?
	8. How is the founder's gradual withdrawal from the company to be managed?
	9. What are the criteria for entry into the company? Do family members want to work in the company? Should in-laws be allowed to join?
	10. What rights have future family members to participation in the business?
	11. What are the roles of different family members in the company, if any?

Table 16.1 *Checklist for a family strategic plan (continued)*

	12. How should family members be remunerated?
	13. How should the performance of family members in the company be evaluated? What if family members do not perform adequately?
	14. Should there be a development programme for potential successors within the company? How are adequate training and experience for family members before they join the business to be assured?
Share ownership	15. Do shareholders regard themselves as owners of an asset that will yield them a capital sum in due time, or simply as custodians of the shares (which are perhaps placed in trust) for the next generation?
	16. If the shares are viewed as a realisable capital investment, is everyone aware of this and are procedures in place to accommodate holders who want to cash in their shares? What are the rights to own, buy, sell and transfer shareholdings – within and outside the family?
	17. Alternatively, if the shares are seen as a non-transferable trust for future generations, is everyone aware of this and is the company geared up to provide income and pension rights in place of capital asset status for the shares?
	18. What should the dividend policy be? How is the revenue generated by the business to be shared?
	19. Who should have voting control?
	20. What will happen as regards share ownership in the next generation?
	21. Should family members who are active in the business be treated differently from those who are inactive? What degree of control should family shareholders who are not active in the business exercise?
Relationships within the family	22. How should differences within the family be dealt with?
	23. Who has responsibility for unpalatable company financial or personnel decisions with a direct family impact?
Other matters	24. Should the business have independent directors? How are such people to be attracted, motivated and remunerated?
	25. How can the family protect the security of loyal employees?
	26. What role should the business have in the community?

16.10 REMUNERATION AND TAXATION MATTERS

The director of a family company will typically also be a significant share-holder. This provides a number of alternative ways in which to extract value from the company and also raises the question of tax planning. The discussion in Chapter 14 is relevant to family companies too.

Factors which need to be considered are:

- how and whether to extract value from the company now or retain earnings within the company;
- how and whether to take remuneration in the form of salary or dividend;
- individual pension planning;
- benefits-in-kind;
- whether to employ a spouse or dependant;
- how to minimise capital gains tax;
- individual inheritance tax planning.

These matters are discussed in turn.

16.10.1 RETAINING EARNINGS WITHIN THE COMPANY

Companies currently (1999/2000) pay corporation tax on profits at rates of 20% on profits up to £300,000, 32.5% on profits between £300,000 and £1,500,000 and 30% on profits of £1,500,000 and over. The higher rate personal income tax band is 40% and the company also pays National Insurance at 12.2% of salary.

There is clearly an immediate tax saving from leaving profits within the company rather than taking them as remuneration if, as is likely, the director's marginal income tax rate is 40%. However, leaving profits within the company increases the net assets of the company and ultimately the value of the company. This added value may increase the amount of capital gain if the business is sold in the future and hence capital gains tax, although retirement relief (see section 16.10.6) may reduce this significantly.

16.10.2 SALARY OR DIVIDEND?

Profits can be extracted from the company by way of dividend or salary. Each has different implications for both the company's corporation tax position and the director's income tax position.

Salaries and the associated employer's National Insurance contribution of 12.2% are fully deductible in calculating profits chargeable to corporation tax. The director will pay income tax on his remuneration (less allowances) of 10% on the first £1,500, 23% of the next £26,500 and 40% on amounts over £28,000. He will also pay employee's National Insurance on remuneration up to £26,000.

Dividends are not deductible in calculating chargeable profits of the company. The director pays income tax on the amount of the cash dividend plus the associated tax credit (one-ninth of the cash dividend) at 10% if he is a basic rate taxpayer and 32.5% if he is a higher rate taxpayer. The amount of the tax credit can be set off against any income tax liability.

It follows that the decision whether to pay dividend or salary depends on the marginal tax rates of both the company and the director. Table 16.2 shows the difference in the combined corporation and income taxes paid on £10,000 of profit paid as dividend and £10,000 of profit paid as salary. When the company is paying corporation tax at the lower rate, a dividend is generally more tax efficient. Otherwise, there is only an advantage if the director is paying income tax at the lower rate, as he then avoids employee's National Insurance.

16.10.3 PENSION PLANNING

Pension contributions are a very tax efficient way of taking a benefit from a company, especially when the director is a higher rate taxpayer. The contributions are fully deductible in calculating profits chargeable to corporation tax, there is no employer's or employee's National Insurance to pay, and the director is not subject to income tax on the contributions.

Although pension benefits are subject to income tax, it will often be at a lower rate than the director's marginal rate of income tax at the time when the contributions to the pension fund were made. In addition, the pension fund is not subject to tax on its investment returns and so should grow faster than individual investments.

Pension planning should be done in conjunction with salary planning as, depending on the type of scheme, either the amount of contributions or the level of benefits will be limited by salary level.

16.10.4 BENEFITS-IN-KIND

Directors suffer income tax on the cash equivalent of benefits-in-kind provided either for themselves or their family. The most obvious benefit is

Table 16.2 *A comparison of dividend and salary remuneration*

£10,000 of profit paid as dividend

Profits chargeable to corporation tax	< £300k	£300k–£1,500k	> £1,500k
Marginal rate of corporation tax	20.0%	32.5%	30.0%
Profit	10,000	10,000	10,000
Corporation tax	−2,000	−3,250	−3,000
Available for dividend	8,000	6,750	7,000
Director/shareholder taxed on:			
Net dividend received in cash	8,000	6,750	7,000
Tax credit (1/9th of net dividend)	888	750	777
	8,888	7,500	7,777
If director's taxable earnings < £28,000			
Income tax due (wholly offset by tax credit)	Nil	Nil	Nil
Net cash received by director	8,000	6,750	7,000
Effective overall tax rate	20.0%	32.5%	30.0%
If director's taxable earnings > £28,000			
Income tax due less tax credit	2,001	1,688	1,751
Net cash received by director	5,999	5,062	5,249
Effective overall tax rate	40.0%	49.4%	47.5%

£10,000 of profit paid as salary (not affected by company's tax rate)

Profit	10,000
Salary	8,913
Employer's National Insurance @ 12.2%	1,087
	10,000
If director's taxable earnings < £28,000	
Income tax @ 23%	2,050
Employee's National Insurance @ 10%	891
Net cash received by director	5,972
Effective overall tax rate	40.3%
If director's taxable earnings > £28,000	
Income tax @ 40%	3,565
Employee's National Insurance contribution – limit already reached	Nil
Net cash received by director	5,348
Effective overall tax rate	46.5%

the company car. Some other benefits currently avoid National Insurance and are therefore more tax efficient than paying the director a higher salary so that he may purchase the benefit himself.

However, the tax advantages of providing company cars are progressively being reduced by each successive Finance Act such that, depending on mileage and running costs of the car, a director may be better off taking a higher salary and purchasing his own car. In addition, nearly all benefits-in-kind are now subject to employer's National Insurance.

16.10.5 EMPLOYING A SPOUSE OR DEPENDANT

Paying a salary to a spouse or dependant may be beneficial in order to use their tax allowances and lower tax bands. However, for the remuneration to be deductible in calculating profits chargeable to corporation tax, it must be incurred wholly and exclusively for the purposes of the business. Any remuneration which is regarded as excessive in relation to the duties performed by the spouse or dependant may not be allowed as a deduction.

16.10.6 MINIMISING CAPITAL GAINS TAX

Capital gains tax (CGT) may be chargeable when a director disposes of his shareholding in the family company. The tax is based on the excess of the proceeds over the cost with an allowance for inflation (indexation relief) up to April 1998 and thereafter an allowance for the length of time that the asset has been owned (taper relief).

Gains can be sheltered from CGT by retirement relief which is available if the director is at least 50 years old, or younger if the disposal is made on grounds of ill health, has control of not less than 5% of the voting rights in the company and is a full-time working director. These conditions must be met for at least one year and the relief will be reduced proportionately where they have not been met for ten years. If relief is being claimed on the basis of age rather than ill health, it is not necessary for that individual to have retired from the business from the date of disposal. Thus the individual can obtain relief on the sale of the goodwill of the business even though he remains an employee of the company. Relief is also not forfeited if the individual ceases to be a full-time working director prior to the disposal but continues up to the date of disposal to devote at least ten hours per week to the company in a technical or managerial capacity. In the case of shares, if the company has chargeable assets which are not 'business assets', only the 'appropriate proportion' of the gain is eligible for relief.

For the 1999/2000 tax year, 100% relief is available on gains up to £200,000 and a further 50% relief on gains between £200,000 and £800,000. The relief is being gradually phased out by the end of 2002/2003.

In planning to reduce CGT the following should be considered:

- If commercially sensible, take advantage of retirement relief while it is still available.

- When disposing of part of a holding, consider whether the balance represents at least 5% of the voting rights so that retirement relief will apply to a subsequent disposal.

- Plan the timing of any part disposals to maximise the benefits of the annual exemption (£7,100 of gains for the tax year 1999/2000).

- No capital gain arises on the transfer of assets between spouses and indexation and taper reliefs are not compromised. Consider transferring assets to take advantage of the spouse's annual exemption. In addition, a spouse who works full-time for the company is also entitled to retirement relief assuming that he or she meets the other conditions.

- If the company is being sold, then, assuming it has sufficient distributable reserves, the payment of a dividend immediately prior to the sale will reduce the capital gain. The dividend will be taxed but at a lower rate than the capital gain, assuming retirement relief does not apply. On the other hand, if taper relief is a significant proportion of the gain, it may be beneficial not to pay a dividend and to take the maximum possible capital gain.

- Very importantly, remember that all capital gains are extinguished on death. No capital gains tax is payable and the cost for calculating the capital gain when the inheritor disposes of the shares is the market value at time of death.

16.10.7 INHERITANCE TAX PLANNING

Directors of qualifying unquoted companies (which include those on the Alternative Investment Market) can generally obtain 100% business property relief from inheritance tax when they gift their shares, provided that the shares have been held for at least two years.

Most unquoted companies qualify unless their business consists of dealing in stocks and shares, dealing in land and buildings or holding investments.

16.10.8 VALUATION OF UNQUOTED COMPANY SHARES

The valuation of shares in unquoted companies is a subject which is arguably more art than science. The basis of valuation of the shareholding will depend on such factors as the size of the shareholding, the rights attaching to the shares, the number and identity of the holders of the other shareholdings and the size of their shareholdings, the sort of buyer that might be expected, the company's trading prospects, and all the other factors relevant to the particular case. There is no standard formula.

Majority holdings are likely to be valued by reference to the value of the company as a whole. This will reflect the value of the underlying assets, the estimated maintainable profits and all the other relevant factors. On the other hand, a minority holding in an unquoted company, where no dividends can be expected, might have a value very much less than the proportion of the value of the company as a whole which that holding represents. This is because if there is no prospect of income nor of sale of the shares, a minority holder, who can have little influence on the conduct of the company's affairs, can expect no returns from his or her investment unless and until the company is sold, floated or wound up, none of which may be in prospect. Also, it should be remembered that the Articles of Association of unquoted companies usually regulate and restrict the transfer of shares by members.

16.10.9 SHAREHOLDERS' AGREEMENTS

Family arrangements can be implemented either by amending the company's Articles or by entering into a shareholders' agreement. In practice, a combination of the two is often adopted.

Usually, such family agreements are undertaken in the expectation that the agreement will be a confidential statement of agreed intent rather than a legally binding contract. But, as circumstances change, a view frequently develops that legal enforceability is necessary and even desirable. For example, exit procedures for family shareholders who wish to 'cash in' often make clear their ability to sell their shares but, in order to protect the company against take-over or a large withdrawal of cash, impose restrictions on who they may sell to or state that the consideration for their shares will be paid over an extended period of time. This may well impose a serious burden on the departing family shareholder. This sort of conflict of interest is probably better dealt with via a binding contract rather than by an unenforceable understanding.

Some of the issues that would normally be covered by an agreement between shareholders are:

a) **Pre-emption rights**

When one of the shareholders wishes to sell, the other shareholders may not wish the buyer to be other than a family member. In any event, it might not be possible to find an outside buyer for a minority interest in a family company. Shareholders can decide at the outset on pre-emption rights by which the remaining shareholders are either given the chance, or are obliged, to buy the leaving shareholder's interest.

b) **Valuation provisions**

As noted above, it is very difficult to value shares in a family-controlled company. A valuation provision can set out how the value of those shares should be calculated, or may (for example) provide for an independent expert to value the shares.

c) **Voting mechanisms**

Certain decisions may be thought to be of particular significance. The shareholders may wish to provide special voting rights before those decisions are made – for example, a requirement for all shareholders to consent before a particular asset can be sold, or setting out situations in which minority shareholders have a power of veto over a proposal which has majority consent.

16.11 SUMMARY

1. Historically, family companies have been the seedcorn of commercial activity.

2. Family companies are companies and should be governed as such.

3. Family companies should be careful to distinguish family matters from business matters. If there is a conflict, family requirements may well triumph over commercial interests.

4. Most successful family companies, sooner or later, have to introduce non-family members to the board of directors.

5. Family companies will not benefit from inactive family non-executive directors.

6. In cases where a family company is directed by family members, succession issues should be a major business concern.

7. Family companies benefit from explicit and transparent family plans.

8. Family owners and directors should always take advice on the most appropriate and tax efficient remuneration, dividend policy, retirement and pension packages.

Chapter 17

The Governance of Companies

The subject of the governance of companies may seem rather academic and remote to practising company directors. However, it is important that all directors are broadly acquainted with the issues and can follow the debate, particularly as government is planning a substantial revision of company law to be introduced into Parliament in (probably) 2002.

This chapter considers the ideas underlying some different opinions as to how companies should be governed, discusses the roles of the parties (or 'stakeholders') associated with a company, and ends with a summary of the recommendations of the various Reports which have been commissioned over the past decade.

17.1 WHAT IS CORPORATE GOVERNANCE?

There is no universally accepted view of what 'corporate governance' means. It is an expression capable of wide definition.

> *Corporate governance . . . is concerned with the way corporate entities are governed, as distinct from the way businesses within those companies are managed. Corporate governance addresses these issues facing boards of directors, such as the inter-action with top management, and relationships with the owners and others interested in the affairs of the company, including creditors, debt financiers, analysts, auditors and corporate regulators. Concern about corporate performance through involvement with strategy formulation and policy making, and corporate conformance through management supervision and accountability to the stakeholders fall into the field of governance* (Tricker [1984], p. xi).

> *the relationship among various participants in determining the direction and performance of the company* (Monks & Minow [1995], p.1).

> *the system by which companies are directed and controlled* (Cadbury Report [1992], *para 2.5*).

In order to set corporate governance in context, it is appropriate to review the following issues:

- What is the purpose of companies; what are companies *for*? What is the role of companies in society? In whose interest should companies be run?

- How should power over companies be exercised; to whom should companies be accountable?

- How should the process of governance be organised? For example, what should be the composition of the board? How should boardroom behaviour be regulated? How should director remuneration be decided? What information should companies reveal?

- Should the processes of corporate governance vary according to the particular situation of the company, depending upon, for example, whether it is small or large and whether the owners are family members in a private company, a holding company in a group, or institutional investors and members of the public in a listed company?

The first two issues are logically prior and are discussed below. From the answers to these questions follow the answers to more specific questions about the structure of the governance of companies. The answers provided by the various corporate governance committees with respect to these matters have been discussed throughout this *Guide* and are summarised in section 17.6 below.

17.2 WHAT ARE COMPANIES FOR?

In practice, in order to reap the benefits of specialisation and exchange, individuals co-operate with each other and form associations (in a loose sense) to pursue economic objectives. Modern economies are characterised by many types of possible organisation, for example the joint stock company, mutual societies, co-operative societies, state-owned enterprises, 'Delaware' companies, US limited liability companies, limited liability partnerships, charities, 'independent statutory bodies', partnerships, trusts, non-profit organisations, and others. These different governance arrangements have evolved in competition with each other to suit different circumstances, each form in its own circumstances maximising society's economic surplus net of trans-actions costs and the cost of ownership. (It is an interesting point, but beyond the scope of this book, as to whether modern capitalist societies have the optimal blend of relatively efficient forms of economic organisation. The privatisation debate can be viewed in this context.)

However, in a market economy the limited liability company, with which this *Guide* is mainly concerned, is the major agent of job creation and economic development. Such companies employ people, generate tax income, produce a wide array of goods and services at competitive prices, increasingly manage our savings, and secure our retirement income. How companies are directed, controlled and managed – and in whose interests – is therefore of great significance.

It is important from society's point of view that companies, in pursuing their activities, use economic resources efficiently. A key element in improving economic efficiency is corporate governance, which provides the system by which the objectives of the company are set, the means of attaining the objectives are determined and the means of monitoring performance are assured. Good corporate governance also helps to attract capital by giving investors confidence that their funds will be used honestly and effectively. Corporate governance is thus ultimately concerned with the exercise of power over the use of economic resources with the intention of promoting economic efficiency. An effective corporate governance regime, then, should work to maximise the wealth of the whole community.

Companies have a major and growing impact upon society. As early as the 1930s commentators were writing about the phenomenon of 'the modern corporation' (Berle and Means [1932]). There has been a dramatic growth in the impact of companies on society and in the power of the people who control those companies. Many large firms have become extremely diversified transnational corporations whose riches and influence on occasion over-shadow that of governments.

Further, corporate structures in international business have become increasingly complex. Networks of subsidiary and associated companies, cross-holdings, ownership chains whereby private companies and limited partnerships control public listed companies, large groups like the Japanese keiretsu and many other forms of strategic alliances are more and more replacing the single corporate entity. The issue of control thereby becomes less obvious and more complicated.

Businesses generally impose costs upon others that are not reflected in their profit and loss statements. These are unfavourable 'externalities': costs incurred by a company but paid by others. An example is the cost of pollution caused by emissions from company chimneys which is paid for, either directly or indirectly via health provision, by the taxpayer. Governments attempt in many cases to make companies bear the full burden of these externalities – penalties are levied if levels of pollution are 'too high', for example – but companies still have massive effects upon society. Serious new issues are continually arising – arms exports, water shortages, waste discharges, training of the unemployed, multi-racial workforces, etc. – which are seen by many as legitimate interests of society and areas where companies can damage societal welfare.

The debate about the role of companies has been sharpened in recent years by a number of developments which have prompted increasing interest about those who control companies and what they do with that power. There has been growing public concern about the high levels of executive pay and the terms and amount of compensation that directors receive, particularly when they leave the company. Some of the executive remuneration and compens-ation arrangements revealed in recent years – rolling contracts, share options, 'golden handshakes', 'golden handcuffs', and the rest – are seen as having had little to do with the performance of the senior executives. In the 1980s there were a number of well-publicised corporate scandals, particularly Bank of Credit Commerce International, the Maxwell group of companies, Polly Peck International and Guinness, which seemed to indicate that many very large companies were effectively answerable to no one or controlled by a small coterie with nefarious motives.

The two considerations – the impact of companies upon both society's economic performance and society's non-economic welfare – are at the heart of the corporate governance debate. It may be contended that

The purpose of companies is to maximise the efficient creation of wealth, whilst observing the law and seeking to minimise the negative impacts of corporate activity on participants and society generally. Corporate governance is one of the principal means by which this purpose is achieved. The board of directors is the instrument by which effective corporate governance is achieved. It follows that

the key purpose of the board of directors is to seek to ensure the prosperity of the company by collectively directing the company's affairs, whilst meeting the appropriate interests of its shareholders and relevant stakeholders (IoD [1999]).

17.3 TO WHOM SHOULD COMPANIES BE ACCOUNTABLE?

17.3.1 SHAREHOLDERS

The classical concept of the company is discussed in Chapters 1 and 2. The key concept outlined there is the incorporation of a legal entity, separate from the owners and employees, which has many of the features of a corporeal person. The company has a life of its own, the shareholders can transfer their ownership rights to others, and the owners' liability for the company's debts is limited to their equity investment. Yet ownership is the basis of power. These characteristics of a company – the system of governance of the corporation – are enshrined in company law. This essentially mid-nineteenth-century creation has proved an enormously successful way of organising economic activity.

The shareholders are the members of the company. Their position is different from that of other associated parties in that it is based on property rights. Shareholders lack the leverage that other parties' contractual relationships with the company sometimes supply. Once they have subscribed the capital they forgo any day-to-day or detailed control over how the funds are to be used. Also, the shareholders, ranking last in order for their income and taking the greatest risk of irrecoverable loss of their assets, cannot be satisfied without the company having first satisfied their customers and then all the other parties in terms both of the amount and the security of their income.

These differences provide the main justification for shareholders enjoying rights denied to the other parties associated with a company. Shareholders' interests are specifically protected by company law. In general, the existing structure of law implies an obligation on directors to manage the company for the benefit of shareholders (subject to safeguards to protect actual and potential creditors). Directors owe their duty to the company, but the interest of the company is defined in common law as meaning the interest of the body of shareholders (present and future) as a whole.

As described in Chapter 2, 'ownership' of a company is divided among the shareholders. The conventional model assumes many shareholders, and thus they can exercise control only through a sort of representative democracy. They 'elect' directors as stewards rather than exercising direct control themselves. Directors may be viewed as trustees of the owners, running the company on their behalf and owing them and the company fiduciary duties, but not subject to day-to-day control.

As a consequence, the key elements of a registered company are:

- Shareholders have the power under the Articles of Association to appoint directors. (In practice, at least in the case of public companies, they confirm appointments made by the board between annual general meetings.) The general meeting of shareholders also has an overriding power under the *Companies Act 1985*, which cannot be excluded by the Articles, to remove directors. In this sense, then, ultimate power in the company rests with the members voting in meetings of the company. In practice their power is delegated in order to ensure that the company may undertake its business on a day-to-day basis. Shareholders delegate their power to directors. They call directors to account at general meetings of the company.

- Directors in law have fiduciary duties to ensure they act honestly and use their best judgement only for the benefit of the company. Directors must use their powers only for proper purposes and with care and skill. If a director breaches his duties, he may be sued by the company (and in certain circumstances by the shareholders acting individually or on the company's behalf – though this power is difficult to exercise (see section 8.3)).

- Shareholders also have a right to information about the company and can play a part in the formal decision-making of the company, primarily by participation in general shareholder meetings and by voting.

- An equity share can be bought, sold or transferred, and entitles the shareholder to participate in the profits of the company, with liability limited to the amount of the paid up capital.

There are three important caveats, however:

1. In the circumstance of insolvency or near-insolvency, the duty of directors to shareholders is subordinated to the overriding obligation to ensure that the interests of creditors are protected, particularly through insolvency law (see Chapter 15).

2. Various statutes and regulations made under statute impose some wider duties of accountability to parties associated with the company, especially employees and customers, on both companies and their directors (see Chapter 10).

3. Employees are given a measure of protection under company law as well as by other statutes. Directors' duties are extended to have regard to the interests of the company's employees in general as well as to the interests of its members by s.309 (1) of the *Companies Act 1985* (though it is not clear how this duty could be enforced – see section 10.2).

The accountability of directors to shareholders naturally leads to the question of how shareholders are to exercise their control. This is the so-called 'agency problem', that is, how shareholders are to hold their agents (directors) to account (see Coase [1938], Fama and Jensen [1983] and Easterbrook and Fischel [1991]). (The term 'agent' here has a wider connotation than its legal definition.) Control is necessary because the principal and the agent have different interests. Directors, seeking to maximise their own personal utility, will take actions that are advantageous to themselves but may be detrimental to the shareholders. The principal wants the agent to act in the principal's best interest; the agent wants to act in his own best interest. This probable conflict was recognised over two centuries ago:

> *The directors of companies, being managers of other people's money than their own, it cannot well be expected that they should watch over it with the same anxious vigilance with which the partners in a private copartnery frequently watch over their own* (Adam Smith [1776])

Control is difficult because, first, there is a kind of market failure in that the level of effort by the board (which is costly to the directors) is not directly observable and therefore perhaps cannot be adequately monitored; secondly, principal and agent have different attitudes to risk; and, thirdly, there is an asymmetry of information. However, given rational behaviour by both sides, it may be argued that the transactions costs of appropriate checks and balances are necessary and desirable and that the optimum contract ties executive remuneration to company performance. There has thus been much debate about what should be the mechanisms of shareholder control – disclosure to shareholders, reform of the Annual General Meeting, audit committees, the use of independent non-executive directors, the separation of the roles of chairman and managing director, etc. There has also been great controversy about the merits and mechanics of various systems of rewarding directors. These two issues – control by shareholders and directors' remuneration – predominate in the subject matter of the various corporate governance Reports.

There is some evidence of linkage between various attributes of governance and company performance, but the evidence is very mixed (see Patterson [1998] for a survey of the literature). On balance, the theoretical predictions are, at best, very weakly confirmed, suggesting that in fact shareholder power in quoted companies is not extensive and that current director remuneration systems are not effective in inducing directors to devote their best efforts to maximising shareholder returns.

17.3.2 STAKEHOLDERS

There is, however, a different way of looking at companies. In a market economy a company is an economic and social organisation transforming inputs into outputs and exchanging these in the marketplace. It can be regarded as a system that links customers and all the parties who contribute to the customers' satisfaction. A company, although it has a legal existence of its own, has to act through human agents such as directors, managers and employees. At the heart of the company, therefore, is a complex web of socio-economic relationships. The company can be seen as the nexus of a set of contracts, implicit and explicit, with its many associated parties. These associated parties, sometimes called 'stakeholders', from time to time may take an interest in, and be in a position to influence, the company's goals and operations. The relationship between the business and these parties is sophisticated and only in some aspects specifically defined in law. If a company is to be defined as a nexus of relationships among all the stakeholders (including shareholders), then it may be appropriate to require companies to serve a wider range of interests than shareholders alone.

Before considering the issue of stakeholder accountability, it is appropriate to consider the current position, as delineated in law and good practice, of the major parties with an interest in the company.

17.4 THE MAJOR STAKEHOLDERS

17.4.1 SHAREHOLDERS

The relationship of shareholders with the company has been touched upon in section 17.3 above, and is dealt with throughout this *Guide*. Shareholders are the owners of the business. Ultimate power within the company rests with them. Decisions taken in general meetings are binding on directors and the company. Shareholders have the power to appoint and dismiss directors.

17.4.2 DIRECTORS

Directors, as their title suggests, should collectively provide the direction of the company. As their role is central to this *Guide*, their relationship with the company is dealt with throughout the text, but especially in Chapters 4, 5 and 7.

17.4.3 CREDITORS

The fact of limited liability of shareholders clearly puts creditors – persons who are owed money by the company – at risk. Many features of companies and insolvency legislation (such as the requirement to file information at Companies House) stem from the need to compensate creditors for the limitation of shareholders' liability. Thus, for example, creditors have the power to petition the courts to wind up the company. Creditors have additional protection in law in that from the time that a director knows, or ought to have concluded, that a company has no reasonable prospect of avoiding insolvent liquidation, that director must take all the steps that a reasonably diligent person, having both the skill, knowledge and experience appropriate to a director performing the functions entrusted to the director in question and the general skill, knowledge and experience actually possessed by the director concerned, should take to minimise the loss to the company's creditors. Failure to do so may expose the director concerned to Court action for 'wrongful trading' and a personal liability to contribute to the company's assets for the benefit of the creditors if the company does indeed become insolvent (see section 15.3).

The management of creditors will therefore be a major preoccupation for any company, particularly if it is coming under cash flow strains. The board of directors should be responsible for creating, and monitoring compliance with, the company's policy on terms of payment. It is damaging to a company to get a reputation as a poor payer. Even so, larger companies frequently attempt to fund their working capital requirements at their smaller suppliers' expense.

17.4.4 EMPLOYEES

Employees of companies have contracts of employment with the company. This confers important rights upon the employee (see section 10.2). The *Companies Act 1985* lays a duty upon directors to have regard in the performance of their functions to the interests of the company employees in general, though there is no guidance on what this means in practice. The rights and duties contained in present-day health and safety and employment rights legislation, discussed in Chapter 10, go well beyond the dictates of a buyer/seller relationship. Examples of these are the statutory consultation requirements in the event of redundancies or transfers of undertakings and the requirements to disclose information – not only for the purposes of collective bargaining but also to be in accordance with good industrial relations practice. In recent years there has been a host of regulation and legislation emanating from Westminster and Brussels setting out the rights of employees and the obligations of companies to which the company must adhere.

However, the relationship between an employee and the company is more profound than contractual or statutory issues. The relationship between a company and its employees should not be governed by a merely legalistic approach. It is becoming increasingly unhelpful to regard the relationship in such a simplistic manner. It is true that employees sell their labour to companies; where a company recognises trade unions, collective bargaining over terms and conditions of employment is an expression of this contractual relationship. But in no area of business is treating a contract as being simply about a quantity of a commodity for such-and-such a price more likely to come unstuck. In the first place, as the emphasis in modern economies shifts from manual to mental skills, from a labour-intensive economy to a skills and knowledge economy, the idea that labour can be treated as just one of the factors of production, and an undifferentiated mass at that, loses even the limited validity it might once have possessed. Secondly, employees are rightly concerned about such factors as the security of their employment, the capacity of their employer to recognise and reward their individual contributions to the business, the physical conditions in which they work and the inherent interest of the job, in addition to their remuneration.

Therefore the need to take account of the qualitative and implicit aspects of contractual relationships applies with particular force to a company's relationship with its employees. In a real sense employees are the backbone of the company and securing the highest performance from employees whilst providing a proper remuneration should be a key aim of the board. A committed and motivated workforce is often a key ingredient in a successful company.

17.4.5 CUSTOMERS

All activity within the company should have a simple end – to secure that its products or services are bought in such quantities and at such prices as to provide for the profitable survival and growth of the company. The buyers of the products or services are customers. It is impossible to overstate the importance of customers in the business context; ultimately companies stand or fall to the extent to which they can persuade customers to buy their products or services. The customer is king. Only customers produce revenue for a company; every other party associated with a company through the market involves costs to the company. At the macro-economic level the free enterprise system depends fundamentally on the ability of individuals and organisations to choose to spend their money on the products of one business rather than on those of another. This is a key feature which distinguishes the free enterprise approach from the collectivist model.

There is now a formidable array of legislation in place to protect the interests of customers, both economic and otherwise. Companies must take adequate account of, or provide adequate compensation for, possible dangers to health or safety inherent in a particular product or service, and they must not attempt to secure unfair advantages over customers, whether by price fixing or collusive practices, by failure to disclose information relevant to the customer's choice, or by attempts to set aside statutory safeguards for customers' economic interests. Consumer law applies to both companies and directors, and is backed by powerful enforcing agencies – local Trading Standards Officers and the Office of Fair Trading. In addition, customers may benefit from the guardianship activities of the Competition Commission. The duties of companies and their directors to consumers are discussed in section 10.4.

But there is a wider constraint. Nothing is more calculated to bring a business to disaster than failure to take account of its customers' requirements and interests in the widest sense. Of course, if relationships with consumers could be predicted with certainty, then companies would not fail. They do fail.

Commercial life is uncertain and unpredictable. The marketplace can never be taken for granted. For this reason companies must spend time and money in winning and holding their customer base. There are numerous ways in which the company can devote itself to internal factors to bring about profitable survival – but often customers are fickle and unpredictable. However secure the market base may appear to be, it can and will change.

17.4.6 DEBTORS

Most companies need to view their debtors in different ways according to the state of the company. How important is a particular debtor to the company? Which debtors have to be placated? Which debtors can be pressed? How the balance is drawn will depend upon the relative importance of the debtor to the business, the company's order book, and, most importantly, its cash flow. Cash is the lifeblood of a company. If cash is short, one option is to chase debtors.

It should not, however, be the purpose of a company to be pro or anti debtors. Other companies should be given reasonable time in which to pay their debts and only then pressed for payment.

In any event, all companies should have a debtor book which should be kept under reasonable control as part of their working capital management. The management of debtors is part of the financial efficiency of the company and also plays an important role in establishing creditworthiness.

17.4.7 GOVERNMENTAL ORGANISATIONS

Governments pass laws and should see to it that they are executed. In the field of corporate life, as noted above, there is a host of legislation which affects companies and to which companies must adhere. In particular, there are the requirements of the *Companies Acts* which, if not followed, particularly as to reporting requirements, may result in criminal charges.

On the other hand, governments see the corporate sector as a provider of both employment and tax revenues. To this extent the economic welfare of the nation depends on successful commercial ventures by companies. Governments need companies and need to ensure an economic environment in which they can succeed.

Given the power of government, it is necessary for businesses to maintain links with the government to press for the claims and interests of companies.

To this end, a substantial number of business bodies have been established, including the IoD, the Confederation of British Industry and many Chambers of Commerce. Through membership of such organisations companies and directors can ensure that they promulgate their message. They may or may not succeed, but the medium of such public organisations is of key importance to the survival of companies.

17.4.8 THE COMMUNITY

There is a widely held view that companies should act and be seen to act as good 'corporate citizens' wherever they operate, at both the local and the national level; companies should act 'responsibly' towards society.

Being a good corporate citizen is not entirely easy to define. Plainly it includes scrupulous compliance with the law of the countries in which the company does business, both generally and as it affects their dealings with stakeholders, in the same way as any other person, legal or natural. As companies are legal entities, the only problem that their corporate capacity causes in this aspect of good citizenship is that they can be made subject only to economic penalties. Companies cannot be sentenced to a term of imprisonment, for example. However, where it is necessary to prove that a company acted with criminal intent, the law is generally fully prepared to impute the state of mind of the individuals who can be held to be a company's 'mind and will' to the company itself. The mind and will of a company is normally held to reside in its board of directors (see Chapter 3).

Issues beyond obedience to the law which are raised by the notion of corporate citizenship are taken up in section 17.5.4.

17.5 SHAREHOLDERS VERSUS STAKEHOLDERS – THE DEBATE

In whose interests should companies be directed? An overview of the broad positions taken by participants in the corporate governance debate is given in the following paragraphs. The treatment of the issues is no doubt oversimplified, but no general guide can deal with every permutation of facts and argument. Interested readers are referred to the lists of references and additional reading.

However, before reviewing the shareholder versus stakeholder debate, it should be stated that there is a view of companies which falls outside this particular focus. This line of argument – see, for example, Kay and Silberston [1995] – starts from the non-corporeal, metaphysical nature of the company. As such, there is no compulsion to regard the interests of the company as being identical with the interests of the body of stakeholders. Instead, the company can be taken to have its own interests, independent of any group of stakeholders. Underlying this argument is a rejection of the Anglo-Saxon view that how a company governs itself is largely a matter for the company (in its Articles of Association). By contrast, the structure and organisation of the société anonyme (SA) and the Aktiengesellschaft (AG) are largely laid down in statute and directors are required to exercise their powers in the interest of the company as an entity in its own right, independent of any other interests. The board of directors should be seen as *trustees* of the assets of the company rather than as *agents* of the shareholders or other stakeholders. The fiduciary duty therefore is to preserve and enhance the value of the company's assets and to balance fairly the various claims on the assets and the returns they generate.

17.5.1 THE SHAREHOLDER ACTIVIST VIEW

This is the view that the aim of corporate governance should be to maximise shareholder value, that it is up to the shareholders to define the company's business, and that directors are accountable only to shareholders (though the state may impose responsibilities upon them with regard to wider stakeholder interests). This is broadly the model from which the current legal and regulatory situation has developed, although it has been frequently modified since.

However, activist shareholders would argue that some changes are needed, but only in order to increase shareholder power and to make directors even more accountable to shareholders (see, for example, Monks and Minow [1995]). It is argued that the power of shareholders in practice is not as potent as it once was. In the first place, the Courts recognise that directors must have discretion in the way they manage the company and thus are unwilling to interfere in what they see as the proper exercise of commercial judgement. Secondly, whilst in theory the Annual General Meeting is the major means whereby shareholders examine the record of the board and hold them to account and shareholders can re-appoint and dismiss directors, it is held that in practice shareholders find it difficult to utilise their voting power effectively and often lack sufficient information properly to hold directors to account.

It may be that shareholders in private companies are able to exercise their power, since in most private companies shares will usually be held by a few persons, meetings can be called easily and votes can be quickly arrived at. But this is not the case with large and quoted Plcs. By their nature, share ownership is widely spread. Small shareholders of large companies find it difficult to co-ordinate their actions and votes and, it is sometimes alleged, do not have sufficient and timely information on which to form a coherent view about important matters. Boards are generally able (particularly by their use of proxy votes) to have their way and overrule small shareholders. The Annual General Meeting, therefore, is often not an effective way of holding directors to account.

Deficiencies in shareholder monitoring of boards matter because a great deal of research suggests that in quoted companies there is little identity of interest between owners and 'managers'. The growth of a new professional managerial class (the 'managerial revolution') has meant that owners are remote from the people actually running the business, who usually own only a relatively tiny part of the equity. The result is a weakening of individual shareholder control over large companies and greater autonomy for the directors of the companies.

It is argued that there tends therefore to be a vacuum of accountability in the case of large, publicly quoted companies, so that they often no longer have as a prime purpose the enhancement of shareholder value. The remedy is held to be closer and more powerful shareholder supervision of boards. The need is to give substantive content to the present structure of notional accountability to shareholders by, for example, enlarging the role of non-executive directors, improving the extent and availability of information about the company to shareholders, extending the use of 'independent' board committees, and other means discussed in the various corporate governance Reports.

Over the past 20 years or so there has been a growing movement by institutional investors to attempt to hold boards to account. The rise of shareholder activism began in the USA in the 1980s. Organisations such as Institutional Shareholder Services in the USA have been set up to advise pension funds and other investing institutions on governance issues. The Association of British Insurers and the National Association of Pension Funds have been set up in the UK. Major institutional investors vigorously harry boards of directors of 'under-performing' companies – The Californian State Employees Pension Fund (CalPers) and Hermes Lens Asset Management have been particularly active – and exert great pressure on boards to eliminate

363

corporate governance practices that they see as protecting under-performing boards.

The result has been, some would suggest, that in practice not all shareholders are equal. The large institutional investors – pension funds, unit trusts, and the like – tend to be provided with more, and more timely, information about the company's affairs than other shareholders. These briefings are designed to secure proxy votes in support of the board. There is therefore often no substantive debate at the AGM. The institutional investors do not normally even attend the AGM. The important debates and decisions have happened elsewhere.

One type of important decision is that regarding the composition of the board. In practice, board appointments agreed by the board and the institutional shareholders are not reversed at the AGM. It may be argued that the Combined Code provision that a nomination committee of the board, made up mainly of independent non-executive directors, should recommend appointees is a tacit admission of the failure of shareholder power in this respect.

The activities of institutional investors have been attacked on the ground that 'under-performance' is defined by them only in terms of short-term shareholder returns, whilst the efficient generation of wealth needs companies both to recognise the wider interests of other stakeholders in the company and to pay attention to the long-term performance of the company. It may be that directors are insufficiently responsive to small shareholder concerns (and therefore their companies are relatively inefficient), but it is alleged that the rise in the size and power of institutional investors and consequent pressures from them has led boards to be overly concerned with short-run profitability to the detriment of their companies' long-run performance.

Similarly, it is argued that companies have many intangible assets – the skills of the workforce and a reputation amongst customers, for example – which short-term shareholder pressures force them to neglect. This neglect means that in fact companies do not maximise profitability and the long-run growth prospects of the economy are thereby damaged. If directors were accountable to those who create and possess these intangible assets, then directors would have to tilt the balance of considerations in favour of broad societal issues and towards the long-run maximisation of returns from all the company's assets. Companies are therefore relatively inefficient, not because of insufficient shareholder influence, but by reason of the reverse.

17.5.2 THE STAKEHOLDER VIEW

By about the 1970s the role of the company in society was being questioned, largely on the ground that companies have, or should have, responsibilities beyond their legal duty to their shareholders. Given the size and scale of many companies, it began to be argued that companies should be run for the benefit of, and be accountable to, all their 'stakeholders' (see, for example, Hutton [1997]). A stakeholder is anyone who can affect or is affected by a company's objectives and activities. Shareholders, for example, are just one group of stakeholders among many and should cede some part of their influence and control to all the other interested parties. Directors should, it is argued, be under a duty to operate the company for the benefit of all parties and not just shareholders, and therefore should be accountable to all interested parties. It follows that the corporate governance rules should be changed to require companies to take into account the social effects of their activities.

We can distinguish 'hard' and 'soft' variants of the general stakeholder viewpoint. A 'hard' line is that directors should be required in law to operate the company for the benefit of all stakeholders collectively. The company, to which directors' duties are owed, should not be thought of as the shareholders only, but as embracing all stakeholders. Directors therefore should have an enlarged duty to promote the interests of all parties associated with a company without the interests of one being overriding, to serve a balanced socio-economic purpose. Directors should be obliged to set the interests of another constituency above those of shareholders where they consider this is necessary to satisfy broader ethical or social considerations. This duty would be enforceable by any interested party.

A 'soft' interpretation is that directors should be required to further the interests of stakeholders, even where to do so is to the detriment of shareholders, but only where the directors judge it is appropriate to do so.

Either interpretation, if accepted, would involve major changes in the present company law and the present institutional rules. There would be a need to change the law to allow directors discretion to subordinate the interests of shareholders to wider social considerations ('soft' stakeholderism) or to mandate an enforceable duty on directors to serve a balanced purpose ('hard' stakeholderism). It would mean the end of shareholders' unique right to determine board membership (perhaps all stakeholders would have the right to nominate directors – in the Netherlands and Germany the Works Council has the power of veto over membership of the supervisory board) since it would be inconsistent to leave shareholder powers intact and simultaneously require directors to have regard to wider interests.

Similarly, hostile take-overs would be difficult or impossible, since ownership of a majority of the equity would not confer a right to appoint or dismiss the directors. Proponents of the stakeholder position would welcome this, since it is seen to be unfair that the property rights of the shareholders should confer total control over the outcome of a bid which may have vast consequences for workers, suppliers, the community, etc. (Interestingly, even where the directors, acting in the best interest of the company as they see it, reject a bid, they must still refer the matter to the shareholders. This is not the case in most European countries, where hostile take-overs are very infrequent.) The effects of this change in the market for corporate control – the market where competing groups of executives bid for the right to deploy corporate assets – on the allocation of economic resources and the welfare of society as a whole are likely to be profound, but are beyond the scope of this discussion.

In addition, certain rules of good practice (for example, concerning board composition) and legal requirements relating to general meetings of the company would also need to be changed.

However, it is the view of many commentators – see, for example, Sternberg [1997] – that there are serious weaknesses in the stakeholder interpretation, whether of the 'hard' or 'soft' variety:

1. Directors should, it is argued, act for the benefit of all parties in aggregate. Directors will not be permitted to attempt to maximise the interests of any one group – say, long-run shareholder returns, employees' wages, customer value – but must serve all interests. But there will inevitably be circumstances in which the interests of stakeholders clash. What benefits one group will often harm another. How, then, are directors to strike a balance between the vast array of competing interests, or, alternatively, how is the law to say which are to be regarded as overriding? Different interests can be ranked only by reference to the purpose of the company, but stakeholder theory does not permit this.

2. Accountability to all stakeholders is in reality accountability to none. What would be the yardstick for measuring company performance? By contrast, 'maximizing long-term returns for the owners' is a sharp and unambiguous objective; performance is easily measured against it. It is hard to see how the directors could be held accountable to the stakeholders *en*

masse. In any event there are problems regarding the identification of the groups to whom directors should be accountable. Individuals are simultaneously members of more than one interest group, and the membership of the groups will constantly change. Some stakeholders will be significantly affected by a company's actions, others less so. To which communities should directors pay regard?

3. It would need every stakeholder to accept the objectives set for the company. Otherwise the directors would not be constrained within proper purposes as defined by the constitution of the company. Without legal constraint, directors would have a dangerously broad, unpoliced and unaccountable discretion. Directors would have a major distributive role in allocating the company's resources. Many people are uncomfortable with the notion of company directors playing the part of moral or political arbiters, particularly as this power would be unconstrained.

Cadbury [1990] queried to what extent business has a responsibility to maintain the framework of the society in which it operates and how far business should strive to reflect society's priorities rather than its own commercial ones. The answer, given twenty years earlier, to some is clear. For example, Friedman [1970] argues that it is no business of companies to attempt to take general social concerns into account, and it is mistaken to expect or require them to do so. The purpose of business – what society expects the business system to deliver – is maximum benefits from the minimum use of resources. The operation of a company always imposes costs on society which add to the resources being consumed. Society is concerned with the overall result and uses the law, regulation and other pressures to try to optimise the balance between the net economic goods that companies deliver and the other social goods it desires. Friedman argues that society cannot expect company directors to alter the balance between private 'goods' and public 'bads' that public policy has laid down. In the first place, company directors probably do not know the best actions to take to bring about the desired social result. Secondly, even if they did, in so doing they would be acting as unelected politicians or unauthorised civil servants. The only obligation of boards of directors is to maximise economic efficiency. Directors, Friedman maintains, are not fiduciaries for society as a whole; they have only one constituency – their shareholders. By contrast, government continually makes economic/social trade-offs. We accept this state of affairs on the whole because we hold government accountable through the political process. But there is no corresponding accepted standard in the corporate domain that legitimises a board's economic/social trade-offs. Customers, employees, share-holders, and so on, have not agreed such a standard.

> *Few trends could so thoroughly undermine the foundations of our free society as the acceptance by corporate officials of a social responsibility other than to make as much money for their stockholders as possible.* (Friedman [1962], p.133)

Thus, if stakeholderism is to be practicable, there must be a statutory obligation imposed on directors to take stakeholder interests into account when making commercial decisions. This means that, inevitably, the discretionary power would be handed over to the Courts, and in effect the Courts would redistribute company assets. However, many would argue that the Courts are ill equipped to make these essentially economic decisions. The result might be an undesirable increase in the degree of political or state control over the operations of the market place. Hayek [1979], p. 82, put it this way:

> *So long as the management has the one overriding duty of administering the resources under its control as trustees for the shareholders and for their benefit, its hands are largely tied; and it will have no arbitrary power to benefit from this or that particular interest. But once the management of a big enterprise is regarded as not only entitled but even obliged to consider in its decisions whatever is regarded as the public or social interest, or to support good causes and generally to act for the public benefit, it gains indeed an uncontrollable power – a power which could not be long left in the hands of private managers but would inevitably be made the subject of increasing public control.*

4. In stakeholder theory the directors are accountable to the company's stakeholders. But there is a logical objection. The proposition that companies are affected by, and affect, certain groups does not entail that they should be accountable to those groups. Accountability follows from legitimate authority, not from a mere relationship alone. It is true that companies need employees, customers, creditors, etc., and must pay some attention to stakeholder interests. It may even be true (though it is unproven) that companies which preserve the environment, empower their employees, enjoy great public esteem and so on are generally more successful commercially. But it does not therefore follow that stakeholders have legitimate authority over the directors and hence the company. Stakeholders may withdraw their co-operation, but this is quite different from their holding the company to account. Stakeholders may be powerful in relation to the company, but this does not confer legitimate authority on them. Power does not justify authority.

EXAMPLE

In 1972 Lockheed was in a difficult situation. It was employing 25,000 people making the new wide-bodied L-1011 passenger jet in California and was a crucial economic force in the local community. At the same time the company was suffering from major cutbacks in defence orders; Lockheed's military order book was in a parlous state.

The board of Lockheed desperately needed civil aviation orders; so far there were no orders at all for the L-1011. There was only one large airline in the world which was not committed to a rival Boeing plane, All-Nippon Airways of Japan.

Many analysts at the time recommended that Lockheed cut their losses and abandon the plane. Corporate earnings, and the bonuses and stock options of top management and directors, would undoubtedly have been improved by the closure of the L-1011 plant.

In the event, the board decided to keep the plane, safeguarding the 25,000 jobs at a time of recession, and paid All-Nippon a vast sum of money in return for their ordering some planes. Some commentators even talked of All-Nippon 'extorting' money from Lockheed.

The company subsequently argued that it was good governance to 'buy' the order and put its duty to the community above the self-interest of the company and its board.

17.5.3 A MIDDLE WAY

The overwhelming public interest is that business should be run effectively as a generator of wealth and employment for the participants and thus for the whole community. A widely held view is that this is best accomplished by broadly the present set of arrangements. It is argued that the objective of companies to maximise shareholder value is in practice the most likely way also of securing the prosperity and welfare of the whole community. The basic duty of directors should therefore be unaltered; in particular, directors should not be *obliged* to put the interests of others above the interests of shareholders in any circumstances save where required by specific law, and such laws should be justified on their own merits rather than as part of a general prescription regulating the governance of companies.

Even so, given this, it is argued by many that directors and shareholders should be encouraged to the realisation that shareholders' best interests are not necessarily (or, indeed, often) in conflict with the interests of stakeholders. Undoubtedly, companies sometimes take too short-term a view and neglect intangibles like reputation, goodwill, etc. Directors should be encouraged to appreciate the importance of fostering effective relationships with employees, customers, suppliers and the wider community as a means of promoting their companies. To be commercially successful, companies need to pay attention to stakeholder concerns – not because it is right to do so, but because it is commercially efficient to do so. Shareholder value versus stakeholderism is thus to some extent a non-issue because harmonious and productive relationships with stakeholders can often add shareholder value; in practice, the interests of competitiveness and efficiency often do not conflict with wider public interest benefits. An adequate recognition by shareholders and directors of the importance of a satisfied workforce, loyal customers and suppliers, and a favourable corporate reputation, for example, would embrace both approaches. The fundamental premiss is that maintaining and developing relationships with the key parties with whom the company is associated and recognising and understanding what constitutes the elements and values, often only implicit, in stakeholder concerns and interests, can make a substantial difference to business success.

However, it may not be easy to do this. The relationships between a company and stakeholders are sometimes circumscribed by law and regulation, either in the interest of society as a whole or to take account of actual or perceived inequalities in the bargaining power of different interests, but a large number of relationships are not subject to specific legislation or regulation. In any event the key factors in many relationships are not always obvious, since many qualitative and non-quantifiable factors often need to be considered. Nevertheless, the board of directors, as custodian of the company's prosperity, must recognise and evaluate these qualitative factors in much of its decision-making and adopt policies for its dealings with other parties which take account of more than the commercial aspects of the company's relationship with them and any additional specific pieces of legislation which circumscribe a board's freedom of action in these dealings. This line of reasoning has led the IoD, for example, to include in its Code of Professional Conduct [1998b] an Article enjoining directors to

> *Exercise responsibilities to employees, customers, suppliers and other stakeholders, including the wider community.* (Article 4)

Thus, whilst the obligations of a director are primarily owed to the company, it is also often necessary to take into account the interests of all individuals and groups with a legitimate and direct interest in the achievement of company objectives and the way in which these objectives are achieved. A wise board will identify and know the interests, views and expectations of these stakeholders, will ensure that communications with such stakeholders are timely, effective and unbiased, subject to the needs of commercial security and regulatory compliance where appropriate, and will set up procedures for managing relationships with stakeholders, particularly at times of crisis (e.g. litigation, environmental disasters, take-over bids).

Where the balance is struck is a matter for the board. Even where stakeholder interests are not protected by law, it is the job of the board of directors, as stewards of the company's survival and prosperity, to take a view as to how the company relates to stakeholders, what extra-legal commitments it will make – from holding itself accountable at one extreme, through active co-operation, consideration and explanation, to ignoring at the other extreme. Some boards of directors take the view – sometimes explicitly stated as necessary in the company's own long-term interest – that their companies should act and be seen to act as 'good corporate citizens', and attempt to be a positive force for good in such areas as protection of the physical environment, education, urban renewal, health, racial equality, and other areas of social concern. For example, boards will very often pay greater attention to their customers' needs and concerns than is strictly required by the laws designed to protect consumer interests. Similarly, boards will often come to the view that it is unhelpful to deal with employees simply on the basis of a contractual buyer/seller relationship and will go beyond the rights and duties contained in present employment legislation and company law. On the other hand, some boards take a position much closer to the strict limits prescribed by law and regulation.

Whatever standpoint in relation to stakeholders is adopted by the board will no doubt change as circumstances change. The important point is that the board recognises it has to take a view and maintain what it regards as a proper balance of interests in the light of the law and relevant regulations and the board's judgement of the commercial interests of the company. The stance a board takes will not be immutable. Good practice is evolutionary and should be reviewed as circumstances change. It is for the board to judge, on a case-by-case basis, which stakeholders it treats as relevant and which of their interests it is appropriate to meet. This is one way of remaining competitive.

This line of argument rejects the notion that company directors should in general be moral or political arbiters. This would be unacceptable and

371

inefficient. Rather, it is argued, the corporate governance regime should help the board make sound *business* decisions, not decisions about income and wealth distribution. These latter should be the province of elected politicians.

Unfavourable public externalities as a result of companies' operations is another issue. A moderate and widely held view is that their amelioration is better secured by specific legislation which bears on specific business activities – for example, working conditions, the environment, fair trading and competition, as detailed in Chapter 10 – rather than by changes to the whole system of the governance of companies.

Finally, many commentators stress the need for a *flexible* set of laws, regulations and rules of good practice. Both the ever-changing economic, social and technological conditions of business and the great diversity of companies entail that a rigid regime of corporate governance is unlikely to be effective. This view was strongly endorsed by the Hampel Report, which warned against adopting a prescribed form of corporate structure and a set of rigid standards and rules and applying them to any company. Many argue that directors should observe only the general principles of 'best practice', as set out in the widely accepted corporate governance Reports, and be free to adopt them to the extent and in the manner most appropriate for their particular company. It would then be up to the directors to explain and justify any departure from 'best practice' principles, and up to the shareholders and stakeholders to hold them to account and exert whatever pressures the law allows them.

Small companies are a clear example where the imposition of a rigid corporate governance regime would be inappropriate. Many of the corporate governance provisions are irrelevant or overly burdensome in the case of small companies. There are many details of process – e.g. minimum notice periods for meetings, the need for written resolutions, the capital maintenance rules, the power of directors to issue shares, the filing requirements for accounts – which might usefully be simplified for small companies without serious loss of accountability. This is particularly true in the case of family and owner-managed companies, where the shareholder, employee, director and creditor may all be the same person or only a small group of people.

17.5.4 THE SOCIAL RESPONSIBILITY OF BUSINESS

It is often argued that companies should behave 'responsibly' towards society. At the extreme, this might mean that directors should be responsible for their employees' healthcare, should consciously help the unemployed, should support ethnic minorities, for example, irrespective of shareholder consider-ations. As noted above, however, many commentators take the view that such considerations and tasks are the preserve of government rather than companies:

> *Business's overwhelming contribution to society is by ensuring prosperous and enterprising companies which create wealth and generate jobs – not through social and public works.* (IoD [1998a])

Certainly, directors need to have regard to the communities in which their companies operate, and companies, their directors and their employees often have a great deal to contribute to the solution of many social and environ-mental problems, particularly in such areas as education and training, urban renewal and the stimulation and propagation of an enterprise culture. Nevertheless, directors must remember that their duty is to the company; they do not have a totally free hand to act purely as their personal consciences dictate. Subject to the considerations above, a company can do well by doing good. But directors should consider the interests of all stakeholders only so long as they do so in the context of increasing shareholder value. Companies can be benefactors in their local communities, hire and train uneducated workers, or whatever, but the justification should be that these 'social' activities increase the long-run value of the company. Of course, the relationship between shareholder returns and any particular board decision does not have to be immediate and direct.

An example is the making of charitable, political, and similar gifts. As the law stands, the payment must be for the benefit of the company, reasonably incidental to its business and made *bona fide* in the interests of the company:

> *The law does not say that there are to be no cakes and ale but that there are to be no cakes and ale except such as are required for the benefit of the company.* (Bowen J, *Hutton v West Cork Railway* {22}).

Many boards believe that their philanthropic efforts are good for business. To what extent this is the case is a matter for the board to judge.

One way in which a company's need to be a good corporate citizen has been expressed is the notion of a 'licence to operate'. The argument is that

> *the continued existence of companies is based on an implied agreement between business and society. In effect, companies are licensed by society to provide the goods and services which society needs* (Cadbury [1990], p. 149).

On one level, this is a truism. If no one will work for a company or no one will buy its products, then the company will go out of business. The licensing concept has content only if it means the mandatory imposition of a duty upon companies and their directors to pursue the interests of certain groups in society. In this case, it becomes a form of 'hard' stakeholderism.

17.6 THE CORPORATE GOVERNANCE REPORTS

There are few theoretical insights into the governance of the modern corporation. There is no consistent and comprehensive theory equivalent to the Marshallian theory of markets or Keynes' General Theory, which illuminates the whole subject, explains why companies are governed the way they are and which has high predictive power with respect to board actions. There are only piecemeal attempts to explain how the modern company is directed. This is perhaps why the committees set up to examine and report on corporate governance failed to provide any theoretical underpinnings to their recommendations and showed no sign that they were aware of academic work in the field.

The Reports concentrated on relatively narrow issues concerning the mechanics of controlling the boards of companies and their directors, preventing fraud, improving information about companies, and making boards of directors more accountable to shareholders.

17.6.1 THE REPORTS ON CORPORATE GOVERNANCE

a) The Cadbury Report

The Cadbury Committee [1992] was established largely in response to a number of well-publicised corporate scandals. The Committee was set up jointly by the London Stock Exchange, the Financial Reporting Council and the accountancy Institutes to report on the financial aspects of corporate governance and the responsibilities of directors in relation to accounting matters. The ensuing Report dealt mainly with matters designed to improve management of the board and increase the transparency of the workings of the board. The Report includes a Code of Best Practice. The recommendations of the Report have been incorporated in the London Stock Exchange Listing Rules and have been endorsed publicly by the major shareholder bodies.

b) The Greenbury Report

In 1995 increased public concern over the large compensation packages, pay increases and share option gains in the privatised utility industries led the Confederation of British Industry (CBI) to set up a study group to study how best to decide directors' remuneration. The outcome of this study was the Greenbury Report [1995], which also embodied a Code of Best Practice. The most significant recommendation was the need to set up certain committees of the board. Virtually all the Greenbury recommendations have been incorporated in the Listing Rules of the London Stock Exchange.

c) The Hampel Report

The London Stock Exchange, the CBI, the IoD, the Consultative Committee of Accountancy Bodies, the National Association of Pension Funds and the Association of British Insurers established a further committee in November 1995 to review the extent to which the recommendations in the Cadbury and Greenbury Reports had been implemented and whether they had achieved their purpose (Hampel [1998]). The ensuing Report focused upon measures considered necessary to improve the effectiveness of the board. At the same time, the Report emphasised the need not to damage 'enterprise' by too much 'control' and highlighted the danger that an overly onerous corporate governance regime may stifle enterprise. The Report also stressed that, because of the variety of company circumstances, simply adopting a prescribed set of rules would be inappropriate. Hampel encouraged companies to apply corporate governance principles in the ways that best suited them (and, where there was a deviation from 'best practice', explain the reasons for it in the annual accounts) rather than follow a 'box-ticking' approach to corporate governance.

The Hampel Committee also produced the Combined Code on Corporate Governance [1998]. This is summarised in Appendix B and is annexed to the Stock Exchange Listing Rules.

d) The Combined Code

The Combined Code has a number of provisions relating to internal control. Principle D.2 states that *The board should maintain a sound system of internal control to safeguard shareholders' investment and the company's assets,* and the associated provisions are that the board should annually or more frequently review the effectiveness of the company's system of internal control (D.2.1) and that if the company does not have an internal audit function it should from time to time review the need for one (D.2.2). The Listing Rules of the London Stock Exchange require that a UK registered listed company includes in its Annual Report a narrative statement of how it has applied the internal control Principle of the Combined Code and a statement of compliance with the associated Code provisions D.2.1 and D.2.2 or, in the case of non-compliance, give the reasons.

e) The Turnbull Report

The Combined Code gave little guidance to directors of listed companies on the scope, extent and nature of the review of internal controls required by the relevant provisions of the Code. Consequently the Institute of Chartered Accountants in England & Wales, backed by the Stock Exchange, formed a working party to study the matter. The resulting Turnbull Report [1999] sets out the principal characteristics of a sound system of internal control and how effective review of such a system can be achieved. Specifically, it provides guidance with regard to assessing how the company has applied Code Principle D.2, and implemented the associated provisions. The Turnbull Report further requires that directors must state in the Annual Report that there is an ongoing process for evaluating and managing the company's key risks which is regularly reviewed by the board; how effectiveness of the internal control system has been reviewed, the role played by the audit committee, whether any material losses were suffered and what remedial action or contingency plans were put into effect; or, where the directors are not able to make these disclosures, explain why no such control system has been implemented.

The main features and recommendations of the Combined Code and the Turnbull Report are both summarised briefly in Appendix B.

17.6.2 INTERNATIONAL PRINCIPLES OF CORPORATE GOVERNANCE

There have been two recent attempts to formulate internationally agreed principles of corporate governance.

a) The OECD

The OECD has developed a set of *Principles of Corporate Governance* [1999] which embodies the agreed views of its 29 member countries and therefore represents a common basis of good practice. Each Principle is supported by a number of recommendations and by addenda which explain its rationale and suggest ways in which it may be made operational. The Principles are intended to be used as a benchmark by national governments in developing their own national company law and regulation. The Principles are concerned with protecting shareholders' rights, equal treatment of shareholders, the role of stakeholders in corporate governance, the responsibilities of the board and the need for disclosure and transparency. Appendix D lists the Principles.

b) The Commonwealth Association for Corporate Governance

The Commonwealth Association for Corporate Governance (CACG) was established in April 1998 in response to a Declaration of the Commonwealth Heads of Government meeting in 1997 to promote good standards in corporate governance throughout the Commonwealth and to facilitate the development of appropriate institutions able to advance, teach and disseminate such standards. The CACG has formulated *Guidelines* [1999] to encourage best practice. They are intended to be equally applicable to boards of directors of all sorts of enterprise – public, private, state-owned or family-owned. They are designed to focus particularly on the needs of emerging and transition economies. Each Principle of corporate governance is accompanied by explanatory notes to help the interpretation and application of the Principles. The fifteen CACG Principles are listed in Appendix E.

Neither the OECD nor the CACG Principles are mandatory. The effect of these first 'international' codes remains to be seen, although the CACG Principles are currently being applied to develop codes of corporate governance specifically relevant to individual countries within the Commonwealth.

17.6.3 THE REPORTS AND THE LISTING RULES

The recommendations of the various Reports are technically voluntary. Many of the recommendations are annexed to the London Stock Exchange Listing Rules, but non-compliance with the Combined Code will not automatically result in a de-listing; the obligation is only to make a statement about the degree of compliance and give reasons for any non-compliance. However, the government has explicitly refused to rule out statutory enforcement if voluntary compliance with the Code is inadequate. Pressure from institutional investors has also reinforced the need for a high degree of compliance. In practice, therefore, a growing majority of directors of listed companies comply with the recommendations. Furthermore, many unlisted companies also comply with the principles of the Combined Code and make disclosures on a voluntary basis.

The Listing Rules require the following information to be included in listed companies' reports and accounts:

1. A narrative statement of how the company has applied the principles of the Combined Code, with sufficient explanation for shareholders to evaluate how the principles have been applied.

2. A statement as to whether or not the company has complied with the Combined Code provisions throughout the whole accounting period and, where the company did not comply with a provision for any part of the period, a list of the provisions not complied with and reasons for non-compliance.

Directors are responsible for drafting these statements once they have carried out a review by answering the questions listed in Table 17.1. This list of sample questions is not exhaustive; there may be other matters of importance to the company which need to be reported in the corporate governance statement.

The corporate governance statement must be reviewed by the auditors.

17.6.4 THE MAJOR TOPICS COVERED BY THE REPORTS

As noted above, the Reports beg important conceptual questions. Implicitly, without discussion, the Reports assumed:

1. that the board is and should be accountable only to the company's shareholders;

2. that broad principles rather than prescriptive rules are sufficient to ensure good corporate governance;

3. that additional legislation is not needed.

Their recommendations centre on practical issues to do with the processes of governance and the amount and detail of information disclosed about directors. It is convenient to group the recommendations of the Reports together under four headings: board structure and membership, board management, directors' remuneration and financial control. The main recommendations with respect to these topics are briefly summarised in Table 17.2.

Table 17.1 *Considerations prior to the narrative statement required by the Combined Code*

A Directors	1. How is effectiveness of the board assessed? 2. Have the roles of chief executive officer and chairman been divided? 3. Is there a balance of non-executive and executive directors on the board? 4. Has the board received timely and appropriate information on which to base decisions? 5. Has a nomination committee been established to consider appointments to the board? 6. Are directors subject to re-election every three years?
B Directors' remuneration	7. Has a remuneration committee consisting of non-executive directors been set up with an identifiable procedure for determining executive remuneration? 8. What is the level and make-up of directors' remuneration – is it structured to link rewards to corporate and individual performance without being excessive? 9. Has the company's remuneration policy and the remuneration of directors been disclosed in the accounts?
C Relations with shareholders	10. Has there been any dialogue with any institutional shareholders? 11. Have any changes been made to the AGM to improve communication with private investors and encourage their participation?
D Accountability and audit	12. Has the board presented a balanced and understandable assessment of the company's position and prospects? 13. On review, was there found to be a sound system of internal control to protect the shareholders' investments? 14. Has an audit committee, with written terms of reference and comprising at least three non-executive directors, been formed to review financial reporting and internal control principles?

a) Board structure and membership

i Chairman and chief executive

The Cadbury Report [1992] recommended that:

- The roles of chairman (responsible for the running of the board) and chief executive (responsible for running the company's business) should be divided in order to avoid an excessive concentration of power. If, nonetheless, one director holds both positions, there need to be strong, independent non-executive directors on the board and the board should explain to the shareholders why the roles are combined.

ii Nomination committee

The Cadbury Report recommended that boards should set up nomination committees to report and propose appointments of executive and non-executive directors to the board for approval. This was re-affirmed by the Hampel Report [1998]: the committee would not have the authority to make appointments, but it is recommended that it should create formal job specifications, search for possible candidates and recommend persons for appointment. The Combined Code [1998] requires that a nomination committee be adopted in all but small companies, where the function may be performed by the board. It is also required that the majority of committee members are non-executive directors and that the members are identified in the Annual Report.

iii Re-election

The Hampel Report, supported by recommendations of the National Association of Pension Funds (NAPF) and the Association of British Insurers (ABI), strongly recommends that after the first AGM directors should be required to offer themselves for re-election at least every three years and that no director's service contract exceeds three years without the prior approval of the shareholders. This recommendation has been adopted in the Combined Code. One of the principles of the Code is the need to work towards setting notice and contract periods at one year or less.

The Listing Rules require directors to offer themselves for re-election at the first AGM held following their appointment as a director.

iv Non-executive directors

Boards should contain a mix of executive and non-executive directors, with sufficient of the latter to provide an 'independent' check on the executive directors. The Hampel Report recommended that at least one-third of the board members should be non-executives. Non-executives should have no business or other relationship with the company which might impair the independence of their judgement. Non-executives should be appointed for a specific period, re-appointment should not be automatic and their selection should be by a formal process. These requirements are part of the Combined Code and the Listing Rules [1999].

The Hampel Report also recommended that non-executives should be paid by way of shares in order to align their interests with those of the shareholders.

In addition, the Hampel Report emphasises the need for directors to receive initial instruction on their responsibilities following their appointment and for this to be supported by instruction and training from time to time.

b) Board management

The Cadbury Code and the Hampel Report specify certain measures as important to improving the effectiveness of the board. These are, in brief, that:

- there should be regular board meetings;

- there should be a clear division of responsibility between members of the board, with no single director being allowed unfettered discretion to make decisions;

- each director should be supplied with a formal written schedule, setting out matters for approval by the board;

- directors should be allowed to seek independent legal or professional advice at the company's expense in furtherance of their duties, and the advice and services of the company secretary (who should be knowledge-able about the compliance rules) should be available to all board members;

- all board members should be supplied with good quality and timely management information;

- the company secretary should be removable only by the board as a whole.

c) **Directors' remuneration**

v *Remuneration committee*

Directors' pay should be determined by an independent remuneration committee made up mainly (Cadbury Report) or wholly (Greenbury Report) of non-executive directors. The committee should establish company policy regarding executive directors' reward and should consider each year whether the annual general meeting should be invited to approve the policy. The committee should consult the company chairman and/or chief executive about their proposals and have access to professional advice.

However, the Hampel Report considers that the overall framework and level of directors' remuneration should remain the responsibility of the board and the remuneration committee should determine individual remuneration packages only within this framework. The Combined Code is in agreement with this view, since it is the board, rather than the remuneration committee, which is required to report to shareholders on directors' remuneration. The Combined Code also requires members of the remuneration committee to have no business or other relationship with the company which could affect their independent judgement.

vi *Remuneration details in the accounts*

The Greenbury Report required detailed information on directors' remuneration to be included in the company's accounts to a much greater extent than is required under the *Companies Act 1985*. In particular, the Report recommended that:

a) the company policy on remuneration and its operation as it affects individual directors should be set out in the annual report;

b) details on individual directors' share options, pension entitlements and annual bonuses should be set out in the annual report;

c) the reason for any notice period in a service contract exceeding one year should be made public;

d) long-term incentive schemes should be approved by the AGM.

vii *General principles*

In addition, the Greenbury Report laid down some general principles of good practice. These are:

a) the remuneration committee should look at what comparable companies are offering and take account of the relative performance of the company;

b) the remuneration committee should be aware of the wider environment in which the company operates and employment conditions elsewhere in the company;

c) conditions tied to performance should be designed to enhance the business and any short-term share option schemes need to be weighed against the benefits of longer-term incentives for directors;

d) where the director leaves because of unsatisfactory performance, the compensation commitments may be different and the reasons for leaving should be considered by the remuneration committee as a factor in determining compensation;

e) payment of compensation in instalments should be considered so as to give the company the option of reducing or stopping the payment if a former director mitigates his loss by obtaining new employment;

f) a company with a remuneration committee should have a remuneration policy and the details, if a listed company, should be given in the company's annual report.

d) Financial controls

viii Audit committee

The Cadbury Report, supported by the Hampel Report, recommended that the board sets up an audit committee with formal terms of reference outlining the objectives, responsibilities, composition and authority of the committee. The committee should have full powers of investigation and access to outside advice. The committee should have at least three members, all of whom should be non-executive directors and, where possible, completely independent from the company. The external auditor and the finance director should normally attend meetings of the committee. These requirements about the structure and make-up of the audit committee have been adopted in the Combined Code. Section 5.7.2, above, contains a discussion of the audit committee.

ix Internal controls

The Reports took the view that the board has a duty to present a balanced and understandable assessment of the company's position (Cadbury Report) and its prospects (Hampel Committee). To achieve this, the board is required to implement and maintain an effective system of internal control, covering a whole range of matters, including maintaining proper accounting records, protecting the company's assets, and observing applicable legal obligations.

The recommendation of the Cadbury Report that directors should be required to include a statement in the annual accounts explaining their responsibility for preparing accounts, commenting on the company's internal system of control and confirming that the company is a going concern, was re-affirmed in the Hampel Report and is now embodied in the Combined Code and incorporated in the Listing Rules.

The Combined Code specifically requires directors of listed companies to:

1. Conduct a review at least once a year and report to shareholders on the effectiveness of the company's system of internal control. This review must cover all aspects of internal control including operational and compliance issues rather than purely financial controls.

2. Where there is no formal internal control system, annually review the situation and report to shareholders why the board does not consider such a system necessary and outline other procedures in place to provide information to the board. Directors should periodically assess whether a control system needs to be implemented in response to developing trends or emerging risks.

The Turnbull Report [1999] has been adopted by the Stock Exchange and sets out what is required of listed companies' internal control systems. Compliance is required for accounting periods ending on or after 23 December 2000.

The main features of the approach adopted by the Turnbull Report are:

1. The board of directors should adopt a risk-based approach to establishing a sound system of internal control. The purpose of internal control is to help manage and control risks to which the company is exposed, but not to eliminate all risks, since profits are in part the reward for successful risk-taking in business.

2. The risks to be managed will depend upon the business, but should encompass more than just financial risk – for instance, changes in consumer behaviour, unfavourable legislation, supplier failure, products becoming technologically obsolescent, might be relevant risks.

3. The board should regularly receive and review reports on internal control and undertake an annual assessment.

4. A risk-based internal control system should not be a separate exercise undertaken to meet regulatory requirements but should be embedded in the company's business processes and linked to the business objectives.

Thus the Turnbull Report requires that directors disclose in the annual statement on internal control:

a) that there is an ongoing process for evaluating and managing the company's key risks which is regularly reviewed by the board;

b) how effectiveness of the internal control system has been reviewed (including the role played by the audit committee); *or*

c) where the directors are not able to make the disclosures in a) or b) above, why no such system has been implemented.

Table 17.2 *Summary of corporate governance Reports' recommendations*

Issue	Cadbury [1992]	Greenbury [1995]	Hampel [1998]	Combined Code [1998]
Structure of the board	1. The role of chairman and chief executive should be divided.		1. Reinforces the necessity of a strong, independent 'non-executive' element on the board.	1. Cadbury and Hampel recommendations adopted in the Combined Code, must be implemented by listed companies and the Listing Rules require that any deviation from the Code is explained in a Statement of Compliance in the company's annual accounts.
	2. If one director holds both positions, (a) there should be a strong, independent 'non-executive' element on the board, and (b) the board must explain why the roles are combined.		2. Endorses payment of non-executives by way of shares.	
	3. The board should contain a balance of executive and non-executive directors.		3. The board must consist of at least one-third non-executive directors.	
Management of the board	There should be:		1. Endorses the Cadbury recommendations.	
	1. Regular board meetings;		2. Directors should initially receive instruction on their responsibilities following their appointment and instruction and training from time to time thereafter.	
	2. A clear division of responsibility between members of the board, with no single director being allowed unfettered discretion to make decisions;			
	3. A formal written schedule of matters for approval by the board.			

Issue	Cadbury [1992]	Greenbury [1995]	Hampel [1998]	Combined Code [1998]
	Directors should: 1. Be allowed to seek independent legal or professional advice at the company's expense in furtherance of their duties; 2. Have access to the advice and services of the company secretary; 3. Be provided with good quality and timely management information.			
Board membership	1. Boards should establish nomination committees.		1. Re-affirmed the need for a nomination committee. 2. The nomination committee's role should include reporting on and proposing appointments to the board for approval. 3. After the first AGM directors should be required to offer themselves for re-election at least every three years, and no director's service contract should exceed three years without prior approval of the shareholders.	1. A nomination committee is required. 2. Requires the majority of members of the nominating committee to be non-executive directors and the members to be identified in the annual report. 3. Adopted the Hampel recommendations regarding re-election and contracts. 4. Boards should work towards setting notice and contract periods at one year or less.

Table 17.2 *Summary of corporate governance Reports' recommendations (continued)*

Issue	Cadbury [1992]	Greenbury [1995]	Hampel [1998]	Combined Code [1998]
Remuneration	1. Directors' pay should be determined by an independent remuneration committee made up wholly or mainly of non-executive directors.	1. The remuneration committee should be comprised *entirely* of non-executive directors. 2. Detailed information on directors' remuneration should be included in the company's accounts. 3. The accounts should include a statement that 'best practice' has been followed in determining directors' remuneration.	1. The overall framework and cost of directors' remuneration should remain the responsibility of the board and the remuneration committee should determine individual remuneration packages within this framework. 2. The board (not the remuneration committee) should report to the shareholders on directors' remuneration.	1. A remuneration committee is required and its members are required to have no business or other relationship with the company which could affect the independence of their judgement. 2. The board, rather than the remuneration committee, is required to report to shareholders on directors' remuneration.
Internal controls	1. The board has a duty to present an assessment of the company's financial position. 2. Directors should be required to include a statement in the annual accounts explaining their responsibility for preparing the accounts, commenting on the company's internal system of control and confirming that the company is a going concern.		1. The board's report to shareholders should be expanded to include an assessment of the company's prospects. 2. Re-affirmed the Cadbury recommendations concerning the audit committee.	1. The Cadbury recommendation is embodied in the Combined Code and incorporated in the Listing Rules. 2. Directors of listed companies must (a) conduct a review at least once a year and report to shareholders on the effectiveness of the company's system of internal control, or

Table 17.2 *Summary of corporate governance Reports' recommendations (continued)*

Issue	Cadbury [1992]	Greenbury [1995]	Hampel [1998]	Combined Code [1998]
	3. Boards should establish an audit committee, with at least three members, all of whom are non-executive directors and, where possible, completely independent from the company.			(b) where there is no formal internal control system, annually review the situation and report to shareholders why the board does not consider such a system necessary and outline other procedures in place to provide information to the board. 3. Adopts the Cadbury recommendation in regard to the audit committee

17.7 SUMMARY

1. There is no single, accepted definition of what the expression 'corporate governance' means. It may be interpreted as meaning the system by which companies are directed and controlled.

2. Companies are complex, wealth-producing machines – though in a market economy success is never guaranteed. To whom should they be accountable?

3. Shareholders own claims on the company. In theory they have great power – they can appoint and dismiss directors, they can wind up the company and they can change the nature of its business. 'Shareholder activists' view the key role of directors as being to increase shareholder value.

4. Others take the view that the directors should work in the interest of a wider community – 'stakeholders'. All those persons and organisations which have an interest in the company or its operations, including shareholders, may be called 'stakeholders'. Stakeholders therefore encompass a wider group than directors, employees and shareholders. They include suppliers, customers, the community and governmental organisations. All stakeholders have the potential to influence – for better or worse – the survival and prosperity of the company.

5. Generally, the law as it stands favours a shareholder view of companies. If stakeholders are to be owed duties by companies and/or directors, the law will need to be redrafted and various matters of process will need to be modified.

6. It is up to the board to manage the company's relations with shareholders and other stakeholders, to balance stakeholder interests and the company's interests, in the light of market forces, the law and regulation. It is up to the board to decide how to apply the contents of this *Guide*, taking into account the costs and benefits of governance.

7. There have been a number of corporate governance Reports, and their major recommendations have been incorporated into the Listing Rules of the London Stock Exchange.

Appendix A

Key Aspects of Company Law and Related Provisions

This summary is based largely upon consultation documents from The Company Law Review Steering Group set up by the Secretary of State for Trade and Industry in 1998.

I COMPANY LAW

Subject	Relevant rules	Sanction
Company formation; change of status of company	Companies Act 1985	Refusal to register if requirements not complied with at outset; other defaults are offences punishable by fine.
Company names	Companies Act 1985 and Regulations made under it	Refusal to register or allow business to be carried on under a non-compliant name, and power to direct change of name in certain

Subject	Relevant rules	Sanction
		circumstances. Trading under misleading name in certain respects is an offence punishable by a fine.
Share capital (provisions relating to a minimum capital requirement apply to public companies only).	Companies Act 1985	Compensation for loss resulting from non-compliance; offences concerning false or misleading information, or contravention of financial assistance provisions, punishable by fine or imprisonment; other defaults punishable by fine. Some agreements in contravention of these provisions are void.
Disclosure of interests in shares (applies to public companies only)	Companies Act 1985	Offences of failing to disclose, or giving false information, punishable by fine or imprisonment, and by order of the Secretary of State under Part XV of the Act restricting the shares involved. Other defaults punishable by fine.
Form, content and publicity of company accounts	Companies Act 1985	Failure to comply with procedural provisions on preparation of accounts, and directors' report, and laying before general meeting, are offences punishable by fine. Failure to deliver accounts and reports to the Registrar is also punished by fine. Accounts which fail to comply with the accounting requirements of the Companies Acts may be challenged in court by the Financial Reporting Review Panel (FRRP) or the DTI. If this succeeds, the company must publish revised accounts. Alternatively, subject to criminal sanctions (fine).

Subject	Relevant rules	Sanction
Accounting requirements	Companies Act 1985 and accounting standards	The Accounting Standards board (ASB) sets standards: the FRRP and the DTI are responsible for enforcing them. If the FRRP or the DTI challenge accounts in court, a main focus is material departures from accounting standards where such a departure results in the accounts not giving a true and fair view as required by the Act.
Regulation of auditors	Rules of Recognised Supervisory Bodies (RSBs) and Recognised Qualifying Bodies (RQBs)	Secretary of State may withdraw recognition from RSBs and RQBs. Auditors who contravene RSB rules are subject to sanction by their own RSB or, in serious cases, by the profession's Joint Disciplinary Scheme. Penalties can include withdrawal of registered auditor status.
Technical standards to be employed in audit work.	Statements of Auditing Standards	The Auditing Practices Board has no sanctions. But failure to observe Auditing Standards may render an auditor liable to sanction by the RSB.
Distribution of profits. (Restrictions on distributions by reference to net assets apply to public companies only)	Companies Act 1985	A member of a company who receives a distribution he knows to be unlawful is liable to repay it.
Appointment and removal of directors and secretary.		
Company registered office.	Companies Act 1985	Procedural defaults punishable by fines.

Subject	Relevant rules	Sanction
Fair dealing by directors	Companies Act 1985	Penalties include fines or imprisonment for offences involving dishonesty; fines for procedural defaults; avoidance of contracts in breach of statutory provisions, and personal liability of directors in some circumstances. Breaches of Part X may also constitute grounds for disqualification (see below).
Company administration and procedure (e.g. company name, Register of Members, Annual Return). Private companies may elect to dispense with some requirements.	Companies Act 1985	Procedural defaults punishable by fines
Registration of company charges Unregistered charges void against a creditor, liquidator or administrator.	Companies Act 1985	Procedural defaults by the company punishable by a fine.
Arrangements and reconstructions	Companies Act 1985	Court has discretion and may not consent to a transaction.
Take-over offers.	Companies Act 1985	Fines for procedural default by companies. Shareholders may appeal to the court against a compulsory buyout.
Company inspections	Companies Act 1985; Company Directors Disqualification Act 1986	Disqualification of a director. Restrictions on shares. Criminal offences of supplying false information or destroying documents.

Subject	Relevant rules	Sanction
Fraudulent trading	Companies Act 1985; Insolvency Act 1986	Criminal sanctions under s458; liability to contribute to the company's assets under s213.
Wrongful trading	Insolvency Act 1986	Liability to contribute to the company's assets.
Protection of members against unfair prejudice	Companies Act 1985	At the court's discretion. May include regulation of company's future conduct; requiring company to do or refrain from specific acts; authorising civil proceedings against the company; requiring company to buy out minority shareholder.
Overseas companies	Companies Act 1985	Various, as in Parts of the Act applied to the companies concerned.
Unregistered companies	Companies Act 1985	Various, as in the Parts of the Act applied to the companies concerned.
Solvent winding up of a company	Insolvency Act 1986	A director making a solvency statement without good grounds is liable to a fine, to imprisonment and may be liable to pay the company's debts in full. Procedural defaults by the liquidator are punishable by fine.
Disqualification from acting as a company director	Company Directors Disqualification Act 1986	Criminal penalties for acting while disqualified. Personal responsibility for company debts incurred when acting while disqualified.

II SECURITIES REGULATION

Subject	Relevant rules	Sanction
Supervision of competent authority for listing of securities	Financial Services Act 1986	Withdrawal of designation
Admission of securities to listing	The Listing Rules	Refusal of listing.
Continuing obligations of listed companies. These include: • General disclosure obligation • Announcement of major transactions (acquisitions and disposals) • Shareholder approval for the largest transactions • Shareholder approval of related party transactions • Disclosure of financial information • Circulars • Purchase of own securities • Approval of documents • Directors	The Listing Rules	Breaches of the Listing Rules are punishable by private or public censure or ultimately by delisting. Censure can in some circumstances apply to an individual director. (A power to fine a company has been proposed.)

Subject	Relevant rules	Sanction
Overseas companies	The Listing Rules	Imposes disclosure obligations additional to the Companies Act 1985 on overseas companies with a secondary listing on the London Stock Exchange.
Supervision of non-statutory listing of securities	Financial Services Act 1986	
Offers of securities not falling under Listing Rules	Public Offers of Securities Regulations; Companies Act 1985	The issuer or offeror of the securities, and the directors of such persons, are liable to pay compensation to those suffering loss as a result of untrue or misleading statements in the prospectus or the omission of any matter required to be included. An authorised person under the Financial Securities Act 1986 involved in any contravention of the regulations is treated as having breached the rules of his regulatory body and is therefore liable to be disciplined by that body. Failure of any other person to prepare and file a prospectus where required is a criminal offence punishable by imprisonment or a fine, and any such contravention is actionable at the suit of a person who suffers as a result.
Holding and transfer of securities in uncertificated form	Uncertificated Securities Regulations	
Insider dealing	Criminal Justice Act 1993	Criminal penalties.

III TAKEOVERS AND MERGERS

Subject	Relevant rules	Sanction
Regulation of take-overs. (The aim of the Take-over Code is to ensure fair and equal treatment of shareholders. It is not concerned with competition aspects.)	Take-over Code and associated Financial Services Act 1986, SRO and RPB rules.	The Take-over Panel can issue a private reprimand or public censure. It can also report an offender to a relevant regulatory authority. Firms and individuals regulated under the Financial Services Act 1986 can be penalised for breaches of rules relating to the Code including by withdrawal of authorisation.

IV CORPORATE GOVERNANCE

Subject	Relevant rules	Sanction
Good practice in the structure and operation of boards of directors of listed UK companies, including the setting of directors' pay and the relations between directors, shareholders and auditors. Among specific requirements is the inclusion in the annual report of • narrative on the application of governance principles; • statement on compliance with code provisions with auditor review of certain points;	The Financial Services Act 1986; the Combined Code; the Listing Rules.	Failure by companies to comply with the disclosure provisions of the Code is a breach of the Stock Exchange Rules, and subject to censure or, ultimately, delisting.

Subject	Relevant rules	Sanction
• remuneration report, including specified details of director remuneration.		

Code provisions
addressed to
shareholders are not
subject to formal sanction.

Appendix B

Summary of the Combined Code on Corporate Governance and the Turnbull Report

1. INTRODUCTION

The remit of the Committee on Corporate Governance (Hampel [1998]) was to review and consolidate the earlier work of the Committee on the Financial Aspects of Corporate Governance (Cadbury [1992]), the work of Directors' Remuneration: Report of a Study Group (Greenbury [1995]) and develop clear guidelines on corporate governance standards. In addition to issuing a Final Report, it also drafted The Combined Code on corporate governance, based on the work of the Cadbury, Greenbury and Hampel Committees. The report *Internal Control: Guidance for Directors on the Combined Code* (Turnbull [1999]) suggests how companies can comply with the internal control provisions of the Combined Code. The major elements of the Combined Code and the Turnbull Report are summarised here.

- The London Stock Exchange's Listing Rules require listed companies to provide a statement of compliance with the Code and a detailed directors' remuneration report. Any areas of non-compliance must be disclosed in the company's Annual Report and Accounts and explained fully in the compliance statement.

- Unlisted companies, although they are unaffected by the Listing Rules, are still likely to benefit from the ideas and prescriptions in both the Combined Code and the Turnbull Report.

2. THE COMBINED CODE

In general terms, the Code is designed to:

- encourage shareholders, non-executive directors and auditors to accept their legal responsibilities and scrutinise the stewardship of companies; and

- impose adequate checks and balances on executive directors without restricting unduly the exercise of enterprise by boards of directors.

2.1 BOARDS OF DIRECTORS

Every listed company should be headed by an effective board of directors which governs the company. The Code provides that:

2.1.1 The board

- The board should meet regularly.

- The board should have a formal schedule of matters specifically reserved to it for decision.

- The board should have timely information in a form and of appropriate quality to enable the board to discharge its duties effectively.

- The board should have a formal, transparent procedure for the appointment of new directors; and, unless the board is small, a nomination committee should be established to make recommendations to the board on all new board appointments. A majority of the members of this committee should be non-executive directors and the chairman should be either the chairman of the board or a non-executive director. The chairman and members of the nomination committee should be identified in the Annual Report.

- An individual should receive appropriate training on the first occasion that he or she is appointed to the board of a listed company, and subsequently as necessary.

- Non-executive directors should be appointed to the board for specified terms and reappointment should not be automatic. All directors should be subject to election by shareholders at the first opportunity after their appointment, and to re-election thereafter at intervals of no more than three years. Biographical details of directors submitted for election or re-election should be provided to shareholders.

2.1.2 The company secretary

- The Code supports the Cadbury view that the company secretary should play an important role in providing advice to directors. All directors should have access to the advice and services of the company secretary.

- The company secretary should also be responsible to the board for ensuring that board procedures are followed and that applicable rules and regulations are complied with.

- The dismissal or removal otherwise of the company secretary should be a matter for the board as a whole.

2.1.3 Board committees

- Listed companies are required to maintain separate, independent committees dealing with audit, remuneration, and nomination, each of which should have written terms of reference.

2.1.4 The chairman

- There should be a clearly accepted division of responsibilities at the head of the company between the chairman and the managing director. The justification is to try to ensure a balance of power and authority, such that no one individual has unfettered powers of decision. A decision to combine the posts of chairman and managing director in one person should be publicly explained.

- The chairman has an obligation to disseminate information properly and ensure that all directors are adequately briefed on issues arising at board meetings.

2.1.5 Board composition

- Both the Cadbury and Hampel Reports stress that the board should include independent non-executive directors of sufficient calibre and number for their views to carry significant weight in the board's decisions. 'Independent' directors are defined as persons who 'apart from directors' fees and shareholdings [are] independent of the management and free from any business or other relationships which could materially interfere with the exercise of the independent judgement' (Cadbury). The majority of non-executive directors should be independent. Non-executive directors considered by the board to be independent should be identified in the Annual Report.

- The balance of executive and non-executive directors should be such that no individual or small group of individuals can dominate the board's decision-taking. Non-executive directors should comprise not less than one-third of the board.

2.2 REMUNERATION

- Levels of remuneration should be sufficient to attract and retain the executive directors needed to run the company successfully. The component parts of executive directors' remuneration should be structured so as to link rewards with corporate and individual performance. Recommendations on the design of performance-based remuneration are included as a schedule to the Combined Code.

- Companies should establish a formal and transparent procedure for developing policy on executive remuneration and for fixing the remuneration packages of individual directors. No director should be involved in determining his or her own remuneration.

- The company's annual report should contain a statement of remuneration policy and details of the remuneration of each director.

2.3 RELATIONS WITH SHAREHOLDERS

- According to Cadbury, 'the shareholders' role in governance is to appoint the directors and auditors and satisfy themselves that an appropriate governance structure is in place'. To meet their obligations, shareholders must participate actively in the affairs of the company and make considered use of their votes. In order to do this effectively, they must be fully informed. The Hampel Report emphasises that the overriding objective of listed companies is 'the preservation and . . . enhancement over time of their shareholders' investment'.

- The Code states two key principles:

  - Companies should be ready, where practicable, to enter into dialogue with institutional shareholders based on a mutual understanding of objectives. Section 2 of the Code contains recommendations on improving the dialogue between listed companies and institutional investors, as well as encouraging institutional investors to make considered use of their votes.

  - Boards should use the Annual General Meeting to communicate with private investors and encourage their participation.

- The Code also requires, *inter alia*, an end to the practice of bundling resolutions, such that shareholders have to reject sound proposals in order to vote down one unacceptable element. Distinct issues require separate resolutions.

- At least 20 working days' notice of the AGM (the *Companies Act 1985* specifies 21 calendar days) must be given, and the chairmen of each of the three key governance committees (audit, remuneration and nomination) should be present to answer questions.

2.4 ACCOUNTABILITY AND AUDIT

The Code makes recommendations in three main areas of accountability:

- *Financial reporting.* The board should present a balanced and understandable assessment of the company's position and prospects by ensuring that:

  a both directors and auditors explain their reporting responsibilities in financial reports;

  b interim and other price sensitive reports are balanced and understandable; *and*

  c financial reports are on a 'going-concern' basis, including an explanation of assumptions and qualifications.

- *Internal control.* The board should maintain a sound system of internal controls to safeguard shareholders' investment and the company's assets by:

  a conducting an annual review of such controls and reporting to shareholders;

  b reviewing the need for an internal audit function on a regular basis, where the company does not have one.

- *Relationship with the auditors.* The Hampel Report follows its predecessors in viewing external checks on the consistency and reliability of financial statements as a key to investor confidence. The task of the auditor is seen as being to report to shareholders on whether the company's annual accounts are properly prepared and give a true and fair view, and to review the directors' 'going concern' statement, the extent of Code compliance, and the remuneration committee's report.

- The board should establish formal and transparent arrangements for considering how the financial reporting and control principles should be applied and for maintaining an appropriate relationship with the company's auditors. The Code recommends that

  a the audit committee should review the scope, results and effectiveness of the audit and ensure that, where the auditor also provides non-audit services, this is carefully reviewed.

  b the independence of the audit committee, which is essential, is enhanced by its having at least three non-executive director members, a majority of whom should be independent and named in the annual accounts.

3. THE TURNBULL REPORT

3.1 THE ISSUE

- As noted above, the Combined Code has a number of requirements relating to internal control. In addition, the London Stock Exchange Listing Rules require that a UK-registered listed company includes in its Annual Report a narrative statement of how it has applied the internal control Principle (Principle D.2) of the Combined Code and a statement of compliance with the associated Code provisions (provisions D.2.1 and D.2.2) or, in the case of non-compliance, gives reasons.

- The Turnbull Report provides guidance as to

  - assessing how the company has applied Code Principle D.2 (the board should maintain a sound system of internal control to safeguard shareholders' investment and the company's assets);

  - implementing the Code provisions D.2.1 (that the board should annually or more frequently review the effectiveness of the company's system of internal control) and D.2.2 (that companies which do not have an internal audit function should from time to time review the need for one); *and*

  - reporting on these matters to shareholders in the Annual Report.

3.2 THE APPROACH

- Internal control includes financial, operational and compliance controls and risk management.

- The board of directors should adopt a risk-based approach to establishing a sound system of internal control. This involves conducting an assessment of risks faced by the company, determining what control activities are required to avoid or reduce the impact of those risks and ensuring that appropriate and timely information is communicated to directors to enable them to monitor performance and respond rapidly where change is required. The purpose of internal control is to help manage and control risk appropriately rather than to eliminate all risks, since profits are in part the reward for successful risk-taking in business.

- The risks to be managed will depend upon the business, but should encompass more than just financial risk – for instance, changes in consumer behaviour, supplier failure and products becoming obsolescent might be relevant risks.

- The board should regularly receive and review reports on internal control and undertake an annual assessment.

- The adoption of a risk-based internal control system should be embedded in the company's business processes, linked to the business objectives and not be just a separate exercise undertaken to meet regulatory requirements. In order to ensure the system is not just left to run on its own, managers are required to report on specific areas assigned to them.

- Procedures and the frequency of reporting required should be communicated and agreed so that major control weaknesses may be reported immediately.

3.3 BOARD RESPONSIBILITIES

- The board must set appropriate policies on internal control, seek regular assurance that the system is working satisfactorily, and ensure that the system is effective in managing risks.

- In setting its policy the board should consider the following factors:
  - the nature and extent of the risks facing the company and which risks, and to what extent, are acceptable;
  - the likelihood of the risks concerned materialising;
  - the company's ability to reduce the incidence and impact on the business of risks that do materialise;
  - the cost of operating particular controls relative to the benefits of managing the associated risks.

- The board is responsible for reviewing the effectiveness of the internal control system and for ensuring that it is effective, although the audit committee may review financial controls and provide a 'focal point' for wider control issues. The Appendix to the Report sets out key questions that a board may wish to consider when assessing the effectiveness of the company's internal control system.

- The Report recognises that smaller companies are not able to justify the cost of an internal audit department and does not insist that companies should have internal auditors, though those without them must review the need for them annually.

- The disclosures required by the directors are as follows:
  a that there is an ongoing process for evaluating and managing the company's key risks which is regularly reviewed by the board;

  b how effectiveness of the internal control system has been reviewed, the role played by the audit committee, internal audit function, managers and others suitably placed, whether any material losses were suffered and what remedial action or contingency plans were put into effect; *or*

  c where the directors are not able to make the disclosures in (a) or (b) above, then an explanation of why no such system has been implemented.

Appendix C

Summary of Directors' Personal Liabilities and Sanctions

Directors should know that they may incur personal liability, both civil and criminal, for their acts or omissions in directing the company. Throughout the text, particularly in Chapters 8, 9, 10, 11 and 15, attention has been drawn to the range of penalties that directors may suffer if they breach either the common or statutory law. This Appendix briefly summarises the possible **personal** penalties. A full list of the offences which may involve personal liability by directors and the penalties to which directors may become liable is given in Hutchinson and Farmery [1992], Appendix B.

PENALTIES

A director who fails in his duties to the company may

- have unlimited liability for any loss suffered by the company, even if he himself has not made any personal gain;

- be directly accountable to third parties for any loss or damage suffered by them as a result of his actions, omissions or in respect of information supplied by him.

Any attempt by a company to exempt a director (for example, by provision in the Articles) from liability for negligence, default, breach of duty or breach of trust in relation to the company is void. (However, the company may take out insurance against certain liabilities; see section 12.18).

Directors who have breached either the common law or their statutory duties may be subject to

- personal liability for their acts or omissions;

- the imposition of civil and criminal penalties;

- removal from office; *or*

- disqualification from holding office as a director.

Each of these sanctions is discussed in the following paragraphs.

PERSONAL LIABILITY

Care should always be taken to make it clear to a third party that a transaction is with the company and not with the directors themselves, so that the directors will be considered to be acting as 'agents' for their company. In this case they will not incur personal liability should any breach of contract or tortious act be committed by the company. But if this is not done, or if the directors have personally guaranteed the company's obligation, then they may incur personal liability if the company defaults.

The more important circumstances where directors may find themselves personally liable to third parties for any loss resulting from a breach of duty or a statutory offence are:

- knowingly giving preference to a creditor on a winding-up;

- acting as a director whilst disqualified;

- fraudulent trading;

- where, in winding up the business of the company, it becomes apparent that it has been conducted with intent to defraud;

- 'wrongful trading';

- failing to show the company name clearly on promissory notes, cheques, etc. (the director is liable to the third party where the company fails to pay);

- failing to observe shareholders' rights of pre-emption;

- making false or misleading statements or omitting information from listing particulars or a prospectus;

- irregularities in allotments;

- failing to obtain a trading certificate for a public company before entering into a transaction with a third party;

- where a director of an insolvent company carries on business using a prohibited name;

- non-payment of betting or gaming duties by the company;

- fraudulent evasion of VAT;

- making a dishonest declaration or failing to register for VAT;

- employing illegal immigrants;

- non-payment of national insurance contributions where the company is insolvent and the directors are found to have acted fraudulently or negligently (the *Social Security Act 1998*).

Finally, in addition, directors may also be required to account to the company, as opposed to a third party, for any loss or damage suffered by their failure to observe their duties to the company. For example, circumstances in which directors would be held liable to compensate the company as well as being criminally liable for their actions are:

- authorising an unlawful loan to a director;

- failing to disclose their interest in a contract;

- in an insolvency situation misappropriating the company's money or property.

BREACH OF STATUTORY DUTIES

Generally, criminal liability for acts of the company rests with the company and not the directors. However, there are many duties of the company where directors and other officers of the company who consent to or connive at an offence or, if the offence does not require proof of criminal intention (and most do not), is negligent, may be held accountable for the offence. Schedule 24 of the *Companies Act 1985* contains approximately 250 offences imposing a parallel liability on directors for offences committed by the company. The penalty may be a fine, imprisonment or both.

In addition, there are some requirements under the *Companies Act 1985* which are the responsibility not of the company but of the directors – for example, responsibility for delivering annual accounts to Companies House, disclosing their interest in shares, and disclosing interests in contracts to be made with the company. In these instances the directors are directly liable for their failure to comply, and the penalties and action to be taken are stated in the Act.

There are many statutes protecting employees, consumers, the environment, etc. which impose duties on directors, each detailing the sanctions that can be taken if the duties are breached. Some of these are described in Chapter 10. For example, a director may be held liable for offences committed under the *Theft Act 1968* (obtaining property or pecuniary advantage by deception), the *Trade Descriptions Act 1968* (making misleading trade descriptions to consumers), the *Health & Safety at Work etc Act 1974* (health and safety in the workplace), the *Insolvency Act 1986* (fraudulent and wrongful trading), and the *Criminal Justice Act 1993* (dealing in company securities at a time when he has 'insider information').

BREACH OF COMMON LAW DUTIES

If a director breaches his fiduciary duty or his duty of care and skill to the company, he will be liable to civil action instigated by the company for any loss suffered or undisclosed profit made or advantage taken.

The company may take legal action to obtain:

- an injunction to restrain the director and prevent him from carrying out or continuing with the action constituting the breach of duty in the future;

- damages by way of compensation where the director's action is considered negligent;

- restoration of the company's property, provided it does not prejudice an innocent third party, where the director's fiduciary duty has been broken and assets have been misappropriated;

- an account and repayment of profits made by the director;

- rescission of a contract in which the director has an undisclosed interest; *or*

- dismissal of the director.

Where directors give out information in brochures, accounts, prospectuses, offer documents, etc. issued on behalf of the company to third parties, the purpose of such documents being to persuade third parties to buy securities of the company or deal or contract with it, and the information given is inaccurate, misleading, false or unsubstantiated, the directors may be liable for breach of duty (*Financial Services Act 1986*, s.47). If the mis-statements are made as a result of careless omission or neglect, the directors may face a civil claim for negligence. Alternatively, where there is evidence of intentional fraud or recklessness in compiling the information, the directors may be liable for criminal penalties.

If a director is found guilty of fraud, misrepresentation or other tort, he will be personally liable alongside the company.

In the case of an insolvent company, if a director is found to have misapplied the company's assets, the liquidator may pursue the director for restoration of the company's property or compensation. Furthermore, if it transpires in the course of winding up that the company's business has been conducted with intent to defraud creditors, itself considered as misapplication of funds, the Court may impose personal liability on those directors party to the fraud for all debts and liabilities of the company, without limitation.

DISMISSAL OF THE DIRECTOR

On occasion, shareholders may seek to remove a director from office to protect the company and their investment, perhaps because they become aware that he is not carrying out his duties properly. Whatever the circumstances, the members have the power to remove a director by ordinary resolution, notwithstanding anything in the Articles of Association or in the director's service agreement (ss.303 and 304, *Companies Act 1985*).

Dismissal of a director is discussed more fully in section 7.6.2.

DISQUALIFICATION

Directors may be disqualified from holding office either automatically as a result of certain defined acts or by a Court after application by a complainant.

The grounds for disqualification are discussed in Chapter 11.

RATIFICATION OF BREACHES OF DUTY

The company has power in certain circumstances, whether by resolution of the director or members, to ratify a director's breach of duty after the event. The most common instances probably are where:

- shares were allotted for an improper purpose;
- the director failed to disclose his interest in a contract;
- the director's personal profit or advantage from a transaction was not disclosed;
- the director's duty of care and skill was not exercised, provided there was no fraud;
- the act was outside the company's powers.

However, breaches cannot be ratified where they

- infringe shareholders' rights;
- are fraudulent or dishonest; *or*
- involve a secret profit being made by a director at the direct expense of the company.

Appendix D

OECD Principles of Corporate Governance

There are five Principles. Each Principle is supported by a number of recommendations. There are also addenda to the Principles which explain their rationale and suggest ways in which they may be made operational. Only the Principles are listed here.

I. The corporate governance framework should protect shareholders' rights.

II. The corporate governance framework should ensure the equitable treatment of all shareholders, including minority and foreign shareholders. All shareholders should have the opportunity to obtain effective redress for violation of their rights.

III. The corporate governance framework should recognise the rights of stakeholders as established by law and encourage active co-operation between corporations and stakeholders in creating wealth, jobs, and the sustainability of financially sound enterprises.

IV. The corporate governance framework should ensure that timely and accurate disclosure is made on all material matters regarding the corporation, including the financial situation, performance, ownership, and governance of the company.

V. The corporate governance framework should ensure the strategic guidance of the company, the effective monitoring of management by the board, and the board's accountability to the company and the shareholders.

Appendix E

Commonwealth Principles of Corporate Governance

The *CACG Guidelines* [1999] encompass 15 Principles of corporate governance with explanatory notes to help the interpretation and application of the Principles. The Principles are:

The board should:

Principle 1 – exercise leadership, enterprise, integrity and judgement in directing the corporation so as to achieve continuing prosperity for the corporation and to act in the best interest of the business enterprise in a manner based on transparency, accountability and responsibility;

Principle 2 – ensure that through a managed and effective process, board appointments are made that provide a mix of proficient directors, each of whom is able to add value and to bring independent judgement to bear on the decision-making process;

Principle 3 – determine the corporation's purpose and values, determine the strategy to achieve its purpose and to implement its values in order to ensure that it survives and thrives, and ensure that procedures and practices are in place that protect the corporation's assets and reputation;

Principle 4 – monitor and evaluate the implementation of strategies, policies, management, performance criteria and business plans;

Principle 5 – ensure that the corporation complies with all relevant laws, regulations and codes of best business practice;

Principle 6 – ensure that the corporation communicates with shareholders and other stakeholders effectively;

Principle 7 – serve the legitimate interests of the shareholders of the corporation and account to them fully;

Principle 8 – identify the corporation's internal and external stakeholders and agree a policy, or policies, determining how the corporation should relate to them;

Principle 9 – ensure that no one person or a block of persons has unfettered power and that there is an appropriate balance of power and authority on the board which is, *inter alia*, usually reflected by separating the roles of the chief executive officer and chairman, and by having a balance between executive and non-executive directors;

Principle 10 – regularly review processes and procedures to ensure the effectiveness of its internal systems of control, so that its decision-making capability and the accuracy of its reporting and financial results are maintained at a high level at all times;

Principle 11 – regularly assess its performance and effectiveness as a whole, and that of the individual directors, including the chief executive officer;

Principle 12 – appoint the chief executive and at least participate in the appointment of senior management, ensure the motivation and protection of intellectual capital intrinsic to the corporation, ensure that there is adequate training in the corporation for management and employees, and a succession plan for senior management;

Principle 13 – ensure that all technology and systems used in the corporation are adequate to properly run the business and for it to remain a meaningful competitor;

Principle 14 – identify key risk areas and key performance indicators of the business enterprise and monitor these factors;

Principle 15 – ensure annually that the corporation will continue as a going concern for its next fiscal year.

Useful Addresses

ACAS
Brandon House
180 Borough High Street
London SE1 1LW
Tel: 020-7210 3613
Website: www.acas.org.uk

Alternative Investment Market
Old Broad Street
London EC2N 1HP
Tel: 020-7179 4404
Fax: 020-7797 2001
Website: www.londonstockex.co.uk

British Chambers of Commerce
22 Carlisle Place
London SW1
Tel: 020-7565 2000
Fax: 020-7565 2049
email: info@britishchambers.org.uk

British Venture Capitalists Association
Essex House
12–13 Essex Street
London WC2R 3AA
Tel: 020-7240 3846
Fax: 020-7240 3849
email: bvca@bvca.co.uk

The Chartered Institute of Management Accountants
63 Portland Place
London W1N 4AB
Tel: 020-7637 2311
Fax: 020-7631 5309
Website: www.cimaglobal.com

The Commission for Racial Equality
Elliot House
10–12 Allington Street
London SW1E 5EH
Tel: 020-7828 7022
Fax: 020-7630 7605
email: info@cre.gov.uk

Companies House
Crown Way
Cardiff CF4 3UZ
Tel: 01222-388588
Fax: 01222-380900
email: enquiries@companieshouse.gov.uk

Companies House
37 Castle Terrace
Edinburgh EH1 2EB
Tel: 0131-535 5800
Fax: 0131-535 5820
Website: www.companieshouse.gov.uk

Company Registration Firms
See your local Yellow Pages

Competition Commission
Carey Street
London WC2A 2JT
Tel: 020-7271 0100
Fax: 020-7271 0367
Website: www.competition-commission.org.uk

Confederation of British Industry
Centre Point
New Oxford Street
London WC1
Tel: 020-7379 7400
Fax: 020-7240 1578
email: enquiry.desk@cbi.org.uk

Data Protection Registrar
Springfield House
Water Lane
Wilmslow
Cheshire SK9 5AX
Tel: 01625-545745
Fax: 01625-535777
email: data@wycliffe.demon.co.uk

Department of Social Security – see under Department of Social Security in your local telephone directory or phone Freephone helpline Tel: 0800-393539

Department of Trade and Industry Regional Development and Inward Investment
Kingsgate House
66–74 Victoria Street
London SW1E 6SW
Tel: 020-7215 2578
Fax: 020-7222 0612
email: dti.enquiries@imsv.dti.gov.uk

Economist Intelligence Unit
15 Regent Street
London SW1Y 4LR
Tel: 020-7830 1000
Fax: 020-7499 9767
email: london@eiu.com

Enterprise Grants
Regional selective assistance:
Tel: 020-7215 8460

Equal Opportunities Commission
Overseas House
Quay Street
Manchester
Tel: 0161-833 9244
Fax: 0161-835 1657
email: info@eoc.org.uk

Health and Safety Executive
Rose Court
2 Southwark Bridge
London SE1 9HS
Tel: 020-7717 6000
Fax: 020-7717 6717
Website: www.open.gov.uk/hse/hsehone.htm

HMSO
The Stationery Office
119 Kingsway
London WC2B 6PQ
Tel: 020-7242 6393
Fax: 020-7242 6394
Website: www.hmso.gov.uk

The Insolvency Practitioners Association
Moor House
London Wall
London EC2Y 5ET
Tel: 020-7329 0777
Fax: 020-7329 2204
email: admin@ipa.co.uk

Institute of Chartered Accountants in England and Wales
Chartered Accountants Hall
Moorgate Place
London EC2P 2BJ
Tel: 020-7920 8100
Fax: 020-7920 0547
email: webmaster@icaew.co.uk

Institute of Chartered Accountants of Scotland
27 Queen Street
Edinburgh EH2 1LA
Tel: 0131-225 5673
Fax: 0131-225 3813
Website: www.icas.org.uk

Institute of Chartered Accountants in Ireland
87/89 Pembroke Road
Ballsbridge
Dublin 4
Tel: 00 3531 668 0400
Fax: 00 3531 668 0842
email: ca@icai.ie

Institute of Chartered Secretaries and Administrators
16 Park Crescent
London W1
Tel: 020-7580 4741
Fax: 020-7323 1132
email: icsa@dial.pipex.com

Institute of Directors
Regional – Branch Support
Tel: 020-7766 8870
Fax: 020-7766 8777
email: branches@iod.co.uk
Director Development
Tel: 020-7766 8800
Fax: 020-7766 8765
email: directordev@iod.co.uk
Professional Development
Tel: 020-7451 3106
Fax: 020-7839 9264
email: profdev@iod.co.uk

Institute of Management
Management House
Cottingham Road
Corby NN17 1TT
Tel: 01536-204222
Fax: 01536-201651
Website: www.inst-mgt.org.uk

Institute of Personnel & Development
35 Camp Road
London SW19 4UX
Tel: 020-8971 9000
Fax: 020-8263 3333
email: ipd@ipd.co.uk

The Law Society of England and Wales
113 Chancery Lane
London WC2A 1PL
Tel: 020-7242 1222
Fax: 020-7831 0344
Website: www.lawsoc.org.uk

The Law Society of Northern Ireland
Law Society House
98 Victoria Street
Belfast BT1 3JZ
Tel: 02890-231614
Fax: 02890-232606
email: info@lawsoc/ni.org

The Law Society of Scotland
26 Drumsheugh Gardens
Edinburgh EH3 7YR
Tel: 0131-226 7411
Fax: 0131-225 2934
email: lawscot@lawscot.org.uk

Office of Fair Trading
Field House
Breams Buildings
London EC4A 1PR
Tel: 020-7211 8000
Fax: 020-7211 8800
email: enquiries@oft.gov.uk

PIRC
4th Floor, City Side
40 Adler Street
London E1 1EE
Tel: 020-7247 2323
Fax: 020-7247 2457
email: info@pirc.co.uk

Race Relations Commission
Elliot House
10–12 Allington Street
London SW1E 5EH
Tel: 020-7828 7022
Fax: 020-7630 7605
email: info@cre.gov.uk

The Registrar of Companies
Department of Economic Development
IDB House
64 Chichester Street
Belfast
Tel: 02890-234488
Fax: 02890-544888
Website: www.companies-house.gov.uk

Scottish Enterprises
120 Bothwell Street
Glasgow G2 7JP
Tel: 0141-248 2700

Small Firms Advice Bureau
dial 100 and ask for
Freephone Enterprise

TEC National Council
Westminster Tower
Albert Embankment
London SE1
Tel: 020-7735 0010
Fax: 020-7735 0090
email: info@tec.co.uk

VAT – see under HM Customs and Excise in your local telephone directory

Welsh Development Agency
Principality House
The Friary
Cardiff CF10 3FE
Tel: 0845-7775577
Fax: 0-1443-845589
email: enquiries@wda.co.uk

3i
31 Waterloo Road
London SE1
Tel: 020-7928 3131
Fax: 020-7928 0058
Website: www.3i.com

References

Andrews, John M., *Taxation of Directors and Employees* (Institute of Chartered Accountants in England and Wales, London, 1995).

Association of British Insurers and National Association of Pension Funds, *Responsible Voting – A Joint ABI-NAPF Statement* (www.insurance.org.uk).

Berle, A.A. and Means, G.C., *The Modern Corporation and Private Property* (Macmillan, New York, 1932 (2nd edn 1967)).

Bloom, B., *Taxonomy of Educational Objectives* (Longmans, New York, 1956).

Cadbury, Adrian, *The Company Chairman* (Fitzwilliam Publishing, Cambridge, 1990).

Cadbury, Adrian, *Report of the Committee on the Financial Aspects of Corporate Governance* (Gee Publishing Ltd, London, 1992).

Coase, R., *Published Balance Sheets as an Aid to Economic Investigation* (Accounting Research Association, London, 1938).

Commonwealth Association for Corporate Governance, *CACG Guidelines: Principles for Corporate Governance in the Commonwealth* (CACG, New Zealand, 1999).

Department of Trade and Industry, *The Companies {Tables A to F} Regulations 1985* (HMSO, London, 1985).

427

Dulewicz, V., 'Directorial Competence: A Response and Up-Date', *Competency*, 1994, vol. 2, no. 1, pp. 39–40.

Dulewicz, V., Macmillan, K. and Herbert, P., 'The Development of Standards of Good Practice for Boards of Directors', *Executive Development*, 1995, vol. 8, no. 6, pp. 13–17.

Easterbrook, F. and Fischel, D., *The Economic Structure of Corporate Law* (Harvard University Press, Cambridge, Mass.,1991).

Fama, Eugene F. and Jensen, Michael C., 'Separation of Ownership and Control', *Journal of Law and Economics*, vol. 26, no. 2, June 1983, pp. 301–26.

Freedman, J., 'Small Businesses and the Corporate Form: Burden and Privilege', *Modern Law Review*, 1994, vol. 57, no. 1, p. 555.

Friedman, Milton, *Capitalism and Freedom* (The University of Chicago Press, Chicago, 1962).

Friedman, Milton, 'The Social Responsibility of Business is to Increase its Profits', *New York Times Magazine*, Sept. 13 1970.

Greenbury, R., *Directors' Remuneration: Report of a Study Group* (Gee Publishing Ltd, London, 1995).

Hampel, R., *Committee on Corporate Governance: Final Report* (Gee Publishing Ltd, London, 1998).

Harper, J., *Chairing Boards Today* (Kogan Page, London, 2000).

Harvey-Jones, J., 'The Troubleshooter and the Company Secretary', *Administrator*, April 1995, pp. 6–9.

Hayek, F.A., *Law, Legislation, Liberty, vol. 3: The Political Order of a Free People* (The University of Chicago Press, Chicago, 1979).

HM Inland Revenue, *Residence and Non-Residents – Liability to Tax in the UK* (HMSO, London, 1999).

HM Inland Revenue, *National Insurance Contributions for Company Directors* (Inland Revenue, London, 2000).

Hutchinson, E.A.S. and Farmery, P., *Directors' Personal Liabilities* (The Director Publications Ltd, London, 1992).

Hutton, W., *Stakeholding and its Critics* (Institute of Economic Affairs, London, 1997).

Institute of Chartered Accountants in England and Wales, 'Financial and Accounting Responsibilities of Directors', *Accountancy*, vol. 19, no. 1241, January 1997.

Institute of Directors, *Getting the Family to Work Together* (The Director Publications Ltd, London, 1995).

Institute of Directors, *Succession Management in Family Companies* (The Director Publications Ltd, London, 1996).

Institute of Directors, *The Role of 'Outsiders' in Family Companies* (The Director Publications Ltd, London, 1997).

Institute of Directors (Lea, Ruth), *Business Matters* (The Director Publications Ltd, London, 1998a).

Institute of Directors, *The Code of Professional Conduct* (The Director Publications Ltd, London, 1998b).

Institute of Directors (Renton, Tony), *Good Practice for Directors: Standards for the Board* (The Director Publications Ltd, London, 1999).

Kay, J. and Silberston, A., 'Corporate Governance', *National Institute Economic Review*, August 1995.

Law Commission and Scottish Law Commission, *Company Directors: Regulating Conflicts of Interest and Formulating a Statement of Duties* (HMSO, Cm 4436, London, 1999).

London Stock Exchange, *The Combined Code: Principles of Good Governance and Code of Best Practice* (Gee Publishing Ltd, London, 1998).

London Stock Exchange, *The Listing Rules: commentary on the listing rules and tables of destination and derivation; the Unlisted Securities Market rules* (London Stock Exchange, London, 1999).

Management Charter Initiative, *Senior Management Standards* (MCI, London, 1998).

Monks, Robert A.G. and Minow, Nell, *Corporate Governance* (Blackwell, Oxford, 1995).

Muzyka, D. F., De Koning, A. and Churchill, N., 'Transforming the Entrepreneurial Corporation, Creating and Sustaining Entrepreneurship' (Babson Entrepreneurship Research Conference, London, 1995).

Neubauer, Fred, and Lank, Alden, *The Family Business: Its Governance for Sustainability* (Macmillan Press Ltd, London, 1998).

Organisation for Economic Co-operation and Development, *OECD Principles of Corporate Governance* (OECD, Paris, 1999).

Patterson, Jeanne, *The Link Between Corporate Governance and Performance* (Report Number 1215-98-RR, The Conference Board Inc., New York, 1998).

Smith, Adam, *The Wealth of Nations*, ed. George J. Stigler (University of Chicago Press, Chicago, 1976).

Sternberg, Elaine, 'The Defects of Stakeholder Theory', *Corporate Governance: An International Review*, vol. 5, no. 1, January 1997.

Tricker, R., *Corporate Governance* (Gower Publishing, Aldershot, 1984).

Turnbull, R., *Internal Control: Guidance for Directors on the Combined Code* (The Institute of Chartered Accountants in England and Wales, London, 1999).

Additional Reading

Blake, Allan, *Dynamic Directors: Aligning Board Structure for Business Success* (Macmillan Press Ltd, London, 1999).

Browing, Robert, *Setting up your own Limited Company: How to Run Your Business as a Director and Shareholder* (Oxford How To Books Ltd, Oxford, 1997).

Bruce, Martha, *Rights and Duties of Directors* (Reed Elsevier (UK) Ltd, London, 1999).

Chinn, Richard and Jones, Martyn E. (eds.), *The Corporate Governance Handbook* (Gee Publishing Ltd, London, 1999).

Clayton, Patricia, *Forming a Limited Company: A Practical Guide* (Kogan Page, London, 1998).

Coulson-Thomas, C., *Developing Directors: Building an Effect* (McGraw-Hill, London, 1993).

Demb, A. and Neubauer, F., 'Subsidiary Boards Reconsidered', *European Management Journal*, 1990, vol. 8, pp. 480–487.

Dunne, P., *Running Board Meetings: Tips and Techniques for Getting the Best from Them* (Kogan Page, London, 1997).

Easterby Smith, M., *Evaluating Management Development, Training and Education* (Gower, London, 1994).

Garratt, R., *The Learning Organisation* (HarperCollins, London, 1994).

Garratt, R., *The Fish Rots From the Head: The Crisis in Our Boardrooms* (HarperCollins, London, 1996).

Garratt, R., 'Changing Values in Corporate Governance', *Organisations and People*, 1998, vol. 5, no. 3, pp. 4–11.

Ghaiwals, S. (ed.), *Tolley's Health and Safety at Work Handbook 2001* (Butterworths Tolley, London, 2000).

Ginman, P., *The Guide to Directors' Duties and Responsibilities – Your Questions Answered* (Kogan Page, London, 1992).

Grier, Nicholas, *UK Company Law* (John Wiley & Sons, Chichester, 1998).

Hilmer, Frederick G., *Strictly Boardroom – Improving Governance to Enhance Company Performance* (Information Australia, Melbourne, 1993).

Hilmer, F. and Tricker, R., 'Board Effectiveness', *The Australian Company Director's Handbook* (Australian Institute of Company Directors, 1991).

Howorth, S. and Mcneil, P., *Company Penalties* (Financial Times, London, 1993).

Impey, David and Montague, Nicholas, *Running a Limited Company* (Jordan Publishing Ltd, Bristol, 1998).

Institute of Directors in Southern Africa, *The King Report on Corporate Governance* (Institute of Directors in Southern Africa, November 1994).

Institute of Directors, *Criteria for NHS Boards* (The Director Publications, London, 1995).

Institute of Directors, *Standards for Magistrates Courts Committees* (The Director Publications, London, 1996).

Institute of Directors, *A Development Guide for Business Link Board Members* (The Director Publications, London, 1998).

Institute of Directors, *Assessing Board Effectiveness* (The Director Publications, London, 1998).

Institute of Directors, *Board Development for Business Links* (The Director Publications, London, 1998).

Institute of Directors, *Ethics in Business* (The Director Publications, London, 1999).

Institute of Directors, *The Stakeholder Debate* (The Director Publications, London, 1999).

Institute of Directors, *The Independent Director* (The Director Publications, London, 1999).

Jenkins, Richard, *Companies Act Handbook and Index* (Ernst & Young, 4th edn, London, 1997).

Kendall, N., *Good Corporate Governance: An Aid to Growth for the Smaller Company* (ICAEW, Milton Keynes, 1994).

Kriger, M., 'Creating Strategic Windows: The Increasing Role of Subsidiary Boards in Japanese, European and North American MNC's', *Academy of Management*, vol. 46, 1986, pp. 92–96.

Lai, Jerry, *Tolley's Company Secretary's Handbook* (Tolley Publishing Company Ltd, Croydon, 1998).

Lindon Travers, K., *Non-Executive Directors* (The Director Books, Cambridge, 1990).

Loose, P., Yelland, J. and Impey, D., *The Company Director: Powers and Duties* (Jordan Publishing Ltd, Bristol, 1993).

Mautz, R.K. and Neumann, F.L., *Corporate Audit Committees – Policies and Practices* (Ernst and Ernst, New York, 1977).

Monks, Robert A.G., *The Emperor's Nightingale – Restoring the Integrity of the Corporation* (Capstone Publishing, Oxford, 1998).

Peters, *Corporate Governance in the Netherlands* (Netherlands Committee on Corporate Governance, Amsterdam, June 1997).

Sheridan T., and Kendall N., *Corporate Governance: An Action Plan for Profitability and Business Success* (Pitman Publishing, Croydon, 1992).

Sinclair, Neil, Vogel, David and Snowden, Richard (eds.), *Company Directors: Law and Liability, Vols. 1 and 2* (FT Law & Tax, London, 1997).

Slade, Elizabeth A., *Tolley's Employment Handbook 1999–2000* (Butterworths Tolley, London, 2000).

Souster, P., *Directors: Your Responsibilities and Liabilities,* (ICAEW, Milton Keynes, 1999).

Tricker, R., *The Independent Director – A Study of The Non-Executive Director and of the Audit Committee* (Tolley with Deloitte, Haskins and Sells, London, 1978).

Tricker, R., *International Corporate Governance: Text, Readings and Cases* (Prentice-Hall, Singapore, 1994).

Tricker, R., *The Pocket Director* (Profile Books & The Economist Publications, London 1998).

Wareham, R. and Smailes, D., *Tolley's Company Law Handbook 1999* (Tolley Publishing, Croydon, 1999).

Wright, D and Creighton, B., *Rights and Duties of Directors* (Butterworth, London, 1991).

Index